The Government of Scotland
1560–1625

TO MY PARENTS

The Government of Scotland
1560–1625

JULIAN GOODARE

OXFORD
UNIVERSITY PRESS

OXFORD
UNIVERSITY PRESS

Great Clarendon Street, Oxford OX2 6DP

Oxford University Press is a department of the University of Oxford.
It furthers the University's objective of excellence in research, scholarship,
and education by publishing worldwide in

Oxford New York

Auckland Bangkok Buenos Aires Cape Town Chennai
Dar es Salaam Delhi Hong Kong Istanbul Karachi Kolkata
Kuala Lumpur Madrid Melbourne Mexico City Mumbai Nairobi
São Paulo Shanghai Taipei Tokyo Toronto

Oxford is a registered trade mark of Oxford University Press
in the UK and in certain other countries

Published in the United States
by Oxford University Press Inc., New York

British Library Cataloguing in Publication Data

Data available

Library of Congress Cataloging in Publication Data

Data available

ISBN 0-19-924354-9

1 3 5 7 9 10 8 6 4 2

Typeset by SNP Best-set Typesetter Ltd., Hong Kong
Printed in Great Britain
on acid-free paper by
Biddles Ltd,
King's Lynn, Norfolk

The best reason why monarchy is a strong government is, that it is an intelligible government. The mass of mankind understand it, and they hardly anywhere in the world understand any other. It is often said that men are ruled by their imaginations; but it would be truer to say they are governed by the weakness of their imaginations. The nature of a constitution, the action of an assembly, the play of parties, the unseen formation of a guiding opinion, are complex facts, difficult to know and easy to mistake. But the action of a single will, the fiat of a single mind, are easy ideas: anybody can make them out, and no one can ever forget them.

Walter Bagehot, *The English Constitution* (1867)

Acknowledgements

I AM MOST GRATEFUL to the scholars who kindly agreed to read draft chapters and made numerous helpful suggestions: Professor Michael J. Braddick, Professor J. H. Burns, Dr Jane Dawson, Professor Maurice Lee, Professor Michael Lynch, Dr Athol Murray, and Mr W. D. H. Sellar. Particular mention should be made of Dr Murray, who read some drafts more than once and whose inexhaustible knowledge of archives and administrative procedure has been invaluable.

I have benefited from valuable advice and encouragement from many other scholars, too many to list individually, but I must mention Dr Sharon Adams, Dr Steve Boardman, Dr Pauline Croft, Dr John Finlay, Dr Mark Godfrey, Dr Alan R. MacDonald, Dr Hugh V. McLachlan, Dr Lauren Martin, Dr Joyce Miller, Professor Conrad Russell, Dr Michael Wasser, Professor Christopher A. Whatley, Dr Jenny Wormald, and Dr Louise Yeoman. Any remaining errors are my own.

Papers based on early versions of Chapters 2, 4, 5, and 11 were presented to the Scottish Legal History Group, the Institute of Historical Research, the Conference of Scottish Medievalists, and the Modern History Seminar, University of Dundee.

This book, like its predecessor, has a distant but detectable relationship to my unpublished 1989 Ph.D. thesis. That thesis addressed a wide range of topics, and I have come to see it as an interim report on a very long-term research programme which is still far from complete. Materials from the thesis, heavily reworked, may be found in various places below, particularly in Chapters 2, 3, and 5.

Oxford University Press has been a patient and supportive publisher, with special thanks due to Anne Gelling and Ruth Parr.

My wife, Jackie, has exercised a social scientist's welcome influence, particularly on Chapter 12. The dedication acknowledges a longer-term debt.

J.G.

Edinburgh
December 2003

Contents

Conventions and Abbreviations

Money: All sums are in pounds (£s) Scots unless otherwise stated, sometimes rounded to the nearest £. In 1560 the English £ (sterling) was equal to about £4. 10s. Scots at par, and the French crown to £1. 6s. 8d. Scots; by 1601 they were worth £12 Scots and £3. 6s. 8d. Scots respectively. The Scottish currency was pegged to the English in 1603, and between then and 1625 there were no major fluctuations in currency values.

Dates: These are given in old style (i.e. Julian calendar), but with the year beginning on 1 January.

Style: Contemporary documents are quoted in the original spelling, but the letters i/j and u/v are modernized; 3 (yogh) is given as y. Contractions are expanded, and modern capitalization and punctuation used. In the text, names of people and places use the standard modern form where one exists. Translations not otherwise attributed are my own.

The following abbreviations are used:

Aberdeen Letters	*Aberdeen Council Letters*, 6 vols., ed. L. B. Taylor (London, 1942–61)
Add. MS	Additional MS (BL)
Adv. MS	Advocates' MS (NLS)
APS	*Acts of the Parliaments of Scotland*, 12 vols., ed. T. Thomson and C. Innes (Edinburgh, 1814–75)
Balfour, *Practicks*	Sir James Balfour of Pittendreich, *Practicks*, 2 vols., ed. P. G. B. McNeill (Stair Society, 1962–3)
BL	British Library, London
BUK	*Booke of the Universall Kirk: Acts and Proceedings of the General Assemblies of the Kirk of Scotland*, 3 vols., ed. T. Thomson (Bannatyne and Maitland Clubs, 1839–45)
Calderwood, *History*	David Calderwood, *History of the Kirk of Scotland*, 8 vols., ed. T. Thomson and D. Laing (Wodrow Society, 1843–9)
Carnwath Court Book	*Court Book of the Barony of Carnwath*, 1523–1542, ed. W. C. Dickinson (SHS, 1937)
Craig, *De Unione*	Thomas Craig of Riccarton, *De Unione Britanniae Tractatus*, ed. C. S. Terry (SHS, 1909)
Craig, *Jus Feudale*	Thomas Craig of Riccarton, *Jus Feudale*, 2 vols., ed. J. A. Clyde (Edinburgh, 1934)
CSP Dom.	*Calendar of State Papers, Domestic Series*, 94 vols., ed. R. Lemon et al. (London, 1856–)
CSP Scot.	*Calendar of the State Papers Relating to Scotland and Mary Queen of Scots*, 1547–1603, 13 vols., ed. J. Bain et al. (Edinburgh, 1898–1969)

CSP Venetian	*Calendar of State Papers . . . in the Archives and Collections of Venice*, 38 vols., ed. R. Brown et al. (London, 1864–1940)
Eccles. Letters	*Original Letters Relating to the Ecclesiastical Affairs of Scotland*, 2 vols., ed. D. Laing (Bannatyne Club, 1851)
Edin. Recs.	*Extracts From the Records of the Burgh of Edinburgh*, 13 vols., ed. J. D. Marwick et al. (SBRS and Edinburgh, 1869–1967)
ER	*Exchequer Rolls of Scotland*, 23 vols., ed. J. Stuart et al. (Edinburgh, 1878–)
Falkirk Court Book	*Court Book of the Barony and Regality of Falkirk and Callendar*, i: *1638–1656*, ed. D. M. Hunter (Stair Society, 1991)
Fife Court Book	*Sheriff Court Book of Fife, 1515–1522*, ed. W. C. Dickinson (SHS, 1928)
Gordon, *Sutherland*	Sir Robert Gordon, *Genealogical History of the Earldom of Sutherland* (Edinburgh, 1813)
HMC	Historical Manuscripts Commission
HMC, *Mar & Kellie*	HMC, *Report on the Manuscripts of the Earl of Mar and Kellie*, 2 vols., ed. H. Paton (London, 1904–30)
HMC, *Salisbury*	HMC, *Calendar of the Manuscripts of the Marquis of Salisbury*, 24 vols., ed. S. R. Bird et al. (London, 1883–1976)
Hope, *Major Practicks*	Sir Thomas Hope, *Major Practicks*, 2 vols., ed. J. A. Clyde (Stair Society, 1937–8).
HP	*Highland Papers*, 4 vols., ed. J. R. N. Macphail (SHS, 1914–34)
James VI & I, *Political Writings*	King James VI & I, *Political Writings*, ed. J. P. Sommerville (Cambridge, 1994)
JR	*Juridical Review*
Lindsay, *Works*	Sir David Lindsay of the Mount, *Works*, 4 vols., ed. D. Hamer (Scottish Text Society, 1931–6)
LP James VI	*Letters and State Papers during the Reign of King James VI*, ed. J. Maidment (Abbotsford Club, 1838)
Melros Papers	*State Papers and Miscellaneous Correspondence of Thomas, Earl of Melros*, 2 vols., ed. J. Maidment (Abbotsford Club, 1837)
Melville, *Diary*	James Melville, *Autobiography and Diary, 1556–1610*, ed. R. Pitcairn (Wodrow Society, 1842)
Melville, *Memoirs*	Sir James Melville of Halhill, *Memoirs of His Own Life*, ed. T. Thomson (Bannatyne Club, 1827)
NAS	National Archives of Scotland, Edinburgh
NLS	National Library of Scotland, Edinburgh
Pitscottie, *Historie*	Robert Lindesay of Pitscottie, *Historie and Cronicles of Scotland*, 3 vols., ed. Æ. J. G. Mackay (Scottish Text Society, 1899–1911)

RCRB	*Records of the Convention of Royal Burghs of Scotland,* 7 vols., ed. J. D. Marwick and T. Hunter (Edinburgh, 1866–1918)
RMS	*Register of the Great Seal of Scotland (Registrum Magni Sigilli Regum Scotorum),* 11 vols., ed. J. M. Thomson et al. (Edinburgh, 1912–)
Row, *History*	John Row, *History of the Kirk of Scotland, 1558–1637,* ed. D. Laing (Wodrow Society, 1842)
RPC	*Register of the Privy Council of Scotland,* 37 vols., ed. J. H. Burton et al. (Edinburgh, 1877–)
RSS	*Register of the Privy Seal of Scotland (Registrum Secreti Sigilli Regum Scotorum),* 8 vols., ed. M. Livingstone et al. (Edinburgh, 1908–)
SHR	*Scottish Historical Review*
SHS	Scottish History Society
Skene, *DVS*	John Skene, *De Verborum Significatione: The Exposition of the Termes and Difficill Wordes Conteined in the Foure Buikes of Regiam Majestatem and Uthers . . .* (Edinburgh, 1599)
SME	T. B. Smith (ed.), *The Laws of Scotland: Stair Memorial Encyclopedia,* 25 vols. (Edinburgh, 1987–1995)
Stair, *Institutions*	James, Viscount Stair, *Institutions of the Law of Scotland,* ed. D. M. Walker (Edinburgh, 1981)
TA	*Accounts of the (Lord High) Treasurer of Scotland,* 13 vols., ed. T. Dickson et al. (Edinburgh, 1877–)
TGSI	*Transactions of the Gaelic Society of Inverness*
Trials, ed. Pitcairn	*Criminal Trials in Scotland, 1488–1624,* 3 vols., ed. R. Pitcairn (Bannatyne and Maitland Clubs, 1833)

RMS and *RSS* are cited by document number without comment; all other citations are to page numbers unless otherwise stated. Parliamentary statutes in *APS* have a chapter number as well as a page number; references to *APS* lacking such a number are not to statutes. Titles of secondary works, and of primary sources not listed here, are given in full on their first citation, and thereafter shortened. Full citations of abbreviated titles will be found in the Bibliography.

Introduction

This book has three aims. The first is to put Scotland on the map for those interested in the history of European government. To illustrate the need for this, we may visit Sicily. Sicilians in the early seventeenth century believed that only two parliaments still retained their traditional rights and powers: their own, and that of England. A distinguished historian offers the comment:

> Clearly, these enthusiasts knew nothing about the States-General of the United Provinces of the Netherlands, nor of the Polish Diet, the Swedish Riksdag, or of several of the German Landtage. But then, why should they have known about the distant north of Europe?[1]

Why indeed? But the omission here of one major institution in the 'distant north of Europe', the Scottish parliament, suggests that Scotland has been *terra incognita* not just to contemporary Sicilians, but to historians too.[2] The role that parliament continued to play in the government of Scotland, the growth of personal monarchy notwithstanding, will be one of the themes of this book. Both personal monarchies and representative assemblies are themes of interest in a European context. It should be added that the book is not narrowly constitutional, but concentrates on how monarchies and assemblies, and other central and local institutions of government, were *used* by the political classes. It is a case study of how a late medieval European kingdom was transformed into an integrated state by the development of a more dense matrix of public authority.

The second aim is to provide materials for those interested in British history. Historians of England have found it useful to look beyond their own borders for the dynamics of early Stuart government: studies have exploited the explanatory power of the interaction between the different kingdoms of the British Isles, to elucidate such things as power politics in the court and early parliaments of James I, the restructuring of the church in three

---

[1] H. G. Koenigsberger, 'The Parliament of Sicily and the Spanish Empire', in his *Estates and Revolutions* (Ithaca, NY, 1971), 80.

[2] A fuller census of European parliaments, also omitting Scotland, is given by R. Zaller, 'Parliament and the Crisis of European Liberty', in J. H. Hexter (ed.), *Parliament and Liberty from the Reign of Elizabeth to the Civil War* (Stanford, Calif., 1992), 202. There are signs that the neglect of Scotland's parliament is passing; it receives welcome attention in M. A. R. Graves, *The Parliaments of Early Modern Europe* (London, 2001). It also gained some contemporary international recognition, at least outside Sicily. The Venetian ambassador to France in 1561 wrote: 'If any authority in France can control the absolute power of the king it is the assembly of the three estates, who represent the whole kingdom, like the parliament in England and Scotland and the Diet in Germany.' *CSP Venetian*, vii. 326.

kingdoms, and the collapse of Charles I's regime in England in 1640.[3] This book, although it deals just with Scotland, attempts to do so in awareness of these issues, and draws attention where possible to connections with them. The treatment of such matters as the nature of allegedly 'absentee' Scottish kingship after 1603 (where a major revision of conventional views is undertaken in Chapters 4 and 6) may help to foster understanding of the interactions between the kingdoms. English historians are becoming less insular—or should that be more insular?—and seeking to enrich their work by taking account of developments in a neighbouring polity that was often influenced by English pressure or English example.

Thirdly, I hope that this book will contribute to Scottish history. Later in this introduction there is a discussion of the historiography of Scottish government which indicates some of the main approaches which scholars have taken to the subject. Many areas of Scottish history require an understanding of government; this book may help to provide it.

Government is often believed to be about institutions. These cannot be ignored; but it is also about *processes*. I could have written separate chapters on the crown, parliament, privy council, central administration . . . there are worthy English precedents for such an approach.[4] However, I have structured the book as far as possible to bring out the processes that took place within and around institutions, rather than hopping from one institution to another. For instance, various institutions had a representative role, lobbying central government on behalf of their members. That process is discussed in Chapter 2. Some of the same institutions were also specialist executive agencies of government, enforcing and even creating rules which those subject to them were expected to observe. That aspect of their work is discussed in Chapter 7. Parliament as a consultative body comes in Chapter 2, while its legislative role comes in Chapter 3 and its relationship to the crown in Chapter 4. Institutional machinery usually comes ready labelled and is easy to identify; I have tried to go beyond mere identification and to discuss the kinds of things that happened when the machinery was set going. The book's title—*The Government of Scotland*—has two complementary meanings, static and dynamic. There was a government: there was government; it was both a thing, and a process.[5]

---

[3] To take just a few examples: N. Cuddy, 'Anglo-Scottish Union and the Court of James I, 1603–1625', *Transactions of the Royal Historical Society*, 5th ser. 39 (1989), 107–24; C. Russell, 'English Parliaments, 1593–1606: One Epoch or Two?', in D. M. Dean and N. L. Jones (eds.), *The Parliaments of Elizabethan England* (Oxford, 1990); C. Russell, *The Causes of the English Civil War* (Oxford, 1990), ch. 5; J. Morrill, 'A British Patriarchy? Ecclesiastical Imperialism under the Early Stuarts', in A. Fletcher and P. Roberts (eds.), *Religion, Culture and Society in Early Modern Britain* (Cambridge, 1994); C. Russell, *The Fall of the British Monarchies, 1637–1642* (Oxford, 1991), ch. 2.

[4] Notably A. G. R. Smith, *The Government of Elizabethan England* (London, 1967), and D. Loades, *Power in Tudor England* (London, 1997).

[5] 'Historians should therefore think less of *government* as an institution or as an event, than of *governance* as a process': S. Hindle, *The State and Social Change in Early Modern*

The nearest thing to the fully institutional study that I might have written comes in the core of the book, beginning in Chapter 3. Here, government is broken down into its component parts, from crown and parliament to local commissaries and baron courts. Chapter 3 traces the unintended rise of a sovereign legislature. The late sixteenth century saw regular attempts to codify Scotland's venerated but unusable medieval laws in order to adapt them to current conditions. Meanwhile, parliament began to pass a large volume of legislation. When the codification projects failed, it became clear that the law was fundamentally statutory rather than immemorial. Chapter 4 shows the rise of parliament being paralleled by the rise of a more powerful personal monarchy, in which the crown began to do more things using the royal prerogative, and even to exclude parliament from certain areas. The possibility of sustained conflict between crown and parliament began to arise. The continuing influence and involvement of the crown after 1603 casts doubt on the concept of 'absentee monarchy'.

The next few chapters trace the way in which law and policy were implemented. The institutions that did most of the work are all discussed, but Chapter 5 is not about specific institutions at all; it is about styles of government, and particularly about different ways in which laws could be enforced. Not all laws were expected to be enforced in full, and a typology of enforcement patterns is given. There is also a critique of conventional accounts of 'central' and 'local' power, arguing that 'centralization' was not experienced by the localities as an external force; it occurred *in* the localities. Chapter 6 is the only chapter to be about a specific institution—the privy council. From its origins in 1545, this gradually became the central coordinating body of daily government. It worked by consensus with the monarch (something that changed little even after 1603), and coordinated the executive government departments. These departments receive their own detailed discussion in Chapter 7, showing that there were several new policy-making bodies.

Executive governmental machinery in the localities is dealt with in the next two chapters. Chapter 8 looks at traditional institutions, notably the sheriff, baron, and regality courts controlled by the nobility. These courts gained some new powers but mainly became much more accountable to the centre. Meanwhile Chapter 9 shows a number of completely new powers being created alongside the old ones, notably the local courts of the church but also some new civil administrators. This was one of the most significant periods ever for the growth of local government in Scotland.

The book's core is framed by two sections that are less about institutions and more about people and processes. The first section consists of two chapters dealing with the political community—the propertied elite. Chapter 1

England, c.1550–1640 (London, 2000), 23 (emphasis in original). Of course, they should think of both.

discusses how the various components of government—monarchy, parliament, privy council, and so on—were legitimized in the course of political practice. 'Righteous' government was highly valued, not least because it was recognized that rulers and governmental agencies might do things that would be undesirable or wrong. The various social and political groups constituting Scottish government are introduced, and they receive fuller discussion in Chapter 2. This begins with the traditional 'three estates' of clergy, nobles, and royal burghs, showing how they functioned as interest groups and how their privileges became more dependent on the state. Three new interest groups gained in influence: lawyers and lairds, the latter of whom became a fourth estate in 1587, and agents of England. All related to government, either through participation in its internal processes, or through lobbying to get what they wanted.

We also need to look beyond the political community, to see what a more active and interventionist government was like for those on the receiving end. This is the subject of Chapters 10 and 11. The costs of state formation were low in Scotland—which may be an indirect indication of the weakness of the state. Few people died in creating it; few (in the core of the state at least) were deprived of important political rights; it did not even cost much money. But there were certainly some who lost out—mainly from outside the charmed circle of the elite. Chapter 10 deals with the experience of the political elite of the Highlands, who were not welcome or respected members of the Scottish body politic, and who came to experience a quasi-colonial relationship with the authorities. A typology of colonies shows the various ways in which this operated. Chapter 11 discusses the common people, and particularly certain groups whose encounter with government proved memorable. A 'new violence of the state' emerged in certain policies of central government.

Chapter 12 draws various threads together and weaves them into what may be a recognizable and even familiar pattern. As I write, it is fifty years since Geoffrey Elton published *The Tudor Revolution in Government*, and his ideas—generally in significantly modified form—have exercised a compelling influence ever since. No scholar interested in early modern government can ignore them. The Scotland of Mary and James VI, both of whom hoped to succeed to the English throne, experienced almost unprecedented détente and then regal union with England, and one cannot avoid asking the question: was there a 'Stewart revolution in government'? My answer, briefly, is that there was. But brief answers are inevitably simplistic, and in the chapter I draw attention to certain modifications of the 'revolution in government' hypothesis that are necessary in order to apply it to Scotland. 'Revolution in government' has never been an entirely satisfactory phrase or hypothesis, and is best treated as a thought-provoking point of departure for analysis. Most of my modifications reduce the scale of the 'revolution' as it occurred in Scotland, although one or two of them actually increase it.

In a previous book I argued for the development of an 'absolutist state'—a concept which, like 'revolution in government', had been developed elsewhere but which I found helpful to apply to the Scottish evidence.[6] The chapters that follow provide further support for this case, although I am not going to argue it all over again. It may be helpful to clarify the relationship between the terms 'absolutist state' and 'revolution in government'. They are to some extent different ways of looking at the same thing—or rather, not at a thing, but at a process. The 'revolution in government' was a series of loosely related changes, spread over half a century or so, that transformed many aspects of Scottish government. The 'absolutist state', too, was in practice a series of trends towards a ideal type that could never be completely realized. Simple ideals are never realized, but they help us understand complex and messy reality.

The 'absolutist' trend in the period 1560–1625 was for government to become more centralized and focused on the monarch. The monarch would govern nominally alone, and in practice with the advice and support of a landed nobility whose client networks animated the bureaucracy at the centre and in the localities. This can be distinguished from the characteristic medieval polity in which the monarch governed as a coordinator of nobles who were not only landed, but also equipped with private armies that made them power centres. Medieval power was decentralized and states lacked sovereignty. The absolutist state can also be distinguished from its successor, a parliamentary regime that controlled a centralized state but did not rely solely on landed power; instead it gave a distinct role to financial, trading, and manufacturing interests. It should be mentioned that the term 'state' is used conventionally in this book, to mean the system of institutions and personnel by means of which government (as a process) was exercised over a given territory. It is thus somewhat more abstract than the term 'government', which can refer to the particular people operating the system.

The 'revolution in government' focuses less on the interests of social groups as articulated in systems of power, and more on the practicalities of constitutional, legal, and administrative change. Parliamentary sovereignty was established over a territorially unified state, with parliament (including the crown) as a body that made laws and imposed taxes rather than just providing a consultative forum. Daily government ceased to consist of the king giving personal orders after taking advice; it came to operate through an executive privy council, coordinating specialist and sometimes bureaucratic departments that could generate policy rather than just pen-pushing.

---

[6] J. Goodare, *State and Society in Early Modern Scotland* (Oxford, 1999), ch. 3 and *passim*. The term 'absolutist state', like 'revolution in government', is not ideal, but it is familiar. It can give rise to misunderstanding—critics occasionally assume, for instance, that 'absolutism' involved some kind of total power that removed the need for local consent, although no proponent of the idea has said this. But on balance it seems better to use these terms, carefully defined and qualified, than to develop new and perhaps unfamiliar ones.

Meanwhile the number of public administrators in the localities soared. But one of the essential modifications of the original 'revolution in government' hypothesis involves the recognition that, while the territorial nobility were integrated into the centralized state, they were not superseded. On the contrary, their client networks animated the state machinery. All this nevertheless meant that the institutions of government became more tightly integrated, and able—so long as political consensus prevailed—to get more things done.

The most important group in Scottish political society was the nobility, and it is worth discussing how I define and deploy this term. It is not really possible to manage with a single definition of it for all purposes.[7] Within the broadest definition of 'the nobility' there were always gradations or subdivisions, and defining these is if anything more important than defining 'the nobility' as a whole. Definitions can be based on personal status, on relationship to other members of the political elite, or on relationship to land and resources.

Personal status meant, broadly, that a noble was a son of a noble. This large and inclusive group was heavily stratified. The basic division within it was between peers and non-peers. Within the peers there were also different titles: mainly earls and lords, with a handful of dukes, marquises, and viscounts. Within the non-peers—usually known as lairds—there were knights, baronets (from 1620), and others. Peers were personal members of parliament, lairds were not. Precedence within and between these various status groups was deeply felt and sometimes keenly contested.

Nobles' relationship to other members of the elite was relevant because government, and indeed aristocratic society as a whole, operated through patronage and clientage. The basic division was between greater lords—magnates—who had clients, and lesser lords who *were* clients. Lesser lords who wanted to participate in national politics, or who had some request to make of the central government, would tend to do so via a greater lord, perhaps the dominant regional magnate or the head of their own surname. Again the greater lords were usually peers and the lesser ones were usually lairds, but some were not. This dimension of definition of the nobility thus relates to political function.

Nobles' relationship to land and resources meant that there were richer and poorer nobles. Those with the highest status—the earls—do seem usually to have been richer, though there were a few rich lairds and poor peers. Some resources were more desirable than others: land brought tenants who might furnish fighting men, while coal mines did not. Nevertheless, there was much

---

[7] The difficulties of attempting to do so are illustrated by K. M. Brown, *Noble Society in Scotland: Wealth, Family and Culture, from Reformation to Revolution* (Edinburgh, 2000), 1–21. In the English language we have the particular problem that words like 'noble', 'peer', 'baron', and 'gentleman' did not always mean the same thing on both sides of the Border.

common ground among all nobles economically. They all had landed rents, and possessed similar jurisdictions (often baron courts) along with their lands. They might differ in their formal tenurial status: peers and other richer landlords were usually feudal tenants in chief of the crown, while lesser landlords might be feudal vassals of another noble, or might even be feuars (heritable tenants who were in practice proprietors). But the fact of their all being landlords is central to any practical understanding of 'the nobility'.

So much for Lowland nobles. Highland chiefs were sometimes similar, but the differences were also significant. Hardly any of them were peers; nor did they generally elect representatives to sit in parliament, unlike Lowland lairds. Highland chiefs were heads of ruling families which maintained more of a collective identity than Lowland surnames, giving chiefs a different relationship to their leading clansmen. The rents of ordinary folk were not necessarily paid to the chief personally. And highlanders were generally reluctant participants in 'Scottish' national politics.

When I write of 'nobles' or 'the nobility', therefore, I aim for the definition that best suits the context. Often the context is political society at a national level, and here a status-based definition may be appropriate. The peerage, closest to the monarch and with personal membership of parliament, should be distinguished from lairds with less immediate access to high politics. 'The nobility' is a better term for the leading members of political society than 'the peerage', however, because a peerage was not actually essential to personal participation in high politics; it was normal for leading politicians to be peers, but a few were not. Those whose primary function was to be close to the monarch may be described as 'courtiers'. When nobles' relationship to landed resources is crucial I sometimes refer to 'the nobility' meaning all landlords; the term 'lords' also means this. The noble status of the unlanded younger son of a laird does not seem to have been politically significant, and unlanded 'nobles' are not generally comprehended in my definition of the 'nobility'. Finally, I use the term 'magnates' to mean greater nobles who had other nobles as their clients.

There is no chapter dedicated to the nobility. Similarly, there is no chapter on the church, and for the same reason: it comes into every chapter.[8] The matrix of authority within which early modern Scots were governed included a variety of courts and officials. In organizing these thematically I have made various divisions which I have found helpful, such as between traditional and newer local authorities (Chapters 8 and 9). The local courts of the church, kirk sessions and presbyteries, feature prominently in Chapter 9, because they were powerful new institutions of government. Justices of the peace are also found in that chapter, because they were also new. They generally regulated different aspects of people's lives, but one of the points

---

[8] The church features least in Ch. 10, on the Highlands, because its presence in the Highlands was limited.

that emerges from considering them together is how much practical overlap there was in membership and jurisdiction between ecclesiastical and secular authorities. Even when there was no overlap there was usually active cooperation.

So the lack of a separate chapter on the church also means that there is no distinction drawn between 'church' and 'state'. Governmental authority flowed downwards to all authorities, both civil and ecclesiastical, from the sovereign body controlling Scottish government—the crown in parliament. This was the body that made the ultimate rules, both civil and ecclesiastical, by which the Scots were governed. It not only set the rate of interest and laid down regulations for the customs, it also defined the religion that they were to practise and laid down rules for the financing and polity of the church. It is sometimes said that 'state' authority was ineffective over the church, but this authority was decisive.

But surely there have been many accounts of conflict between 'church' and 'state'? Indeed there have, but none of them have troubled to define the 'state', treating the word simply as shorthand for the crown and other civil members of the government when they came into conflict with elements within the church. This is not an acceptable use of the term 'state' for the purposes of a book about government. Accounts of 'church–state conflict' in this period generally turn out to be about a movement of committed Protestants which gained much support (although not universal support) among ministers in the general assembly. This movement naturally provoked political confrontation with the government, as radical movements tend to do, but any suggestion that it was not governed by that government would be absurd.

The idea of 'church–state conflict' can be exposed as unsound by taking it to its logical conclusion. James VI sometimes had problems governing the church, but he had problems governing heritable regalities too. Perhaps we should label these problems 'heritable regality–state conflict'. And when he gaoled the magistrates of Montrose in 1599, perhaps that was 'Montrose–state conflict', with the implication that the burgh of Montrose was somehow not part of the state either. Clearly this will not do. What has been carelessly called 'church–state conflict' was certainly conflict, but it was conflict between political groups who were all comprehended within the state. It was even conflict within the church itself, since although James faced opposition from many churchmen he also received support from other churchmen. Similarly, some civil politicians could support the church opposition. To separate out 'the church' as a unitary thing distinct from 'the state' is a fundamental error that can easily lead to misunderstanding in the history of Scotland after the Reformation.

It may be helpful at this point to review past scholarship on the subject of government in early modern Scotland. Some distinguished historians have discussed the subject, and although the resulting body of work is not extensive it includes some material of high quality. Produced sporadically over a long period, however, it does not always address current concerns.[9]

This is certainly so with earlier scholarship on the Reformation, which provides the context for much of the historiography of government. Current concerns are, however, very much present in the work of the formative modern influence on the subject, Gordon Donaldson. He saw the key issues of the Scottish Reformation as being administrative and financial, and took a keen interest in questions of polity—notably whether the church was to be constituted on episcopalian or presbyterian lines, and the impact of ecclesiastical concerns on broader politics. These were evidently fruitful lines of enquiry, having been followed by several other scholars who have sometimes, but not always, accepted Professor Donaldson's conclusions.[10]

These are not the only governmental questions raised by the Reformation. The impact of church discipline was crucial, and a recent group of scholars has delved into parish records to see what happened when ordinary people were confronted by the Reformers' demands for godly discipline.[11] One

---

[9] What follows is an indicative rather than comprehensive survey, concentrating on leading works. These are often books, though a number of articles are also discussed, especially on subjects where there are few or no books. These works do not all deal directly with the period 1560–1625, but they are relevant to its broader context. Although the editing and publishing of primary documents has been a significant tradition in Scottish historiography, and several of the scholars mentioned have contributed to it, record publishing as such is not noted here. A few editions are noted because of the significance of their introductions.

In a special category is the vitally important survey of the governmental archives: Scottish Record Office, *Guide to the National Archives of Scotland* (Edinburgh, 1996). Much of the relevant material in this work was contributed by Athol L. Murray, who also provides an important survey of archival issues in his introduction to *Acts of the Lords of Council*, iii: *1501–1503*, ed. A. B. Calderwood (Edinburgh, 1993).

[10] An emphasis on Protestantism and episcopalianism is found in G. Donaldson, *The Scottish Reformation* (Cambridge, 1960), id., *Scottish Church History* (Edinburgh, 1985), and W. R. Foster, *The Church before the Covenants, 1596–1638* (Edinburgh, 1975). Episcopacy is problematized by D. G. Mullan, *Episcopacy in Scotland: The History of an Idea, 1560–1638* (Edinburgh, 1986), and the politics of ecclesiological controversy are further discussed by A. R. MacDonald, *The Jacobean Kirk, 1567–1625: Sovereignty, Liturgy and Polity* (Aldershot, 1998). An older constitutional study is D. Shaw, *The General Assemblies of the Church of Scotland, 1560–1600* (Edinburgh, 1964). A presbyterian perspective on Professor Donaldson's original agenda is found in J. Kirk, *Patterns of Reform: Continuity and Change in the Reformation Kirk* (Edinburgh, 1989). Important local studies along these lines are F. D. Bardgett, *Scotland Reformed: The Reformation in Angus and the Mearns* (Edinburgh, 1988), and M. H. B. Sanderson, *Ayrshire and the Reformation: People and Change, 1490–1600* (East Linton, 1997).

The continuing contribution of the late medieval Catholic heritage is taken seriously by I. B. Cowan, *The Scottish Reformation* (London, 1982), and limits to what Protestantism could achieve are indicated by M. Lynch, *Edinburgh and the Reformation* (Edinburgh, 1981), and id., 'Preaching to the Converted? Perspectives on the Scottish Reformation', in A. A. MacDonald et al. (eds.), *The Renaissance in Scotland* (Leiden, 1994). A remarkable study holding much interest for our period as well as its own is W. Makey, *The Church of the Covenant, 1637–1651* (Edinburgh, 1979).

[11] M. F. Graham, *The Uses of Reform: 'Godly Discipline' and Popular Behavior in Scotland and Beyond, 1560–1610* (Leiden, 1996); R. Mitchison and L. Leneman, *Girls in Trouble: Sexuality and Social Control in Rural Scotland, 1660–1780* (2nd edn., Edinburgh, 1998); L. Leneman and R. Mitchison, *Sin in the City: Sexuality and Social Control in Urban Scotland, 1660–1780*

branch of such scholarship has concentrated on witch-hunting, one of the
most distinctive governmental operations of this period, which demonstrates
links between central and local authorities as well as between ecclesiastical
and secular authorities.[12]

The early twentieth century was keenly interested in constitutional history.
This topic is now little studied in its own right, but an understanding of it remains crucial. The key institution providing Scotland with a constitution was
parliament, the subject of a magisterial early monograph by Robert S. Rait.[13]
The project to compile parliamentary biographies like those of the English
History of Parliament was initiated in this period, but took a long time to
reach publication.[14] Professor Rait's work remains essential reading on the
mechanics of parliament, but he wrote at a time when English scholars were
at the height of their optimism about the constitutional importance of their
early modern parliament, and he drew a sharp contrast between what he perceived as an effective English body and an ineffective Scottish one.[15] Scholarship in both countries has now moved on, and a recent revival in the study of
the Scottish parliament has felt no need to endorse Professor Rait's pessimism
about its effectiveness.[16]

(Edinburgh, 1998); and M. Todd, *The Culture of Protestantism in Early Modern Scotland* (New
Haven, 2002).

[12] This is the subject of the classic C. Larner, *Enemies of God: The Witch-Hunt in Scotland*
(London, 1981), and more recently there are S. Macdonald, *The Witches of Fife: Witch-Hunting
in a Scottish Shire, 1560–1710* (East Linton, 2002); J. Goodare, 'Women and the Witch-Hunt in
Scotland', *Social History*, 23 (1998), 288–308; id. (ed.), *The Scottish Witch-Hunt in Context*
(Manchester, 2002); and id. et al., 'The Survey of Scottish Witchcraft, 1563–1736' (Jan. 2003),
www.arts.ed.ac.uk/witches/.

[13] R. S. Rait, *The Parliaments of Scotland* (Glasgow, 1924). An earlier work, C. S. Terry, *The
Scottish Parliament: Its Constitution and Procedure, 1603–1707* (Glasgow, 1905), was largely
superseded by Rait.

[14] M. D. Young (ed.), *The Parliaments of Scotland: Burgh and Shire Commissioners*, 2 vols.
(Edinburgh, 1992–3). This work contains much valuable information, but its limitations for
parliamentary history are pointed out in a review article: J. Goodare, 'Who was the Scottish
Parliament?', *Parliamentary History*, 14 (1995), 173–8. The main problem is the shortage of
evidence for voting and debates, so that links between members' parliamentary and extra-
parliamentary behaviour and affiliations are hard to establish. This problem is also apparent in
J. R. Young, *The Scottish Parliament, 1639–1661: A Political and Constitutional Analysis*
(Edinburgh, 1996), which is nevertheless a useful work of reference detailing the membership
and constitution of parliament and its committees in the 1640s. Some broader conclusions are
offered by id., 'The Scottish Parliament and the Covenanting Revolution: The Emergence of a
Scottish Commons', in id. (ed.), *Celtic Dimensions of the British Civil Wars* (Edinburgh, 1997),
which are characterized as at best provisional in the introduction to this volume by John Morrill
(pp. 11–12).

[15] This also helped to legitimize the Anglo-Scottish union of 1707. One of the leading English
scholars then emphasizing the importance of parliament was Albert V. Dicey, who collaborated
with Professor Rait to produce A. V. Dicey and R. S. Rait, *Thoughts on the Union between
England and Scotland* (London, 1920). This is now little more than a period piece, but it eluci-
dates Rait's general approach to the subject.

[16] Notable here is a special issue of *Parliamentary History*, 15 (1996), also published as
C. Jones (ed.), *The Scots and Parliament* (Edinburgh, 1996). See also I. E. O'Brien, 'The Scottish

The constitutional tradition also produced studies of other institutions, notably the college of justice[17] and the convention of royal burghs.[18] Local government was not neglected, and some editions of the records of sheriff courts, baron courts, and burgh of barony courts contain introductions of lasting significance.[19] Particular attention was paid to government in the royal burghs.[20] Ian Rae's study of the Borders deserves special mention.[21]

Related to constitutional history is administrative history. The Scottish administration, and especially the financial administration, has been the subject of numerous detailed studies, with the copious works of Athol Murray having particular importance.[22] Some other scholars have also illuminated

Parliament in the 15th and 16th Centuries' (Ph.D. thesis, Glasgow, 1980); J. Goodare, 'The Scottish Parliament of 1621', *Historical Journal*, 38 (1995), 29–51; id., 'The Scottish Parliamentary Records, 1560–1603', *Historical Research*, 72 (1999), 244–67; id., 'Scotland's Parliament in its British Context, 1603–1707', in H. T. Dickinson and M. Lynch (eds.), *The Challenge to Westminster: Sovereignty, Devolution and Independence* (East Linton, 2000); id., 'The Admission of Lairds to the Scottish Parliament', *English Historical Review*, 116 (2001), 1103–33; id., 'The Scottish Parliament and its Early Modern "Rivals"', *Parliaments, Estates and Representation*, 24 (2004, forthcoming); and A. R. MacDonald, 'Deliberative Processes in Parliament, c.1567–1639: Multicameralism and the Lords of the Articles', *SHR* 81 (2002), 23–51.

[17] The importance of the 1933 monograph on this by Robert K. Hannay was marked by its reprinting, along with six essays on parliament and other constitutional topics, as *The College of Justice: Essays by R. K. Hannay* (Stair Society, 1990).

[18] T. Pagan, *The Convention of the Royal Burghs of Scotland* (Glasgow, 1926).

[19] *Sheriff Court Book of Fife, 1515–1522*, ed. W. C. Dickinson (SHS, 1928); *Court Book of the Barony of Carnwath, 1523–1542*, ed. W. C. Dickinson (SHS, 1937); *Court Book of the Burgh of Kirkintilloch, 1658–1694*, ed. G. S. Pryde (SHS, 1963). There is an isolated but valuable survey of these institutions from a socio-economic point of view: T. C. Smout, 'Peasant and Lord in Scotland: Institutions Controlling Scottish Rural Society, 1500–1800', *Recueils de la Société Jean Bodin pour l'Histoire Comparative des Institutions*, 44 (1987), 499–524.

[20] D. Murray, *Early Burgh Organization in Scotland*, 2 vols. (Glasgow, 1924–32); *Ayr Burgh Accounts, 1534–1624*, ed. G. S. Pryde (SHS, 1937); id., 'Scottish Burgh Finances before 1707' (Ph.D. thesis, St Andrews, 1928); id., *The Burghs of Scotland: A Critical List* (Glasgow, 1965).

[21] T. I. Rae, *The Administration of the Scottish Frontier, 1513–1603* (Edinburgh, 1966). See also M. Wasser, 'The Pacification of the Scottish Borders, 1598–1612' (M.A. diss., McGill University, 1986).

[22] Dr Murray's main financial studies relevant to this period are A. L. Murray, 'The Exchequer and Crown Revenue of Scotland, 1437–1542' (Ph.D. thesis, Edinburgh, 1961); id., 'The Procedure of the Scottish Exchequer in the Early Sixteenth Century', *SHR* 40 (1961), 89–117; id., 'The Customs Accounts of Kirkcudbright, Wigtown, and Dumfries, 1434–1560', *Transactions of the Dumfriesshire and Galloway Natural History and Antiquarian Society*, 3rd ser. 40 (1963), 136–62; id., 'The Customs Accounts of Wigtown and Kirkcudbright, 1560–1660', *Transactions of the Dumfriesshire and Galloway Natural History and Antiquarian Society*, 3rd ser. 42 (1965), 114–32; id., 'The Scottish Treasury, 1667–1708', *SHR* 45 (1966), 89–104; id., 'The Revenues of the Bishopric of Moray in 1538', *Innes Review*, 19 (1968), 40–56; National Archives of Scotland, id., 'The Comptroller, 1425–1610' (David Berry prize essay, 1970), GA355.93 (cf. id., 'The Comptroller, 1425–1488', *SHR* 52 (1973), 1–29); id., 'Sir John Skene and the Exchequer, 1594–1612', *Stair Society Miscellany*, i (1971); id., 'The Pre-Union Records of the Scottish Exchequer', in F. Ranger (ed.), *Prisca Munimenta: Studies in Archival and Administrative History Presented to A. E. J. Hollaender* (London, 1973); id., 'Notes on the Treasury Administration', *TA* xii (1980); id., 'Financing the Royal Household: James V and his Comptrollers, 1513–1543', in I. B. Cowan and D. Shaw (eds.), *The Renaissance and Reformation in Scotland* (Edinburgh, 1983); id., 'The Salmon Fishings of Strathnaver, 1558–1559', *Review of Scottish Culture*, 8 (1993), 77–83; id., 'Exchequer, Council and Session,

aspects of the financial administration,[23] while Dr Murray has also written a number of other administrative studies.[24] A study of the privy council is badly needed.[25]

Also poorly served has been legal history.[26] There is no early modern equivalent to Hector MacQueen's splendid study of the late medieval common law.[27] Debate has been vigorous on certain issues in scholarly journals, notably foreign influence on Scots law, and how the court of session acquired its jurisdiction.[28] There are two books on legal aspects of the early sixteenth century. One, on the court of the bishop's official, tends to look backwards—these courts had existed for centuries but were abolished at the

1513–1542', in J. H. Williams (ed.), *Stewart Style, 1513–1542* (East Linton, 1996); id., 'Dirty Work at the Exchequer: Inverness's Charter and Accounts, 1592–1594', *Scottish Archives*, 4 (1998), 85–90; and id. (ed.), 'A Memorandum on the Customs, 1597', *SHS Miscellany*, xiii (2004, forthcoming).

[23] These include R. Nicholson, 'Feudal Developments in Late Medieval Scotland', *JR* NS 18 (1973), 1–21; C. Madden, 'The Finances of the Scottish Crown in the Later Middle Ages' (Ph.D. thesis, Glasgow, 1975); id., 'Royal Treatment of Feudal Casualties in Late Medieval Scotland', *SHR* 55 (1976), 172–94; J. E. L. Murray, 'The Organisation and Work of the Scottish Mint, 1358–1603', in D. M. Metcalf (ed.), *Coinage in Medieval Scotland, 1100–1600* (British Archaeological Reports, no. 45, 1977); J. Goodare, 'Parliamentary Taxation in Scotland, 1560–1603', *SHR* 68 (1989), 23–52; id., 'Thomas Foulis and the Scottish Fiscal Crisis of the 1590s', in W. M. Ormrod et al. (eds.), *Crises, Revolutions and Self-Sustained Growth: Essays in Fiscal History, 1130–1830* (Stamford, 1999); and id. (ed.), 'Fiscal Feudalism in Early Seventeenth-Century Scotland', *SHS Miscellany*, xiii (2004, forthcoming).

[24] These include A. L. Murray, 'The Lord Clerk Register', *SHR* 53 (1974), 124–56; id., 'Huntly's Rebellion and the Administration of Justice in North-East Scotland, 1570–1573', *Northern Scotland*, 4 (1981), 1–6; and id., 'The Scottish Chancery in the Fourteenth and Fifteenth Centuries', in K. Fianu and D. J. Guth (eds.), *Écrit et pouvoir dans les chancelleries médiévales: Espace français, espace anglais* (Louvain-la-Neuve, 1997).

[25] W. Taylor, 'The Scottish Privy Council, 1603–1625: Its Composition and its Work' (Ph.D. thesis, Edinburgh, 1950), is based on outdated assumptions. P. G. B. McNeill, 'The Jurisdiction of the Scottish Privy Council, 1532–1708' (Ph.D. thesis, Glasgow, 1960), is effective though narrowly focused. T. M. Chalmers, 'The King's Council, Patronage, and the Government of Scotland, 1460–1513' (Ph.D. thesis, Aberdeen, 1982), addresses a more up-to-date agenda and provides a model of what could be done for the period after the creation of a lasting privy council in 1545.

[26] There is a survey of the major works on the law of this period in J. W. Cairns et al., 'Legal Humanism and the History of Scots Law: John Skene and Thomas Craig', in J. MacQueen (ed.), *Humanism in Renaissance Scotland* (Edinburgh, 1990).

[27] H. L. MacQueen, *Common Law and Feudal Society in Medieval Scotland* (Edinburgh, 1993). In comparison, D. M. Walker, *A Legal History of Scotland*, iii: *The Sixteenth Century* (Edinburgh, 1995), and iv: *The Seventeenth Century* (Edinburgh, 1996), are disappointingly superficial. There is however much historical material in T. B. Smith (ed.), *The Laws of Scotland: Stair Memorial Encyclopedia*, 25 vols. (Edinburgh, 1987–95). Two older publications remain valuable: H. McKechnie (ed.), *Introductory Survey of the Sources and Literature of Scots Law* (Stair Society, 1936), and Lord Normand (ed.), *An Introduction to Scottish Legal History* (Stair Society, 1958). One important aspect is well covered by I. D. Willock, *The Origins and Development of the Jury in Scotland* (Stair Society, 1966).

[28] Recent works on these issues are W. D. H. Sellar, 'Scots Law: Mixed from the Very Beginning? A Tale of Two Receptions', *Edinburgh Law Review*, 4 (2000), 3–18, and A. M. Godfrey, 'Jurisdiction in Heritage and the Foundation of the College of Justice in 1532', *Stair Society Miscellany*, iv (2002).

Reformation. The other, on the beginnings of the legal profession, looks forward to the further rise of that profession throughout the early modern period.[29]

There is a good deal of recent scholarship on the Highlands, particularly two important books on the structure of clan society.[30] Michael Lynch and I have studied aspects of government policy towards the Highlands, in work that complements Chapter 10 below.[31] Other than that, straightforward political history has not been high on the agenda of Highland historians, and Donald Gregory's narrative, first published in 1836, has not been superseded in its entirety.[32] Jane Dawson's fine book on the fifth earl of Argyll shows what can be achieved with careful study and a modern research agenda, and there are other books on the later seventeenth century which offer some perspective on what came before.[33]

Pre-eminent in the government of Scotland, it has seemed, were kings. The 'Stewart Dynasty in Scotland' series, edited by Norman Macdougall, has produced a number of books assessing late medieval kings' relations with their magnates. The assumption has been that 'kingship' could work effectively if the king involved his magnates in his governing and distributed patronage wisely. Since Stewart monarchs were more often not governing than governing—minorities, captivities, and other incapacities took up over half their time—there are clearly further questions to be asked about late medieval politics and government, but the usefulness of the 'crown and magnates'

---

[29] S. D. Ollivant, *The Court of the Official in Pre-Reformation Scotland* (Stair Society, 1982); J. Finlay, *Men of Law in Pre-Reformation Scotland* (East Linton, 2000). See also G. Donaldson, 'The Legal Profession in Scottish Society in the Sixteenth and Seventeenth Centuries', *JR*, NS 21 (1976), 1–19.

[30] R. A. Dodgshon, *From Chiefs to Landlords: Social and Economic Change in the Western Highlands and Islands, c.1493–1820* (Edinburgh, 1998), and A. I. Macinnes, *Clanship, Commerce and the House of Stuart, 1603–1788* (East Linton, 1996).

[31] J. Goodare and M. Lynch, 'The Scottish State and its Borderlands, 1567–1625', and M. Lynch, 'James VI and the "Highland Problem"', both in J. Goodare and M. Lynch (eds.), *The Reign of James VI* (East Linton, 2000); J. Goodare, 'The Statutes of Iona in Context', *SHR* 77 (1998), 31–57; Goodare, *State and Society*, chs. 7–8. A further related study focuses more on images than on policies: A. H. Williamson, 'Scots, Indians and Empire: The Scottish Politics of Civilization, 1519–1609', *Past and Present*, 150 (Feb. 1996), 46–83.

[32] D. Gregory, *History of the Western Highlands and Isles of Scotland, 1493–1625* (2nd edn., London, 1881), complemented by W. C. Mackenzie, *History of the Outer Hebrides* (Paisley, 1903).

[33] J. E. A. Dawson, *The Politics of Religion in the Age of Mary Queen of Scots: The Earl of Argyll and the Struggle for Britain and Ireland* (Cambridge, 2002); D. Stevenson, *Alastair MacColla and the Highland Problem in the Seventeenth Century* (Edinburgh, 1980); and P. Hopkins, *Glencoe and the End of the Highland War* (Edinburgh, 1986).
Histories of individual clans are usually cited in more general works, but mention should be made of some recent Ph.D. theses: J. A. Stewart, 'The Clan Ranald: History of a Highland Kindred' (Ph.D. thesis, Edinburgh, 1982); M. D. W. MacGregor, 'A Political History of the MacGregors before 1571' (Ph.D. thesis, Edinburgh, 1989); F. A. MacDonald, 'Ireland and Scotland: Historical Perspectives on the Gaelic Dimension, 1560–1760' (Ph.D. thesis, Glasgow, 1994); and D. A. Watt, 'Chiefs, Lawyers and Debt: A Study of the Relationship between Highland Elite and Legal Profession in Scotland, c.1550 to 1700' (Ph.D. thesis, Edinburgh, 1998).

approach for that period seems established.[34] Early modern scholars sometimes seem to feel that they should adopt this approach, but attempts to apply a 'crown and magnates' agenda after the death of James IV in 1513 have not yet proved entirely convincing.[35] By the time of the Reformation, the increased importance of religion and diplomacy—not to mention parliament and even perhaps the political community—meant that the issue of 'kingship' was in some ways merely one among several.[36]

The Reformation came in 1560, and in the same year Scotland's 'auld alliance' with France was repudiated in favour of a virtually unprecedented 'amity' with England. Both these issues had been creating ideological fault lines in the political community for some time, but now the divisions were out in the open. A revolution had taken place, and while some people were happy about this, others were not. Patterns of politics came to be dominated by issues of *allegiance*. No longer did magnates simply relate individually to the king (or queen) and to their local rivals; they formed parties, took sides, and sought support on ideological grounds from those below them. This comes out clearly in a magisterial study by Gordon Donaldson.[37]

Along with issues of allegiance came the constitutional questions raised by the deposition of Mary queen of Scots in 1567, and the rise of 'resistance theory' in Scotland and on the Continent. People now gained new and sophisticated reasons for disobeying their kings—and, in response, new

---

[34] The 'Stewart Dynasty in Scotland' series, and the related debate on late medieval kingship, are discussed by M. Brown, 'The Taming of Scotland? Kings and Magnates in Late Medieval Scotland: A Review of Recent Work', *Innes Review*, 45 (1994), 120–46. N. Macdougall, *James IV* (Edinburgh, 1989), is a magisterial study in this series of a king whose reign raises issues of direct relevance to the late 16th c. An alternative approach to the period is offered by A. Grant, 'Crown and Nobility in Late Medieval Britain', in R. A. Mason (ed.), *Scotland and England, 1286–1815* (Edinburgh, 1987). The importance of parliament to magnate governance is shown by R. Tanner, *The Late Medieval Scottish Parliament: Politics and the Three Estates, 1424–1488* (East Linton, 2001).

[35] J. Cameron, *James V: The Personal Rule, 1528–1542* (East Linton, 1998), is vitiated by inattention to the role of parliament in connecting the king to the political community, not to mention the omission of religious policy. Also disappointing is P. E. Ritchie, *Mary of Guise in Scotland, 1548–1560* (East Linton, 2002), the main value of which is for diplomacy. M. Merriman, *The Rough Wooings: Mary Queen of Scots, 1542–1551* (East Linton, 2000), wisely ignores the 'crown and magnates' agenda and concentrates on diplomacy.

[36] The works most resembling studies of 'kingship' all address these broader issues rather than concentrating on 'crown and magnates': G. Donaldson, *Mary Queen of Scots* (London, 1974); M. Lynch (ed.), *Mary Stewart: Queen in Three Kingdoms* (Oxford, 1988); G. R. Hewitt, *Scotland under Morton, 1572–1580* (Edinburgh, 1982); M. Lee, *Great Britain's Solomon: James VI and I in his Three Kingdoms* (Urbana, Ill., 1990), and Goodare and Lynch (eds.), *The Reign of James VI*.

[37] G. Donaldson, *All the Queen's Men: Power and Politics in Mary Stewart's Scotland* (London, 1983). This deeply researched (if frustratingly under-referenced) work deals with the period *c.*1550–84, and concentrates not on Mary herself but on contested allegiances within the political community. The 16th-c. relevance of the scholarly literature on 'kingship' is discussed by J. Goodare, 'The Scottish Political Community and the Parliament of 1563', *Albion*, 35 (2003), 373–97. For a broader review article see S. Boardman and M. Lynch, 'The State of Late Medieval and Early Modern Scottish History', in T. Brotherstone and D. Ditchburn (eds.), *Freedom and Authority: Scotland, c.1050–c.1650* (East Linton, 2000).

and sophisticated reasons were developed for obeying them. Much work on the late sixteenth century has discussed political ideas.[38] Ideas became more important with the union of crowns in 1603, raising contentious issues with which contemporaries grappled with varying degrees of success.[39]

Finally there is the multi-faceted question of the changing nature of the Scottish political regime. The background to this was the changing relationship of the nobility with the state, since the regime was constituted in association with the nobility. Nobles abandoned autonomous military power, and the government demonstrated increasing ability to get them to obey a wide range of laws, in the period *c.*1584–1625. The change was traumatic but eventually decisive.[40]

This raises other questions: what the nobles did once they ceased feuding, and whether other social groups were involved in government. Maurice Lee first opened up this topic with a remarkable study of James VI's outstanding secretary and chancellor, John Maitland of Thirlestane, who he argued was instrumental in reforming Scotland in the late 1580s and early 1590s so as to lay the foundations of an integrated state focused on monarchical authority.[41] Professor Lee's later works have been concerned, not only to establish a political narrative for the early seventeenth century, but also to show this integrated state in action and to explain the making of government policy by the crown and privy council in partnership with the nobility.[42] Other scholars have developed aspects of this, in particular a study of James VI's non-noble administrators, and an account of government

[38] A. H. Williamson, *Scottish National Consciousness in the Age of James VI* (Edinburgh, 1979); J. H. Burns, *The True Law of Kingship: Concepts of Monarchy in Early-Modern Scotland* (Oxford, 1996); and R. A. Mason, *Kingship and the Commonweal: Political Thought in Renaissance and Reformation Scotland* (East Linton, 1998). Some of these works also discuss the pre-Reformation period, but they show the raising of the ideological temperature in the late 16th c.

[39] W. Ferguson, *Scotland's Relations with England: A Survey to 1707* (Edinburgh, 1977); B. Galloway, *The Union of England and Scotland, 1603–1608* (Edinburgh, 1986); B. P. Levack, *The Formation of the British State: England, Scotland and the Union, 1603–1707* (Oxford, 1987); J. Wormald, 'The Creation of Britain: Multiple Kingdoms or Core and Colonies?', *Transactions of the Royal Historical Society*, 6th ser. 2 (1992), 175–94; R. A. Mason (ed.), *Scotland and England, 1286–1815* (Edinburgh, 1987); id. (ed.), *Scots and Britons: Scottish Political Thought and the Union of 1603* (Cambridge, 1994); B. Bradshaw and J. Morrill (eds.), *The British Problem, c.1534–1707* (London, 1996); and David Hume of Godscroft, *The British Union*, ed. P. J. McGinnis and A. H. Williamson (Aldershot, 2002).

[40] J. Wormald, *Lords and Men in Scotland: Bonds of Manrent, 1442–1603* (Edinburgh, 1985); K. M. Brown, *Bloodfeud in Scotland, 1573–1625* (Edinburgh, 1986); and M. B. Wasser, 'Violence and the Central Criminal Courts in Scotland, 1603–1638' (Ph.D. diss., Columbia University, 1995).

[41] M. Lee, *John Maitland of Thirlestane and the Foundation of the Stewart Despotism in Scotland* (Princeton, 1959). The term 'despotism', which Professor Lee has since dropped, indicates a concept similar to what I and others have later called 'absolutism'.

[42] M. Lee, *Government by Pen: Scotland under James VI and I* (Urbana, Ill., 1980), and id., *The Road to Revolution: Scotland under Charles I, 1625–1637* (Urbana, Ill., 1985).

policy under Charles I and how it became so unpopular as to provoke revolution.[43]

I have tried in this book to interpret the Scottish scholarship in the light of wider studies of state formation. Studies of England are particularly interesting because of England's close connection with Scottish history and because English scholarship on the subject is well developed; two recent books have focused fruitfully on the development of state power as it was articulated in the localities and amongst the common people.[44]

There is no shortage of broad social theories of the state. These can help to organize the evidence in thought-provoking ways, though they were rarely developed with Scotland in mind, and can never be pressed further than the evidence will permit. Perry Anderson's concept of the absolutist state, with a centralized administration grafted onto a peasant economy dominated by landlords, has been much cited.[45] Ernest Gellner's model of the articulation of power, poised between material economic realities and patterns of culture and cognition, is breathtaking in its broad sweep.[46] Michael Mann's typology of separate but interdependent forms of social power has considerable analytical value.[47] There are numerous other such works.[48] Finally, the 'Origins of the Modern State in Europe' series, sponsored by the European Science Foundation, is a carefully planned series of works by a large group of scholars, lacking the single synoptic view of a Gellner or a Mann but bringing to the subject a range of detailed expertise.[49]

---

[43] R. R. Zulager, 'A Study of the Middle-Rank Administrators in the Government of King James VI of Scotland, 1580–1603' (Ph.D. thesis, Aberdeen, 1991), and A. I. Macinnes, *Charles I and the Making of the Covenanting Movement, 1625–1641* (Edinburgh, 1991). For my own studies related to this see J. Goodare, 'The Nobility and the Absolutist State in Scotland, 1584–1638', *History*, 78 (1993), 161–82, and id., *State and Society*, chs. 2–3.

[44] M. J. Braddick, *State Formation in Early Modern England, c.1550–1700* (Cambridge, 2000); S. Hindle, *The State and Social Change in Early Modern England, c.1550–1640* (London, 2000). For the debate on the 'Tudor revolution in government', see Ch. 12 below.

[45] P. Anderson, *Lineages of the Absolutist State* (London, 1974).

[46] E. Gellner, *Plough, Sword and Book: The Structure of Human History* (London, 1988).

[47] M. Mann, *The Sources of Social Power*, i: *A History of Power to AD 1760* (Cambridge, 1986).

[48] These include P. Corrigan and D. Sayer, *The Great Arch: English State Formation as Cultural Revolution* (Oxford, 1985); T. Ertman, *Birth of the Leviathan: Building States and Regimes in Medieval and Early Modern Europe* (Cambridge, 1997); S. E. Finer, *The History of Government from the Earliest Times*, 3 vols. (Oxford, 1997); C. Tilly (ed.), *The Formation of National States in Western Europe* (Princeton, 1975); and id., *Coercion, Capital and European States, AD 990–1990* (Oxford, 1990). Two seminal articles are H. G. Koenigsberger, 'Monarchies and Parliaments in Early Modern Europe: *Dominium regale* or *Dominium politicum et regale*', *Theory and Society*, 5 (1978), 191–217, and J. H. Elliott, 'A Europe of Composite Monarchies', *Past and Present*, 137 (Nov. 1992), 48–71.

[49] P. Blickle (ed.), *Resistance, Representation, and Community* (Oxford, 1997); R. Bonney (ed.), *Economic Systems and State Finance* (Oxford, 1996); J. Coleman (ed.), *The Individual in Political Theory and Practice* (Oxford, 1996); P. Contamine (ed.), *War and Competition between States* (Oxford, 2000); A. Ellenius (ed.), *Iconography, Propaganda, and Legitimation* (Oxford, 1998); A. Padoa-Schioppa (ed.), *Legislation and Justice* (Oxford, 1997); and W. Reinhard (ed.), *Power Elites and State Building* (Oxford, 1996).

In studying the history of government, we have to think ourselves into the minds of the policy-makers. Mary and James VI, the regents in the latter's minority, their chancellors, secretaries, and treasurers, and their subordinates, all knew themselves to be governors and worked at their tasks deliberately. We must grasp what options they saw themselves as having in the light of the information available to them and the value system within which they operated. Only thus can we explain why the Scottish government did one thing and not another.

But having thought ourselves into the policy-makers' minds, we ought to think ourselves out again. It is all too easy, immersed in government papers, to adopt the government's own value system. We view the world as if from the throne, or from the chancellor's desk, and say: These were the problems facing Scotland. We ought rather to say: These were the problems facing Scotland's *rulers*. Many histories, otherwise enlightening, have failed to make this distinction, and have assumed that the problem of early modern Scotland was 'lawlessness', 'disorder', 'lack of effective control', or some such phrase. James VI and his councillors thought they had a problem of 'disorder' when people would not obey them; the people themselves may have perceived a problem of unreasonable royal demands and interference. Or perhaps not: perhaps the people too, or some of them, agreed that there was 'disorder' and that laws against it needed enforcement; but that is something that can be discovered only through case-by-case study of the evidence, and only by taking into account the perspective of the people. From their perspective, government could solve problems, but it could also create them.

Problem-solving and problem-creation could even be symbiotic. Governmental expansion into new areas might be forced in order to protect parts of the state's structure—as when taxes had to be increased to pay for governmental activities. This might solve problems, but equally, it might create new ones. The restructuring of the church after 1596, originally undertaken with the limited aim of curbing ecclesiastical dissidents, took on a life of its own and ended up threatening the beliefs of many. Expansion of the state could lead to instability.

So the growth of the state is not necessarily something to celebrate. This may be confirmed from a brief glance at an even broader perspective on state structures and processes of power—the perspective of civilization as a whole. Human history is far more than the history of people living in states, and more even than the history of civilization. As Michael Mann has commented, the state has been part of civilization, and perhaps an unwelcome part:

Civilization was an abnormal phenomenon. It involved the state and social stratification, both of which human beings have spent most of their existence avoiding.[50]

---

[50] Mann, *Sources of Social Power*, i. 124. The same point emerges if we regard 'civilizations' as essentially plural rather than singular, as in F. Braudel, *A History of Civilisations*, trans. R. Mayne (Harmondsworth, 1993).

This point should be borne in mind, not only in connection with Chapter 11 when the official treatment of some of those in the lower social strata is discussed, but also more generally. Governments are constituted as vehicles for broader social interests—particularly, although not exclusively, the interests of the propertied. Today this presents itself as a contrast between the formal choice of a government by the voters and the practical influence of corporate lobbyists. The contrast is particularly stark when so many of the voters decline to vote. In early modern times, powerful economic interests openly and directly constituted themselves central and local governors. But they did not govern *as* economic interests; they had to take on a more public form. They needed the public infrastructure that only a government could provide: laws, and means to enforce them.

Some of the ways in which early modern economic interests used government will emerge in the pages that follow. Versions of the issues thus raised are sometimes still with us, as when we are told that 'McDonald's cannot flourish without McDonnell Douglas, the designer of the US Airforce F-15'.[51] This is often discussed these days in terms of 'globalization', with the implication that it is something new. In fact, the idea that trans-global influences are new is hardly borne out by the historical record. The names just quoted are bound to remind Scottish historians of a previous phase of 'globalization', the expansion of the British empire. Broad global interconnections can be traced back to the early modern period and even further.[52]

So it would be a mistake to equate the state—public authority—with individual states; neither civilization nor social stratification are confined within national boundaries, and there is no reason to think that the exercise of power can be studied in hermetically sealed compartments. If we study individual states, as by and large we must, it cannot be bad for us from time to time to reflect on what we are doing. Why is this geographical expression we know as Scotland a valid field of historical enquiry, in the early modern period or in any other? What, if anything, distinguished it from England, France, or western Europe, and what did it share with them? Might we not do better, for instance, to look at a 'complex of interacting cultures' within the British Isles?[53] In many ways we should. The states of early modern Europe were in certain crucial ways more similar to one another than they were to the medieval kingdoms—and other political entities—that had preceded them. The impact of the early modern state was not very different for the people of Lanarkshire from what it was for those of Lancashire, and to that extent I can only plead convenience for restricting my enquiry to the former; what I have to say is also relevant in a general way to the latter.

[51] Thomas Friedman, *New York Times* columnist, quoted in W. Bello, *Deglobalization: Ideas for a New World Economy* (London, 2002), 8.

[52] A. G. Frank and B. K. Gills (eds.), *The World System: Five Hundred Years or Five Thousand?* (London, 1993).

[53] H. Kearney, *The British Isles: A History of Four Nations* (Cambridge, 1989), 4.

Have I just said that southern Scotland and northern England were the same? I think not; but those to whom this question occurs will know that the political identity of the Scottish nation has been much discussed in recent decades. The key question has been the nature of the relationship that Scotland has, or ought to have, with a powerful southern neighbour that is in some ways similar, in others different, and is often unsympathetic to special Scottish characteristics. This was an important question in the sixteenth and seventeenth centuries too, though usually in different ways. But I hope it does not diminish the importance of the Scottish national question to say that this book is primarily about an even more important issue— the expansion of government until it was supreme over older, more private, more local forms of authority. Whether the 'centre'—the ultimate source of supreme public authority—was located in Edinburgh or London was for most purposes less important than whether it should exist at all. Feudal magnates on both sides of the Border exercised their own authority in the fifteenth century; they did not ask permission in either capital before acting. The two kingdoms had been frequently at war since 1296, and warfare forced people to take sides, yet day-to-day government was carried on with little reference to central authority. The Border ballads celebrated the values of kinship, and were contemptuous of wardens and officials. Public authority was eventually established on both sides of the Border by 1603, but the transfer of overall authority from Edinburgh to London at that date was a less significant event than the integration of the magnates into a matrix of state authority.

This state emerged unproclaimed and unplanned. Many historians have assumed that the union of crowns, so often proclaimed and celebrated at the time, was actually the cause of the governmental developments that began to manifest themselves in Scotland later in the reign of James VI. This assumption is challenged in Chapters 4 and 6, which try to cut the union of crowns down to size. But there were some people who did work hard at the serious business of governing, and whose efforts gradually brought change, even if it was not always the change that they intended. It is worth considering who they were and how they operated. The king, obviously, would expect to benefit—but in practice he might not, since governmental specialization and complexity might make it harder for him to lay his hands on the levers of power. As Norbert Elias pointed out long ago, increasing specialization tends to lead both to centralization, increasing the power of the central rulers, *and* to those rulers becoming dependent upon their subordinates. He wrote repeatedly of a 'human web with high and increasing division of functions'.[54] The state was a matrix of authority, penetrating society intimately but also (and for that reason) dispersed widely through it. Just because the mesh

[54] N. Elias, *The Civilizing Process*, trans. E. Jephcott (Oxford, 1994), 345–55.

became narrower over time, that does not mean that the influence wielded from any one point on the mesh was more decisive.

It is more useful to look at the people connected with central government as a whole, both those involved in it directly, and (to a lesser but relevant degree) those who used its services. They would include legislators, who discovered the power that could be wielded by a statute; beneficiaries of legislation, who were enabled to do new things; litigants in the central courts and petitioners to the privy council, who sought from the crown something that they thought would be justice, and who were willing to pay for this service that the crown was now beginning to provide; courtiers, whose standing in the country was enhanced by their influential position at court and the profits this brought from clients; and Protestant churchmen, who aimed to capture the church, and then govern it, at a national level (with the support of the crown, or without it). National integration, through law, through national institutions, through centrally orchestrated client networks, and through religion, made the business of government more hectic and even exciting. Meanwhile, for traditional, autonomous forms of authority in the localities, the story was sometimes of quiet decay, sometimes of reconstruction in a new form, and occasionally of deliberate demolition.

Scotland lagged behind in many of those governmental developments that it shared with England. Scotland in the 1580s looks in some ways like England in the 1530s. We may well not accept that English governmental restructuring occurred primarily in the 1530s;[55] equally, there is no need to confine Scottish developments to the 1580s. Countries coming late to state formation might feel pressure from more advanced neighbours—but they had some advantages. Administrative structures had a tendency to diverge from their original purpose, and to become less responsive to demands from the centre; those states that created their institutions early might be at a disadvantage a century or two later. States following in their wake could adopt the latest administrative methods.[56]

The proliferation of institutions and of authority was a series of waves, but not merely an oscillation up and down. Each wave moved forwards, and was followed by another one behind it and then above it. This produced a complex pattern. If we concentrate on the forward movement of certain individual waves, we may feel that they carry the whole story of governmental development. On closer inspection we may find these same waves losing their force or even receding in later periods. Waves of governmental authority recede less readily than hydraulic ones, but there was still (and is still) a long-term

---

[55] As argued by Professor Elton in *The Tudor Revolution in Government*. One line of criticism of the 'Tudor revolution' is that the changes cited by Professor Elton did occur, but not primarily in the 1530s or in a planned way: D. Starkey, 'After the "Revolution"', in C. Coleman and D. Starkey (eds.), *Revolution Reassessed: Revisions in the History of Tudor Government and Administration* (Oxford, 1986), 199–201. This is discussed in Ch. 12 below.

[56] Ertman, *Birth of the Leviathan*, 26–8, 318–19.

tendency for laws to lose their relevance to current issues and for taxes to decline in value. In its time a particular wave may still have hit the beach quite
hard, so its subsequent withdrawal may not be a reason for dismissing it. But
the point is that it cannot carry the whole story. It is essential to understand
individual waves, but we must also look beyond them to grasp the general
pattern of governmental development. New laws and new taxes were flood-
ing forwards. The long-term pattern was formed by the cumulative effect of
many waves, and by the fact that in our period, the tide was coming in.

CHAPTER ONE

Legitimacy

> As the head is ordeined for the body and not the body for the head, so
> must a righteous king know himselfe to bee ordeined for his people, and
> not his people for him.
>
> James VI & I, speech to parliament, 1604, in *Political Writings*, 143

Queen Mary returned to her native land in 1561 with three ships and a few
dozen unarmed servants and companions. She came to take over the government of a kingdom in which a provisional administration had been formed in
the previous year by the Protestant insurgents, the 'Lords of the Congregation', who had overthrown the regency of her mother, Mary of Guise. They
thus had a lot of explaining to do, both to their queen and to the world. How
had their rebellion been justified? How had it been able, as it gathered
momentum, to turn itself into a government?

An outline of the new administration had first taken shape on 1 August
1559, when the Lords of the Congregation made a bond not to communicate
with the regent. In September, the English ambassadors pointed out to the
Congregation that 'the worlde can make nae other exposycion of it, but that
they be as it were a faction gathered togither, contending agenst th'auctoryte'.
But by October they had claimed to be more than a faction: they had described themselves as 'the lawful heads and born councillors of this realm',
and referred to their leadership as a 'Great Council', a phrase implying governmental authority. They had summoned a convention of estates (consisting
only of their supporters, but they had many supporters) which deposed the
regent—in the name, but without the permission, of the king and queen. The
convention had heard a rousing speech from the leading minister John
Willock, declaring that 'as subjects are commanded to obey their magistrates,
so are magistrates commanded to give some duty to the subjects', and that
'albeit God hath appointed magistrates his lieutenants on earth . . . yet He
did never so establish any but that, for just causes, they might have been
deprived'.[1]

---

[1] John Knox, *History of the Reformation in Scotland*, 2 vols., ed. W. C. Dickinson (London,
1949), i. 206–7, 239, 245, 249–51; Sir Ralph Sadler and Sir James Crofts to Sir William Cecil, 8
Sept. 1559, *State Papers and Letters of Sir Ralph Sadler*, 3 vols., ed. A. Clifford (Edinburgh,
1809), i. 432–3. Knox at the time referred to the establishment of the 'Great Counsall' as

The queen was thus presented with an explicitly contractual view of government. Her mother had been justly deposed for neglecting her subjects' rights. The provisional administration claimed to have God on its side; this was common to all sixteenth-century governments and would-be governments, and was not insignificant. More immediately noteworthy is the variety of other sources on which the administration drew to legitimize its authority. It was based on the innate rights of the nobility (the 'born councillors'); it had been endorsed by the three estates (not just the partisan convention of October 1559, but the well-attended Reformation Parliament of the following August); it had a morsel of dynastic credibility (in using Mary's name, and in the adherence of the heir presumptive, the duke of Châtelherault); and it had diplomatic recognition from the English (whose troops had helped to install it). And it was in *power*—something that always commands a certain respect.

Mary's arrival shows us a monarch adding herself to an already constituted government. The secretary, William Maitland, had been jittery at the prospect of her coming, because she had not yet established a relationship with the council; he feared that others might influence her to the council's detriment.[2] But he need not have worried. The council she appointed was a 'Greit Counsale', continuing the existing structure and terminology, and the leaders of the provisional government were all members of it (although there was some broadening of membership). Two weeks later the council started calling itself by the normal term, 'Secreit Counsale' or privy council, the council specifically of the monarch.[3] The smoothness of this transition reminds us that it was never simply the queen who constituted the government, just as the multifarious justifications for that government's authority caution us against ascribing unilinear monarchism to all sixteenth-century thinkers and propagandists. The queen herself had an important dual role. She personally validated the government (for which her name sufficed) and coordinated its various components (for which political skills and activity were required).

How had she acquired this role, and how was it maintained on her behalf? It was through a set of formal rules and informal customs: rules governing her succession to the throne, rules governing what commands she was entitled to issue (on her own account, or in conjunction with other bodies such as parliament), and conventions as to what the guiding principles of her

subsequent to the regent's deposition: Knox to Gregory Railton, 23 Oct. 1559, *Sadler Papers*, ii. 218. For an early decree issued by the Lords of the Congregation in Oct. 1559 laying down penalties for adultery, see Dundee City Archive and Record Centre, Dundee council minutes, vol. i, p. 11. For the ideology of the religious revolution, see Burns, *The True Law of Kingship*, 153–72, and R. Mason, 'Covenant and Commonweal: The Language of Politics in Reformation Scotland', in N. Macdougall (ed.), *Church, Politics and Society: Scotland, 1408–1929* (Edinburgh, 1983).

[2] M. Loughlin, 'The Career of Maitland of Lethington, c.1526–1573' (Ph.D. thesis, Edinburgh, 1991), 99–101.   [3] *RPC* i. 157, 163.

commands should be. She was of course the legal monarch by the formal rules; her own accession in 1542, a female aged one week, in the middle of a war, provides the clearest illustration of the Scots' attachment to these rules. There were also powerful informal customs telling the queen, and those who acted in her name, how they were expected to govern. Adherence to these rules and customs showed the government to be, in James VI's words above, 'righteous'.

James VI made his speech long after he had repudiated any suggestion of a contractual basis for his government. He was shocked at the 'popular tumult and rebellion' of 1559–60, and regarded himself as an absolute king.[4] And yet, as he well knew, a government's power to do things was hedged round by a myriad of practical restraints. He had the right to issue binding commands, but he did not just get up in the morning and start issuing whatever commands he felt like. He ascertained whether a command was likely to be respected before acting. So long as he did this successfully, he would draw little attention to the practical restraints on his theoretical power, simply because he made sure that he acted within them. What he and his government did was not just legal, but widely accepted. It was *legitimate*.[5]

This chapter, then, has as its starting point the acceptance of government by the political community. People agreed, on the whole, that they ought to be governed; this formed the basis for the legitimacy of the government they had. In investigating this, we should consider law and government as a reflection of a set of shared values. People were just as capable in the sixteenth century as they are today of recognizing that a law might be formally legal but undesirable or even unjust. They might still argue for obedience to such a law; many, then as now, included the value of obedience *per se* among their political values, and it was harder then to advance utilitarian arguments for disobedience, although God could be invoked. On the other hand, to say that government is accepted as legitimate is not necessarily to say that it is welcomed. People's expectations of government may be low, and they may put up with it as they put up with the weather. If they accept what the government has just done as normal behaviour for a government, that may be enough for legitimacy in practice; but it may fall well short of saying that they think the government did what it ought to have done.[6] Clearly, people thought that some laws and governmental actions were better than others. How were *good* government and *good* laws to be identified, either by legislators or by subjects?

[4] James VI, *Basilicon Doron*, in *Political Writings*, 25; R. A. Mason, 'James VI, George Buchanan, and *The True Lawe of Free Monarchies*', in his *Kingship and the Commonweal*.

[5] What follows on this subject has been influenced by R. Barker, *Political Legitimacy and the State* (Oxford, 1990); D. Beetham, *The Legitimation of Power* (London, 1991); and, for discussion of the concept's applicability to this period, Braddick, *State Formation in Early Modern England*, 68–85.

[6] L. R. Della Fave, 'Towards an Explication of the Legitimation Process', *Social Forces*, 65 (1986), 476–500.

Legitimacy is ultimately about what people think about government. But it cannot be so directly. What they think is irrelevant unless their thoughts are manifested in action; if they keep their thoughts to themselves, not only will they have no effect on the government, but they will leave no trace in the historical record. We are interested in whether they act to endorse or participate in the government (even distantly, such as by paying taxes), or whether they act to undermine it (even indirectly, by passive non-cooperation). Historical evidence is available for this; and if people act to endorse the government, their precise inner motives for doing so matter less. If people's government-endorsing actions arise wholly from cynical self-interest, or from fear of retribution, they may rapidly desert the government in a crisis. But even if political actors' publicly expressed beliefs are insincere, the fact that they have expressed them still gives them a motive for adhering to them; both politicians and ordinary people wish to avoid being seen as insincere or inconsistent. It is at any rate normal for people's government-endorsing actions to be sincere enough to indicate that they intend to continue endorsing it.

What people do about government extends to what they *say* about it. Expressing an opinion about the government is tantamount to supporting or undermining it. Routine grumbling about tax bills is common enough, but if the grumbling gets a bit louder it will strengthen people's reluctance to pay, making tax collection harder. The grumblers may also question why the government needs the money, moving into the field of criticizing government policy. Enough of this can inspire broader anti-government movements. From routine grumbling about taxes there is a lengthy but clear continuum ending in mass non-payment campaigns, ideologically charged and with the explicit design of bringing down the government. The Netherlands experienced such a campaign against the 'tenth penny' in 1571–2, which proved crucial in the successful revolt of the northern provinces against Spanish rule. The Dutch victory reverberated round Europe, and the Scots were fully aware of its significance.[7]

It is more normal for people to pay their taxes. If they do, this confers legitimacy on the government. Payment acts as a public affirmation that the taxpayers have accepted the government as legitimate. They may actually be glad to pay if they are keen on the cause for which the government is levying the taxes, but even if (as is probably more common) they pay with reluctance, the point is that they do pay. Every time they do so they affirm, to themselves and to anyone else who knows about their action, that the government is something that ought in general to be obeyed. Success in collecting taxes also strengthens the government by giving it financial resources, but this is separate from the issue of legitimacy. All forms of active participation or acquiescence in government confer legitimacy. In early modern times, people

---

[7] Craig, *Jus Feudale*, I.16.16.

attended coronations, royal entries and other ceremonial occasions, participated in parliaments and other political assemblies, and swore political
oaths.[8]

The legitimation of government was a dynamic process. The government
was continually doing things that would demonstrate its legitimacy;
laws came forth trailing clouds of rhetoric announcing them as just, wise,
and beneficial, and everybody (of course) welcomed them as such.[9] For
historians, this is usually just verbiage through which to wade in search of
other things. In considering the statute of 1606 on the royal prerogative,
what we want to know is how parliament actually changed royal power over
the church; we are impatient when, instead of getting to the point, the act tells
us that

God ... hes endewed his majestie with sa mony extraordinar graces and maist
rare and excellent virtues as he is not onlie knawin by daylie and manifest experiences
in materis of greatest difficultie and consequence, to the unspeakable conforte of
all his faithfull subjectis, to be capable of the happie governement of his saidis
kingdomes, bot be his maist singular judgement, foirsicht and princelie wisdome,
worthie to posses and habill to governe far greater dominionis . . . God hes manifestlie
expressit his heavinlie will to be that his majesties imperiall power, quhilk God hes sa
gratiouslie inlarged, sall nocht by thame [i.e. the estates] in ony sorte be impared,
prejudged or diminissed, bot rather reverenced and augmented sofar as possible they
can.[10]

Et cetera. In fact this act's concrete force was small; the rules were unclear,
and remained so. The verbiage, filling the air with monarchist rhetoric, *was*
the point. It was on this that the legitimacy, not just of the law, but of the king
and his dynasty, depended.

We can thus identify a hierarchy—or perhaps a matrix—of elements of
government, for each of which in turn legitimacy had to be established. The
legitimacy of the dynasty was basic enough, and dynasticism grew more
insistent with the desire of Mary and James to succeed Elizabeth on purely
dynastic grounds; but more fundamental yet was the institution of monarchy
itself. This was not often questioned, but thinkers knew that there was nothing necessary about it, and Roger Mason points out how basic was the question that the upheavals of the 1560s and 1570s posed for James: 'Why should
we obey you?'[11] People could also weigh the pros and cons of elective and

---

[8] Beetham, *Legitimation of Power*, 90–5.

[9] The development of preambles to statutes, explaining and justifying them, took place
gradually in the middle decades of the 16th c. The innovatory preambles produced in the
parliament of 1540 may be linked with the experimental printing of that parliament's statutes.
Cf. a comparable development in England: S. J. Gunn, *Early Tudor Government, 1485–1558*
(London, 1995), 188.

[10] *APS* iv. 281, c. 1.

[11] R. A. Mason, 'George Buchanan, James VI and the Presbyterians', in id. (ed.), *Scots and
Britons*, 119. Cf. Williamson, *Scottish National Consciousness*, 50–2.

hereditary kingship.[12] The greatest political theorist of that period, George Buchanan, envisaged a radical reduction in the monarch's power. Things were very different by the time of the 1606 prerogative statute, and although this flew high in its obsequious royalism, the privy council soared yet higher in conveying parliament's sentiments to James:

This acknauledging of the princes soverayne prerogative wes dew to all the kingis that ever rang in this realme, bot so mekill more to your majestie, nor to any uther that ever possessed that royal dignitie, as be the merite of your majesties awin peculiar qualities and most rare vertewes, thay thocht gif the kingdome had bene elective, that of all that leivis in this aige, your majesties self wald be fund wourthiest to be chosin be election to ressave and posses all soverane power.[13]

So even if Buchanan had won, they would still have elected James: a reassuring thought, no doubt. The presbyterian David Calderwood, noting that the act offered James's personal qualities as its rationale, commented sourly, 'But this respect is not hereditarie.'[14] Both the official ideology and the presbyterians were extreme, however, and most people probably accepted monarchy pragmatically. Thomas Craig thought that 'kings were first instituted by God', but that monarchy was 'settled on an hereditary basis in order that the ambition and strife of men might be stayed'.[15]

The monarch as ultimate terrestrial symbol of political legitimacy had in our period both a long future and a long past. Especially with Scotland's long royal minorities, the symbol might almost as well have been an inanimate object, like the conch shell in Golding's *Lord of the Flies*. When political differences became so severe, in 1570–3, that the factions could not even agree on the ultimate source of authority, it is hard to say which faction had the more impressive symbol: the queen's party, whose parliaments were held with the correct regalia and who could refer to an adult monarch even if she was inadvertently absent, or the king's party, who could produce an infant but no regalia.[16] The regents who ruled in the name of the young king never claimed to be more than ordinary nobles bearing a temporary and elective responsibility. In theory they could have attained a higher status, as with the much-flattered royal favourites who exercised power in the absolute monarchies of early seventeenth-century Europe, so their modesty may have as much to do with the general position of the Scottish crown in the sixteenth century as with their lack of royal blood. At any rate, the adult reign of James VI would enhance the monarch's personal authority in the government (see below, Chapter 4). Monarchs, more than any other form or component of government, could appeal to divine sanction and tradition.

[12] Burns, *True Law of Kingship*, 38–9.
[13] Council to James, 4 July 1606, *Melros Papers*, i. 16. 'Rang' = reigned.
[14] Calderwood, *History*, vi. 495.   [15] Craig, *De Unione*, 229.
[16] Donaldson, *All the Queen's Men*, 121.

Theory, while granting a high authority to monarchs, recognized that such authority could be misused. In doing so, the monarch would become a tyrant: the simplest definition of a tyrant, indeed, was that she or he failed to rule in the interests of the 'people' (that is, broadly, the propertied classes). Buchanan argued that Mary, in common with many of her predecessors, had been a tyrant of this type.[17] But although it was not tyranny, or even a reputation for tyranny, that caused Mary's downfall, James knew that he could not afford to be typecast as a tyrant. Early in his reign, he put much effort into justifying this. In 1591 he issued a coin depicting the sword and scales of Justice, with the legend 'In these a king differs from a tyrant'.[18] Later, he felt more secure on the question, and discussion of tyranny was deliberately muted. The Geneva Bible of 1560, which James regarded as seditious, frequently used the word 'tyrant'; it was omitted from the Authorized Version of 1611.[19] It was still possible to recognize publicly that some kings were somewhat better than others, so long as the current occupant of the throne was awarded top marks. Bishop William Cowper, preaching before the king in 1617, linked his praise of James with lengthy passages discussing the difference between good and bad kings.[20] The government needed to give the impression of recognizing that it was possible for a king not to be legitimate, but it tried to control the terms of debate. James might claim not to be a tyrant, but his subjects could not freely discuss whether he was one or not.

When it came to specific royal measures, then, it was not just a matter of appealing to divine sanction, or to tradition, or to the necessity of obedience. James justified his actions not only in terms of his prerogative—that he had the right to do as he did—but in utilitarian terms too—that he was doing what was best for the people. He argued the case for his measures, 'power being joyned to reasoun (as hes ever bein our constant forme of proceiding in all our governament)'. But he added that if anyone had 'ony scruple of the justice and necessitie of his hienes proceidings heirin, it doth only proceid of ignorance or mistaking the trewth of his hienes actions'.[21] Similar conceits may be found lodged in the minds of rulers down to this day.

Still, it would be as well not to be too cynical. The relationship between the ultimate, divine source of authority and the actions of the government was a two-way one. Conventional accounts of legitimacy have it working to get people to agree to obey a government measure because it had divine sanction. Certainly this might persuade devout people to accept it. But God was

---

[17] W. A. Gatherer (ed.), *The Tyrannous Reign of Mary Stewart: George Buchanan's Account* (Edinburgh, 1958). One could also be a tyrant through conquest, but this type of tyranny was not an issue in Scotland.

[18] I. Stewart, 'Coinage and Propaganda: An Interpretation of the Coin-Types of James VI', in A. O'Connor and D. V. Clarke (eds.), *From the Stone Age to the 'Forty-five* (Edinburgh, 1983), 458; Burns, *True Law of Kingship*, 284–6.

[19] C. Hill, *The English Bible and the Seventeenth-Century Revolution* (London, 1993), 59–60.

[20] William Cowper, *Workes* (2nd edn., London, 1629), 782–3, 788–90.

[21] *RPC* vii. 193, 190.

supposed to be good. Might not the terrestrial goodness of a measure persuade devout people that it had divine sanction? Instead of saying, 'I can't see the practical value of this measure, but I will support it because I have been persuaded that it comes from God', they might sometimes say, 'I *can* see the practical value of this measure, and this persuades me that it comes from God.' Both types of reasoning probably occurred on occasion, and could even be mutually reinforcing. If governments did enough things that had self-evident practical value for their subjects, then the subjects would be more likely to take other more questionable measures on trust.

Monarchs needed servants and advisers. The privy council, including the great officers of state, could expect to have the legitimacy of its composition subjected to critical scrutiny. The usual theme (endless variations were possible) was: should the monarch choose the privy council personally and without constraint, or should he or she be advised and served primarily by the greatest magnates? Put like that, the two options were ultimately incompatible, but nobody could say so; the correct answer to both questions was yes. James VI was wholly conventional in envisaging his son 'choosing your servants for your own use, and not for the use of others . . . indifferently out of all quarters', and also that he would 'delight to be served with men of the noblest blood that may be had'.[22] If either option were felt to be absent, the legitimacy of the council's composition might be doubted, especially by those who disapproved of its latest activities. Mary's government was criticized both for allegedly making her the pawn of a baronial clique (too much influence for the earls of Moray or Bothwell), and for allegedly being a royal tyranny in contempt of the nobility (too much influence for David Riccio). Both views—though historians of Mary's reign are sometimes tempted to take one or other of them at face value—tell us less about political practice in the 1560s than about the language in which political debate was conducted. The creative tension between the two views was at the heart of a polity that was both monarchical and aristocratic.

The legitimacy of parliament was also important. This was established not only by willing participation among its members, but also by large-scale attendance by non-members. Nobles brought retinues with them to maintain their prestige. Crowds of townsfolk gathered to watch the ceremonies and to hear the acts proclaimed. In our period, the acts began also to be printed, and people who bought them were also conferring legitimacy on them.

Parliament's legitimacy was rarely if ever contested directly. In 1578, when parliament was held in Stirling Castle, it was 'murmurit' by 'disfavorars of his grace['s] gubernament and regiment' that there could be 'na frie acces' for people to present their grievances.[23] The importance of this complaint will emerge shortly, when processes of petitioning and lobbying are discussed; it

[22] James VI, *Basilicon Doron*, in *Political Writings*, 36–7.   [23] APS iii. 94, c. 1.

was evidently an expression of support for ideal parliaments. James liked to imply that parliaments were not essential, but controversies raged less over the existence of parliament than (as with the privy council) over its composition. There was uneasiness at the admission of shire commissioners in 1587, and conflict throughout our period over the presence of bishops as the ecclesiastical estate. It was the attempt to shore up the bishops' position in the 'Black Acts' of 1584 that led to the most far-reaching assertion of parliamentary authority: 'the honour and auctoritie of his [i.e. the king's] supreme court of parliament, continewit past all memorie of man unto thir dayis as constitute upoun the frie votis of the thrie estatis of this ancient kingdome', by which 'the lawis and actis of parliament (be quhilkis all men ar governit) [were] maid and establisit'.[24]

Parliamentary decisions had to be reached through the correct procedure, as the mention of 'frie votis' reminds us. In fact, formal divisions seem hardly ever to have been taken in the sixteenth century, and parliament operated by consensus—based usually on the leadership of the king or queen (if an adult) and that of their magnates (at all times). When James VI abandoned the search for consensus in parliamentary decision-making after about 1598, he transformed the practical exercise of power; but he did so in accordance with the formal rules, for nobody could say that parliament should not take votes.[25] They might feel that there was something wrong, but there were no words in which it could be articulated.

Or were there? Formal rules are not everything, and people may feel that what a government does is illegitimate even if it has followed the rules. New modes of political discourse grow up to meet the new situation; these in turn, if widely accepted, can become new rules. Scarcely anybody had talked about 'free parliaments' before the early seventeenth century; but when it was claimed in 1606 that parliament should have a 'solemne and free advice and vote' (and that bishops were corrupting this), and doubts were expressed about how the king obtained his parliamentary majorities, they too did so according to the rules, for nobody could say that parliaments ought not to be free.[26]

What is striking is how indirectly, even though persistently, the dissidents criticized parliament in the early seventeenth century. There was grumbling about proxies; about the number of newly created peers; about the banning of meetings of individual estates during parliament's sitting; about the bishops' role in election of lords of the articles; about courtiers caballing with the lords of the articles; and about corrupt recording of the votes; but there was no frontal attack on the legitimacy of any early seventeenth-century

---

[24] *APS* iii. 293, c. 3.
[25] J. Goodare, 'Scottish Politics in the Reign of James VI', in id. and Lynch (eds.), *The Reign of James VI*, 36–7, 49, 52; A. R. MacDonald, 'Deliberative Processes in Parliament'.
[26] Calderwood, *History*, vi. 530.

parliament as there was on the parallel general assemblies of the church. Either this was because parliament was not so heavily manipulated, or the dissidents still hoped to control it after they had abandoned hope in the general assembly. Such probing of parliament's legitimacy could penetrate deeply. In the general assembly of 1600, when the church's parliamentary representation was under discussion, 'They beginne to reasoun the mater *ab ovo*, to defyne a parliament, and what it is to vote in parliament. The king hearing of it, discharged them to meddle with that point.'[27]

The legitimacy of individual laws was also asserted—or denied. This was a less perilous and more frequent topic of discussion. How did people decide whether a particular law was beneficial? They did not usually do so from first principles, whereby they might have reasoned (following James) that because God's purposes in instituting monarchy and placing the king on his throne were good, therefore the king's latest action must also be good. In fact, they used common sense and self-interest; and if what the king had just done was not good (or not good for them), they often said so. They agitated: they petitioned. And a king who wished to be seen as good had to listen. The privy council register contains frequent protests against specific government policies; examples of policies being changed or abandoned in response can also be found, although not in such numbers. The most absolute and unquestioned monarch could not carve chunks out of the revenues of monasteries and bishoprics in order to finance the royal guard in 1584, even with parliamentary sanction, because enough influential people thought that this would be unjust (or at least that it would hit their pockets unreasonably).[28]

Accounts of the legitimation of power can give the impression that the success or failure of governmental measures depends solely on their acceptance as legitimate, or not, by the political community. But government does not act only by persuasion; it is also directly coercive. It may *force* people to do things that they would rather not do. So the failure of a measure may primarily indicate a lack of adequate coercive resources. Government also achieves some of its aims through the deployment of economic power. Here the failure of a measure may indicate a lack of adequate money. State power, like other forms of power, is threefold. It can be military, in which the characteristic sanction for non-compliance is death or physical punishment; it can be economic, deployed either by material rewards for compliance or by confiscation for non-compliance; or it can be ideological, deployed by persuasion in terms of values professed in common by ruler and ruled, and with sanctions ranging from public disapproval to eternal damnation. These forms of power, although always conceptually separate, are usually deployed in combination, and one can be converted into another. The scheme to finance the royal guard involved both economic and military power; to the extent that people refused

---

[27] Ibid. 2–3 and *passim*.   [28] *APS* iii. 298–9, c. 13; Goodare, *State and Society*, 147.

to pay because they believed the scheme to be unjust, then ideological power was involved too. Legitimacy, in effect, is ideological power.[29]

There are nevertheless good grounds for analysing the legitimation of government. Not only does it represent power in itself, but it also forms the best starting point for an understanding of the political processes by which decisions were taken. Legitimation of government depended on regular contact and participation. This made Scottish politics fully 'political' in Bernard Crick's classic (and classical) definition:

Politics, then, can be simply defined as the activity by which differing interests within a given unit of rule are conciliated by giving them a share in power in proportion to their importance to the welfare and survival of the whole community. And, to complete the formal definition, a political system is that type of government where politics proves successful in ensuring reasonable stability and order.[30]

Politics in this sense does not exist everywhere: only where decisions are made through negotiation, consensus, and compromise among competing but established interest groups. A detailed discussion of these groups' activities must wait until Chapter 2, but here we can identify some of the ways in which leading members of the political community interacted to maintain the government's legitimacy. In Scotland, parliament was the supreme and most obvious place for such political activity. That Scotland was a parliamentary monarchy had been enough for Sir John Fortescue, in the fifteenth century, to regard it (like England) as a *dominium politicum et regale*, a term cited by Professor Crick and with similar Aristotelian overtones.[31] But parliament was far from being the only forum for political participation, so political processes should be placed in a broader framework.

First, though, we need to identify the political community itself. They can be defined using the concept of legitimacy: the members of the political community were those *for whom* government was legitimate, and in whose interests government was carried on. Individuals within that community may not have had a direct share in the government, and even if they had, they probably did not agree with everything it did; but they had at least a voice. They could bring their grievances to it, and expect a hearing. Under certain circumstances they did also have the right to participate, possessing actual membership of the forums in which politics was carried on. This chapter began with James VI's quite conventional statement that a 'righteous king' should 'know himselfe to bee ordeined for his people'. The 'people' were those who had this right to be heard or to participate. Government, for them, was a matter of reciprocal obligations. They might be taxed, but it was agreed that they could expect benefits in return; taxation was granted unconditionally by parliament, but parliament discussed it first. It was not a matter of

[29] Goodare, *State and Society*, ch. 9.
[30] B. Crick, *In Defence of Politics* (5th edn., London, 2000), 21–2.
[31] Burns, *True Law of Kingship*, 16.

arbitrary tribute, as it was with the exactions of the Ottoman Empire from its subject peoples.

The corollary here was that anyone who lacked a voice in government was not part of the political community, and they would experience government differently. The main excluded groups were the common people, and almost all women except queens. The political elite of the Highlands also came into this category, though they could participate in the govermental traditions of their own region. 'All subjects are legitimately governed, but some are more legitimately governed than others.'[32] If the common people were legitimately governed, it was in highly indirect ways. To the extent that legitimacy was conferred through acts of consent to government, few such acts were open to them to undertake. They could come to watch coronations and royal entries. They could attend church—though there were many reasons for doing so, and desire to register a willingness to undergo kirk session discipline was not necessarily one of them. They could complain to the local courts of wrongs done to them, and sometimes act as witnesses in court.[33] Other than that, for them, government *was* arbitrary, and they could not participate in it. Their experience of it deserves to be discussed separately (see below, Chapters 10 and 11).

How, then, did the political community participate in governmental processes? Two modes of participation have been postulated: voice and membership. The second mode can be subdivided, since some members of governmental forums had only a subordinate position, while other members had the power to take the lead in decision-making. That gives us three modes: voice—the ability to lobby or petition; subordinate membership—the ability to attend governmental assemblies; and leading membership—the ability to steer governmental assemblies. Participation might be hollow, and petitions were easily rejected; but a legitimate government had to be seen to offer the realistic possibility of genuine participation and of responsiveness to petitions. So long as that was maintained, the government had the prospect of winning support or at least acquiescence for its policies.

In fact the three modes of participation overlapped in more than one way, and thus require further subdivision. Some people were members of parliament, but exercised most of their influence as lobbyists. A few were not even members, but still took the lead in shaping its activities. And there was much more to participation in government than parliament; government itself operated in different modes. There were components of government in which members of the political classes could participate directly—parliament,

---

[32] Barker, *Political Legitimacy*, title of ch. 6.

[33] Among those barred from being witnesses were women and the 'puir': Balfour, *Practicks*, ii. 378. Women were admitted in 1591 as witnesses in cases of treason and heresy (in practice meaning mainly witchcraft): Hope, *Major Practicks*, VII. 13. 56. The main exceptions here were the kirk session and higher church courts, which proceeded inquisitorially and were thus free to interrogate anyone.

general assembly, some local courts—and others in which they were accepted as having a right to petition—parliament again, privy council, royal court. Direct participation was infrequent, even though when it occurred it could be crucial. Local courts might meet frequently, but parliament did not. Everyday central government meant the privy council and royal court, in which only a few people were actively involved. Regular participation by the rest of the political nation involved having a voice, not direct membership.

This conceptual structure may seem complicated, and indeed it can be simplified. There was a single, basic division in the political community, between those powerful interest groups who took the lead in decision-making, and everyone else. The leading groups used both voice and membership: so did everyone else. But the leaders got very different results from their efforts, because they were basically partners in government. The government would be very unlikely to do anything that any of them would regard as seriously illegitimate. The remainder of the political community could not be ignored, and the government had to acknowledge obligations to them; but they did not have to be conciliated on every single governmental measure.

The political leaders in everyday central government comprised the monarch, the privy council, courtiers, leading nobles, and representatives of the English government. (The latter were involved in the government of Scotland, both before and after 1603, because of Scotland's satellite status since 1560.) All of these had strong shared interests and normally did their best to cooperate. This can be seen, first, in the business of everyday central government; how it worked in parliament will be seen later.

Everyday decision-making involved questions like who should be granted a wardship and on what terms, or which of two feuding lairds should be ordered to find caution not to molest the other, or what should be said to the king of France, or which way to tilt the scales of justice in a legal case. Many of these decisions required the monarch's signature, or sometimes a warrant from the privy council; some could be implemented by word of mouth.

The people Mary or James VI had round them to make these decisions varied. The privy council (including the officers of state) was often supremely important, and when we speak of everyday central government we speak, more often than not, of monarch and privy council. This is noteworthy because the privy council was a new body—Mary was the first adult monarch to maintain one. Together with privy councillors, and partly overlapping with them, there were leading courtiers. These included people holding honourable offices in the royal household that brought them into contact with the monarch, and other courtiers with no formal function—effectively guests of the monarch. Not all of these would be in government, however. Some would be seekers, rather than wielders, of governmental power, while others would be lobbyists aiming to promote the interests of the group they represented.

Within the privy council and royal court, but to some extent also forming a distinct group beyond, were leading nobles. They had a more or less automatic entrée to the court, and might well be at least nominal members of the council. When they actually attended court or council, and exerted political influence, they were formally members of everyday government. But they remained part of a community of nobles with distinct local interests— both collective, as concerning nobles' status, and individual, as concerning the assertion of their interests against rivals who typically were other nobles. When they acted in the capacity of members of everyday central government, they were not expected to do so disinterestedly. A noble privy councillor who put in a rare appearance at the council to pursue a feud was functionally little different from a lobbyist. But if he stepped up his council attendance gradually, and eventually became a leading statesman, there would be no definite point at which he crossed the line from being outside to being inside the government. The government was not only pervaded by aristocratic interests, it also possessed an aristocratic penumbra.

Also a distinct interest within the Scottish court were representatives of England. English ambassadors were usually resident at the Scottish royal court until 1603.[34] They gave advice and exerted political influence in a way directly comparable to Scottish nobles at court. In a period of Anglo-Scottish 'amity' (from 1560) and formal alliance (from 1586), the assumption behind their presence was that it would be beneficial to both countries to consult one another's interests. After 1603, the king himself functioned as the coordinator of this beneficial joint interest. Although Scotland remained a largely sovereign state, even after 1603, its government's activities were systematically constrained by the presence of English interests which it was dangerous to ignore. When the English were flouted, the consequences could be dire, in the form of sponsorship of *coups* and occasional direct military intervention.

These four interest groups at the core of the state—privy council, royal court, leading nobility, and English representatives—were the crucial ones with whom the king had strong shared interests. He could not afford seriously to fall out with any of them, and they in turn had to take his interests very much into account. They also had many interests in common with one another—privy councillors were related to nobles, as were gentlemen of the chamber; members of all three groups might receive English pensions. If the king's interests diverged from those of one group, that was usually not because of his personal wishes, independent of any other factor; it was because he was an important link between the groups, and chose to satisfy one group rather than another. The ability to make such a choice (provided it is a real choice) does represent power, but the 'king's power' was always and inevitably shared with, and dependent on, the power of these core interest groups. All these groups operated by consensus with the crown and with one

---

[34] For an overview of diplomatic arrangements towards the end of the period see *CSP Scot.* xiii, I, pp. xix–xvi.

another; any failure of that consensus would hit the headlines, and might even endanger the stability of the regime.

Beyond these groups at the heart of everyday central government, we find a further collection of interest groups, and again we may focus on four: the church, the burghs, the lawyers, and the lesser members of the landed classes. The first of these, the church, was a large but amorphous body. A distinction should be drawn between the general assembly, which led the church up to about 1600 but did not have a close relationship with the crown, and the bishops after about 1600, who did. The bishops, when they took over control of the church from the assembly, brought it closer to the centre of power, though at the price of loss of autonomy. The leading bishops were sometimes privy councillors and occasionally courtiers, but probably only one bishop (Archbishop Spottiswoode) ever carried real weight in decision-making.[35] The result was that the church did not have a consensual relationship with the government, even under episcopacy; it usually had to do what it was told, with a good deal of local protest and non-compliance. The church's local bodies, presbyteries and synods, might try to maintain the former arm's-length relationship, or might work more closely with the bishops. Their choices here, and the conflicts they generated, would have a long string of consequences all down the seventeenth century.

The other three interest groups were more straightforward. The royal burghs were a rare presence at court. Although the king got to know some of the magistrates of Edinburgh quite well, he could treat them high-handedly without distempering the entire body politic. Their own recourse tended to be to the privy council rather than to the royal court or nobility; they were merely lobbyists, and increasingly unsuccessful ones at that. Lawyers had connections with the court of session through their leaders' membership of the college of justice. Again this familiarized privy councillors with their point of view, since privy councillors were so often senators of the college. Finally, members of the landed classes below the leading nobility were not regular courtiers. A mere laird, or even a lesser peer, would normally approach the corridors of power through an intermediary. That intermediary could be anyone in the central core—a councillor or a courtier, perhaps a bishop—but it would most naturally be a territorial magnate with whom the laird had ties of kinship or clientage. So these four groups—church, burghs, lawyers, and lairds—had more distant connections with government, but still had ways in which they could seek a voice in everyday decision-making.

Things became more serious when the big, formal decisions had to be taken. The questions here would affect more people and for longer: questions

---

[35] Lee, *Government by Pen, passim*; cf. A. S. W. Pearce, 'John Spottiswoode, Jacobean Archbishop and Statesman' (Ph.D. thesis, Stirling, 1998). Andrew Knox, bishop of the Isles, and James Law, bishop of Orkney, deserve mention as agents of royal authority in their dioceses, but were not leading figures in the church, let alone the privy council. Bishops gained more influence under Charles I.

like who should be the regent, or whether a treaty with England should be negotiated and on what terms, or how the church should be governed, or what the rate of interest should be. This was when the estates were involved in a formal way, and a parliament was summoned. We thus need to examine parliament's role in political decision-making.

Parliament had two separate though related functions: as a debating forum, and as a legislative body. In the first capacity it was in some ways a forum where representatives of the propertied classes negotiated with the everyday central government—it offered 'advice' to the government. This could produce disagreement and provide a platform for opposition. Parliament was not actually governing at the moment at which it was debating. But the debate was intended to produce legislation, and here what was involved (in the words of the enacting clause of a statute) was 'advice and consent'.

Legislation was an act of all the members of parliament, from the monarch down to the humblest burgh commissioner. Even the lesser members carried a real responsibility for parliamentary decisions, which were the most solemn and authoritative acts that a Scottish government could take. Parliament, defined in its full sense as crown plus estates, was sovereign (see below, Chapter 3). Parliaments should not be assumed to be a natural feature of the political landscape, since large and growing numbers of other countries managed without them.[36] Still, parliaments were well established in Scotland, although in Chapter 4 we shall encounter tendencies towards absolute monarchy that might eventually have eclipsed them. In 1562 the general assembly mentioned, quite seriously, that divine law was pronounced by 'the eternall God in his parliament'.[37] People evidently accepted the principle that binding decisions should be reached in parliament, by some combination of consensus and majority vote—though the details of the combination might not always command assent among those who did not prevail.

Parliament could legitimize even the very biggest decisions. In 1560, the adoption of the Protestant faith was legislated by parliament. In 1567, the transfer of the crown to the infant James VI was ratified by a convention of estates and then by parliament. It was made clear that parliament was not actually electing him, but its endorsement was nevertheless significant: it was 'fundin and declarit' by parliament in December 1567 that Mary's abdication in her son's favour 'was, and is, and salbe in all tymes cuming haldin, repute and estemit lauchfull and perfyte'.[38] If the political classes in parliament had refused to acquiesce in the transfer of power it is hard to see how the new regime could have survived. To be sure, that parliament was summoned only once the regime was more or less established. Perhaps a better example of an

[36] M. A. R. Graves, *The Parliaments of Early Modern Europe* (London, 2001), 127–32.
[37] *BUK* i. 21. Cf. the English ambassador's satirical and widely circulated comment that John Knox thought himself to be 'of God's privy council': Knox, *History*, i. p. lxxii.
[38] *APS* iii. 11, c. 1.

assembly *choosing* a regime would be the convention of estates of June 1578 that ratified the earl of Morton's headship of the council by a vote of 25 to 23.[39] If the vote had gone the other way, Morton would probably have lost his position.

Since the government did not depend directly on a parliamentary majority, what would happen if the government and a parliamentary majority came to disagree? The sizeable advantage possessed in parliament by any government of the period made such a development unlikely; but it (or something like it) did happen after 1638, and led to a complete change of regime. Yet the *possibility* of such a thing had actually helped to legitimize the regime up to that date. Parliament consisted of influential people making real decisions; that impressed the public in a way that a collection of painted marionettes in the parliament house (no matter how loyal) would not have done. The debate helped to legitimize the outcome. Those who disapproved of the decision could feel that they had been heard, or at least could plausibly be told that they had been heard and should now shut up. Parliaments did not discuss withdrawing cooperation from the regime, any more than James VI's subjects discussed publicly whether he was a tyrant or not; but the perception that its commitment to the regime was both real and freely given aided the regime's legitimacy, just as it helped to have a manifestly non-tyrannical monarch.

It was certainly widely accepted that parliament could legitimize opposition, and even resistance, to a regime. All that was necessary was to accept what has been called the 'magistrate theory' of authority, by which authority was vested not in the crown alone but also in the lesser magistrates who, collectively, made up parliament. Scotland, with its wide support for the ideas of Knox and Buchanan, was one of the prime locations in Europe for the 'magistrate theory', which was never entirely suppressed despite the best efforts of James VI. But probably the main effect of parliamentary contact with government in our period (in which, after all, parliament did not withdraw its sanction from the government, at least after 1559–60) was to further the process of integration of the body politic, helping to bury the older idea of authority being exercised by autonomous nobles.[40]

The concepts of court and country are helpful here. The 'court' encompasses those who identify their interests with the royal court; the 'country' encompasses everyone else among the political classes. The concepts were developed to explain a division between the two, but even if they were

---

[39] *APS* iii. 120–1; *CSP Scot.* v. 295–6; Goodare, 'Scottish Politics', 36.

[40] Burns, *True Law of Kingship*, chs. 6–7; W. Schulze, 'Estates and the Problem of Resistance in Theory and Practice in the Sixteenth and Seventeenth Centuries', in R. J. W. Evans and T. V. Thomas (eds.), *Crown, Church and Estates: Central European Politics in the Sixteenth and Seventeenth Centuries* (London, 1991), 165–71. In England too, 'resistance theory' or what Patrick Collinson prefers to call the 'polemical critique of monarchy' was much in evidence in certain Elizabethan parliaments, notably those of 1572 and 1584: P. Collinson, 'The Monarchical Republic of Queen Elizabeth I', in his *Elizabethan Essays* (London, 1994), 43–56.

broadly united it may be worthwhile looking for potential fault lines. One point about the legitimation of government is that the 'country' may also be divisible into two groups: those who want government to leave them alone, and those who have ideas of what they would do if *they* were in government.[41] Just as the present governors had to explain and justify their actions, so too those who aspired to replace them had to explain and justify why their programme was preferable.

Parliament was not a thing in its own right, but a meeting place—a crossroads, even—where the matrix of governmental authority was reconfigured and broadened. Some extra groups were invited in to help take decisions, because the core groups for everyday government could not take them on their own. Sometimes the core groups were themselves divided over what to do; sometimes they had a clear solution to the problem but it required legislation or taxation that only parliament could provide.

Formally, the matrix of parliamentary authority was quite different from the everyday pattern involving privy council, royal court, leading nobility, and English representatives. Of these groups, neither courtiers nor the English had any official status in parliament. Privy councillors, or at least the officers of state, did form an influential group—they usually sat in the lords of the articles, parliament's key committee. The nobility, too, were usually peers and thus personal members of parliament, although those who attended may not always have been the same as those who hung around the royal court. Parliament also admitted to membership all prelates; the bishops were creatures of the crown, but many monastic commendators in the sixteenth century were not really clergymen but backwoods noblemen. And that was only two of parliament's estates; there were two more—burgesses and (after 1587) shire commissioners—with their own representatives on the lords of the articles. Neither group was involved much in everyday central government, or had close connections with the crown. The dependence of government on the crown, it would seem, was eclipsed when the estates met.

However, this eclipse was more apparent than real, and to many contemporaries it would not even have been apparent. For one thing, the dependence of everyday government on the crown was a formality that concealed the true interplay of political influence. The monarch as a human being was as likely to be influenced as to influence others. And in formal terms, parliament also depended on the monarch, without whose approval it could not meet, even though withholding that approval might be dangerous.[42]

Moreover, when it came to the realities of political influence, parliamentary government was like everyday central government in depending on a similar

---

[41] These tendencies become clear when in 1621 a parliamentary voting record becomes available: Goodare, 'The Scottish Parliament of 1621'.

[42] Cf. Mary's manoeuvres to avoid, or at least delay, a parliament in her early years: J. Goodare, 'The First Parliament of Mary Queen of Scots', *Sixteenth Century Journal*, 36 (2005, forthcoming).

configuration of interest groups. Just as the royal burghs were not members of the inner circle of everyday central government, so they were not influential members of parliament. The same applies to the shire commissioners after 1587. Time and again they found themselves at odds with the proposals of the government. Occasionally they got their way—notably with the destruction of a tax revision scheme in 1600. Burgh commissioners were usually able to get private acts of parliament for their burghs (so long as the government did not object), though shire commissioners seem rarely to have done this. When taxes were imposed, or when religious innovations were made by statute, burgh and shire commissioners may well have wished that their presence in parliament did not confer quite so much legitimacy on the process.

One thing that these four more distant groups had in common was that they tended to relate to government, not directly, but via representatives. There were hundreds of parish ministers, and they could not all come to parliament; the general assembly itself was considered to consist of representatives of the ministers (though the representation was often uneven). It usually sent its own delegates to petition, or negotiate with, both everyday central government (monarch and council) and parliament. There were thousands of individual burgesses, who were represented (again unevenly) by their burgh magistrates and councils. The burgesses' voice in government came through those councils, either directly or via a further intermediary, the convention of royal burghs. Lawyers in Edinburgh were mostly members of the college of justice, who on most matters were represented by the lord president and fourteen senators of the college (the judges of the court of session). Lesser landlords also required representation, which in parliament came (after 1587) via the elected shire commissioners. But they might also be 'represented' as clients of the magnates, and their relationship with the magnates requires further consideration.

The nobility—or at least the magnates—were highly influential in parliament, as out of it. One might expect them to have shared the point of view of their fellow-landlords, the shire commissioners, with whom they had so many interests in common. Probably in other contexts (in local politics, or in relationships with their peasant tenants) they did act in much the same way as lesser lairds—except that some of the lesser lairds might also be their clients. But when it came to central government, the nobility had a special relationship with it that lesser landlords lacked. Along with the nobility, the influential members of parliament were the monarch, the officers of state (the most important privy councillors), and to a lesser extent the bishops. But there were other influential interest groups in the corridors of power when parliament met: the English ambassadors, for instance; or the court of session, which could exert behind-the-scenes influence on the shaping of legislation.

Parliament, then, was never a rubber stamp, but the people who controlled everyday central government were also the people who carried most influence in the parliament house. This both legitimized the regime and exposed some of the fault lines dividing the various interest groups on which it depended; the government listened more attentively to some groups than to others. It will be the task of the next chapter to show in more detail why this was so.

CHAPTER TWO

The Body Politic

I will do nocht without the conveining
Ane parliament of the estaits all:
In thair presence I sall but feinyeing
Iniquitie under my sword doun thrall.
Thair may no prince do acts honorabill,
Bot gif his counsall thairto will assist:
How may he knaw the thing maist profitabil,
To follow vertew and vycis to resist,
Without he be instructit and solist?

Lindsay, 'Ane satyre of the thrie estaitis',
in *Works*, ii. 165

The body politic in sixteenth-century Scotland, as elsewhere in Europe, was a segmented creature. To be members of the Scottish political community, people had also to be members of another, more limited, community: their estate. The division of society into three orders—those who prayed, those who fought, and those who worked—was a medieval and Renaissance commonplace. That these orders were in some sense represented in parliament was also accepted, though the correspondence between the three orders of society and the three estates of parliament was never exact; those who worked, in particular, were largely unrepresented, and in Scotland the third estate of the medieval parliament was made up of burgesses, mainly merchants. There were, nevertheless, three estates, and very highly they thought of themselves too.[1]

The traditional rights of the estates did not depend on the crown. The essence of a medieval parliament was an assembly of the privileged classes, defending the special rights of their estate against both common people and crown.[2] Many parliamentary peerages had emerged in the minority of James II with little royal input.[3] Later peers had received their titles from the crown, but even in 1562, Mary could not sustain the creation of her half-brother as

---

[1] The estates as constitutional entities in our period are surveyed by J. Goodare, 'The Estates in the Scottish Parliament, 1286–1707', *Parliamentary History*, 15 (1996), 11–32 at 17–24. As we shall see below, the admission of shire commissioners to parliament in 1587 meant that there were four estates thereafter. For relations between government and the common people, see Ch. 11 below.

[2] V. G. Kiernan, *State and Society in Europe, 1550–1650* (Oxford, 1980), 4.

[3] A. Grant, 'The Development of the Scottish Peerage', *SHR* 57 (1978), 1–27.

earl of Mar in the face of protests from Lord Erskine, who had a hereditary claim to the earldom. Lord James had to make do with the earldom of Moray, traditionally possessed by members of the royal family, while Erskine would himself be created earl of Mar in 1565.[4] And once an earl, always an earl; the assembled earls in parliament knew that the crown could not take their titles away. The same applies, *mutatis mutandis*, to the other estates in parliament: the bishops (always appointed by the crown in our period), and the royal burghs.

The reaffirmation of the estates' individual privileges was a traditional parliamentary proceeding. Each estate could receive an act ratifying its 'liberties'. These might include the right not to have their status diluted; for Fraserburgh to be created a royal burgh was against the 'liberties' of the burgh of Aberdeen, or so the Aberdonians claimed.[5] Parliamentary ratifications of the 'liberties' of the estates became frequent in the mid-sixteenth century, only to slow to a trickle towards the century's end. They gave the assembly something of the air of a mutual-admiration society, as each estate assured itself and its associates how important they all were to the body politic. It was all very gratifying, but also vague and even ambiguous. On the face of it, a parliamentary ratification of 'liberties' could signify either a promise of non-interference in free-standing status communities, or the *creation* of privilege by the state. The story of the estates in our period is to some extent a shift from the former to the latter.

One of the functions of corporate bodies representing the estates was to sort out certain matters without bothering parliament—resolving internal disputes, and making rules for the conduct of their own business and allocation of their own resources. All these forums (even, usually, the general assembly) knew their place: they willingly submitted serious internal disputes to the sovereign parliament. Moreover, they sought parliamentary legislation to protect themselves against other interest groups in society, thus recognizing parliament's function as the supreme arbiter of the political system. Instead of seeking to cut itself free of parliament, each estate aimed to develop channels through which it could lobby parliament for what it wanted. Lobbyists ask for things, but the holder of power does not have to grant them, and if they are granted it may be for a variety of reasons. It can be argued that, however well connected, lobbyists are not actually *in* government; if they are, they cease to be lobbyists. But this statement needs to be qualified. Lobbyists of parliament could also be members of some other component of government. The burghs were assiduous lobbyists, both individually and through their

---

[4] M. Lee, *James Stewart, Earl of Moray* (New York, 1953), 97; D. H. Fleming, *Mary Queen of Scots* (2nd edn., London, 1898), 309–10; *The Scots Peerage*, ed. J. B. Paul, 9 vols. (Edinburgh, 1904–14), v. 596–614.

[5] Aberdeen City Archives, William Kennedy's 'Alphabetical index to the first 67 volumes of the council register of the city of Aberdeen, 1398–1800', vol. i. pp. 284–5. The claim was unsuccessful.

representative body, the convention of royal burghs. Yet individual burgh
councils governed their towns; the convention of royal burghs was among
the bodies governing the individual burghs. We shall meet the individual
estates again as sectional and local governors later in this book; in the present
chapter we shall examine them as political actors on the national stage.

The church, traditionally, was the first estate, which is as good a reason as
any for beginning with it. The Protestant church, however, was not a traditional entity. From the outset of the Reformation it took a clear stand against
many commonly cited grounds of legitimate authority: 'nouther antiquitie,
tytle usurpit, lineall discente, place appointit, nor multitude of men approv-
ing ane errour'.[6] The general assembly was a completely new body that was
hard to fit into conventional models of authority. It even had some characteristics that might have enabled it to rival parliament: it could regard itself as
representing the entire body of the realm, constituted as 'the haill generall
kirk of this realme . . . asweill of all members therof in all estates as of the
ministers'. But although this aspect has been stressed by Duncan Shaw among
others, it should not obscure the fact that the church behaved in practice like
a single estate. The document just quoted, an address to the Regent Morton
in 1574, referred to the practice of holding two general assemblies a year, 'be
act of parliament authorized'.[7] The general assembly in the years up to 1597
spent endless time and effort negotiating with the government, petitioning it,
and making demands and protests to it, as almost every page of its register
testifies. The non-ecclesiastical members were there not as representatives,
but because they were interested in, and concerned with, ecclesiastical affairs;
they were expected to see things through the eyes of the ministers. Rather
than regarding the general assembly as a parallel body to parliament, we
should think of it as a body that, in order to obtain most of the things that it
held dear, routinely lobbied parliament.

This lobbying led to a regular relationship between the church and parliament. The synod of Lothian asked in 1590 'that his majestie wald let thame
understand quhen a parliament salbe, that the commissioners of the kirk may
convene to a generall assemble before the sam'.[8] The parliament of May 1584
was unprecedented, according to David Calderwood, in passing the Black
Acts without giving the general assembly a chance to object: 'ever since the
reformation, nothing concerning the effaires of the kirk was treated or concluded till first the generall assemblie was made privie thereto, and their commissioners heard to reasoun and agree to the same'.[9] Calderwood provides an

  [6] *APS* ii. 531 (the Confession of Faith of 1560). For John Knox's vision of the Scottish Protestant church as connected, not to the pre-Reformation history of Scotland, but to the biblical
Jewish church, see R. A. Mason, 'Usable Pasts: History and Identity in Reformation Scotland',
SHR 76 (1997), 54–68.
  [7] *BUK* i. 292; Shaw, *General Assemblies*, 19–20.
  [8] *Records of the Synod of Lothian and Tweeddale, 1589–1596, 1640–1649*, ed. J. Kirk (Stair
Society, 1977), 18.   [9] Calderwood, *History*, iv. 62.

excellent description of how a political system should operate: the church, as an interest group, should be consulted in advance about the government's plans, and should have the opportunity to 'agree to the same'. Of course, parliament had the final say.[10]

For a brief phase in the 1570s, the assembly tried to occupy a slightly different space in the body politic. Instead of going to lobby the government, the government would come to it. Several assemblies invited the regents, or commissioners from the crown, to attend, in the hope that their presence might commit the government to supporting the assembly's proceedings. They hardly ever came. After the Second Book of Discipline of 1578 established a more clerical view of the ministry, the invitations ceased, although ad hoc negotiations between assembly and government continued.[11]

Advance consultation before a parliament did not just mean the assembly having the opportunity to object to government plans; it could also mean the assembly making its own proposals to parliament. In 1597, the commissioners of the general assembly noted that 'it has been the continual custome of the kirk at parliaments to crave such things as were found necessary to pass in lawes for their well and priviledges'.[12] The long series of statutes to impose every aspect of the Reformation on a sometimes recalcitrant populace bears witness to one aspect of this. Acts on the church's own 'privileges', however, were more rare, and by 1597 the church was already becoming in effect a department of state.[13]

Presbyterian radicals thereafter continued to champion 'church liberties', but only from the fringes. The bishops who actually controlled the church spoke instead of the manifold benefits of royal protection of the church. When two nobles were added to the commission on stipends in 1607, 'and the number of the temporal and spiritual state maid unequal', the bishops did not demand their *rights* as the 'spiritual state', but 'referrit the interpretatioun of the sam to your most sacred majestie, quhiche we ar assurit wilbe maist favorable and beninge towardis ws'.[14] The alliance with the crown (and not parliament) was essential to the bishops, who had no other source of authority, but it also benefited the whole church in some matters: better stipends—though these might have come anyway, and were not *that* generous—and more effective persecution of Catholics—though the persecutors found that the king kept them on a leash which he could tighten or loosen as his needs required.[15]

---

[10] There was also church lobbying of council and royal court: e.g. Calderwood, *History*, v. 291.

[11] Shaw, *General Assemblies*, 52–7.

[12] *BUK* iii. 931.

[13] The last general ratification of the liberties of the English church had been in 1462, so the Scottish state had some catching up to do: Gunn, *Early Tudor Government*, 169.

[14] Bishops to James, n.d. [c.Aug. 1607], *Eccles. Letters*, i. 101.

[15] On stipends, see M. Lynch, 'Preaching to the Converted? Perspectives on the Scottish Reformation', in A. A. MacDonald et al. (eds.), *The Renaissance in Scotland*, 306–14; Foster,

The church, as an estate of parliament, expected to have representatives in it. Traditionally the prelates—bishops, and commendators of monasteries—sat in parliament. They continued to do so throughout our period, but often had little connection with the church. Bishops were few and marginal for most of the period up to 1600, while the commendators of the secularized monasteries were almost all laymen. The leaders of the general assembly showed little interest in church representation in parliament before about 1578. Parliament generally cooperated in passing legislation for the church. The government rarely intruded in the work of the general assembly, and even Mary refrained from systematic interference. That was seen as enough.

In the 1580s and early 1590s the church's position came to be that any parliamentary representatives it had should be appointed by, and answerable to, the general assembly. Various schemes were discussed. The most striking, in 1596, was for each of the fifty-one presbyteries to send commissioners to parliament to make up the spiritual estate—they would in theory have received the revenues of the pre-Reformation bishoprics and monasteries, of which there were also fifty-one, as they fell vacant. None of these schemes, however, was implemented. After 1596 the radical presbyterian minority, who had always been suspicious of them, realized that any scheme for church representation was now likely to facilitate royal control over the church rather than church influence in the state. From 1600 onwards, the king gradually restored bishops, both as leaders of the church and as church representatives in parliament. In fact, being all royal nominees, they were royal representatives in parliament at least as much as church representatives.[16] Bishops were prominent managers of the court's programme in all early seventeenth-century parliaments.

The general assembly (or its majority view: the assembly was not a homogeneous body) therefore maintained no separation from parliament, and certainly did not hold itself to be parallel to parliament or co-equal with it. It asked parliament for things; it met before parliament to prepare a lobbying programme; and it showed interest in having representatives within parliament to speak for the church. In this the general assembly behaved much like the convention of royal burghs. The burghs, as we shall see, both lobbied parliament from the outside and briefed their representatives within it. They played politics as effectively as they could. The church did the same.

The Church Before the Covenants, ch. 8; and V. T. Wells, 'The Origins of Covenanting Thought and Resistance, *c*.1580–1638' (Ph.D. thesis, Stirling, 1997), ch. 1. Examples of curtailment of persecution of Catholics include *APS* iv. 116 (1597), and James to Chancellor Hay, 12 Jan. 1625, *Eccles. Letters*, ii. 774. See in general A. I. Macinnes, 'Catholic Recusancy and the Penal Laws, 1603–1707', *Records of the Scottish Church History Society*, 23 (1987–9), 27–63.

[16] A. R. MacDonald, 'Ecclesiastical Representation in Parliament in Post-Reformation Scotland: The Two Kingdoms Theory in Practice', *Journal of Ecclesiastical History*, 50 (1999), 38–61.

In a feudal age, the nobles had less need of sectional freedoms: the whole of society was their privileged playground. There was only one act ratifying their 'privilegeis and liberteis', in December 1567. It favoured the 'nobilitie and barrounis' (not just the peers), and probably the most specific privilege it had in mind was their right to hold baron courts.[17]

The nobility did have two vital and exclusive privileges. The first—so obvious that it tends to be forgotten—was the right of personal attendance in parliament for peers. The nobles, indeed, were manifestly the most important estate. The second, less immediately obvious but no less essential, was that of unrestricted access to the king.[18] Propinquity to the crown brought obvious benefits: a constant flow of patronage, and (as noble indebtedness began to bite, from the 1590s onwards) an element of protection from creditors. In 1624, after the suicide of the deeply indebted second earl of Lothian, James urged the creditors 'to yeild to a continewatioun [i.e. deferment] of thair principall sowmes without urgeing the rigourous advantage of the law in caise of not payment thairof'.[19]

If the nobles stood little in need of acts confirming sectional privileges, no more did they need a sophisticated institution to gain access to governmental structures. Just as there were conventions of the royal burghs, however, there were conventions of the nobility. They are normally invisible as a constitutionally defined sectional interest, for the crown's authority was bound up with the nobility, but conventions of the nobility can be identified if the records of conventions are examined carefully.

The earl of Mar claimed, in order to defeat a 1598 scheme for regular twice-yearly conventions, that 'conventions' were parliaments in all but the ceremonies. If he meant the formal conventions of estates, he was certainly right. But Thomas Craig, considering conventions at the same date, was doubtful about their powers: he suggested that their acts had once had the validity and authority of statutes, but no longer did.[20] He perceived conventions and parliaments to be divergent—and he, too, was right.

The solution to this paradox is the emerging, if never clear-cut, distinction between ordinary conventions (of the nobility only) and conventions of estates. Conventions of estates, which succeeded 'general councils' in the mid-sixteenth century, were the only bodies that shared with parliament the right to impose taxation, and to decide war and peace. They could also make temporary legislation, but taxation formed a growing proportion of their

---

[17] *APS* iii. 33, c. 32; Balfour, *Practicks*, i. 41. For privileges of 'nobles' and an attempt to define nobility, see K. M. Brown, *Noble Society in Scotland*, 7.

[18] Goodare, 'The Nobility and the Absolutist State', 165–6.

[19] James to council, 9 Apr. 1624, *RPC* xiii. 488–9. Cf. K. M. Brown, 'Noble Indebtedness in Scotland between the Reformation and the Revolution', *Historical Research*, 62 (1989), 260–75.

[20] George Nicolson to Sir Robert Cecil, 16 Dec. 1598, *CSP Scot.* xiii, I. 353–4; Craig, *Jus Feudale*, I. 8. 10.

limited business.[21] However, there were more and more 'conventions' that lacked one or more estates and were never intended to be conventions of estates. Parliaments declined in frequency as their legislative importance increased in the 1580s; the reverse happened with conventions. In the twenty-eight years from 1560 to 1587 there were thirty-one 'conventions'; in the next fifteen years there were forty-nine.[22] Of the twenty-five of the latter with recorded sederunts, only three had more than ten burgesses present, and these were definitely conventions of estates with agendas of direct commercial interest (one, in 1594, voted a tax, and the other two, in 1597, imposed customs on imports). For our purposes it is more significant that the average burgess attendance for the others was *fewer* than four, and that seven had no burgesses at all. Moreover, nine had no bishops, and none more than three. The bishops had been eclipsed; the commendators had been assimilated to the peerage as actual or prospective lords of erection; a handful of burgesses might turn up through personal involvement in the politics of the day; it is clear that these conventions were really conventions of the nobility.

　　The nobility attended, not to legislate, not to tax, not to take judicial decisions, but to discuss politics—mostly gravy train politics. The nucleus of these conventions was usually the privy council; not always, but the indefinite constitutional form is less important here than the concrete political function. In April 1593 a convention met, described formally as a 'conventioun of the nobilitie', and said informally to have been 'gathered of fewe chosen persons at th'apetytes of the present courtiers'.[23] Its main business was day-to-day political questions, and it also discussed in outline some of the matters to be brought before parliament in June. Another example comes from November 1596, when a proclamation referred to the 'ordour tane at the Conventioun at Falkland upoun the xii day of August last, and thaireftir ratifeit be ane uther Conventioun of the Esteatis, at Dunfermling the penult day of September last bipast'.[24] At the August meeting, which was thus distinguished from a convention of estates, there had been eleven nobles present. The act it issued was in the name of 'the kingis majestie and lordis of his secreit counsaill', speaking of the king as 'haveing at lenth ressonit and conferrit with the saidis lordis of his secreit counsale and sindrie of his nobilitie, and with sum of the ministerie, being alsua personalie present'. These ministers had been invited, but with them came the uninvited and unwelcome Andrew Melville, who took the opportunity to call the king 'God's sillie vassall'.[25] The proceedings combined informality and exclusiveness (though the latter failed on this

---

[21] *APS* ii. 543, c. 20; R. K. Hannay, 'General Council and Convention of Estates', in his *The College of Justice* (Stair Society, 1990), 244–5.

[22] J. Goodare, 'Parliament and Society in Scotland, 1560–1603' (Ph.D. thesis, Edinburgh, 1989), app. A, which gives references to numerous conventions not recorded in *APS* or *RPC*. For parliament's growing legislative importance, see Ch. 3 below.

[23] *BUK* iii. 796; Robert Bowes to Lord Burghley, 19 Apr. 1593, *CSP Scot.* xi. 80.

[24] *RPC* v. 328.　　　[25] *RPC* v. 310–11; Melville, *Diary*, 369–71.

occasion). The nobles wanted unrestricted access to the king for themselves, and this sort of relaxed convention suited them exactly.

Conventions of the nobility under James VI fulfilled many of the functions of the medieval parliament—elite political contact to sort out routine problems. They were a kind of annual general meeting, or even sometimes a policy and resources committee, for the feudal ruling class.[26] They made few laws—if they wanted a law they would get the next parliament to enact it; and they had no need of formal lobbying. The conventions were just like those of the burghs in the way they dealt with internal disputes among their members: in the nobility's case, these disputes were of course feuds. Reconciling feuds involved wide-ranging negotiations, and from the 1590s the king himself took an active part.[27] Many of the discussions must have taken place at the frequent conventions of these years, and at least one convention (in 1602) was held specifically to negotiate the ending of a single feud.[28]

After 1603, these frequent, informal conventions of the nobility came to an end, partly because the king was no longer available to preside, and partly because they were less necessary: a new understanding between crown and nobility had grown up since 1598.[29] Instead, the nobles developed new forms of contact with the crown, using the king's Scottish courtiers as intermediaries. These men, like John Murray of Lochmaben (later earl of Annandale) and Thomas Erskine of Gogar (later earl of Kellie), were themselves marginal to Scottish political history, but they served as the channels of communication for influential friends and relatives in Scottish government, like the earls of Melrose and Mar.[30] However, this left high and dry those nobles lacking a court connection, who were now deprived of their main channel of participation. Sir Colin Campbell of Glenorchy, who spent the whole of the 1630s lobbying in vain for a peerage, may have failed because of his reluctance to attend the royal court in person.[31] An incipient division between court-connected nobles and others became increasingly significant, and was obvious at the voting in the parliament of 1621.[32]

The nobles gained control of the monasteries during the sixteenth century, in a trend that antedated and paralleled the Reformation. Nobles' kinsmen

---

[26] Cf. P. M. Ribalta, 'The Impact of Central Institutions', in W. Reinhard (ed.), *Power Elites and State Building* (Oxford, 1996), 20–1; Tanner, *The Late Medieval Scottish Parliament*.

[27] K. M. Brown, *Bloodfeud*, 216–18.

[28] Nicolson to Cecil, 4 July 1602, *CSP Scot.* xiii, II. 1014–15; Brown, *Bloodfeud*, 171.

[29] Goodare, 'The Nobility and the Absolutist State', 169–70. The main such conventions after 1603 were (i) a convention of 1606 that preceded the controversial 'general assembly' of that year: Calderwood, *History*, vi. 588–90; (ii) two conventions of 1620–1, in which the nobility were asked to tax themselves without the other estates, but refused: *Melros Papers*, ii. 376–92; *RPC* xii. 378–80, 404–7; *APS* iv. 589–90.

[30] See *Melros Papers*, i–ii, and HMC, *Mar & Kellie*, ii, *passim*. More study of this process is required. There is, however, an excellent overview of the functioning of political contact after 1603 in Lee, *Government by Pen*.

[31] D. A. Watt, 'Chiefs, Lawyers and Debt', 149–51.

[32] Goodare, 'Scottish Parliament of 1621', 38–42.

became commendators of monasteries, lay substitutes for abbots and priors who increasingly became outright possessors of the monastic property. As a result the estate of the nobility received a large boost in numbers at the expense of the church. The claim of the First Book of Discipline (1561) to the revenues of the old church tacitly omitted the monasteries.[33] Nevertheless, the church still claimed some degree of supervision over the commendators. In 1572, the general assembly felt that 'becaus the possessoure of the same [monasteries] mon supplie the place of ane of the ecclesiasticall estate in parliament, neidfull it is, that he quha sall have the stile, title and place of abbot, priour, or commendatar, be well learnit and qualifeit thairfore'; it was proposed that the bishop should examine his 'learning and habilitie' before his appointment. There was no suggestion that the commendator should be a minister, or appointed by the church, but monastic chapters were to be made up by ministers serving the parishes annexed to the monastery.[34] Even this claim could not be sustained in the face of steady secularization.

Eventually there was a series of creations of 'lords of erection', converting the monastic properties one by one into secular lordships, mainly in the 1590s and 1600s. The new lords joined the noble estate for most purposes. There was one exception: 'the awneris thairof may clame to be taxt with the barounes of the temporall estait, and thairthrow his hienes will be defraudit of a great part of the samin taxatioun', so they had to continue being taxed with the benefice-holders at a higher rate.[35] Thus there was a certain mingling of the clerical and noble estates of parliament.

The creation of the 'lords of erection' was so manifestly a government operation that the nobility could no longer so easily see their privileges as innate; they now, like the other estates, depended on the state. The king in 1612 thought that 'the great number of noblemen there [in Scotland] doe more harme then goode to that state'—although he had created many of them himself. Next year he was informed that 'theye begin to talke in Scotland of ancient nobiletye and there previledges must not be brokin', which 'dois mutche discontent his majestie'.[36] Privilege, thought James, should depend on his grace alone.

The story of the relationship between burghs and government is a multifarious one. Much of the story is one of royal interference in burghs, and attempts to resist this; but the government could also grant rewards and privileges to burghs. Traditionally, burghs saw themselves as a free-standing estate like the other two, with innate privileges. As royal burghs, it was difficult to deny that they in some sense derived these privileges from the crown;

---

[33] M. Dilworth, 'The Commendator System in Scotland', *Innes Review*, 37 (1986), 51–72; I. B. Cowan, *The Scottish Reformation* (London, 1982), 120.   [34] *BUK* i. 210.

[35] *APS* iv. 292, c. 19. There is no detailed account of the 'lordships of erection', but see Lee, *Government by Pen*, 63–4.

[36] James to earl of Mar, 26 Sept. 1612, and Viscount Fenton to Mar, 27 Oct. 1613, HMC, *Mar & Kellie*, i. 68; ii. 55.

but that they depended on the crown's *will* or *pleasure* was far from their thoughts. The court of session had held in 1550 that the crown had no power to grant trading rights to non-burgesses.[37] This particular privilege rested on common law; increasingly, however, the burghs' privileges were seen as statutory. As listed in 1633, the chief privileges were the monopoly of foreign trade and the restriction of most trade to resident burgesses.[38] In return for this privilege, the royal burghs paid a regular share (one-sixth) of direct parliamentary taxation, while the foreign trade on which they depended was also subject to increasing customs duties.

The burghs during the sixteenth century built up an elaborate mechanism of participation in parliament, and lobbying both of government and of parliament.[39] From the middle of the sixteenth century this was done through the convention of royal burghs. This was a largely new institution (though founded on the medieval 'court of the four burghs') which enabled the burghs to develop common policies both on matters of interest only to themselves, and on matters which involved the government. The convention of royal burghs met more frequently than parliament (typically twice a year), but when parliament did meet, the burgesses would usually hold their convention shortly beforehand to agree a lobbying programme. Increasingly the delegates to the convention were also the commissioners to parliament.[40] As a result the burghs had a direct input even to the lords of the articles. In 1597 the convention of royal burghs instructed the burgesses on the articles in their negotiations with the other lords on the import of bullion.[41]

Individual burghs, and even individual guilds, could also approach parliament. They had done so regularly in the fifteenth century, before the convention of royal burghs was established.[42] The Edinburgh council appointed a committee of six leading burgesses to prepare legislation 'for the

---

[37] Balfour, *Practicks*, i. 49. As well as royal burghs there were burghs of barony, small market centres with only local trading rights, which did not participate in national politics; for them, see Ch. 8 below. A few of the 'royal' burghs discussed here (notably St Andrews and Glasgow) were technically ecclesiastical burghs, holding of the church rather than the crown, but they had long been accepted as honorary royal burghs, paying royal taxation and participating in the convention of royal burghs. All the active royal burghs were real towns (though some were small), unlike in England where some parliamentary 'boroughs' had only a parchment existence.

[38] *APS* v. 42, c. 24. Along with these went the right to search for infringements of these privileges, and to require non-burgesses to find caution to observe these restrictions.

[39] A. R. MacDonald, '"Tedious to rehers"? Parliament and Locality in Scotland, *c*.1500–1651: The Burghs of North-East Fife', *Parliaments, Estates and Representation*, 20 (2000), 31–58. For a study of London showing similar patterns, see I. W. Archer, 'The London Lobbies in the Late Sixteenth Century', *Historical Journal*, 31 (1988), 17–44.

[40] Pagan, *The Convention of the Royal Burghs*; J. D. Mackie and G. S. Pryde, *The Estate of the Burgesses in the Scots Parliament and its Relation to the Convention of Royal Burghs* (St Andrews, 1923), 17–34. For some lists of requests to parliament, see *RCRB* i. 75–7, 197, 240–1, 468; ii. 89.   [41] *RCRB* ii. 21–2.

[42] M. Lynch, 'Towns and Townspeople in Fifteenth-Century Scotland', in J. A. F. Thomson (ed.), *Towns and Townspeople in the Fifteenth Century* (Gloucester, 1988), 174–5.

weill of the toun' in 1593. These may not have been commercial matters: town government was, after all, government, and when the council decided in 1595 that seduction was too common in the burgh they drew up an article against it for parliament.[43] An Edinburgh skinner was admitted to the craft incorporation 'fre for 40s. deburst of befoir for ratificatioun of the act of parliament', probably the act of 1594 which ratified an earlier act against exports of calf and kid skins, hutherons, and shorelings. Lobbying had its sorrows as well as its joys: the skinners spent over £43 on 'fortificatioun of the act anent the purssis' in May 1599, but no such act emerged from the convention of that date.[44] The convention of royal burghs supervised this process of local lobbying, and burghs that refused to toe the agreed line in parliament could be disciplined.[45]

Burghs and crown sometimes had a difficult political relationship. This topic has been illuminated by the work of Michael Lynch and others.[46] Faction struggles at court could easily spill over into the burghs, as each party sought to place its clients in burgh office or to enforce the political line of the day. Burghs that took the wrong line, or had too close an association with the losing faction, could find themselves in trouble, even though burghs themselves never supported any sixteenth-century rebellions. There had been factional turmoil in the 1540s and 1550s, and would be again in the 1570s and early 1580s—all years of royal minorities. Burghs were fined or otherwise penalized for having taken the wrong side, their councils were purged, and provosts from outside (often prominent nobles) were imposed on them. Some factions within burghs, however, benefited—such as committed Protestants, who were often in a minority within their own burgh, and gained power using leverage provided by the crown. This type of conflict died away during the adult reign of James VI, as the issues involved were gradually settled. A statute of 1609, by restricting burgh office-holding to resident burgesses, reduced the political temperature by excluding noble politicians.[47]

The stability of government by an adult monarch did not, however, mean that burgesses could return to workshop, booth, and counting-house undisturbed. It might have meant that in earlier times; but the government from the 1590s onwards wished to achieve more. A memorandum by a councillor at this time sounded a characteristic note:

---

[43] *Edin. Recs.* v. 90, 141.

[44] *APS* iv. 75–6, c. 47; 'The Incorporated Trade of Skinners of Edinburgh, with Extracts from their Minutes, 1549–1603', ed. W. Angus, *Book of the Old Edinburgh Club*, 6 (1913), 11–106 at 74–5, 99.   [45] *RCRB* i. 469.

[46] M. Lynch, 'The Crown and the Burghs, 1500–1625', in id. (ed.), *The Early Modern Town in Scotland* (London, 1987); id., 'From Privy Kirk to Burgh Church: An Alternative View of the Process of Protestantisation', in Macdougall (ed.), *Church, Politics and Society*; A. L. Juhala, 'The Household and Court of King James VI of Scotland, 1567–1603' (Ph.D. thesis, Edinburgh, 2000), ch. 4.   [47] *APS* iv. 435–6, c. 15.

That the burrows (who seeks well enough to their own commonwealth) be put to order: not that I mean [them] to be in any sort hurt or oppresst, but that they and everie an of the estates may be so ordered as brethren in one society to the wellfare of the whole body, whereof the king is the head; the commonalitie being rich the king cannot be poor, and *e contra*.[48]

One form of interference was with the jurisdiction of the burgh court. New central and local jurisdictions were created by the crown, and the burghs had to adapt to them. The biggest threat was the new admiral's court, chartered in 1587, which would have taken over large tracts of burgh court business if it had ever become fully operational. Fortunately for the burghs, they were able to exploit the downfall of the hereditary admiral, the earl of Bothwell, in 1592, when they obtained a statute cancelling the obnoxious innovation. A more minor jurisdiction, the constable's court, inconvenienced the burgh of Edinburgh in the 1630s and the burgh failed to rid itself of the interloper.[49] In the 1610s, burgh courts also had to adapt to the introduction of justices of the peace: demarcation between them had in 1613 to be supervised by the privy council.[50]

The crown also began to interfere with the burghs' trading privileges by granting monopolies. Most were trading monopolies, in which trade in particular commodities could be carried on only with the permission of the patentee, who was thus able to extract commissions from merchants. Some were regulatory monopolies, in which the patentee's agents were typically empowered to check on quality of manufacture (for which they could charge a fee). Either way, the burgesses saw monopolies as eroding their livelihoods and campaigned staunchly, if not very successfully, against them.[51] Some monopolies transferred responsibilities from the government to private individuals, making it harder for those with grievances against them to seek redress. This was noticeable with the customs, which after 1598 were usually set in tack (i.e. leased out). In 1602, the merchants wanted an allowance of 10 per cent for leakage: their representatives had to argue not with the privy council but with the tacksmen. The councillors remained loftily above the dispute, listened to each side making its case, and then issued a decision in favour of the tacksmen.[52]

Of course the system of royal burghs was itself a giant trading and regulatory monopoly—the people who held the monopoly comprised the great majority of traders—and it might be difficult to object to monopolies

---

[48] BL, 'Proposalls for reformation of certain abuses in the state', in Harl. MS 4612, fo. 47ᵛ. This disordered but fascinating document dates from the late 1590s. No details were given of how the burghs were to be 'put to order'. Cf. the royal attack on the autonomy of French towns in the late 16th and early 17th cc.: D. Parker, *The Making of French Absolutism* (London, 1983), 66–7.

[49] For the admiral's court, see Ch. 7 below. The constable's court is discussed by Goodare, *State and Society*, 80–1.

[50] *RPC* ix. 496, 525–6.   [51] *RCRB* ii. 300, 307–8.   [52] *RPC* vi. 513–14.

without jeopardizing the burghs' existing privileges, now regarded as depending more on the crown. This was one reason why the crown could get away with so much here. Another reason was that the government also offered benefits to burghs in maintaining their own monopoly. Suppressing unprivileged traders in suburbs beyond the burgh limits could best be done by legal actions in the court of session. The expansion of credit from the 1590s onwards also meant legal actions against debtors; here, creditors benefited regularly from statutes enabling debt collection, and the privy council's willingness to order the arrest of defaulting debtors. To that extent there was some reciprocity between burghs and government.[53] That was not the case, however, in the most significant of the new forms of interference: fiscal demands. From the 1590s onwards, not only did parliamentary taxation (payable by the landed classes as well as the burghs) expand; the fiscal burden specifically on commerce increased.[54]

The active governmental economic and fiscal policy of the 1590s onwards involved the use of parliament in a new way—a way that the burghs found both unwelcome and confrontational. Their laboriously developed techniques of lobbying were exposed as dismayingly ineffectual. The government now announced a policy, listened politely (more or less) to the burghs' objections—and went ahead anyway. The imposition of customs duties on wine imports from 1590 onwards is a good example of this.[55] The burghs' proud and entrenched position in parliament worked against them, because they had to turn up and watch damaging decisions being made, and then see the resulting act published in the name of the 'estates'. They protested in 1586 against 'the greitt abuse usitt of laitt be the uther twa estaitis concluding actis thairatt, by [i.e. without] the voitt and consentt of the estaitt of burrowis, and they affirming the samyn in the narrative of the saidis actis to be universallie concludit be the thre estaitis consentis thairto'.[56] The illusion that this was an 'abuse' would soon be permanently dispelled.[57] Unable to quit parliament, the burghs had to watch their presence in it legitimize burden after burden being heaped on commerce. Their only consolation was that just occasionally—notably in 1600 when a revised tax assessment was blocked—they could use their strength to swing a decision in their favour. But the dominant position of crown and nobility in parliament made such moments rare.

---

[53] For debt collection in connection with enforcement of hornings, see Ch. 8 below.

[54] Goodare, *State and Society*, 115–17.

[55] Ibid. 114–15.

[56] *RCRB* i. 210. Cf. the burghs' instructions to their union commissioners in 1604 that they wanted to retain Scottish parliaments, 'and that na thing be concludit in the saidis parliamentis bot be the adwyse of all the estaitis and grittest number of ilk estaitt': *RCRB* ii. 190.

[57] A faint echo of consent by a single estate is found in the statute of 1621 permitting Sir George Hay of Kinfauns to export his iron from Letterewe without it having to go through a royal burgh. The statute narrated that the burghs had consented to this, and that it was not to prejudice their other rights: *APS* iv. 686, c. 100.

By 1623, the exasperated burghs' attitude to royal economic policy was tantamount to 'Find out what little Jimmy's doing and tell him to stop it'. Any government initiative would be likely to damage their interests, and the best (if, alas, far from infallible) remedy lay in lobbying privy council and parliament. The convention of royal burghs, 'understanding that betuixt conventiounes thair doeth occur divers and sindrie particulars quhairin the haill borrowis of this realme ar interest[ed], and becaus of thair not compeirance, gettis so far way and goes on without remeid', granted power to the burgh of Edinburgh 'to compeir in thair names and mak such laufull resistance as they may till they be farder hard'.[58]

Not only was this a sweeping indictment of recent government policy, but the mistrust was reciprocated. In 1621, 'upone that subject of the borrowes, ... his majestie is cawtious anewche to prevent onye hairme he maye have bye the [forthcoming] parlament'. Well might he be 'cawtious': a majority of burghs would vote against the crown in the struggle over the five articles of Perth.[59] This mistrust is too broad a topic to be treated fully here, but we may focus on the burghs' belief that 'resistance' (by which they meant lobbying, not insurrection) could be 'laufull'. This says much about the political culture of the period—both that it was possible to resist, or at least complain, and that once the complaints had been heard, the government could choose to ignore them. 'Laufull resistance' sometimes limited what the government might do; but it also legitimized it.

Clergy, nobility, and burgesses were the three medieval estates. With the expansion of government activity, three were no longer enough: a wider range of social groups was brought into direct contact with government, and they were enabled—or driven—to make their own decisions on the government's legitimacy instead of following the lead of their superiors. A wider range of town-dwellers paid tax. Lawyers grew in numbers and status as the pace of litigation accelerated. Lairds, if feudal freeholders, actually entered parliament in 1587. Kirk sessions, many of whose members were not from the feudal classes, claimed a role in regulating local society. Traditions of deference and hierarchy laid heavily on them, but in time they would come to demand a say in the government commensurate with their social position.

The two key social sectors which had to be drawn into a closer relationship with the government were the lawyers and the lairds. Lawyers were not

---

[58] *RCRB* iii. 143. For an example of the kind of thing that provoked 'laufull resistance', consider the government's recent policy on the 'infective weade callit tabacco', which had oscillated between attempting to ban all imports of it, and enforcing a monopoly (in effect a levy on the trade). The burghs objected vigorously to both policies: *RPC* xii. 397–8; xiii. 28–30, 102–4; *Aberdeen Letters*, i. 204–6; *Edin. Recs.* vi. 242. Cf. the contemporary English assumption that financial 'projects' were bad news for the subject: J. Cramsie, *Kingship and Crown Finance under James VI and I, 1603–1625* (Woodbridge, 2002), 87–8.

[59] Kellie to Mar, 11 Apr. 1621, HMC, *Mar & Kellie*, ii. 107; Goodare, 'Scottish Parliament of 1621', 41, 50–1.

exactly an estate—but they came close to being one. In preparation for the reforming parliament of 1587, the councillor John Lindsay of Menmuir drafted
a proposal that the lords of session should sit in parliament as members of the
clerical estate, which (he pointed out) had been weakened in numbers by the
eclipse of the bishops.[60] The proposal was not adopted, but it shows how high
the judges had risen in their sense of corporate identity, privilege, and influence. Lawyers and judges were in many ways the heirs of medieval church
administrators, and some of them were used in similar roles by the government. The legal profession looked to the government to enhance its role,
and it is no accident that the lawyers overwhelmingly supported the winning
side in the civil wars of 1567–73.[61] And while on the subject of lawyers and
lairds, it is worth pointing out that most lords of session were from lairds'
families.[62]

The court of session had been since 1532 an endowed corporate body, the
college of justice, including not just the president, fourteen 'ordinary' and
four 'extraordinary' judges (the 'lords of session' or 'senators' of the college)
but also a host of advocates, clerks, writers to the signet, and commissaries.
Together they formed an influential professional corporation. In 1593, 1594,
and 1606 the members of the college of justice obtained acts ratifying their
institutional privileges, comparable to the ratifications of the privileges of
estates.[63]

The relationship of parliament and session was one of fruitful cooperation.
The court had been set up partly to take over judicial business from parliament, a process largely completed in the 1540s; cases arising in parliament
and conventions continued to be referred to it.[64] The court used its links with
parliament in a variety of ways. As well as improvements to the substantive
civil law (and here the lords of session probably lobbied for many or most of
the statutes) there were statutes to enhance the authority of the session itself,
and to bring the local courts under central control: matters like the register of
sasines (on which see Chapter 9 below). On one occasion the lords of session
were commissioned by parliament to make legislative decisions on a number
of articles which parliament itself had been unable to deal with.[65] During a
parliamentary session, when inferior courts did not sit, the lords of session
could be drafted in to assist the lords of the articles—the lobbyist's dream.[66]

[60] [Alexander,] Lord Lindsay, *Lives of the Lindsays*, 3 vols. (London, 1849), i. 488–9.
Similarly, the French magistrates ('those who judge') were nearly made an official fourth estate
of the realm in the mid-16th c.: F. J. Baumgartner, *France in the Sixteenth Century* (London,
1995), 83, 124–5.
[61] M. Lynch, *Edinburgh and the Reformation* (Edinburgh, 1981), 133–4.
[62] Donaldson, 'The Legal Profession in Scottish Society', 9.
[63] *APS* iv. 22, c. 24; 67, c. 21; 305, c. 38. For more on the court of session, see Ch. 7
below.
[64] P. J. Hamilton-Grierson, 'The Judicial Committees of the Scottish Parliament, 1369–70 to
1544', *SHR* 22 (1925), 1–13 at 12; *RPC* iv. 101.   [65] *APS* iii. 214–15, c. 9.
[66] *RPC* iv. 194–5.

The court's excellent lobbying ability depended partly on its best-connected members—the 'extraordinary', non-professional lords who were often nobles or privy councillors. Extraordinary lords increased royal influence, but the magnates seem to have wanted them too.[67] Everybody, in fact, seems to have loved the court of session, one of the sixteenth century's great success stories. In about 1600–25 it reached the apogee of its corporate influence in government, through the gradual assimilation of its membership to that of the privy council.[68] The two bodies remained functionally distinct, but when they consisted of the same people they could hardly disagree. This was abruptly reversed in 1625–6, when Charles I separated the membership of the two bodies. The implication that the lords of session held their posts at royal pleasure had not been the accepted view under James VI, and it led to protests. By giving the king a wider choice of advisers, the separation aimed to elevate his personal discretion—and also enhanced the influence of those who had access to his ear.[69]

By 1629 the extraordinary lords were said to be 'butt as spyes over the rest to marke theire doinges, and informe the king of it'.[70] That, of course, did not make the court poorly connected—arguably the reverse—but it demonstrated its dependence on the crown. Still, the relationship was a two-way one. The government needed the court of session to legitimize its heavily legalistic programme, and the court's own legitimacy was now a fragile thing. At a time when there was a large amount of litigation passing through the court, its privileges as an institution were sustained by public opinion. The government knew that if it were seen to interfere in its privileges, this might be tantamount to demonstrating that it was perverting the course of justice, or even ruling unjustly.[71]

The admission of shire commissioners to parliament was an event of seismic significance.[72] The relevant legislation, passed in 1587, recognized and regularized the irruption of lairds onto the political scene that had taken place in 1560. It is well known that about a hundred lairds attended the Reformation Parliament; this was unprecedented but not unique. Over fifty-eight lairds attended a convention in February 1570, thirty-four attended another in July, and over eighty-one came to a third in November 1572. At least eleven conventions between 1560 and 1587 included lairds. The lairds made

---

[67] Hannay, *College of Justice*, 128–34.

[68] All the forty-six lords of session between 1603 and 1625 also became privy councillors, and twelve were also officers of state: Taylor, 'Scottish Privy Council', 37.

[69] Lee, *The Road to Revolution*, 18–23; P. G. B. McNeill, 'The Independence of the Scottish Judiciary', *JR*, NS 3 (1958), 134–47. For the effect of this on the privy council, see Ch. 6 below.

[70] H. L. MacQueen (ed.), 'Two Visitors in the Session, 1629 and 1636', in *Stair Society Miscellany*, iv (2002), 165.

[71] For the failure of a frontal attack on a decision of the court in 1599, see T. M. Cooper, 'The King versus the Court of Session', *JR* 58 (1946), 83–92.

[72] For more details of what follows, see Goodare, 'Admission of Lairds'.

repeated efforts to gain representation, bidding unsuccessfully in 1567 and 1579 before finally succeeding in 1587.

Parliament thereafter could never be quite the same. It had derived its authority from ancient tradition; but now, despite the claim to be reviving a still-born act of 1428, representation in parliament would be based on a manifest innovation. The shire commissioners were not a traditional body. They never penetrated the most traditional temple of status, the form of the royal coronation. Even in the seventeenth century, this was restricted to the three medieval estates, including a requirement for non-existent 'abbots'.[73] Tampering with parliament's immemorial three estates to add a fourth could hardly fail to shake conservative beliefs about the wellsprings of parliamentary authority, helping people to think of government as looking to the future as well as to the past. The term 'the three estates' dropped out of use, to be replaced by the arithmetically neutral 'the estates'.[74]

Once safely ensconced in the estates, the shire commissioners could lobby successfully for the cancellation of a proposed parliament in 1595.[75] This, and the frequent lobbying on taxation, required some kind of informal networking mechanism. This probably arose naturally from the ways in which public issues were discussed. The mid-sixteenth century saw an increase in letter-writing that was no doubt connected with the rise of widespread vernacular literacy. The sending of letters was accompanied by personal contact and by the delivery of oral messages by trusted messengers. The network of correspondence around the Campbells of Glenorchy in Highland Perthshire indicates how these processes operated.[76]

The lairds' networking was not formal enough to be an institution like the convention of royal burghs, but that was not for want of trying. In 1599, a petition from the shire commissioners to the other estates made a number of demands, mainly for reduced taxes, but also for the right to hold their own twice-yearly convention like the royal burghs.[77] It is significant that the shire commissioners' political leaders thought in these terms, and especially that they identified with the burghs, with whom they were taking concerted action against taxation. But perhaps it is equally significant that such a convention was never set up. The destiny of the lairds was not to create another medieval institution, but to undermine existing ones by blurring distinctions of status like those between baron, feuar, and burgess.

---

[73] BL, 'Forme of the coronation of the kings of Scotland', 1625 × 1685, Add. MS 19797, fos. 57ᵛ–58ᵛ. Shire commissioners did, however, have their own representatives in the group that 'fenced' each parliament (formally constituting it as a law court): Sir Thomas Hamilton, 'Memoriall anent the progres and conclusion of the parliament haldin at Edinburgh in October 1612', *Maitland Club Miscellany*, iii (1843), 113.

[74] Goodare, 'Estates in the Scottish Parliament', 17–24.

[75] John Colville to John Carey, 18 Mar. 1595, *CSP Scot.* xi. 553.

[76] *Clan Campbell Letters, 1559–1583*, ed. J. E. A. Dawson (SHS, 1997), 4–8 and *passim*. The Campbells of Glenorchy were unusual in preserving their correspondence but not in writing it.

[77] NAS, misc. parliamentary papers, PA7/1/48.

The lesser estates, burgh and shire commissioners, were representatives of wider communities who were not personally present in parliament, and the strength of their connections to these communities is itself likely to have diluted their connections with the government. A separation between governors and governed does not exist everywhere, but it did exist in early modern Scotland. Representativeness may mean typicality, but need not; today's 'elected representatives' are not typical of the people who elect them. What it does have to mean is responsiveness. It is a reasonable conjecture that, as in contemporary county representation in England, commissioners were selected for their local prestige and so *were*, in an oligarchical sense, representative.[78] Shire commissioners had been introduced because the consent of the peers to legislation and taxation was no longer sufficient to bind lesser landlords, but probably it was the greater of these lesser landlords who most often sat in parliament.[79]

The shire commissioners were not the only lairds who came to Edinburgh for a parliament. The nobles brought their followers with them, to demonstrate their status. Lord Maxwell wrote to Sir John Maxwell of Pollok, enjoining him to join his following of 'kyn, freyndis, varsallis, serweandis and dependaris, during the tyme of the parliament now approaching'. The earls of Huntly and Errol in 1597 brought an enormous following of four hundred horsemen, including several other peers and many lairds.[80] How the lairds in a noble's following related to the lairds who were personal members of parliament we do not know. Probably some of the latter were also the former. Since parliament itself did not sit every day during its existence, but waited upon the deliberation of the lords of the articles, most of the shire commissioners will have spent part of their time mixing with these other lairds, the nobles' followers, and part of it (until 1621) holding unminuted but more formal meetings of their separate estate.[81] All this probably tended to connect the shire commissioners to the nobles' estate. When the lairds' and nobles' estates found themselves at odds, as they periodically did, the most likely explanation for the shire commissioners' independent behaviour is that the leading nobles were closely connected with the government, and indeed were

---

[78] M. A. Kishlansky, *Parliamentary Selection: Social and Political Choice in Early Modern England* (Cambridge, 1986), pt. I.

[79] This point might be elucidated by extensive prosopographical analysis, for which the starting point would be provided by Young (ed.), *The Parliaments of Scotland*. Scottish shire commissioners were drawn from a narrower social stratum than their English counterparts, because more of the greater landlords were titled peers, and because the franchise was more restricted (40s. of old extent, a traditional valuation usually worth much more than the English 40s. sterling of current rentals).

[80] Lord Maxwell to Maxwell of Pollok, 30 Apr. 1578 and 9 Oct. 1591, in W. Fraser, *Memoirs of the Maxwells of Pollok*, 2 vols. (Edinburgh, 1863), ii. 143, 166; Nicolson to Cecil, 9 Dec., and Ashton to Cecil, 12 Dec. 1597, *CSP Scot.* xiii, I. 128, 131.

[81] For what is known on this subject see MacDonald, 'Deliberative Processes in Parliament'. Separate meetings of the individual estates, banned in 1621, were allowed again in 1630: 'Diary of the Convention of Estates, 1630', ed. J. Goodare, *SHS Miscellany*, xiv (forthcoming).

often functioning components of it. Lairds were not. Their connections were with the propertied community at large.

Burghs too sometimes sent sizeable delegations to parliament. Sometimes up to three would be registered on the parliamentary sederunt, even though they had only one vote. Or only one would be registered, although we know the other members of the delegation from the burgh records.[82] Such delegates were not necessarily qualified to act as commissioners: St Andrews in 1612 sent its minister as part of its parliamentary delegation.[83] As with the shire commissioners, this did not in any way make them unrepresentative. It is certain that burgh commissioners represented their burgh councils. The latter were themselves increasingly oligarchical in our period, and were losing their close ties with the burgess community; still, in a similar sense, burgh councils did represent burgh communities.[84] In a rough and ready way, the Scottish body politic got the representation it deserved; few political communities can say much more.

Scotland's status as a dependent state meant that it had a certain amount of alien material lodged in its body politic. English influence was indirect, both before and after the union; there was no English right (or power) to issue orders to the Scottish government. But it still makes sense to consider the English interest—represented by the ambassadors of Queen Elizabeth before 1603, and thereafter by James VI himself in his capacity as James I—as an influence on Scottish government and politics. The ambassadors Thomas Randolph in the 1560s, or Robert Bowes in the 1580s and 1590s, wielded political influence that none could discount. Usually this involved putting pressure on the monarch directly, but the English sometimes used the Scottish parliament in pursuit of their aims. During the parliament of 1593, some of the earl of Huntly's dependants had to negotiate with Bowes, as well as with the king and church, in order to preserve their interests when their chief was in trouble. Like other interest groups, the English ambassadors were lobbyists.[85] They benefited from English penetration of James's court, notably by Roger Ashton, an English gentleman of the chamber. He reported regularly to Elizabeth's ministers and is sometimes described as an 'English

---

[82] e.g. the three commissioners from Ayr in 1579, only one of whom was registered in the sederunt: *Ayr Accounts*, 145; *APS* iii. 128. Several other such cases were noted by W. C. Dickinson, 'Burgh Commissioners to Parliament', *SHR* 34 (1955), 92–5; he suggested that the unrecorded commissioners must have failed to attend, but this seems unlikely in the cases where (as in Ayr) they were paid expenses.   [83] Pryde, 'Scottish Burgh Finances', 276.
[84] M. Lynch, 'Continuity and Change in Urban Society, 1500–1700', in R. A. Houston and I. D. Whyte (eds.), *Scottish Society, 1500–1800* (Cambridge, 1989), 87–8.
[85] 'The Straloch Papers', *Spalding Miscellany*, i (1841), 6–7. See also Bowes to Burghley, 8 and 28 May 1593, *CSP Scot.* xi. 87, 93. Evidence for direct lobbying of members of parliament is scanty, probably because ambassadors were too discreet to mention it in their correspondence. Protocol expected that formal requests should go through the monarch or privy council: G. Mattingly, *Renaissance Diplomacy* (Pelican edn., Harmondsworth, 1965), 235.

agent', but he was primarily James's servant. It suited James to have someone close to him in communication with England.[86]

Although the English were a quite different kind of interest group from those we have considered so far, their function from this point of view was similar: to exert pressure, to negotiate, and to seek the best possible government policies from the Scottish government. In the period after 1560, the English found themselves in the virtually unprecedented position of having a friendly, and somewhat dependent, Scottish government. Did they exploit this unreasonably? Did they ride roughshod over Scotland?

There are occasional examples of English insensitivity. At least one English official could not distinguish between England and Britain—a problem not confined to the early modern period. The English agent in Mainz described the English parliament of 1624 as 'le Parlement de la Grande Bretagne'.[87] But this was exceptional. A more familiar pattern was manifested by some of the blatant interventions of the late sixteenth century, such as Sir William Cecil's scheme, in 1570, to have Elizabeth named as 'defender' of the Scottish parliament as part of an English-sponsored political settlement in Scotland.[88] During the siege of Edinburgh Castle in 1573, the Regent Morton was heavily dependent on his English allies. The ambassador, Sir Henry Killigrew, and commander, Sir William Drury, regularly intervened to modify Morton's policy, and eventually directed the fates of the defeated 'Castilians'.[89] Or, again, Sir Robert Melville of Murdochcairny, the Scottish envoy to England in 1593, had to promise that James would not pardon the dissident Catholic earls without Elizabeth's approval. Next year, James even offered to allow Elizabeth to appoint the officers for an army to fight the earls, if only she would pay for it. Elizabeth, however, would not release money unless an army had already been mustered.[90]

It might be thought that the English had more influence after 1603, when their own king could be persuaded to exert his influence as king also of Scotland. There is a sense in which this may have been so, but the matter is not straightforward. Foreign policy was important to the English, and it was obviously gratifying that the possibility of Scotland reviving an anti-English foreign policy had now been removed. But James's foreign policy (it can be described as his because he was always actively involved in it) was not simply

---

[86] Juhala, 'Household and Court of King James VI', app. 1; A. R. MacDonald, 'Ecclesiastical Representation', 50.

[87] Quoted in T. Cogswell, *The Blessed Revolution: English Politics and the Coming of War, 1621–1624* (Cambridge, 1989), 143. The agent was himself German.

[88] *CSP Scot.* iii. 363–5. This did not take effect, but it could not even have been suggested if the English had not been well entrenched in the Scottish political system.

[89] Hewitt, *Scotland under Morton*, 28–30, 169–74.

[90] Bowes to Burghley, 30 Nov. 1593 and 30 Apr. 1594, *CSP Scot.* xi. 234, 324.

English; he pursued dynastic as well as national interests, and employed a number of Scots in his diplomatic affairs.[91]

In domestic policy, James's English ministers seem to have observed proprieties in dealing with Scotland. They were sometimes keen on a policy and pushed for it to be adopted there, but there was nothing sinister or underhand about this—and often it failed. Because Scotland, from the English point of view, was a small, poor, and remote country, there were only a few matters where the English really wanted an influence. Scotland was strategically placed to help (or hinder) the consolidation of English hegemony in Ireland; it had potentially rich fishing grounds; it produced one or two export commodities (such as wool) which the English might want to buy; and it was a noted supplier of fighting men. Other than that, thought most English ministers, Scotland could be left to itself so long as it was not actually causing trouble.

The king himself was interested in religious conformity—perhaps the main area in which one might seek a 'British' policy in the early seventeenth century. His favourite churchmen, whatever their nationality, seem to have been willing to adopt a British perspective. This was rarely simple anglicization, however much the Scots may have feared this; rather, it was a matter of taking whatever opportunities offered in the three kingdoms to introduce the best practice. This would tend to mean more changes to the churches of Scotland and Ireland than to the church of England, but it was not intended to create a greater England in ecclesiastical matters.[92] Borrowing between the churches thus went in various directions. The revised Scottish confession of faith, introduced in 1616, was based not on the English Thirty-Nine Articles but on the Irish Articles of 1615, presumably because these offered a more up-to-date statement of Jacobean Calvinism.[93]

How was Anglo-Scottish policy coordination achieved in practice? Take two examples from the year 1605. Firstly, the Highlands and Ireland. The Scottish secretary, Lord Balmerino, sent a draft Scottish proclamation for the Western Isles to Sir Robert Cecil, his English opposite number, asking for suggested amendments before the document went to the king.[94] Secondly, military recruitment. Cecil, now earl of Salisbury, was considering whether to allow the Spanish Netherlands to recruit troops in Britain. He seems to have assumed that he and the king would make the decision, even though the scheme was to recruit 2,000 men in England, 1,500 in Scotland, and 500 in

[91] S. Murdoch, 'Diplomacy in Transition: Stuart-British Diplomacy in Northern Europe, 1603–1638', in A. I. Macinnes et al. (eds.), *Ships, Guns and Bibles in the North Sea and Baltic States, c.1350–c.1700* (East Linton, 2000).

[92] Morrill, 'A British Patriarchy?'.

[93] J. Perry, 'John Spottiswoode, Archbishop and Chancellor, as Churchman, Historian and Theologian' (Ph.D. thesis, Edinburgh, 1950), 14–17. The Irish Articles had themselves been based on the unofficial Lambeth Articles of 1595.

[94] Balmerino to Cecil, 13 Jan. 1605, HMC, *Salisbury*, xvii. 12.

Ireland. There is no record of the Scottish privy council ever discussing the issue. In August the English privy council wrote to the Scottish, asking that Scottish recruits should embark from Scottish ports and not travel through England. This was, however, a request and not a command. The first signature on the letter was that of the duke of Lennox, perhaps one of the few genuine Britons of the period.[95]

Neither of these examples amounts to much more than a concern to develop and maintain a coordinated policy. Chancellor Dunfermline wrote to Salisbury in 1608, raising issues which encapsulate the coordination of three kingdoms. Two hundred Scottish troops had been raised for service in Ireland; they were paid by Scotland for the first two months, and the Scots arranged for them to be shipped to Carrickfergus, where they were to be commanded by the governor. Their rates of pay would have to be adjusted to those prevailing in Ireland. Dunfermline, meanwhile, wanted reimbursement for Scotland from the English treasury. In a postscript he asked if the arrears of his own English pension could be paid.[96]

Mention of money reminds us that a genuinely subordinate state often has financial surpluses extracted from it by the colonial state. This was not so for Scotland; the English had little desire to lay hands on Scottish royal revenues, and the king was content to have those revenues spent north of the Border.[97] There was instead regular largesse to individual Scottish nobles and courtiers from *English* royal revenues, which may be regarded as an indirect subsidy to Scotland. A particularly clear example comes from 1605, when the duke of Lennox was granted English crown lands worth £900 sterling, on condition that he surrendered the equivalent amount in Scotland—evidently his archbishopric lands, which were now being restored to the church.[98] But this cannot be considered as intervention by the English in their own interests. Elizabeth, with her subsidy to James, had paid the piper and called the tune; the subsidy to Lennox, by contrast, was the king buying support for his Scottish policy. This policy—restoration of episcopal revenues—was perhaps a British policy, but it was not an English one.[99]

Turning from fiscal to economic policy, there were two attempts at English interference—though both failed. English courtiers concocted a scheme in 1617 to infringe the monopolies of the Russia Company and East India Company by forming a new, rival company, chartered under the great seal of Scotland. The scheme did not proceed, but if it had, it would have exploited Scottish rights to benefit the English, or at least some of the

[95] BL, Salisbury to Sir Thomas Edmondes, 11 May 1605, Stowe MS 168, fo. 17^r; *RPC* vii. 742; cf. 130.
[96] BL, Dunfermline to Salisbury, 13 July 1608, Add. MS 32476, fos. 9^r–11^r.
[97] Goodare, *State and Society*, 129–30.   [98] *CSP Dom., 1603–10*, 270.
[99] This distinction between English and British policies is discussed more fully in Goodare, *State and Society*, 244–6. For subsidies to Scotland up to 1603, see id., 'James VI's English Subsidy', in id. and Lynch (eds.), *The Reign of James VI*.

English.[100] More worryingly for the Scots, the economic crisis of the early 1620s saw an effort to convert part of the Scottish economy into a specialist and complementary branch of the English one. In late 1621, the English government planned to restrict wool exports, to succour the struggling cloth industry. A ban on exports of Scottish wool except to England was soon suggested. A proclamation restricting English wool exports, and announcing a plan to do the same for Scotland, was issued in England in July 1622. It was sent to the Scottish council in August asking them to send commissioners to negotiate on the details. Scottish commercial interests, both urban and rural, opposed the scheme, and it seems that the privy council took their side, although would-be monopolists were attracted to it.[101] There were negotiations with English commissioners in the spring of 1623, and the Scots persuaded them to drop the scheme.[102] This disappointed the king, but he agreed to the logical next step: for a commission to be set up within Scotland to encourage the manufacture of woollen cloth there.[103] The scheme had not been outrightly colonialist, but it had been very much an English government initiative, promoted with English interests in mind. Still, the Scottish government was equally able to promote Scottish interests, and the issue was settled—in favour of the Scots, be it noted—by negotiation.

The impression given by all this is that there were hardly any attempts to govern Scotland as an appendage of England. Attempts even to coordinate policies were sporadic and usually based on common sense. It was only natural that, when the king decided to establish consuls in Spain, the Scots should be asked to contribute to the cost through an imposition on trade with Spain like that planned by England.[104] It was a decent gesture by the English ambassador in Constantinople when he sought to prove that the Scots were entitled to the same trading privileges as the English in Turkey.[105]

The court was Anglo-Scottish, and this might have led to some blurring of lines of communication. The earl of Angus, exiled for Catholicism, approached Salisbury in 1609 in hope of getting his banishment rescinded.[106] It was a good try, but there is no record of any response from Salisbury. In 1619, Sir George Calvert, joint secretary of state, wanted his colleague Sir Robert Naunton to deal with an emissary from the merchants of Scotland

---

[100] W. R. Scott, *The Constitution and Finance of English, Scottish and Irish Joint-Stock Companies, to 1720*, 3 vols. (Cambridge, 1912), i. 147–8.

[101] *Stuart Royal Proclamations*, i: *1603–1625*, ed. J. F. Larkin and P. L. Hughes (Oxford, 1973), no. 229; *CSP Dom., 1619–23*, 334, 439; *Edin. Recs.* vi. 238; *Aberdeen Letters*, i. 201–3; *RPC* xiii. 839–40.

[102] *RPC* xiii. 70, 106, 110, 117, 141–2, 148, 172, 176–7, 233, 773–7; *CSP Dom., 1619–23*, 450, 493–4, 505.

[103] *RPC* xiii. 234–36, 298–302; *RCRB* iii. 144; cf. A. D. Nicholls, *The Jacobean Union: A Reconsideration of British Civil Policies under the Early Stuarts* (Westport, Conn., 1999), 160–1.

[104] Salisbury to Dunfermline, Oct. 1611, *CSP Dom., 1611–18*, 83. No such imposition appears to have been made in Scotland.   [105] *CSP Dom., 1623–5*, 428.

[106] Angus to [Salisbury], 12 Oct. 1609, *CSP Dom., 1603–10*, 550.

(probably concerning a scheme to restrict their trade to Scottish-owned ships); the emissary would otherwise go to the king.[107] The trade scheme had British dimensions, so it is understandable that the emissary thought it worthwhile to pull English strings; it would be more interesting to know why Calvert thought that dealing with him fell within Naunton's remit. Still, these were rare and exceptional events, surely indicating James's failure to turn his court into a crucible that would forge a new cadre of Britons.

We may well ask how much of this was good for Scotland; but contemporaries, by and large, did not, at least publicly. Nationalism as a legitimating principle ('do this because it is good for Scotland') was rarely invoked in political discourse. One exception might be the appeal of Sir Richard Maitland to the warring parties in the civil war of the early 1570s not to invite in foreign troops—'Thai help you not for luif thai have to you'; but his anti-political mock-naivety hardly constituted a developed political programme.[108] The Scottish wool-growers, discussed above, seem mainly to have objected to the king's scheme because it would have astricted them to a smaller group of purchasers, who would have been able to hold down prices. The fact that those purchasers would have been English may have been a further demerit of the scheme for some, but there is no proof of this. More ideological was the advocate John Russell's treatise of 1604 on the union, which, formally and deferentially unionist, in fact sounded the alarm for Scottish liberty against English encroachment:

Sall ane frie kingdome possessing sua ancienne liberteis become ane slave, furth of libertie in bondage and servitude—and that of thair auin proper uill, uncompellit or coactit, to the heich honor of Ingland, perpetuall desolatioun of Scotland . . . ? Sall Scotland now eftir many ages ressave schame, and amit hir ancienne beautie? The Lord forbid.[109]

Russell is interesting because his career periodically indicates distrust of the government.[110] Those thinkers who adopted a 'British' vision in the late sixteenth and early seventeenth centuries saw this as fully compatible with Scottish patriotism, and the essentialism and separatism characteristic of modern nationalism were absent.[111] The separatist strand detectable in

---

[107] Calvert to Naunton, 21 June 1619, *CSP Dom., 1619–23*, 54; cf. *RCRB* iii. 75–6.

[108] *The Maitland Folio Manuscript*, 2 vols., ed. W. A. Craigie (STS, 1919–27), i. 310.

[109] John Russell, 'A treatise of the happie and blissed unioun', in *The Jacobean Union: Six Tracts of 1604*, ed. B. R. Galloway and B. P. Levack (SHS, 1985), 89–90. 'Amit' = lose.

[110] He had opposed a reorganization of the business of the court of session by the clerk register in 1585: BL, Add. MS 33531, fos. 199ʳ–200ᵛ. He penned a memorandum suspicious of the crown's taxation claims in 1587, discussed by Goodare, 'Parliamentary Taxation in Scotland', 41. He successfully defended Robert Bruce, the king's *bête noire*, in 1599, whereupon the king swore to have the decision reversed: Cooper, 'The King versus the Court of Session'.

[111] A. Williamson, 'Patterns of British Identity: "Britain" and its Rivals in the Sixteenth and Seventeenth Centuries', in G. Burgess (ed.), *The New British History: Founding a Modern State, 1603–1715* (London, 1999), 138–43; M. Lynch, 'A Nation Born Again? Scottish Identity in the Sixteenth and Seventeenth Centuries', in D. Broun et al. (eds.), *Image and Identity: The Making*

Russell's thought was marginal to the key ideologically charged issues of the period. The dynasticism of the government and the internationalism of its presbyterian opponents precluded the construction of debates between them in terms of nationalism—as indeed was normal for the elites of dependent territories in early modern Europe.[112] Much unionist imagery concentrated on courtly ceremonial, which was hard to gainsay and which had no obvious anti-union equivalent.[113] The usual official view of national sentiment in the early modern composite monarchy was forcefully expressed by the count-duke of Olivares, minister of Philip IV of Spain: 'Cursed be nations, and cursed the men who are *nacionales*! . . . I love all the vassals of the king . . . I am no *nacional*—that is for children.'[114] James VI, and perhaps even more the cosmopolitan Mary, would have agreed.

The rise of a personal monarchy was paralleled by a decline in official tolerance for corporate status groups. We shall examine this from the monarchy's own point of view in Chapter 4. James VI aspired to draw all individuals in the body politic into a direct dependence on the crown, and one effect of this was to undermine the autonomous privileges of individual estates and corporate bodies. Courtiers and other royal servants were distanced from the interests of individual estates. After 1603 the court was physically more distant, but the phenomenon being discussed here was one of functional differentiation rather than geographical division.

In earlier generations, nobles serving the crown were still nobles; serving the crown and being a noble were felt to be synonymous. Some nobles would be more in favour at court, and others less in favour would be jealous, but nobles were nobles whether in or out of favour. From time to time, late medieval kings might foster the creation of political figures who owed more to them than to local landed society—though such figures would still normally have some links with the local elite. Possible examples from the reign of James V are Sir James Hamilton of Finnart and Oliver Sinclair of Pitcairn. But they were exceptional. More commonly, even kings' younger sons acquired titles, estates, and local power bases, rapidly becoming indistinguishable from the nobles around them. The earl of Moray under James V was the king's half-brother and had been inserted into the vacant earldom, but in his

and Re-making of Scotland through the Ages (Edinburgh, 1998), 94–5. For a view of the 17th-c. Scottish literati lamenting the demise of court patronage while demonstrating inadvertently that they could do well without it, see D. Allan, 'Prudence and Patronage: The Politics of Culture in Seventeeth-Century Scotland', *History of European Ideas*, 18 (1994), 467–80.

[112] A. M. Rao and S. Supphellen, 'Power Elites and Dependent Territories', in Reinhard (ed.), *Power Elites and State Building*, 80–1.

[113] K. M. Brown, 'The Vanishing Emperor: British Kingship and its Decline, 1603–1707', in Mason (ed.), *Scots and Britons*; C. W. J. Withers, *Geography, Science and National Identity: Scotland since 1520* (Cambridge, 2001), 56–67.

[114] Quoted in J. H. Elliott, *The Count-Duke of Olivares: The Statesman in an Age of Decline* (New Haven, 1986), 564. On presbyterian internationalist thinking, see Williamson, *Scottish National Consciousness*, ch. 1.

career as a regional magnate in royal service he seems little different from other magnates with established kinship networks.[115]

Now, however, the outlines emerged of a functional differentiation in the body politic: between those with a primary connection directly to the crown, and those whose primary attachments were to traditional privileged groups—particularly the nobility. By the 1590s there were sometimes clear differences between courtiers who were neither magnates nor related to magnates, like Sir William Stewart of Grandtully, and magnates who were not courtiers, like his local neighbour the sixth earl of Atholl.[116] Other non-courtier magnates included the seventh earl of Argyll, whose defeat at the battle of Glenlivet (1594) ended his chances of advancement outside his Highland heartland.[117] After the seventh earl of Glencairn participated in the Ruthven Raid of 1582, his political career was largely a blank for the next forty-nine years.[118] Sharon Adams's pioneering regional study of the south-west has identified 'developing faultlines' between old and new nobles and between courtiers and nobles with established local power bases.[119]

The process of differentiation was aided by the regal union, making the court more remote and expensive, but the differentiation discussed here was essentially functional rather than geographical and had begun before 1603. The point was that those connected most closely to the centre tended to be connected least to particular localities. John Murray, earl of Annandale, acquired property in Dumfriesshire but no local connections; his son and successor found no support when he and Montrose raided Dumfries in 1644. The process of differentiation was never complete, and some early seventeenth-century courtiers did have local roots; but these were less necessary than they had been a century earlier.[120]

By the seventeenth century the distinction between courtiers and magnates, though never total, had become familiar. Sir Robert Gordon advised his nephew, the thirteenth earl of Sutherland: 'If yow hawe two or thrie sones, make one of them a courtiour after his trawells abrod in other countreys. Let him be bred in England; for it is requisite that some of our nobilitie be about

---

[115] Cameron, *James V*, 53–5, 119–22, 191–227, 244–5, 273–4.

[116] Stewart was a royal page, and later a gentleman of the bedchamber. He seems not to have been beholden to any magnate: W. Fraser, *The Red Book of Grandtully*, 2 vols. (Edinburgh, 1868), i, pp. lxxix–lxxxvi. For enmity between his and Atholl's families see *RPC* vi. 299–300.

[117] For the king's distrust of him see Thomas Douglas to Cecil, 26 Mar. 1602, *CSP Scot.* xiii, II. 961.

[118] He long remained a privy councillor but attended council rarely; his lack of influence was not due to lack of interest or ability. S. Adams, 'James VI and the Politics of South-West Scotland, 1603–1625', in Goodare and Lynch (eds.), *Reign of James VI*, 230.

[119] S. Adams, 'A Regional Road to Revolution: Religion, Politics and Society in South-West Scotland, 1600–1650' (Ph.D. thesis, Edinburgh, 2002), 64.

[120] K. M. Brown, 'Courtiers and Cavaliers: Service, Anglicisation and Loyalty among the Royalist Nobility', in J. Morrill (ed.), *The Scottish National Covenant in its British Context* (Edinburgh, 1990); K. M. Brown, 'Aristocracy, Anglicisation and the Court, 1603–1637', *Historical Journal*, 36 (1993), 543–76. For a critique of the concept of 'absentee monarchy' see Ch. 4 below.

ther prince.'[121] The 'courtiour' would be a younger son, like Gordon himself, rather than the head of the house. Some courtiers preferred not to have any connection with a noble house and to seek an immediate dependence on the crown. Dependence on a magnate could be suspect unless that magnate's own loyalty was unimpeachable. Sir William Stewart of Traquair boasted to the king that 'in all my lyftyme I nevir haid na secundarie dependance bot as I restit only bund to your majestie'.[122]

All this tended to exalt the position of the crown. By 1611 the privy council could write of 'this commounwelth, being bot one body, participating of lyffe and lustre derivat frome your majestie, the sole head and essence of the same, and thairfra conveyed to all the memberis thairof'.[123] Head and body were standard medieval metaphors, but the substance behind them seems to have been shifting. All authority descended from the king, which increasingly tended to make everyone else into undifferentiated 'subjects', even the nobility and other groups whose privileges had previously been thought to be innate.[124] Additionally, the council stressed that the state was now a *single* body politic, united by the king—not a collection of interest groups jostling for position. Such groups still existed, of course, but they had lost much autonomy. In the prevailing political culture, any assertion of sectional interests, even by the nobles, could now be seen as corroding the state's mystical unity.

The reality behind the council's dazzling metaphors was the absolutist state. From being a decentralized kingdom based on the power of a landed aristocracy, Scotland had become a centralized kingdom based on the power of a landed aristocracy. The nobles ruled, but they were no longer all in all to their tenants, clients, and followers; they ruled as cogs in a state machine. The key to this transformation was their abandonment of private warfare, and acceptance of the king's courts as the normal means to resolve their disputes. Their tenants, clients, and followers still looked to them as lords and patrons, but in a different way; instead of serving in their lords' armies, they served in royal armies or worked in law courts and administration. A proliferation of patrimonial bureaucracy, most of it nominally royal bureaucracy, allowed nobles as patrons to scatter networks of their clients through the system in an advantageous way. Other sectional interest groups, like lawyers and burgesses, also found roles within the system of patronage and clientage. The system of military recruitment outlined at the end of the Conclusion below relied on recruiters who might have local connections, but did not need them. What they did need was a court patron.

---

[121] W. Fraser, *The Sutherland Book*, 3 vols. (Edinburgh, 1892), ii. 344.

[122] NLS, Stewart to James, 10 Oct. 1604, Denmylne MSS, Adv. MS 33.1.1, vol. i, no. 17.

[123] Council to James, 24 Jan. 1611, *RPC* ix. 593.

[124] Q. Skinner, *The Foundations of Modern Political Thought*, 2 vols. (Cambridge, 1978), ii. 351–2.

So there was now a more integrated national structure of authority, rather than a series of regional structures presided over by territorial magnates. There was rather more differentiation of function, especially through the proliferation of lawyers at the centre, than there had been in the earlier regional structures. Meanwhile, the new dispensation involved the collection and circulation of a good deal more money, and those tenants who were no longer required for military service might find themselves having to pay economic rents. Military service continued, and indeed the nobles themselves still served in royal armies, but they now did so as officers in a state-controlled regimental structure, rather than as leaders of their own feudal followings. The transformation and integration of the body politic was part of the emergence of a single unified state.

CHAPTER THREE

Law and Legislation

Juges be war, pretend na ignorance:
Excuse is nane, the lawis ar to yow knawin.
The michty Lord, quha gevis governance,
His law, his word, into your eir is blawin;
The princis lawis befoir yow heir is schawin.
Gif ye do wrang do nocht your self abuse;
Heir is your reule, ye can have na excuse.

When Alexander Guthrie, burgh clerk of Edinburgh, acquired a copy of the newly printed parliamentary statutes in 1566, he was so excited that he penned this verse in the flyleaf.[1] This edition contained all the statutes from the first parliament of James I, in 1424, up to the most recent; almost all were being printed for the first time. An unassuming octavo volume, it was nevertheless an impressive legal edifice, as Guthrie immediately realized. It became an enzyme within the body of Scots law. As its implications began to seep into Scottish legal practice and juristic thinking, it began to animate and transform the nature of the law from within. But in 1566, that was in the future, and even the provenance of the law was unclear. Guthrie himself attributed the statutes first to God and then to the queen; we may be more inclined to connect them first with parliament, but if so, that is one of the things we need to discuss.

Before considering who made the law, however, perhaps we should ask what it was. Here we need a wider perspective on the matter, beginning in the fifteenth century. The system of formal rules by which Scotland was governed had long been a single, national one; a statute of 1504, for instance, ordered that 'all our soverane lordis liegis beand under his obeyance, and in speciale the Ilis, be reulit be our soverane lordis aune lawis and the common lawis of the realme, and be nain uther lawis'.[2] This made it recognizably royal law: the crown gave authority to it. Some laws—statutes—received their authority also from parliament, but there was no sense at the outset of our period that this was so for law in general. Law was an autonomous and largely fixed

---

[1] *Actis and Constitutionis of the Realme of Scotland . . .* (Edinburgh, 1566), copy in NLS, H.33.c.24.
[2] *APS* ii. 252, c. 24. This made Scotland comparable to England, but unlike France, with its regional systems of law. Scots law may not have been *applied* in remote regions like the 'Ilis', but that is a separate issue, examined in Ch. 10 below.

system, validated (like the crown itself) by ancient tradition. Hector MacQueen's detailed study of late medieval law shows that although there was some legal change, it was not primarily driven by governmental initiative, and he finds it unnecessary to offer any extended discussion of parliament.[3] Law was constituted in the courts, and evolved through procedural adaptation rather than being altered by legislation. In our period this changed, and parliamentary legislation emerged as the dominant force in the shaping of the law.

There was already a demand for central justice in the fifteenth century—a demand, however, that neither parliament nor council was keen to meet, preferring to remit cases to the 'judge ordinary' (usually the sheriff) wherever possible. It is understandable that a parliament dominated by magnates with their own feudal courts would do this—and in parliament's case it was a *choice* to refuse to hear cases, for it clearly had jurisdiction if it chose to exercise it. But at least from the time of James IV, the royal council began to be willing to entertain more cases. The pace quickened in the 1530s, when the court of session—a conciliar body, established as a professional college of justice in 1532—obtained the sole right to decide cases concerning 'fee and heritage' (title to land), over which its predecessors, the 'lords of session', had possessed little or no jurisdiction.[4]

This change, like the earlier (and possibly related) abandonment of process by pleadable brieve in the local courts, was not part of any legislator's master plan. Once in place, however, the existence of an active central court paved the way for further legal developments to be enacted by statute. A central court not only had a better overview of problems in the law; it was also (as shown in the previous chapter) well connected to propose that parliament should intervene to remedy these problems through legislation.

Meanwhile, parliament delegated its own routine judicial functions to the court of session, enabling it to concentrate more on its legislative role. Previously it had been common for parliament to appoint judicial committees of 'auditors' to hear cases, in effect a parallel central court to the (conciliar) lords of session. But after 1532 the bench of 'auditors' was increasingly drawn from the judges of the session; after 1544 no further auditors were appointed.[5] A differentiation and specialization of governmental functions had taken place.

Or so it appears with hindsight. At the time, however, it might have seemed that parliament was *losing* functions, and becoming less necessary to the government of the country. The fifteenth-century parliament had had important political functions, being the normal forum where the king had met with his

---

[3] MacQueen, *Common Law and Feudal Society*, 265–6 and *passim*.
[4] Ibid. 219, 239–42; Godfrey, 'Jurisdiction in Heritage'.
[5] Hamilton-Grierson, 'Judicial Committees'.

magnates. But the late fifteenth and early sixteenth centuries were a bad time
for Europe's parliaments, several of which were downgraded or even
abolished. Scottish parliaments ceased to be annual after 1496; Norman
Macdougall has argued that James IV simply found less need for them. He
could consult his magnates at his court—an elaborate court that was gaining
in political functions. He developed general councils—enlarged meetings of
the royal council, over the membership of which he had more control than
over parliaments. He developed his non-parliamentary revenues, so that another occasional function of parliament, taxation, was even less necessary.
Only its function as a supreme court was still important to the king. The first
parliament after 1496, in 1504, was summoned, not to tax, and not primarily
to legislate (although his ministers took the opportunity to have some legislation passed), but to forfeit some of the king's opponents for treason.[6] Attendances also declined: fifteenth-century parliaments could have over a
hundred members, but after 1490 none exceeded sixty. The nadir was
reached in 1527, when only twenty-seven turned up.[7]

   This, of course, was during a period of political turmoil during the minority of James V; and this is a clue to why parliament survived. At Flodden in
1513, much of the achievement of James IV's reign had perished: its political
harmony and its complex, glittering court centred on the royal household.
Renewed political instability meant more work for parliament in finding so-
lutions for a variety of problems concerning the regency and the succession.
This might mean lower attendances at parliament, since only the dominant
faction would be likely to come, but at least the institution was still meeting.
Then, in the 1530s, a need arose to define the country's religious orientation
in response to the Reformation challenge, and this was done through legislation.[8] James V seems to have had less distaste for parliament than his father,
and the 1530s saw slowly increasing attendances and a temporary recovery
almost to annual parliaments.[9]

   Legislation was only a minor task for fifteenth-century parliaments. A typical parliament would pass a dozen or so acts, of which many or most would
be temporary administrative orders of the kind that would later be the responsibility of the privy council.[10] Some of the measures that have attracted
most attention from historians, such as the act on feu-ferme tenure of 1457,
or the 'Education Act' of 1496, had little or no discernible effect, impressive

---

   [6] Macdougall, *James IV*, ch. 7; cf. L. O. Fradenburg, *City, Marriage, Tournament: Arts of
Rule in Late Medieval Scotland* (Madison, Wis., 1991).   [7] *APS* ii. 318–19.
   [8] Cf. J. Wormald, *Court, Kirk and Community: Scotland, 1470–1625* (London, 1981), 21–2.
   [9] This decline in parliamentary membership, followed by revival in the second quarter of the
16th c., is close to the pattern found in England: J. Loach, 'Parliament: A "New air"?', in
Coleman and Starkey (eds.), *Revolution Reassessed*, 121.
   [10] When in 1450 there are eighteen new acts and reissues of eight more, this is such a large
volume of business as to call for special comment: Tanner, *The Late Medieval Scottish Parliament*, 122–3. Of these, about fourteen were administrative orders that the 16th-c. privy council
could have issued: *APS* ii. 33–4, cc. 2, 3, 5; 35–7, cc. 2, 4, 7, 8, 10–15, 17.

though they may have looked on paper.[11] But at least parliament was recognized as a legislative body. James IV had omitted to develop any alternative mechanism—such as the proclamation or royal edict—for issuing new laws. So once a demand for legislation arose, parliament was well placed to spring into action once more.

And this is what happened. From the 1580s, the Scottish parliament became almost a different assembly. No parliament before 1579 passed as many as fifty acts; but after that date, only a small number enacted fewer, and many exceeded a hundred. The law was transformed by an explosion of legislative activity. One does not need even to open the published *Acts of the Parliaments of Scotland* to see that volume 2 spans nearly a century and a half (1424–1567), while volumes 3 and 4, of equal bulk, cover twenty-five and thirty-two years respectively (1567–92, 1593–1625). But while this was in progress, what it meant was debatable. Contemporaries knew that the law was in flux, but were uncertain about what type of law would or should emerge. Nobody *planned* to reshape the law through legislation; it was proverbial wisdom that 'few lawes and well put in execution, are best in a well ruled common-weale'.[12]

Although these new statutes were certainly laws, they were not the basis of Scots law as commonly understood. Scotland was well supplied with ancient texts and collections of laws—the 'old laws'—which had been thoughtfully provided by venerable lawgiving kings like David I (1124–53) or Malcolm II (1005–34). In fact the 'old laws' attributed to these kings were all much later and not of royal origin, but this is how sixteenth-century jurists saw them. To David I was attributed the best-known text, *Regiam Majestatem*, a general code of law and procedure on all the main civil and criminal matters. It was the most systematic treatment of its law that Scotland possessed, and the jurists universally held it in high regard.

The one thing they did not do with the *Regiam*, however, was to *use* it. It and the other 'old laws' were obscure and little understood—they were centuries old, often fragmentary, and sometimes not what they purported to be. Even the relatively straightforward *Quoniam Attachiamenta*, a fourteenth-century text on legal procedure, relied heavily on procedure by brieve, which had been the standard form of action in the royal courts in the fourteenth and fifteenth centuries but had declined sharply since. Of the seven brieves given by the main version of *Quoniam* known in the sixteenth century, four were defunct, and the most common surviving brieve, that of succession or mortancestry, was given in an obsolete form (on which more in a moment).

---

[11] *APS* ii. 49, c. 15; 238, c. 3. On the implementation of these acts, see A. L. Murray, 'The Comptroller', 14; Macdougall, *James IV*, 174–5. Of course there were *some* important statutes in the 15th c., though they seem to interest lawyers more than historians. Two examples still partially in force are the 'Leases Act' of 1450 and the 'Prescription Act' of 1469: *APS* ii. 35–6, c. 6; 95, c. 4.
[12] James VI, *Basilicon Doron*, in *Political Writings*, 21–2.

Quoniam also contained material on such obviously medieval topics as serfdom, trial by battle, and procedure by the 'laws of Galloway'—which were
no longer extant.[13] As for *Regiam Majestatem*, it was yet more arcane and
impenetrable. It has even been argued that it was compiled primarily as a
symbol of Scottish national identity in the early fourteenth century, rather
than for practical use.[14]

And yet it was, in a profound sense, the law. It could not be repudiated
without doing violence to the structure of the law as that was understood.
What lawyers craved was not a new law that they could actually use, but a *Regiam* that they could actually use. They wanted the old laws *codified*, not superseded. Thus the story of the development and reform of the law in our
period is in large part the story of the various projects to codify the law, combining the old laws with the parliamentary statutes so as to produce a single
complete code of law. It is also—to anticipate—the story of how those projects failed.

Law codification raised a conceptual problem. The parliamentary statutes
were expected to fit into the framework provided by the old laws—but how?
The authority of the old laws stemmed from their virtually immemorial
antiquity. Although the *Regiam* was thought of as the law of David I, this did
not mean that David had introduced it; the prologue said that he had commanded the laws 'in habitual observance in our courts' to be put into writing.
The editor and greatest protagonist of the old laws, Sir John Skene, did not
articulate the explicit view that the laws were literally immemorial, as his
English contemporary Sir Edward Coke did, but he probably thought along
similar lines.[15] This was based on a view of society as fundamentally static;
the best law was the oldest, and anything new was likely to be an innovation
of doubtful authority. But where did this leave statute?—the best statute was
surely the most recent. Could a statute contradict the old laws? If so, it was
but a short step to the vertiginous suggestion that the old laws, being the
oldest, were the *least* authoritative because least relevant to changing current
conditions.

---

[13] *Quoniam Attachiamenta*, published with *Regiam Majestatem*, ed. Lord Cooper (Stair
Society, 1947), cc. 49–57 (brieves), 56 (serfdom), 61, 74 (battle), 72–3 (Galloway). This version
of *Quoniam* had evolved some distance from earlier ones; for an edition that aims to come as
close as possible to the original, see *Quoniam Attachiamenta*, ed. T. D. Fergus (Stair Society,
1996). For the texts of the 16th-c. brieves see Balfour, *Practicks*, ii. 644–51. Like *Regiam*,
Quoniam was attributed to David I.
[14] A. Harding, '*Regiam Majestatem* amongst Medieval Law Books', *JR*, NS 29 (1984),
97–111. Mild scepticism is expressed by H. L. MacQueen, '*Regiam Majestatem*, Scots Law and
National Identity', *SHR* 74 (1995), 1–25 at 6. For the few occasions when it was used in the late
Middle Ages, see MacQueen, *Common Law and Feudal Society*, 89–93; for the rarity of its use
in the 1540s, see A. L. Murray, 'Sinclair's Practicks', in A. Harding (ed.), *Law-Making and Law-
Makers in British History* (London, 1980), 101. The *Regiam* certainly did not occupy the central
position in legal practice that it had in legal theory.
[15] For Coke see J. G. A. Pocock, *The Ancient Constitution and the Feudal Law* (2nd edn.,
Cambridge, 1987), ch. 2 and *passim*. We shall return to Skene shortly.

The most logical way back from the brink of this conceptual abyss would have been to argue that the role of statute was to declare pre-existing law. The idea of statute as declaratory might have been encouraged by the conservative religious legislation of the reign of James V. Parliament did not think that it was innovating when it ordered that 'all the sacramentis be haldin and honourit', that 'the glorius virgine Mary' be 'reverendlie worschippit', and so on.[16] But these forays into the field of religion, once begun, could not be so easily stopped—although the bishops tried to do so in 1543, when they objected unsuccessfully to religious legislation on the grounds that it was invalid without the consent of the church.[17] When in 1560 the time came for these timeless doctrines to be altered, there seemed nothing unusual in having the job done by parliament. There were no debates about the competence of statute like those which the English Reformation prompted.[18] Indeed, the English themselves (to look no further afield) had helped to settle the issue; statutory power to declare the true faith had become a commonplace, and More, Fisher, and others who had opposed it had long been cold in their graves. This is one effect of the often-remarked fact that the Scottish Reformation came late. The debate that did occur demonstrates that statute was accepted in principle: Catholics pointed out that the queen had never ratified the legislation of the Reformation Parliament, so that, as John Knox wrote furiously in 1563, 'some say that we have nothing of our religion established, neither by law or parliament'.[19] The implication was that if Mary had ratified the acts, even Catholics might have thought them valid.

But so long as the conventional wisdom expressed itself in demands for codification of the law, on the basis of the old laws, there could be no full recognition of the supremacy of statute. This was the most common reaction in the sixteenth century by those who thought about the potential contradiction between statute and old laws. They recognized the limitations of the old laws in their current obscure form, using them when they could in specific cases, and hoping that the question would be made irrelevant by a code based on the old laws and approved by parliament. After all, *Regiam Majestatem* itself said that it had been compiled by King David 'with the advice and consent of the whole realm, spiritual as well as temporal'.[20] Now the process would be repeated.

In the fifteenth century, there had already been some proposals to codify the law. The commission of 1426 'to mend the lawis that nedis mendment' seems to have aimed to 'mend' procedure, 'swa that the causis litigious and pleyis be nocht wrangwisly prolongyt', rather than to produce a code of

---

[16] *APS* ii. 370–1, cc. 1–9.   [17] *APS* ii. 415, c. 12; cf. Ch. 2 above.
[18] G. R. Elton (ed.), *The Tudor Constitution* (2nd edn., Cambridge, 1982), 239.
[19] Knox, *History of the Reformation in Scotland*, ii. 81; cf. Goodare, 'The First Parliament of Mary Queen of Scots'.   [20] *Regiam*, ed. Cooper, p. 58.

substantive law.[21] The 'commission' of 1473, sometimes referred to, was merely a proposal to the king.[22] The one serious effort seems to have been in 1469, with a dramatic commission for 'the reductione of the kingis lawis, Regiam Majestatem, actis, statutis and uther bukis to be put in a volum and to be autorizit and the laif to be distroyit'.[23] But no such 'volum' emerged. Some of the commissions may have done some work, and their existence may be part of a broader concern for law reform which saw some revision (but not codification) of *Quoniam Attachiamenta*. However, the total amount of usable law codification in the fifteenth century seems to have been zero.[24]

Sometimes revision or codification was not thought necessary; simply printing the laws would do. Chapman and Millar, the first printers in Scotland (1507), were to print the 'bukis of our lawis' (i.e. the old laws) and 'actis of parliament'. This did not happen, but it was evidently thought feasible by one of the country's foremost lawyers, William Elphinstone, who was involved in the project.[25] Law codes were printed in huge quantities on the Continent in the early seventeenth century; they were more common than Bibles.[26] Printing was, indeed, all that the statutes needed to leap to prominence in 1566; but this would not have been sufficient for the obscurities of the old laws.

The subject of law codification revived in the 1560s, perhaps spurred by Scotland's French connections (especially strong during the regency of Mary of Guise and the personal reign of Mary): 1561–7 was a key period for French law reform.[27] A Scottish law reform commission of May 1566, the first actually to achieve anything, included three lawyers known to have studied in

---

[21] *APS* ii. 10, c. 10.

[22] The lords 'wald beseke our soverane lord' to appoint a commission: *APS* ii. 105, c. 14. There is no more evidence that James III did so than that he took the other advice offered by this parliament. Cf. Tanner, *Late Medieval Scottish Parliament*, 201–4.

[23] *APS* ii. 97, c. 20.

[24] *Quoniam*, ed. Fergus, 90–5. The topic of attempted law reform is further discussed by MacQueen (*Common Law and Feudal Society*, 89–93) in the context of establishing the actual use made of the *Regiam*. The suggestion has also been made that the 1469 commission was responsible for engrossing the statutes of earlier parliaments and then destroying the original register, which might explain why this register is lacking before 1466: O'Brien, 'The Scottish Parliament in the 15th and 16th Centuries', 20–2. For MSS that may have resulted from the work of the 15th-c. commissions, see Scottish Record Office, *Guide to the National Archives of Scotland* (Edinburgh, 1996), 12–13.

That the project was not a hopeless one from the start may be suggested from the fact that a comparable if much smaller project did succeed. This was the scheme to codify the traditional laws of Ettrick Forest, where the forest court issued a comprehensive code of revised laws in 1499. But Scots law as a whole would have required more than the twelve laws in this code. 'The Statutes of Ettrick Forest, 1499', ed. J. M. Gilbert, *Stair Society Miscellany*, ii (1984).

[25] *RSS* i. 1546; L. J. Macfarlane, *William Elphinstone and the Kingdom of Scotland, 1434–1514* (Aberdeen, 1985), 236–7.

[26] G. Parker, *Europe in Crisis, 1598–1648* (2nd edn., London, 1981), 59–60.

[27] J. H. M. Salmon, *Society in Crisis: France in the Sixteenth Century* (London, 1975), 151–62; cf. J. Durkan, 'The Royal Lectureships under Mary of Lorraine', *SHR* 62 (1983), 73–8 at 74.

France among its key members: John Leslie, bishop of Ross, who initiated and chaired the commission, Edward Henryson, editor of the printed statutes that resulted, and David Chalmers, recently appointed a lord of session.[28] Also important was Sir James Balfour, recently appointed clerk register. According to Henryson, the commission planned to start with the post-1424 statutes, and then go on to codifying Scotland's old laws.[29] The edition of the statutes was a landmark in the development of Scots law: had the commission concentrated on the old laws, later legal history might have been very different. The next stage, the codification of the old laws, was never reached, and the commission itself is not known to have been active after 1566.

One member of the commission did produce a work using the *Regiam* and many other old laws: Chalmers's 'Dictionary of Scots law'. This was a digest collection of old laws, statutes, and decisions of the court of session. Presented to the queen (according to the preface) in July 1566, the 'Dictionary' may have been a preliminary report on this second stage of the commission's work. However, it was far from restricting itself to the old laws; more likely it was an independent work, on the strength of which Chalmers had been put on the commission. In its clear presentation—a chronological summary of significant laws arranged under alphabetical subject headings—it could have been a most useful handbook for legal practitioners.[30]

But the 'Dictionary' was not a codified law, still less a codified version of the old laws. How could it have been, when the material Chalmers worked with was unsystematic? The old laws needed more than diligent compilation. Chalmers included a number of laws 'collectit out of the cronickillis, alss out of the majestie [i.e. *Regiam Majestatem*] and wtheris wolumis that presentlie ar not in use'; he explained that they were still 'worthie to be wnderstand, and will serff at the leist in place of ane histoir'. By the 'cronickillis' Chalmers mainly meant that of Hector Boece; the fact that Boece's fabulous 'laws' of his equally fabulous early 'Scottish kings' were then taken seriously did not mean that these laws—such as one requiring that 'the sow eittand hyr gryssis to be stanit to deid, and na man to eit hir fless'—were in force. Chalmers knew this, but could not solve the problem that it posed.[31]

---

[28] *Actis and Constitutionis of the Realme of Scotland . . .*, introduction; J. Durkan, 'The French Connection in the Sixteenth and Early Seventeenth Centuries', in T. C. Smout (ed.), *Scotland and Europe, 1200–1850* (Edinburgh, 1986), 25; G. Brunton and D. Haig, *An Historical Account of the Senators of the College of Justice* (Edinburgh, 1836), 123.

[29] *Actis and Constitutionis of the Realme of Scotland . . .*, introduction.

[30] BL, David Chalmers, 'Dictionary of Scots law' (1566), Add. MS 27472. Chalmers, a Catholic and partisan of Queen Mary, was exiled after her downfall in 1567. The only known copy of his book came into the hands of the Regent Moray, and carries his binding; but such interest as Moray had in law reform seems to have taken other directions, and there is no evidence that Chalmers's book went into circulation.

[31] BL, David Chalmers, 'Dictionary of Scots Law' (1566), Add. MS 27472, fos. 3ʳ, 63ʳ, and *passim*. Chalmers later claimed to have seen the chronicle by 'Veremund' which Boece had cited as his source for information about Scotland's early (and mythical) kings: N. Royan, 'Hector Boece and the Question of Veremund', *Innes Review*, 52 (2001), 42–62.

Even if all this activity in her reign hardly justified Chalmers's later con-
gratulations to Mary for 'reducing to order' the laws, more had been achieved
in the 1560s than ever before.[32] The work continued in the 1570s. In 1575, an
act 'anent the sichting, collectioun and reformatioun of the lawis of this
realme' lamented 'the harme quhilk this commoun weill sustenis throw want
of a perfyte writtin law', and appointed a commission to draft 'ane certain
writtin law'.[33] The expected transition from 'lawis' to 'ane law' indicates that
codification was still intended. The key commissioners were James Balfour,
who provides a link with the 1566 commission, and John Skene; what eventually emerged was Balfour's 'Practicks'.

Balfour's 'Practicks' was compiled very much on the plan laid down by the
act: from the 'bukis of the law' (that is, the 'old laws'), the 'actis of parliament', and 'decisionis befoir the sessioun'. Balfour's work was thus similar to
Chalmers's—not a code but a magpie-like collection of all the Scots law he
could find, the older the better; though it was somewhat less jumbled, and
much larger.[34] Balfour probably began with a digest of the old laws, divided
it roughly into subject headings, and like Chalmers added statutes and session
decisions chronologically under each heading. The arrangement of his headings within larger themes seems more sophisticated to modern eyes, but it was
not always appreciated at the time; some contemporary copyists of the
'Practicks' rearranged it on Chalmers's alphabetical plan.[35]

Balfour did make some advances over Chalmers. Though his collection
was still founded on the old laws, he tilted its balance towards recent times:
its vast size arose from the inclusion of many more decisions of the court of
session.[36] He also relegated the luxuriant fantasies of Boece to an appendix
where they could safely be ignored, instead of putting them proudly at the
head of each chapter. He may have intended to incorporate them in the body
of the text (he died in 1583 with it unfinished), but even if so, he clearly had
his doubts about his Boece.

The first writers to apply critical standards to the old laws were Balfour's
protégé Skene and Thomas Craig, both working in the 1590s and 1600s; and
they reached different conclusions. They had to grapple with the dawning re-
alization, reached by Skene and others between 1601 and 1604, that the text
of Scotland's cherished *Regiam Majestatem* was suspiciously similar to the
old English legal treatise known as Glanvill's *Tractatus*, attributed to the

---

[32] David Chalmers, *La Recherche des singularitez plus remarquables concernant l'estat
d'Ecosse* (Paris, 1579), introduction.   [33] *APS* iii. 89.

[34] Balfour and Chalmers were familiar with Continental law—the 'theorik of the legistes and
canonistes'—but this only serves to underline the paucity of the *Scots* law that they recorded:
Finlay, *Men of Law in Pre-Reformation Scotland*, 89; J. W. Cairns, 'The Civil Law Tradition in
Scottish Legal Thought', in D. L. Carey Miller and R. Zimmermann (eds.), *The Civilian
Tradition and Scots Law* (Berlin, 1997), 199–200.

[35] Balfour, *Practicks*, i. pp. lviii, xxxv–xxxviii.

[36] For the scale of his achievement here see W. M. Gordon, 'Balfour's *Registrum*', *Stair Society
Miscellany*, iv.

justiciar of Henry II (1154–89). Of course David I antedated Henry II, and one could claim, as Skene was obliged to do, that the English and not the Scots were the plagiarists; but it was an argument unlikely to carry universal conviction.[37]

These problems for the reputation of the old laws perhaps contributed to their absence from the greatest legal issue of the early seventeenth century: Anglo-Scottish union. Proposals for a union of laws had to discuss the extent to which English and Scots law were customary systems, whether the alleged immemoriality of English law made it unique, and whether the greater influence of civil law in Scotland was an impediment to union; but the old laws themselves had little significance. Anti-unionists could have used the old laws to argue for the distinctiveness of Scots law, but such arguments were rarely if ever deployed. If the old laws had retained their fifteenth-century prominence, they would have dominated the debate.[38]

Thomas Craig, a leading participant in the union debate, made his major contribution to legal scholarship in his *Jus Feudale*. This celebrated book took a much broader view of the subject of Scots law, past and present, than the works considered so far. Completed about 1605 towards the end of the author's long career as an advocate and justice depute, it was professedly a 'commentary on feudal customs . . . a scientific formulation of our Scots law'.[39] Its ingredients were not merely current local practice, but included history from classical times and much of the west European legal tradition. He erected feudal law into a system to answer a wide variety of legal questions, from the rights of third parties in debt cases to the succession to kingdoms.

Craig, like Skene, used and esteemed old laws, but different ones—the Lombardic 'Books of the Feus'. Despite his own devotion to antiquity—or perhaps because of it—he was the first to grasp the nettle of the new discovery about the *Regiam*, repudiating the work without hesitation as 'a blot on the jurisprudence of our country . . . useless as an aid to judicial decision'.[40] A rational humanist, he felt that his own feudal laws were important not because ages of use had given them authority (they were not, after all, any more Scottish in origin than the *Regiam*), but because when looked at objectively they had something to offer the times in which he lived. Unhampered by Scotland's own mildewing medieval laws, he was free to serve up a fresh synthesis of law, derived from the most useful laws medieval Europe had to offer,

---

[37] H. L. MacQueen, '*Glanvill* Resarcinate: Sir John Skene and *Regiam Majestatem*', in A. A. MacDonald et al. (eds.), *The Renaissance in Scotland*. The *Tractatus* had indeed been written under Henry II, although probably not by its traditional author, Ranulph de Glanvill. *Regiam Majestatem* was an adapted copy of it, made at an uncertain date but perhaps shortly after 1318.

[38] For Scots law and the union see B. P. Levack, 'English Law, Scots Law and the Union, 1603–1707', in Harding (ed.), *Law Making and Law Makers*; id., *The Formation of the British State*, ch. 3; and id., 'Law, Sovereignty and the Union', in Mason (ed.), *Scots and Britons*.

[39] Craig, *Jus Feudale*, i. p. xii.   [40] Ibid., I.8.11.

for a seventeenth-century audience. This, however, distanced him from his Scottish contemporaries, and it is hard to assess his standing—is it more significant that the privy council praised the *Jus Feudale* and recommended its printing, or that the recommendation was ignored?[41] Craig in due course achieved a European reputation, but his chief impact on Scots law at the time was probably a negative one: to undermine the idea that a code of law based on the old laws would be essential or even desirable. By contrast, Chalmers, Balfour, and their colleagues were consciously concerned to adapt the law to the needs of a changing society, but had not as yet developed the intellectual and critical tools to achieve this.

In Skene's later work, some of these tools can be seen in the process of development. His *De Verborum Significatione* (1597) was not intended to be a synthesis of the old laws, merely a collection of pathways which he had discovered through some of their more overgrown and tangled thickets. But it would have been an essential precondition for revival of the old laws— indeed, together with his bilingual edition of the old laws themselves (published under the title of *Regiam Majestatem*, 1609), it was perhaps the most single-minded effort yet made. Skene wished the old laws to be seen in a broad comparative framework, adding marginal references not just to Scottish statutes, but also to many English ones.[42] Although he resisted Craig's contention that the *Regiam* was not indigenous to Scotland—that would have undermined the whole project as he conceived it—he did drop some of the more awkward of the other old laws, such as the *Liber de Judicibus*, which Chalmers and Balfour had often cited but which was in the main a rearranged and modified version of the *Regiam*. He established intelligible texts of many obscure passages. He showed particular interest in Highland laws, apparently with the idea that they might be integrated into any future system.[43] He provided a splendid index, making the material in his edition much more accessible.

But Skene did not codify the laws themselves, nor did he attempt to identify which of them were outdated. Anyone who inherited land in Scotland knew that the brieve of succession—sometimes known as the brieve of mortancestry—was directed to the sheriff, not (as *Quoniam Attachiamenta* had it) to the justiciar, and that he then summoned an assize of thirteen men, not (as *Regiam Majestatem* had it) of twelve. Skene did not realize that the late medieval brieve of mortancestry had been a different brieve, designed to deal with a dispute over succession to lands rather than simply to enable heirs to be infefted in their lands. By our period, that brieve of mortancestry had been eclipsed, and writers like Balfour had succeeded in confusing it with the

---

[41] Council to James, 14 Apr. 1608, *Melros Papers*, i. 43–4.

[42] Skene's marginalia were omitted from Lord Cooper's edition of the *Regiam*, which was otherwise based on his work.

[43] For contemporary thinking on this subject, see Williamson, *Scottish National Consciousness*, ch. 6.

brieve of succession.[44] One can only sympathize with Skene, able neither to alter his traditional text, nor to add a footnote explaining that it had gone out of date. His works were still not a usable code. Rather they provided the material from which a code might have been constructed.

There were indeed two further law reform commissions in the early seventeenth century, but they achieved less than their predecessors, and little need be said about them. The commission of 1628 was mainly concerned with establishing which statutes were current, *Regiam Majestatem* being tacked on as an afterthought. Although the commission claimed to have done some work and was renewed in the 1633 parliament, it published no results: it was 'not muche reguardit, and is licklie to be desertid'.[45] Neither this nor the final commission (1649) produced the *Code Napoléon* which by then was the only alternative to statute, and in 1681 Lord Stair made the codification project redundant by producing an authoritative synthesis of the law without using the old laws.[46]

Even as successive law commissions wrestled with the intractable old laws in vain, Scots law was being refined, updated, and extended. No single code of 'perpetuall lawes' was produced, but every parliament passed statutes to solve the problems of some branch of law and extend the competence of statute over other branches which had previously relied on old laws or custom. By the seventeenth century, most criminal prosecutions were based on statute.[47] The true law reformers were the drafters of the statutes—who no doubt counted Chalmers, Balfour, Skene, and Craig among their numbers. Skene had done his best with the *Regiam*; but the statutes he had helped to print (he brought out the second collected edition in 1597) made it irrelevant, and it came half a century too late.

The old laws were now being reduced to talismans. Or perhaps they had been talismans for a long time, but people now began to notice it. In practice, the old laws could be overridden even by lesser authorities like the convention of royal burghs, which in 1581 told Inverness that it had no right to levy an

[44] *Quoniam*, c. 52, and *Regiam*, c. III.28, in *Regiam*, ed. Skene. Cf. *Regiam*, ed. Cooper, pp. 225–6. The brieve of succession was also known in the 16th c. as the brieve of inquest, as well as the brieve of mortancestry. The assize for it usually numbered thirteen; it could be fifteen or some other odd number, but not twelve: *Fife Court Book*, pp. xcvii–xcviii. For the original brieve of mortancestry, a pleadable brieve (unlike the brieve of succession), see MacQueen, *Common Law and Feudal Society*, ch. 6.

[45] *RPC*, 2nd ser. viii. 365–7; *APS* v. 46–7, c. 32; William Maxwell, advocate, to Sir John Maxwell of Pollok, 14 June 1633, in Fraser, *Memoirs of the Maxwells of Pollok*, ii. 226. Similarly, the 1633 commission to print Craig's *Jus Feudale* came to nothing: *APS* v. 57, c. 47.

[46] *Regiam*, ed. Cooper, pp. 3–4, 6–7. Stair's perspective on the law reform commissions was characteristic: 'these books called *Regiam Majestatem* are no part of our law . . . though they be mentioned for to be revised and reformed with our former ancient laws, Parl. 1425, c. 54, Parl. 1487, c. 115, yet these do not acknowledge them, as already become our laws, but as much, as by alteration thereof, may become our law'. Stair, *Institutions*, I.16. The statutes he cited are now printed as *APS* ii. 10, c. 10; 97, c. 20. Stair's modern editor was unable to trace the second of these, not realizing that it is now assigned to 1469 rather than 1487.

[47] G. C. H. Paton (ed.), *Introduction to Scottish Legal History* (Stair Society, 1958), 41.

'excyse boll' on burgesses, 'nochtwithstanding the Lawes of the Majesty [i.e. *Regiam Majestatem*]'.[48] Even when they were of practical use, the old laws' position shifted, and by 1624, we can see why. Montrose, backed by other burghs, challenged Edinburgh over the latter's restriction of trading in its dependent burgh of Leith. Montrose's case rested on one of the old Burgh Laws, 'and this statute is a law publisched in print in the booke callit Regiam Majestatem amongst the burrow lawes, cap. 139'. It would have been in Montrose's interest to claim that this law was irrevocable, since Edinburgh was founding on a later charter of David II; but instead Montrose claimed that the law could be taken away only 'be ane act of parliament'.[49] There was no suggestion that the Burgh Laws were authoritative simply because they were anterior to Edinburgh's charter, or because they formed a complete, integrated system. Instead they were regarded as old statutes, subject to amendment by later statutes but not by royal charters—quite a modern view.

The eclipse of the old laws left statute supreme. Because the statutes were drafted to solve current problems and not fourteenth-century ones, and because they were not expected to form part of a universal law code, they could be used as they stood. They did not have to be edited, just printed. In 1525, a litigant in the session had cited an act of parliament, only to be met with the rejoinder that no such act existed.[50] Such elementary disputes would no longer be possible. The simple fact of printing gave the statutes unparalleled circulation and impressiveness, and they were directly associated with current affairs—each parliament was followed by another printed pamphlet with more statutes, and surviving copies of the 1566 edition are often bound with some of these. The latest parliamentary enactments were just as much news then as now, and good care was taken to maintain interest in them. Parliament itself was a spectacular ceremonial event, the importance of which for their own prestige was well understood by participants.[51] Parliament and legislation were linked with politics and current affairs, as when the dissident earl of Bothwell referred sarcastically in 1592 to his enemy, Maitland, as 'the great legislator the chanceller'.[52]

The chronological arrangement of the printed statutes, underlined by the periodic appearance of supplements, required people to look first to recent times for their laws, and to expect further changes in them. In this alone, the contrast with the old laws was vast. No longer would the oldest law be the most authoritative; now it would be the newest statute. It was recognized that the law needed to evolve and that parliamentary statutes were the driving

---

[48] *RCRB* i. 123.
[49] *Aberdeen Letters*, i. 229. The reference was to Skene (ed.), *Regiam*, which also included the Burgh Laws.   [50] Finlay, *Men of Law*, 101–2.
[51] For the chief ceremony, the opening and closing 'riding' of parliament, see Rait, *The Parliaments of Scotland*, 529–32; for the highly charged atmosphere in which it took place, see Goodare, 'Parliament and Society', app. 5: 'Precedence and ceremonial'.
[52] Calderwood, *History*, v. 152.

force. Sir Thomas Hope, in the early seventeenth century, could discuss *how* statutes changed the law, and whether they could be backdated.[53] At the end of the barren labours of all the law codifcation commissions, it was more than ever possible to agree with Craig: 'it has to be frankly admitted that the Scots acts are practically the only written source of genuine native law we have'. George Buchanan had put it more succinctly: the Scots 'have no laws but their acts of parliament'.[54]

The difference between Craig's careful formulation and Buchanan's rhetorical one, however, is itself illuminating. For in fact the Scots had a great many laws apart from their acts of parliament, and their number was increasing—although they were now directly regulated by statute. Late medieval law had been made by the courts; with the expansion of legal and administrative business in the sixteenth century, there was now more scope for this. Institutions of government by their nature can make rules for their own conduct, and for the people with whom they deal, and there were now more institutions than before. The privy council established its own administrative practices; the court of session and exchequer set legal precedents, and also passed acts which were accepted as subordinate legislation; the commissary courts evolved practice in the field of family and testamentary law, aided in the former field by the general assembly of the church; and local courts were also able to establish rules applicable to their localities.

Some of these developments are evident in the 'Major Practicks' of Sir Thomas Hope, king's advocate, which he compiled between about 1608 and 1633 as a successor to Balfour's 'Practicks'. Hope's work was a collection of laws and decisions, arranged under subject headings like Balfour's—but the balance of its contents had shifted markedly. Balfour had had a fair number of statutes, drawn fairly evenly from the century and a half between 1424 and 1579: Hope also had a fair number, but his came overwhelmingly from the 1580s and later. In many of his topics, the law had been transformed by this new legislation. To prove this point exhaustively would require another book, but as a small example, consider Hope's position on the seemingly traditional subject of teinds, where the pre-1580 statutes occupy a quarter of a page of his printed edition, and more recent statutes three and a half pages.[55] Again, Balfour had had many session cases: so did Hope. Balfour's cases had come mainly from the period 1532–54: Hope's came mainly from the 1610s and 1620s. He cited several of Balfour's cases as well, but the general impression is that the law had moved on.

Equally striking was what Hope left out. He had available to him Skene's edition of the old laws, but made little use of it. He accepted the validity of *Regiam Majestatem*, on the grounds that Scottish statutes had referred to it

[53] Hope, *Major Practicks*, I.1.18.
[54] Craig, *Jus Feudale*, I.8.12; George Buchanan, *The History of Scotland*, 6 vols., ed. J. Aikman (Edinburgh, 1830), ii. 447. Cf. Craig, *De Unione*, 320–1.
[55] Hope, *Major Practicks*, III.18.9–23.

as law (in itself a quiet reversal of the relative authority of statutes and old laws); but he found it unnecessary to give more than a small fraction of Balfour's citations from it. He did have a brief but interesting section 'Of the Chamberlane', about the long-defunct chamberlain ayre. This, the subject of one of the texts of the old laws, had supposedly in the fourteenth century been an annual inquiry into the affairs of the burghs. Hope noted a statute as late as 1491 endorsing the ayre, and commented that 'the chamerlane of old wes the king's officer over all the burrowes of this realme'. As an officer of state himself, he may well have thought that it might be a good idea to revive, or rather reinvent, such a useful disciplinary institution. The constable's court was reinvented on similar lines in 1631. The old laws were no longer everyday law, but a government seeking new ideas might still find a use for them.[56]

The practice of treating the decisions of the court of session as law had been introduced by Chalmers and Balfour—a crucial innovation. But Balfour was not clear exactly *how* they were law: he claimed that cases where the law was unclear had to be remitted to parliament.[57] In 1535 there had indeed been a 'mater referrit be the lordis of sessioun to the lordis thre estatis of parliament for interpretatioun of certane lawis'. The lords of the articles made a decision in the outstanding case, based on 'the use in tymes bigane', and 'findis that the saidis lawis suld be sa interprete and usit in tymes cuming'.[58] This does not seem to have been repeated in our period, probably because the 'use in tymes bigane' could be discerned from Balfour's own work.

Balfour had had few or no sources of recent law other than statutes and session decisions: Hope had a new, intermediate category for 'statutes of session'. As well as its ordinary decisions, the court had begun making what were usually described as acts of sederunt—in effect, subordinate legislation. It was possible for acts of sederunt to become statutes later: Sir George Mackenzie listed a number of instances.[59]

The court of session's practice of making acts of sederunt meant that its ordinary decisions seem not to have been set-piece test cases. There was no explicit doctrine of the single binding precedent. The exchequer, a smaller but parallel court, did hear cases which it treated as test cases. One well-known

[56] Hope, *Major Practicks*, V.5.1–6; *APS* ii. 227, c. 19. On the chamberlain ayre, which had not in practice been annual, see E. L. Ewan, 'The Community of the Burgh in the Fourteenth Century', in M. Lynch et al. (eds.), *The Scottish Medieval Town* (Edinburgh, 1988), 230. For the extensive powers that the chamberlain had in theory (although not in practice) over the burghs, see 'The Chalmerlane Air' in Skene (ed.), *Regiam*, 1st pagination, pp. 147–57. For the constable's court, see Goodare, *State and Society*, 80–1. *Regiam Majestatem* was still recommended, along with the acts of parliament, for purchase by a projected public library in Aberdeen in 1685: M. Lynch and H. M. Dingwall, 'Elite Society in Town and Country', in E. P. Dennison et al. (eds.), *Aberdeen before 1800: A New History* (East Linton, 2002), 181.   [57] Balfour, *Practicks*, i. 1–2.

[58] *APS* ii. 349–50, c. 38.

[59] *Acts of Sederunt of the Lords of Council and Session* (Edinburgh, 1790); Sir George Mackenzie, *Observations on the Acts of Parliament* (Edinburgh, 1686), 293–4.

one, in 1586, set the rate at which former church lands should be valued for parliamentary taxation. It was explicitly subordinate to parliament: the rate was to be applied generally, 'providing alvyis that in cais it be fundin be censiament of parliament that the fewaris of kirklandis be subject to na taxatioun or to less taxatioun, this present decreit to have na forder executioun'. Parliament never did provide a 'censiament', and the exchequer's rate was not always applied; Hope cited it but commented that it 'should be generally used in retoureing of lands, albeit it be not allwayes observed'.[60] Another decision, when in 1599 'the lords fund that four puncheons of French wyne goes to a tunne', also seems to have been a test case.[61]

Scottish judges could also adopt law from outside—particularly Roman law, which expanded in much of sixteenth-century Europe. The Scottish Reformation favoured Roman law; rather than continue the work of the 1566 commission on the old laws, the godly Moray regime next year proposed a new start, with a new commission to codify the law according to the 'fassoune of the law Romane'.[62] There is no evidence that such a commission was set up, but it perhaps became more common to see the principles of Roman law being used to decide cases where the law was unclear. The general assembly of the church gave such a principle, the *lex talionis*, house room in 1568.[63] Almost all Scottish advocates admitted in this period had qualified in civil and canon law in France.[64] William Welwood's *Sea Law of Scotland* (1590), which after the statutes was the first Scottish legal work to be printed, used Roman law extensively. Skene, on the other hand, criticized the encroachment of Roman law into Scotland.[65] Roman-law principles formed a useful adjunct to the collections of session decisions, though they never became any more than that. A crude formulation on this came from John Leslie in the 1570s: 'gif ony cummirsum or trubilsum cause fal out, as oft chances, quhilke can nocht be agriet be our cuntrey lawis, incontinent quhatevir is thocht necessar to pacifie this controversie is citet out of the Romane lawis'. Hope was more thoughtful: 'our king acknowledges no superior, and theirfoir the Roman or civill law hes no auctority among ws to derrogat from our customs. We respect them as good counsellors, bot obey them not as commanders.'[66]

---

[60] T. Thomson, *Memorial on Old Extent*, ed. J. D. Mackie (Stair Society, 1946), appendix; Hope, *Major Practicks*, III.27.13; Goodare, 'Parliamentary Taxation', 32–5.

[61] BL, 'Notes furth of the registers of exchequer, 1583–1674', Harl. MS 4628, fo. 2ᵛ.

[62] *APS* iii. 40.

[63] P. Stein, 'The Influence of Roman Law on the Law of Scotland', *JR*, NS 8 (1963), 205–45 at 215–16; *BUK* i. 130.

[64] Durkan, 'French Connection', 26; Durkan, 'Royal Lectureships', 74. Maitland of Thirlestane and Lindsay of Menmuir organized the endowment of a chair of civil and canon law at the college of Edinburgh in the 1580s: Lee, *Maitland*, 158.

[65] Cairns et al., 'Legal Humanism', 60.

[66] John Leslie, *Historie of Scotland*, 2 vols., ed. E. G. Cody and W. Murison (STS, 1888–95), i. 120; Hope, *Major Practicks*, I.1.21; cf. W. M. Gordon, 'Roman Law in Scotland', in R. Evans-Jones (ed.), *The Civil Law Tradition in Scotland* (Stair Society, 1995), 23–8.

Acts of parliament, made by the crown and estates, were therefore the only ultimate 'commanders' recognized in the government of early modern Scotland. Conventions of estates could tax and issue other temporary measures, but refrained from making permanent legislation. The convention of royal burghs made rules which all the royal burghs were meant to follow, thus disciplining its own members almost as a modern voluntary organization might do. The category of subordinate legislation becomes most clearly visible when we see it in local courts. Sheriff courts, burgh courts, baron and regality courts, burgh of barony courts, even non-baronial courts, could all issue 'acts' or 'statutes'—rules of conduct to be applied within their jurisdiction. These were the equivalent of modern by-laws, as any of their records will illustrate.

The general assembly of the church and the privy council have occasionally been claimed as rivalling parliament as legislative bodies, but their measures on closer inspection always turn out to be subordinate to acts of parliament. Space precludes a full discussion of this, but some evidence may be cited. In 1586, a suggestion that 'the bishops might have preeminence over the brethren' prompted the general assembly to declare that 'it could not stand with the word of God, only they must tolerat it, in case it be forced upon them be the civil power'.[67] That the 'civil power' could make something legal, even if contrary to the word of God, is testimony to its authority. If the general assembly had felt itself to be able to make binding legislation, it would hardly have failed to do so on this occasion. As for the privy council, Craig's view is undoubtedly correct. 'As for ordinances promulgated by the king and privy council . . . they have no legal validity in any point concerning life, liberty, or estate . . . personal and private affairs are unaffected by them.' The same was true, he continued, of conventions of estates. 'Parliament would meet in vain if decisions arrived at by other assemblies were to be allowed the same force and validity as those taken in parliament.'[68] The conclusion must be that parliamentary sovereignty was well understood and rigorously adhered to.[69]

---

[67] *BUK* ii. 647.   [68] Craig, *Jus Feudale*, I.8.9–10; cf. Craig, *De Unione*, 320–1.
[69] This point is documented more fully in Goodare, 'The Scottish Parliament and its Early Modern "Rivals"'.

CHAPTER FOUR

Personal Monarchy

The king, quhat kynde of thing is that?
Is yon he with the goldin hat?

Lindsay, 'Ane satyre of the
thrie estaitis', in *Works*, ii. 379

The man with the 'goldin hat' often seems to dominate the view of early
modern government. It can be hard to see beyond him, or to work out how he
was connected to those beyond him. We may be told, for instance, that it was
'James VI' who restored bishops, or passed the act anent feuding in 1598, or
subjugated the Borders. We may even be told that it was 'James VI' who built
a bridge over the Tweed at Berwick. 'The king' (or occasionally 'the queen')
often serves as a shorthand term for the whole of royal government. As John
Knox noted, 'the thing that is done at the command of any notable persone is
attributed unto him self, althogh it be done be servandes or subjectes at his
command'.[1] This raises a number of obvious questions, and also some less obvious ones. Could the king do it on his own authority, or did he need other
people to endorse his decision? If his own authority sufficed, who helped him
make up his mind, and how? Once he had decided to act, who helped him to
do so, or did so on his behalf? These questions already point towards a reduction in monarchical initiative. In many cases such initiative was absent,
and different questions are appropriate: who acted in the king's name, and
did he have to be told about it afterwards?

This chapter begins with the crown: not simply the person who was
entitled to wear this item of headgear, but the vehicle for the issuing of orders
in that person's name in such a way that they carried effective legal force. The
crown in this sense included not only the king or queen, but also the keepers
of the seals, and anyone else (notably royal lieutenants, commissioners, and
ambassadors) who acted in the monarch's name. These people might have
their own input into the process of issuing one order rather than another,
or drafting an order in a particular way. And even before they became
involved, the actions of the crown were also powerfully influenced during the
process of taking decisions. Monarchs took formal advice from their privy
councillors, and we shall see in Chapter 6 that royal government in our period
did not mean government by the monarch alone, but government by the

[1] John Knox, *Works*, 6 vols., ed. D. Laing (Bannatyne Club, 1846–64), vi. 211.

monarch in conjunction with the privy council. There were also informal advisers, mainly nobles resident at or visiting the royal court. It is worth discussing how far they, too, can be considered as part of the 'crown' in this sense—whether a well-connected or persuasive individual who succeeded in getting James VI to change his mind thereby participated in government. A good absolutist king ought to be counselled by the nobility (although he did not have to be), and even to consult parliament. It was his choice, but that was the right choice.

Although it can be hard to reconstruct the process whereby kings and queens were persuaded to do things, we can be sure that the venue where this happened on a daily basis was the royal court. We need to define the court and to explain how it operated. Monarchs lived their lives in a magnificently contrived arena, seen at its most elaborate during major set-piece events: coronations, royal entries, and baptisms. These were increasingly essential in maintaining the legitimacy of the monarchical system, but were not venues for decision-making.[2] Nor was the royal household usually such a venue. The household was the institution providing the monarch's personal living arrangements—luxurious food, clothing, leisure, and culture. The court included the household but was not restricted to it.

The court was constituted by an arrangement by which the monarch shared his or her personal life with high-born companions who by their birth connected the monarchy with the world of politics. Such companions differentiated kings' and queens' daily lives from the daily lives of rich people living in luxury. High-born companions were about *power*. It was in their presence that monarchs took their everyday political decisions. Principal among these for James VI were the gentlemen of the chamber, initially appointed in 1580.[3] They themselves were not necessarily major figures, but they were linked, by kinship and other ties, to the nobility. Nobles usually had free access to the king, and many of them would often be visiting the court or in temporary residence. Being surrounded permanently with companions linked to a wide range of noble families differentiated the king from a regent, whose household consisted more of his own kinsmen. It could even promote political instability if the various nobles did not get on with one another; but it gave the king a chance to manage them and to encourage them to cooperate. Resentments of a regent would be more likely to simmer inarticulately.[4] After 1603, again, there was no resident court,

[2] M. Lynch, 'Queen Mary's Triumph: The Baptismal Celebrations at Stirling in December 1566', *SHR* 69 (1990), 1–21; id., 'Court Ceremony and Ritual during the Personal Reign of James VI', in Goodare and Lynch (eds.), *The Reign of James VI*. For a less than wholly monarchical ceremony, see A. A. MacDonald, 'Mary Stewart's Entry to Edinburgh: An Ambiguous Triumph', *Innes Review*, 42 (1991), 101–10.

[3] Juhala, 'Household and Court of King James VI', app. 1.

[4] Aspects of the role of courtiers in decision-making are discussed by K. M. Brown, *Bloodfeud*, 116–23; Goodare, *State and Society*, 110–13; N. Cuddy, 'The Revival of the Entourage: The

but significant numbers of Scottish nobles retained court office or court connections.[5]

The royal court was permeable, some of the most important people in it being visitors rather than members of staff. One of the functions of the set-piece ceremonials was to encourage such people to keep coming to court. But that only shows that the court covered a wider field than the crown. Although we can say that royal decisions were made *in* the court, we cannot say that they were made *by* the court. Of course the nobles had their say, either directly or through their connections with the chamber. But so did many other people; that was politics. Decisions were taken with political expediency in mind: we can't do that, it would upset the earl of Atholl; we'd better do this, Queen Elizabeth expects it. But that does not make Atholl, or Elizabeth, part of the Scottish crown or even government. They are better seen as lobbyists, or political interests, within the broader body politic.[6] At this point the history of royal decision-making shades off into the general political history of Scotland.

So the crown was not the court, although it was *in* the court. Even more obviously, the crown was not parliament. But instead of shading off gradually into general political history, the decision-making powers of crown and parliament had a relationship with one another that was precisely identifiable and vitally important. A leading theme of the previous chapter was the emergence of a Scottish parliament that was sovereign and omnicompetent. The doctrine of parliamentary sovereignty will be easily recognized as particularly characteristic of the English constitution in our period.[7] But this is only part of the story, for in Elizabethan and early Stuart England, the crown attempted to demarcate areas which parliament was to keep out of. This was an important component of the royal prerogative: the crown's right to do things independently of parliament. Elizabeth made strenuous and often successful efforts to prevent parliamentary discussion of religious reform, foreign policy, and the succession—although her own religious settlement, and indeed her own title to the throne, rested upon statute. She fostered an increasingly personal monarchy, which attempted with some success to restrict parliament.[8] How much of this was paralleled in Scotland?

Bedchamber of James I, 1603–1625', in D. Starkey et al., *The English Court from the Wars of the Roses to the Civil War* (London, 1987), 178–80; and A. Gibson and T. C. Smout, 'Food and Hierarchy in Scotland, 1550–1650', in L. Leneman (ed.), *Perspectives in Scottish Social History* (Aberdeen, 1988), 33–9.

[5] K. M. Brown, 'Courtiers and Cavaliers'. The allegedly 'absentee' court is further discussed later in this chapter.

[6] Cf. Ch. 2 above.

[7] P. Williams, *The Later Tudors: England, 1547–1603* (Oxford, 1995), 135–6; Elton (ed.), *Tudor Constitution*, 233–41. For contemporary comment, see Sir Thomas Smith, *De Republica Anglorum*, ed. M. Dewar (Cambridge, 1982), 78–9.

[8] J. Loach, *Parliament under the Tudors* (Oxford, 1991), 106–12. In England, as well as roy-alist and parliamentarian theories of sovereignty, there was also a common-law theory which

With hindsight, it can be recognized that the royal prerogative was to rise no higher than to be a special case of subordinate legislation. Things done by the crown alone were always liable to be controlled and regulated by the sovereign legislative body, the crown in parliament. Just as exchequer or general assembly had their own special areas of competence, so did the crown—military matters, for example, or appointment of privy councillors; but it had to defer to parliament whenever parliament chose. Contemporaries would not have seen it like this, however, for three reasons. The main one was that they thought of *all* government as royal government, not parliamentary government; it was done in the name of the crown, after all. The crown held the structure of government together, so that, for instance, officers of state did not litigate against one another in the course of their duties.[9] Secondly, people did not generally recognize government as a process driven forward by legislation; it was only during our period that the power to tax and to legislate became a crucial point of government. Thirdly, and perhaps most significantly, our view is conditioned by our knowledge that as legislation expanded, the crown would never be able to get much of a share of it. The growth of legislation meant the growth of parliament, and the eventual relegation of the crown to a subordinate role in all areas of government.

Whether this long-term perspective is the most helpful in understanding our period—the early seventeenth century in particular—is doubtful, however. This can be seen by looking back from a point when the prerogative was at its height, at least formally: the Restoration. The prerogative was defined by statute, as it related to parliament, in 1661. The crown (and not parliament) had the right of appointment of officers of state, privy councillors, and lords of session; summons and dissolution of parliament, and ratification of its acts; approval of leagues and bonds; military command and the making of war and peace. In addition the prerogative included foreign policy, government of the church, coinage, regulation of foreign trade (including the right to tax it), pardoning of offences, and general oversight of government. There were two alternative theories behind this. Sir George Mackenzie stated that 'our parliaments never give prerogatives to our kings, but only declare what have been their prerogatives'. Alexander Mudie,

---

held that the king—or the parliament—derived their authority from the common law, and that this was derived from judicial interpretation. This probably existed in Scotland too, but as in England, the common law was more often pressed into service to support royalist and parliamentarian theories. Cf. J. Goldsworthy, *The Sovereignty of Parliament: History and Philosophy* (Oxford, 1999), ch. 5.

[9] *SME* vii, para 717. In England too, parliament (i.e. the crown in parliament) was alone sovereign, but people were reluctant to say this because it appeared to downgrade monarchy. They much preferred formulas which appeared to give authority to the crown. M. Mendle, 'Parliamentary Sovereignty: A Very English Absolutism', in N. Phillipson and Q. Skinner (eds.), *Political Discourse in Early Modern Britain* (Cambridge, 1993), 108–9.

however, thought that parliament had *added* to the prerogative in 1661.[10] In that case, what parliament could give, parliament could take away—but this might be difficult in practice: 'once annexed to the crown, who can take the clubbe out of Hercules hand'?[11] It proved possible to disarm Hercules in the later seventeenth century, as it turned out; but what were the trends in the reign of James VI?

One thing that had first to emerge was the idea of *the* royal prerogative, a plenary power inherent solely in the crown. This had first stirred in fifteenth-century England, and gathered strength over the next two centuries, distinct from the older idea of specific, plural prerogatives.[12] Plural prerogatives continued, just as the emergence of the idea of the divine right of kings did not preclude the continuing idea that *all* governmental authorities acted by divine right.[13] An absolute royal prerogative in this new sense scarcely yet existed in sixteenth-century Scotland. The crown had some rights—but *everyone* had *some* rights; and others' rights did not yet derive necessarily from the crown. A form of the royal oath, dating probably from 1445, included the promise to maintain all estates in their privileges,

after the laues and custumes of the realme, the lau Cristine and statuts of the realme, nother to eike nor mynisshe without the consent of the 3 estaits, and nathing to wyrke na use tuoching the comon profitt of the realme bot [i.e. without] consent of the three estaitts.[14]

The word prerogative was used in this older sense as late as 1597, when a statute referred to the king's 'liberteis and prerogativis be the lawis of this realme and privelege of his crown and diademe'. This was still a plural prerogative. Nor was it a matter of the crown's own rights; what the act meant was that the estates' sectional privileges (in this case the 'allegit bipast

[10] *APS* vii. 10–13, cc. 6–7, 12–13; Sir George Mackenzie, *Jus Regium: Or the Just and Solid Foundation of Monarchy in General, and More Especially of the Monarchy of Scotland* (Edinburgh, 1684), 7–8; A[lexander] M[udie], *Scotiae Indiculum, or the Present State of Scotland* (London, 1682), 25–6. This was not just a matter of inflated royalist claims, being echoed even by a contemporary who was suspicious of royal power: 'History of the Macdonalds', *HP* i. 38.

[11] Smith, *De Republica Anglorum*, 87.

[12] S. B. Chrimes, *English Constitutional Ideas in the Fifteenth Century* (Cambridge, 1936), 42–3. The distinction seems to have emerged in the 12th c., when the pope's *plenitudo potestatis* (fullness of power) had been refined into *potestas ordinaria* and *potestas absoluta*, the former bound by positive law and the latter an extraordinary power. These ideas were later transferred to secular rulers. J. H. Burns (ed.), *The Cambridge History of Medieval Political Thought* (Cambridge, 1988), 433–6; cf. F. Oakley, 'Jacobean Political Theology: The Absolute and Ordinary Powers of the King', *Journal of the History of Ideas*, 29 (1968), 323–46.

[13] A point made for England by C. Russell, 'Divine Rights in the Early Seventeenth Century', in J. Morrill et al. (eds.), *Public Duty and Private Conscience in Seventeenth-Century England* (Oxford, 1993). He concludes that as a result there was nothing special about the divine right of kings; this is cogently criticized by J. P. Sommerville, *Royalists and Patriots: Political Ideology in England, 1603–1640* (2nd edn., London, 1999), ch. 1 and pp. 224–65.

[14] R. J. Lyall, 'The Medieval Scottish Coronation Service: Some Seventeenth-Century Evidence', *Innes Review*, 28 (1977), 3–21 at 9, 15–16.

immwnitie' of the merchants from paying customs on imports) could not stand up against the sovereign parliament.[15]

The traditional constitution gave importance to parliament, not generally as a sovereign body, but as a forum for crown and three estates—all separate entities—to meet and negotiate on certain major decisions. These included political decisions as well as legislation. The Lords of the Congregation told a French envoy in 1560

that the kingdom of Scotland is governed differently from others, and if there is a difference between the king and the subjects, it must be debated and decided by the Estates; and even that the kings had no power to make treaties or war without their consent.[16]

This was putting it strongly, but not entirely implausibly. Let us look at a number of potentially contested areas of policy, beginning with the one that the Congregation mentioned specifically: foreign affairs.

Parliament had discussed war, peace, and foreign policy in medieval times.[17] An embassy was sent in 1481 'fra our soverane lordis hienes and fra the estatis of the realme', for instance, while in 1526 no papal legate was to be received in Scotland 'bot be advise of our soverane lord and his thre estatis'.[18] Charles V in 1550 and Henry II in 1552 regarded the concurrence of the three estates as essential to Scottish foreign affairs.[19] In 1563, all conventions discussing questions of war and peace were to have burgesses summoned to them, the implication being that such questions could be decided only in a full convention of all three estates.[20] There was no question of the king having absolute power over foreign policy in 1585, when a convention of estates explicitly 'gevis and grantis to oure said soverane lord, his counsall or sik thairof as his majestie sall chuse, oure full power, privilege, assent and authoritie quhatsumevir competent to us and esteattis foirsaidis' to negotiate an alliance with England; the negotiators were appointed by the convention.[21] Related to foreign policy were military matters. Commanders were answerable to the

---

[15] *APS* iv. 136, c. 22. James had referred to 'the privelege of his crowne' in 1593; this could have been a singular prerogative, and may contain the germ of the idea, although it was not called a prerogative: *BUK* iii. 805. He was referring to a power he held by statute—the right to summon general assemblies—rather than to a power inherent in the crown. The term 'prerogative' was rarely applied to the rights of the monarch before about 1603: *Dictionary of the Older Scottish Tongue*, s.v. prerogative.

[16] Report of the bishop of Valence, May 1560, in A. Teulet (ed.), *Papiers d'État relatifs à l'histoire d'Écosse au XVIᵉ siècle*, 3 vols. (Bannatyne Club, 1852–60), i. 593.

[17] Tanner, *Late Medieval Scottish Parliament*, 165, 230, 265; J. A. Lovat-Fraser, 'The Constitutional Position of the Scottish Monarch prior to the Union', *Law Quarterly Review*, 17 (1901), 252–62 at 254.

[18] *APS* ii. 140, c. 13; 306, c. 16. The embassy of 1481 was sent 'to the king of France and to the parliament of Paris'.

[19] P. E. Ritchie, *Mary of Guise in Scotland, 1548–1560* (East Linton, 2002), 45, 103.

[20] *APS* ii. 543, c. 20.

[21] *APS* iii. 423–4, ratified by parliament, 380–1, c. 18. For more comments on control of foreign policy at this time, see *CSP Scot.* xiii, II. 1115–16.

crown, not parliament, but there were numerous statutes on the army. The summons of the common army (and thus, from time to time, a form of taxation) was a prerogative of the crown.[22] James in 1603 delegated this to the privy council by empowering it to appoint lieutenants as military commanders.[23]

The crown's direct role in religious policy was minimal for several decades after the Reformation. The initial establishment of the Reformation (1560, restated 1567); the assertion of authority over the church (1584); the choice of episcopacy (1584); the choice of presbytery (1592): all were enacted by parliament. The King's Confession (or 'Negative Confession') of 1581, although subscribed by king and nobility, was not ratified by parliament; it recognized the Confession of Faith of 1560 as 'stablished and publictly confirmed by sindrie actis of perlamentis'.[24]

Coinage was accepted in England as a prerogative of the crown, but this was not obvious in Scotland in December 1567, when a statute was passed that the coinage should be 'of sic fynes as utheris cuntreis dois . . . and that na prent, nor cunye of ony layit [i.e. alloy] money be maid or cunyeit in ony tyme cuming, but [i.e. without] avise of the thre estatis of parliament'.[25] The only alloy silver coinage of the reign (minted 1572–80) was indeed authorized by statute;[26] most recoinages up to 1603 (the years of currency debasement) were authorized by parliaments or conventions, and when the crown did debase the currency on its own authority it avoided issuing alloy coins.[27] The act of 1567 was still being cited in 1639, when a similar act regulating copper coins was sought.[28] Coinage was a royal prerogative to the extent that the crown could issue coins on its own authority; but it was not an exclusive prerogative, and the crown could act only within parliamentary constraints.

The role of parliament in supervising daily government could be extensive. In the parliament of 1489, it was 'avisit and sene speidfull that the said consale now chosyn in this present parliament be sworn in the kingis presens and his thre estatis . . . and to be responsable and accusable to the king and his estatis of thare consalis'; the king agreed to 'abid and remane at thare consalis' until the next parliament.[29] The young James IV was not yet recognized as fully in control of his government, although there was no formal minority. Later sixteenth-century parliaments regularly ratified the appointment of the

---

[22] On the fiscal aspect, see Goodare, 'Parliamentary Taxation', 42–3, 48, 51–2.

[23] *RPC* vi. 558–60.

[24] W. C. Dickinson et al. (eds.), *A Source Book of Scottish History*, 3 vols. (2nd edn., Edinburgh, 1958–61), iii. 33. For the 1560 confession alone as the standard of faith in 1584, see *APS* iii. 292, c. 1. [25] *APS* iii. 29, c. 21.

[26] Not in *APS*, this statute is in R. W. Cochran-Patrick (ed.), *Records of the Coinage of Scotland*, 2 vols. (Edinburgh, 1876), i. pp. cxlv–cxlvi.

[27] e.g. *APS* iii. 108, c. 23; 150, c. 31; 191; 215–16, c. 10; 310–11, cc. 28–9; 437, c. 9; 526–7; iv. 48–50; 113; 134–5, c. 20; 154–5, c. 66; 181; 257–8. Cf. C. E. Challis, 'Debasement: The Scottish Experience in the Fifteenth and Sixteenth Centuries', in D. M. Metcalf (ed.), *Coinage in Medieval Scotland, 1100–1600* (British Archaeological Reports, no. 45, 1977).

[28] *Aberdeen Letters*, ii. 146.   [29] *APS* ii. 220, c. 12.

privy council, sometimes adding regulations for its conduct.[30] It is true that
the composition of the council was not decided in the parliament house; but
was the wording of statutes decided there? The point is that parliamentary
approval of councillors was thought desirable, and of more weight than
the mere word of the king, even though the councillors were the king's
councillors.

Parliament occasionally intervened directly in aspects of the administration. Parliamentary commissions for overseeing the expenditure of tax revenue were appointed in 1588 and 1597.[31] In theory, only parliament could
alienate annexed crown property.[32] On one occasion the officers of state were
not to be dismissed without parliamentary approval.[33] These powers fell well
short of full parliamentary control over the executive, of course. There was
no procedure for the Scottish parliament to initiate independent investigations or punish crimes committed by crown officers. Such powers were rare
among European parliaments, being possessed only by the Aragonese *cortes*,
the Polish *sejm*, and the English parliament.[34] The English procedure of
impeachment was a conscious revival in 1621; the Scottish parliament later
followed suit, with the 1642 trial of treasurer Traquair.[35]

It became more important to see the monarchy as permanent, with no in-
terregnum between monarchs. On the death of Queen Elizabeth, there was an
outbreak of raiding on the Borders, justified there by the belief that the authority of the English crown lapsed on the monarch's death. The borderers'
constitutional knowledge was in fact several centuries out of date; the last
English monarch not to date his reign from the day of his predecessor's death
had been Edward I in 1272.[36] However, the idea that a Scottish king was not
fully king until his coronation certainly survived in the early fifteenth century.
In 1412, six years after the death of Robert III, the Scottish government referred to the captive James I as 'the son of the late king'.[37] By 1488, however,
James IV was able to issue a charter in his own name the day after the death
of his father in battle.[38]

There were few more inflammable topics in Elizabethan parliaments than
the succession to the throne and the sovereign's marriage. The main purpose
of the Scottish parliament of 1516 had been to declare the duke of Albany
'secund persoun of this realme'.[39] The second earl of Arran (later duke of
Châtelherault) collected several parliamentary ratifications of his position as

---

[30] *APS* iii. 69, c. 24; 96–8, c. 4; 118–19; 150–1, c. 32; 228–9, c. 38; 378, c. 10; 444, c. 19;
562–3, c. 41; iv. 34, c. 45; 53; 177–8. For more on the privy council, see Ch. 6 below.

[31] *APS* iii. 523; iv. 145–6, c. 48. For a comparable provision in 1586, see *RPC* xiv. 364.

[32] *APS* iii. 89–90.   [33] Ibid. 300–1, c. 16 (1584).

[34] A. R. Myers, *Parliaments and Estates in Europe, to 1789* (London, 1975), 33.

[35] D. Stevenson, *The Scottish Revolution, 1637–1644* (Newton Abbot, 1973), 247.

[36] Wasser, 'Pacification of the Scottish Borders', 87–8; F. Pollock and F. W. Maitland, *The History of English Law*, 2 vols. (2nd edn., Cambridge, 1898), i. 521–2.

[37] Quoted in M. Brown, *James I* (Edinburgh, 1994), 18.   [38] Macdougall, *James IV*, 44.

[39] *APS* ii. 283.

heir presumptive between 1543 and 1560.[40] Sir William Cecil thought in August 1559 that parliament 'may commit the governance' of Scotland 'to the next heir of the crown', whereupon the queen might be deposed if she objected.[41] When the duke of Lennox wanted a ratification of his right to the succession in 1581, this was too controversial for the politicians but parliament's right to make such a ratification was not directly questioned.[42] Royal marriages could be discussed by parliament if they raised constitutional issues, as did that of Mary to Francis in 1558.[43] However, as Queen Elizabeth aged, the dynastic legitimism stressed by James VI as his best claim to succeed her made it harder to express such ideas. When Andrew Melville told the king that Knox, Buchanan, and the Regent Moray had 'sett the crowne upon his head', James retorted that 'it came by successioun, and not by anie man'.[44] In the early seventeenth century, Sir Robert Gordon still thought that a disputed succession should be settled by parliament.[45] This was a dangerous thought for any but the most trusted courtier to express, and then only privately:[46] how could one suggest that there might be a disputed succession without implying that defects might be found in the present royal title? In 1631 the earl of Menteith laid claim to the defunct earldom of Strathearn, inadvertently suggesting that his descent from the last earl (who was descended from Robert II) might give him a better title to the throne of Scotland than Charles I. The suggestion was enough to ruin him.[47]

A strongly dynastic monarchy might have wished to see the heir presumptive as *de jure* regent during a royal minority. This happened, formally, in 1543, when the earl of Arran was declared 'secund persoun of this realme' by parliament, and 'be resoun thairof, tutour laufull to the quenis grace'; but this followed a complex power struggle in which various other configurations of authority were tried. Nor was it repeated in later regencies.[48] Nor, indeed, did it negate the constitutional powers of parliament (or, later, of conventions of estates) over regencies, which were extensive although undefined.[49] The legal

---

[40] Ibid. 411, c. 1; 505–6, c. 2; 605–6, cc. 11–12.   [41] *Sadler Papers*, i. 377.

[42] Occurrents in Scotland, 24 Nov. 1581, *CSP Scot*. vi. 92–3.

[43] *APS* ii. 504–20; Ritchie, *Mary of Guise*, 195–6.   [44] Calderwood, *History*, v. 159.

[45] Fraser, *Sutherland Book*, ii. 357–8.

[46] For his secrecy concerning his major work see D. Allan, ' "An ornament to yow and your famelie": Sir Robert Gordon of Gordonstoun and the *Genealogical History of the Earldom of Sutherland*', *SHR* 80 (2001), 24–44 at 36–7.   [47] Lee, *Road to Revolution*, 119–26.

[48] *APS* ii. 411, c. 1; M. H. B. Sanderson, *Cardinal of Scotland: David Beaton, c.1494–1546* (Edinburgh, 1986), 154–8. For a typology of regencies, see P. G. B. McNeill, 'The Scottish Regency', *JR*, NS 12 (1967), 127–48. There were no regencies after 1578.

[49] Only a convention of estates, not parliament, could elect a regent under James VI. When the Regent Lennox was killed in 1571, parliament was actually in session; but a separate convention (with no doubt the same membership) had to be held to elect a new regent, the earl of Mar. The same parliament then reconvened, and by its first act confirmed Mar's election: *APS* iii. 65–6; 58, c. 1. It seems that parliament could not lawfully be held until a regent had been constituted to hold it. Robert S. Rait claimed that a convention elected the regent because it was a 'more popular assembly', which was true neither for this convention nor for conventions in general, as his own work makes clear: Rait, *Parliaments of Scotland*, 161.

basis of the regency during James VI's minority was Mary's act of abdication, naming a council of seven governors plus the earl of Moray to whom the regency was offered.[50] On the Regent Moray's assassination in 1570, the procedure was unclear (and made more so by the limited recognition of Mary's abdication). A convention of the nobility discussed three alternative methods of electing a regent—by those in Mary's council, by all those who had attended the king's coronation, or by parliament; no agreement could be reached. Scotland was without a regent for six months until the English intervened to get the earl of Lennox elected.[51] Thereupon two successive conventions elected regents in the same way, from among those named in Mary's council, until by 1573 few of these were left, whereupon parliament enacted that any Protestant noble could be elected.[52] There was no official suggestion that the heir presumptive (Lennox or Châtelherault, depending which view was taken of the royal genealogy) had the right to the regency without asking the estates.

Having established all this, we may well wonder why people believed that the monarch was in charge of the government at all. Their belief, however, was entirely correct in several important respects.

Firstly, the monarch appointed most executive officers. She or he could not always act directly; James VI could not sit as a judge in the court of session (not usually, at any rate), but to some extent he appointed the judges.[53] Nor, of course, could he administer the sacraments, but he appointed the bishops. Parliamentary supervision of this was episodic; it was real while it lasted, but it could easily fall into disuse. When the master of Glamis was dismissed as captain of the guard in 1588, he was 'heichlie movit, his office being givin to him be ane parliament, and teane from him without offence';[54] but he was not reinstated.

Secondly, crown and privy council exercised a general oversight of day-to-day government. The two worked closely together, and the growth of central authority enhanced their practical power. The council's business steadily increased. They had needed parliamentary supervision in the days when government had been loose and decentralized, for they could not act without the concurrence of local magnates whose consensual forum parliament essentially was. This older political pattern was gradually replaced by one of political factionalism at the centre, in a closed royal court and in the privy council itself—a pattern supervised by the crown alone. The

<hr/>

[50] *RPC* i. 538–41.

[51] Lord Herries, *Historical Memoirs of the Reign of Mary Queen of Scots*, ed. R. Pitcairn (Abbotsford Club, 1836), 123–4; *Diurnal of Remarkable Occurrents ... Since the Death of King James the Fourth till the year 1575*, ed. T. Thomson (Bannatyne Club, 1833), 180.

[52] *APS* iii. 74, c. 6.

[53] But for some comments, probably from the 1580s, on the crown's limited powers here, see *CSP Scot.* xiii, II. 1115. See also Ch. 2 above.

[54] David Moysie, *Memoirs of the Affairs of Scotland, 1577–1603*, ed. J. Dennistoun (Bannatyne Club, 1830), 71.

privy council was never a mere agency for giving effect to the personal wishes of the monarch. Councillors shaped policy as much as Mary or James did—sometimes more than they did, because it was the councillors who set the agenda and controlled the range of options. But the language employed by all parties observed the proprieties of attributing executive authority to the monarch.[55]

Thirdly, although there was never a need for this to be implemented, the idea took root that the crown was the repository of reserve governmental power in an emergency. John Mair in 1521 had thought that only parliament should declare a state of emergency, 'and thus no way will be opened for the imposition of unprofitable taxes'; James VI thought that only he should have this power.[56]

Fourthly, the crown was itself a component of parliament; it retained the right to summon and dissolve parliament, and to ratify parliamentary legislation. Parliament could not legally act without the crown's cooperation, and although it might often be politically inexpedient to withhold that cooperation, this royal sanction was still a powerful one. This was particularly important because although we know with hindsight that parliamentary control of legislation would survive and grow, there were times—particularly the early seventeenth century—when it looked as though it might decline. It was coming to be more restricted in the kinds of business it dealt with, and it was possible that this trend might continue.

The question, therefore, was coming to be whether ultimate control over government—sovereignty, in fact—should be wielded by crown or parliament. This question arose from the 1590s onwards: not before, because it was only then that sovereignty came fully into being. This happened only gradually; if a symbolic date is needed for its definitive establishment, it might be 1598, when the nobility accepted the act anent feuding. Until then, both crown and parliament had been growing in influence at the expense of other power centres (such as the papacy, or the nobles in the localities), and conflict had not arisen between the two.[57]

Parliament's role had changed during this process; it had lost much of its traditional role as a forum where local magnates kept an eye on things, and gained a new function as a legislative body. But this function the crown might aspire to take over. It has been argued by Helmut Koenigsberger that 'the history of the relations between monarchies and parliaments is the story of a struggle for power'. In this view, consensus between the two was the exception, not the norm. Once they were confirmed as the two biggest frogs in the pond, conflict was more likely. In such a struggle, Professor Koenigsberger

[55] For this, see Ch. 6 below.
[56] John Major (Mair), *A History of Greater Britain*, ed. A. Constable (SHS, 1892), 352; James VI, *Trew Law*, in *Political Writings*, 74–5. Cf. James's disagreement with the general assembly over how a militia should be empowered to act on 'urgent occasioun': *BUK* iii. 833.
[57] Goodare, *State and Society*, ch. 1.

identifies a 'royal mechanism' by which the crown had an inbuilt advantage: it was better placed (because it existed all the time) to absorb parliamentary functions than parliament was to take over royal ones, and it was better equipped for political struggle, being able to play off rival interest groups within parliament against one another.[58] There is no room here for a comprehensive treatment of political struggles from the 1590s to 1625, but some of the results should be noted.

The traditional avenues for parliamentary action were closed off one by one in the 1590s. Foreign policy was not discussed after 1592, when the actions of recent ambassadors to Denmark were ratified by parliament.[59] James VI's marriage, in 1589, was not discussed by parliament. The issues of the regency and succession never arose, but James's thinking on them in 1595 may be gathered from his instruction to the earl of Mar, custodian of Prince Henry, that in the event of his (James's) death, Mar was not to hand over the prince, 'neither for the queen nor for the estates their pleasure', until he reached the age of 18.[60] The last parliamentary commission controlling tax revenue was that of 1597.[61] Appointment of the privy council was last done by a convention of estates in 1598.[62] The appointment of a commission on military discipline in 1599 was the last action on that subject by a convention of estates.[63] The last coinage to be authorized by a convention of estates was that of 1601.[64] Finally, religion continued to be discussed by parliament into the seventeenth century, but the thrust of royal policy was to transfer authority over it to the crown. In 1609, the king received the statutory right to regulate clerical dress on his own authority.[65] A new confession of faith was issued in 1616 on the authority of the general assembly. This was not the same as the authority of the king personally, even

---

[58] Koenigsberger, 'Monarchies and Parliaments', 195, 198–9.

[59] *APS* iii. 566–9, cc. 47–9. The union of crowns effectively deprived Scotland of an independent foreign policy. Even though English parliaments were allowed to debate foreign policy at the end of James's reign, it would have been hard for his last Scottish parliament, in 1621, to do the same, since all knew that they had to follow the English lead. Parliament did, however, debate the royal union scheme in 1604.

[60] James to Mar, 24 June 1595, in *Letters of the Kings of England*, ed. J. O. Halliwell, 2 vols. (London, 1846), ii. 91–2. By contrast, Mar's father, who had had custody of James himself as prince in 1567, had refused to deliver him 'without consent of the thre estaitis': Melville, *Memoirs*, 179.   [61] *APS* iv. 145–6, c. 48.

[62] Ibid. 177–8. The act made regulations for the council, and specified that it was to have thirty-one members, but the names were left blank. Parliament in 1609 ratified a royal commission granting the council some small extra powers: Ibid. 440, c. 21; cf. *RPC* vi. 558–60.

[63] *APS* iv. 188. Both foreign and military affairs could still be influenced indirectly, when parliament was asked to vote taxation to pay for them; but it was no longer able to discuss them directly.

[64] Ibid. 257–8. A parliamentary commission was set up on the coinage in 1621: ibid. 629, c. 34. This was very likely a concession to the opposition: Goodare, 'Scottish Parliament of 1621', 44–5.

[65] *APS* iv. 435–6, c. 15. It was specified that parish ministers were to wear black, but the act was construed more widely by Charles I: *APS* v. 20–1, c. 3.

though the king by this date was in the habit of nominating the members of the assembly.[66]

The crown was active in most of these fields too, but in the 1590s it made as yet no claim to exclusive control over any of them. A small encroachment occurred in 1597, when a supervisory council was instituted for St Andrews University by royal authority alone.[67] It would have been hard to object, for universities had traditionally been free from any form of external interference; there were precedents for parliamentary intervention, but not many. However, parliament continued to legislate for the universities on occasion, so this episode does not show the establishment of an exclusive royal prerogative.[68]

The union of crowns seems to have widened the scope of the prerogative, either through contact with English ideas, or—more probably—because the constitutional flux caused by the union allowed previously unthinkable ideas to circulate. In July 1603, the burghs appointed commissioners to 'wysie' some draft maritime laws, to prepare them for publication, printing—and authorization *by the king*.[69] Possibly parliamentary ratification was envisaged, but this was not made clear. This was a time when people might not have been too surprised to find the new union metamorphosing into an 'Empire of Great Britain'. Both in Scotland and in England, it was expected that an incorporating union would dissolve ancient liberties and fundamental laws, leaving no restrictions on royal power.[70] The burghs expected 'the halding of ane parliament of baith the realmis';[71] that they did not expect unrestricted *parliamentary* power to emerge from the union speaks volumes about the perceived trends in royal and parliamentary authority.

James was no longer going to tolerate the traditional idea that the privileges of the estates existed independently of the crown; they had to acknowledge his superiority. He could always point to the royal origins of the royal burghs, and after about 1597 he had the church more or less nailed down as well. The nobles' privileges could still be seen as innate, and he began to lay more stress on his right to create nobles, as 'the onlie author and founteyne of all dignity in our dominions'. He became more interventionist in disputes over the succession to noble titles—as here, about the earldom of Eglinton.[72] On the bankruptcy of the earl of Atholl in 1617, James on his own initiative offered the title and estates (and the debts) to Lord Lovat; Lovat declined.[73]

---

[66] *BUK* iii. 1132; A. R. MacDonald, 'James VI and the General Assembly, 1586–1618', in Goodare and Lynch (eds.), *Reign of James VI*.

[67] R. G. Cant, *The University of St Andrews: A Short History* (2nd edn., Edinburgh, 1970), 56.

[68] e.g. *APS* iv. 682–3, c. 98.   [69] *RCRB* ii. 164.

[70] C. Russell, 'English Parliaments, 1593–1606: One Epoch or Two?', in D. M. Dean and N. L. Jones (eds.), *The Parliaments of Elizabethan England* (Oxford, 1990), 207–8.

[71] *RCRB* ii. 163.

[72] W. Fraser, *Memorials of the Montgomeries, Earls of Eglinton*, 2 vols. (Edinburgh, 1859), i. 59–62, 170–3, 185–90; quotation at p. 171.

[73] James Fraser, *Chronicles of the Frasers, 916–1674*, ed. W. Mackay (SHS, 1905), 243–4, 253.

An important practical instrument of royal authority was the proclamation. At a time when it was common for statutes to be reiterated, proclamations—which often reiterated statutes themselves—could have a symbolic importance.[74] James once asked Lord Hamilton not to bring his followers to his day of law, 'sen it is ane ill example to brekk the lau baith maide in parliament and reneuit be proclamation'.[75] A memorandum by a councillor just before the parliament of 1612 proposed a number of measures to boost the prerogative, such as one for 'puneisment of transgressours of proclamation'. Power was to be given to the council to appoint lieutenants and make proclamations; sheriffs and heritable officers were to be astricted to execute the council's orders.[76] It is not clear whether anything came of this, but it shows what the government was thinking. Proclamations in 1613–16 (to take a random volume of the privy council register as an example) covered the following major matters. There were proclamations regulating trade by imposing customs duties (on imported grain), by banning export of certain goods (eggs), and by designating certain ports as the only ones allowed to trade with Ireland.[77] A proclamation ordered the celebration of Easter; the royal supremacy over the church was now well established.[78] Most other proclamations dealt with military affairs. None of this was exactly legislation, but it had a real impact on people's lives.

The crown could create new courts of law, and did so with the court of high commission in 1610.[79] There is no reason why the parliament of 1612 should not have been asked to endorse the court, as it did the king's episcopalian programme. James must have chosen to base the court on the prerogative, presumably to prove that he could do it. This court, controlled by the bishops, was to punish ecclesiastical offences and to supervise the lower church courts (presbyteries and kirk sessions) in doing so. It was used both against flouters of godly discipline, such as adulterers, and against presbyterian dissidents. Its creation did not change the law, but directed cases to be decided in a particular court—with procedures that it chose, and with officers appointed by the king personally. In practice, it increased royal authority over the church; it made it easier to proceed against dissidents without trials for treason. Treason had been the main charge available against ministers who declined the jurisdiction of the privy council, which had policed the church until then. This was not only embarrassing; it was also risky, because there was no

---

[74] On the repetition of statutes, see Ch. 5 below.

[75] James to Lord Hamilton, n.d. [?1590s], HMC, *Manuscripts of the Duke of Hamilton*, 2 vols., ed. W. Fraser (London, 1887), i. 66.   [76] RPC xiv. 568–70.

[77] RPC x. 243–4, 325–6, 566–70.   [78] Ibid. 316–17.

[79] For more on the high commission, see Ch. 7. There were initially two courts, one each for the archdioceses of St Andrews and Glasgow, until they were united in 1615. The establishment of the commissary courts had been done by the prerogative in 1564; this was a transfer of jurisdiction from the old church courts rather than the erection of a completely new body. Further regulations for the courts were issued by the court of session. See Balfour, *Practicks*, ii. 655–73.

guarantee that the assize, necessary in treason trials, would cooperate.[80] This was why James Melville wrote that the high commission

putt the king in possessioune of that quhilk a long tyme he had desyrit and huntit for, to witt, of the royall prerogative, and absolut power to use thair bodies and guidis of thair subjectis at pleasure, without forme or proces of the commoun law, even than when the bodie of the realme of England wes in thair parliament compleining of the justice and injurie thairoff.[81]

We begin to hear more of a prerogative right to suspend or dispense with statute. Here the prerogative expanded by popular demand, because the statutes in question were the penal statutes: laws punishing transgressions against the commonwealth, rather than against an individual, and punishable by fines or escheats.[82] They were increasingly prominent and generally unpopular; royal mitigation of their rigour was welcomed. The burghs in 1624 asked the commission for grievances to intercede with the king for the 'suspending' of the recent sumptuary act, claiming that he had promised to do this.[83] As for the dispensing power, James in 1617 received a deputation from Edinburgh on a statute of 1541 on fish exports, and responded by ordering the privy council to consult with the burghs and JPs, and then to issue new regulations, 'to tak effect in all tyme coming, nochtwithstanding of the said act of parliament, or ony thing thairin contenit to the contrair, quhairanent we ar content by these presents to dispens'.[84]

Dispensing with statutes may have been connected with the emergence in England (and perhaps in Scotland too) of the idea of an *inseparable* prerogative, a power or set of powers inherent in the crown which parliament was unable to regulate. The power to dispense with statutes was a crucial case. In England, which had a similar dispensing power, it was generally agreed that the king could dispense even with a statute that said that the king could not dispense with it.[85] The dispensing power was not new, being analogous to the well-understood papal power to dispense from the requirements of canon law. It was used strikingly in 1556. A statute of 1555 banned the election of craft deacons, whereupon after a fierce campaign and local turmoil, particularly in Perth, the crown dispensed the crafts from its effects. This has usually

---

[80] See the discussion over the packing of an assize in 1606, and the need for 'more warye electioun . . . of the nixt assisouris': *RPC* vii. 478–83. The power of the privy council in cases of treason is discussed in Ch. 6 below.

[81] Melville, *Diary*, 792. The point about the prerogative entered the canon of presbyterian objections to the court. Cf. Row, *History*, 273; Calderwood, *History*, vii. 62.

[82] The chief ones in 1610 were usury, firearms, forestalling and regrating, and selling flesh in forbidden time: BL, 'Copies of documents relating to the revenues of Scotland', Add. MS 24275, fo. 9ʳ.

[83] *RPC* xiii. 554–8; cf. *RCRB* iii. 141–2, 149. For the statute, see *APS* iv. 625–6, c. 25.

[84] *Edin. Recs.* vi. 161–2.

[85] Goldsworthy, *Sovereignty of Parliament*, 93–4. Locke would later take the opposite view, that the prerogative could be defined and limited by statute: John Locke, *Two Treatises of Government*, ed. P. Laslett (2nd edn., Cambridge, 1967), 392–3.

been described as a 'revocation' of the statute, but it was really a dispensation.[86] The case appears to be an isolated one at this time. The use of this
power, though more frequent, was still irregular in the 1630s. Charles dispensed with 'the act of parliament maid anent the cheising of the magistrattis
of borrowis' when ordering Edinburgh to elect a provost in 1637, but no such
dispensation is recorded for 1634 when he ordered the election of the entire
council.[87]

On at least one occasion James came close to creating a new crime on his
own authority. By a signet warrant in 1601, he granted a commission of
justiciary to try the crime of conspiracy to murder when the murder had
been 'unexecute'. Noting that 'this fact naikitlie considerit will not appeir
punisheable to the death', he nevertheless ordered 'of our awin absolute
auctoritie and power' that the criminal if convicted should receive the death
penalty.[88]

One prerogative never claimed outright was the right to impose taxes without parliament.[89] There was no Scottish ship money, nor Scottish impositions, and Thomas Craig observed that the Scots would have been indignant
if they had had to endure the English custom of purveyance.[90] But this was not
the whole story, and the point about impositions raises an important issue
about the customs, where the crown's rights were more extensive than in
England. The customs duties had long been regarded as 'our soverane lordis
propirtie', and not as being granted at the discretion of parliament.[91] Before
the seventeenth century this was never seen as giving the crown the right to
change the customs rates. In 1590, lucrative customs duties were imposed on
wine imports by a convention of estates.[92] In 1597, similarly, it was parliament that placed customs on imports, while incorporating the misleading
claims on behalf of the royal prerogative already quoted. However, James in
1610 wrote that 'our customes ar a parte of our annext propertie, and . . . by
the previlege of our crowne we mycht at all tymes haif raised the same'.[93] He
proceeded to do just that. The 'haill borrowes of this realme' were 'havelie
prejudgit be this laitt raising of his majesties customes', but their only remedy
was to send a deputation to the king 'for lamenting the estait and conditioun
of the borrowes'.[94]

---

[86] *APS* ii. 497–8, c. 26; *RMS* iv. 1054; M. Verschuur, 'Merchants and Craftsmen in Sixteenth-
Century Perth', in Lynch (ed.), *Early Modern Town*, 44–6.

[87] *Edin. Recs.* vii. 149–50, 194.

[88] Quoted in Sir David Dalrymple of Hailes, *Annals of Scotland*, 3 vols. (3rd edn., Edinburgh,
1819), iii. 107.

[89] There were some such taxes in 1577, 1596, and 1598, in the form of taxes in lieu of military
service; but they died out, probably because of the disaster that overtook the crown's taxation
policy in 1600. See Goodare, 'Parliamentary Taxation', 48, 51–2.

[90] Craig, *De Unione*, 452.   [91] *ER* xxii. 17.

[92] *RPC* iv. 514. The money was to go to purchase of wine for the royal household—at prices
set annually by parliament. This provision was never enforced, but it shows the degree of parliamentary control that was expected.

[93] James to earl of Dunfermline, 12 Nov. 1610, *RPC* ix. 584–5.

[94] *RCRB* ii. 329; cf. *Edin. Recs.* vi. 74.

The final area for growth of the power of the crown was parliamentary legislation itself. The fact that the crown was a component of parliament began to be important, at least in terms of assertions of royal power.

At this point it used to be conventional to present the argument that parliament became a rubber stamp for the royal will because of the way it was constituted. In particular, the lords of the articles were cited as establishing such a stranglehold over parliamentary business that no dissent could make itself heard.[95] It seems that a cross-election system for the lords of the articles was revived between about 1609 and 1612. By this, the bishops chose the nobles' representatives and the nobles those of the bishops, and these together then chose the burghs' and shires' representatives. Since the bishops were all royal nominees, this allowed the crown in effect to nominate the entire committee, subject only to the proprieties of including the more prestigious members of each estate.

However, recent research has overturned the view of parliament as subservient to the lords of the articles.[96] It is not certain that royal control of the committee grew, because little is known about the late sixteenth-century position. However, the entire chain of reasoning which a focus on the lords of the articles tends to encourage—that the crown controlled the committee, therefore there could be no dissent—rests on faulty premises. There *was* dissent. Sometimes that dissent was so serious as almost to wreck the royal programme. And the lords of the articles seem to have made little practical difference. Parliaments possessed a committee of articles, but conventions of estates did not. The last two parliaments of the pre-covenanting regime, those of 1621 and 1633, both proved appallingly intractable, and the royal legislative programme was enacted only with difficulty and at heavy political cost. One might expect the conventions of estates (1625 and 1630) to have been even more difficult, lacking a committee of articles which was allegedly so necessary; they were certainly uncooperative over some issues, but it is hard to see them as more so than the parliaments.[97] Royal assertiveness is certainly detectable in these developments, but so is parliamentary opposition.

Royal assertiveness can, however, be found in other parliamentary matters. Before the time of James VI, people did not really care whether it was crown or three estates that made statutes. The two had a close and consensual relationship, similar to that of James and his successors with their privy councils (though they argued from time to time, as did James and his council).

---

[95] For instance, we have been told that after 1603, James 'controlled Scotland through the Privy Council and the Committee of the Articles . . . a cabal of sycophants controlled Scotland and through it James circumvented Parliament and the courts'. A. G. Stevenson, 'Claverhouse and the Dalrymples', *JR* (1995), 227–35 at 228.

[96] A. R. MacDonald, 'Deliberative Processes in Parliament', 41–50; Goodare, 'Scotland's Parliament in its British Context', 23–4; R. Tanner, 'The Lords of the Articles before 1540: A Reassessment', *SHR* 79 (2000), 189–212.

[97] Goodare, 'Scottish Parliament of 1621'; 'Diary of the convention of estates, 1630', ed. Goodare; Lee, *Road to Revolution*, 13–14, 99–104, 131–5.

There was a bewildering variety of parliamentary enacting clauses in the fifteenth century.[98] In 1487 there was a foretaste of what was to become a standard formula: 'it is avisit, grauntit and ordanit be our soveran lord be avise of the thre estatis'.[99] But this was still rare. In the 1520s and 1530s, the formula 'it is herefor statute and ordanit be the kingis hienes with avise and consent of the thre estatis of his realme' became standardized (though not yet universal; the briefer 'it is ordanit', or variants thereof, remained more common for a time).[100] By the 1560s, the normal formula was 'the quenis majestie and thre estatis foirsaidis hes statute and ordanit', or 'it is statute and ordanit be our soverane lady with the avise of the thre estatis', or 'oure soverane lady with awyss and consent of the thre estaitis of this present parliament hes ratifiit'.[101] These still represented different concepts; but it did not matter, because crown and estates were not in conflict. It did matter to James VI, however; he insisted that 'the lawes are but craved by his [i.e. the king's] subjects, and onely made by him at their rogation, and with their advise'.[102]

So James's exalted views on the power of a 'free monarch' gave him, in his own view, every right to legislate by royal edict; and he began to sound as if he was doing so. When in 1612 he wanted a parliamentary statute cancelling certain assignations from lordships, he wrote to parliament telling them: 'It is our will' that they should pass such an act. An early example of this sort of thing can be found under the harsh regime of 1584, but otherwise the only surviving royal orders to parliament are subsequent to 1605.[103] The 1616 general assembly, having passed an act against Catholics, supplicated the king 'that it might please his hienes to sett downe ane ordinance for ratificatioun of the former statute, to the effect it may be receivit in all judicatories'.[104] The same assembly ordered the compilation of a book of canons; the compilers were to submit their work firstly to the assembly's commissioners for revision, and then to the king 'that the same may be ratified and approved

---

[98] Here are some from adjacent statutes in 1426: 'it is ordanit be the king ande the parliament'; 'it is ordanit be the king with the consent and deliverance of the thre estatis'; 'it is statute and ordanit be the king and his parliament'; 'it is ordanit' (this uninformative formula was particularly common); 'the king with the consent of the haill parliament forbiddis'. *APS* ii. 9, cc. 2–5. Sometimes either parliament or (more often) the king was omitted: 'it is statut and the king forbiddis' (1424); 'the said day it was decretit be the thre estatis in playn parliament' (1432); 'the parliament thinkis spedful' (1450); 'it is statute, concludit and ordanit in this present parliament be the haill thre estatis' (1493). *APS* ii. 5, c. 18; 20, c. 4; 34, c. 2; 235, c. 21.

[99] *APS* ii. 179, c. 19.

[100] e.g. *APS* ii. 345, c. 20 (1535). This statute also had a recognizable preamble—another new development.   [101] *APS* ii. 541–2, cc. 15, 17; 547, c. 1.

[102] James VI, *Trew Law*, in *Political Writings*, 74. James in his English coronation service had references to the people's possible role in making law omitted: L. L. Peck, 'Kingship, Counsel and Law in Early Stuart Britain', in J. G. A. Pocock (ed.), *The Varieties of British Political Thought, 1500–1800* (Cambridge, 1993), 81–2.

[103] HMC, *Report on the Laing Manuscripts Preserved in the University of Edinburgh*, 2 vols., ed. H. Paton (London, 1914–25), i. 127–8; NAS, royal letters to parliament, PA7/26, nos. 5–7, 10.   [104] *BUK* iii. 1117–18.

by his royal authority'.[105] When there was doubt whether that parliament would be willing to give James statutory authority to regulate the church by edict (with advice from bishops and selected ministers), he commanded 'to pass by that article as a thing no way necessary, the prerogative of his crown bearing him to more than was declared by it'.[106]

The enforced withdrawal of the act to regulate the church was, in practice, a defeat for the king. In other areas, where he and his advisers were more sure of royal authority, they sought, not acts, but ways of avoiding acts. It became accepted among policy-makers that the prerogative should be preferred to statute wherever possible. Archbishop Gledstanes reported to the king that he and others preparing for the 1612 parliament 'have omitted these articles which may seeme to carry envy or suspicion, or which your majesty, by your royall authority, might performe by yourselfe'.[107]

The prerogative also helped governmental functions to diversify, as the business of government became more complex. The same trends were visible in England, where in a seminal article on the 'decline of parliamentary government' Raymond Hinton pointed out the diminishing volume of statute under Elizabeth, James I, and Charles I. Most parliamentary business, he argued, was routine but nevertheless important in its volume; routine government was carried out through parliament. It was at this very time of legislative decline that the business transacted in the privy council and under the great seal and signet reached a peak. It has been argued that this did not distinguish between legislation and administrative orders, and that parliament was happy to supervise the executive, not to run it directly.[108] Whether or not this is true—and it is far from clear that parliament, either in England or in Scotland, *was* happy with the executive's actions in granting monopolies, for example—it does not detract from the fact that the executive was now doing things which earlier had been done by parliament. And the 'decline' identified by Dr Hinton would later be reversed. In the 1640s, and more permanently after 1688–9, parliaments in England and Scotland took the administrative business back again.

Many Scottish statutes, before the 1580s at least, were themselves administrative orders—for instance, a statute of 1551 that burgh magistrates

---

[105] Ibid. 1128.

[106] John Spottiswoode, *History of the Church of Scotland*, 3 vols., ed. M. Napier and M. Russell (Spottiswoode Society, 1847–51), iii. 241–5.

[107] William Scot, *An Apologetical Narration of the State and Government of the Kirk of Scotland since the Reformation*, ed. D. Laing (Wodrow Society, 1846), 236.

[108] R. W. K. Hinton, 'The Decline of Parliamentary Government under Elizabeth I and the Early Stuarts', *Cambridge Historical Journal*, 13 (1957), 116–32; Loach, *Parliament under the Tudors*, 8–9. For the argument that before the 1620s, 'the increase in instruments under the seals is not only an indication of the increasingly interventionist desires of central government; it is also an index of initiatives from individuals in the country at large', presented as an attack on Dr Hinton, see V. Morgan, 'Whose Prerogative in Late Sixteenth and Early Seventeenth Century England?', in A. Kiralfy et al. (eds.), *Custom, Courts and Counsel* (London, 1985), 53. In fact Dr Hinton made a similar point.

should stop artisans charging unreasonable prices.[109] The fact that such measures ceased to be taken in parliament indicates no decline in itself, but rather a differentiation of functions. Government was becoming more intensive, and parliament could not be involved directly in every level of it. There had, indeed, been some differentiation before our period. Border wardens had normally been appointed by parliament up to 1489; thereafter they were appointed by the council.[110] But differentiation might turn into decline if areas of business were established as competent only to the crown and not to parliament. Moves towards this began in the 1590s, and the trend became clear in the early seventeenth century.

If the king was not consulting parliament, was he out of touch with the political nation? Yes and no. The Venetian ambassador, observing the 1617 parliament, certainly thought that 'at the dissolution the king's dissatisfaction with the parliament was as evident as that of the parliament with the king'.[111] This view should be taken seriously, and there was undoubtedly much disaffection; but there were other ways of consulting people. Selected local managers could be summoned to court, or asked to submit reports to the privy council. Such corporatist political practice increased in the early seventeenth century, when interest groups were often invited to resolve their competing claims before the privy council.

The apogee of this tendency was the establishment of a standing commission on manufactures in 1623, with sixty-nine members including officers of state, nobles, lairds, and burgesses.[112] This looks at first sight like a retreat from royal absolutism and a search for wider consensus; but this would be only part of the story. Absolutism was never a matter of arbitrary government, without consultation; the issue was, what kind of consultation? This was the crown's way of expanding into new areas of activity, and doing things that previously parliament (if anyone) would have done. Unlike the members of parliament, the members of the commission were appointed, using the great seal, by the crown. James was always willing to consult people about his projects, so long as he had the final say.

The union of crowns was an important event to the extent that the crown was important. James himself sometimes sounded as if the union had essentially been accomplished in his person, but for our purposes it certainly had not. The union is, in fact, a case study of the prerogative in action. Brian Levack has argued persuasively that James put substantial efforts into an imaginative prerogative programme to foster Anglo-Scottish union. Indeed, after the English parliament rejected a legislative union, the prerogative was all James had to work with. He made various changes to church government and worship in Scotland, of which, however, the erection of the high

---

[109] *APS* ii. 487, c. 18.   [110] Rae, *Administration of the Scottish Frontier*, 25.
[111] *CSP Venetian*, xiv. 549–50.
[112] *RPC* xiii. 298–302. For more on this, see Ch. 7 below.

commission was the only strictly prerogative act; he lifted the customs duties (though most were reimposed in 1611); he fostered a mixture of Scots and Englishmen at his court; he ennobled a few Scots in the English peerage, and Englishmen in the Scottish peerage; he adopted the title 'King of Great Britain', and changed the flag and coinage; and he appointed a cross-Border commission in the Border shires. All to little avail: Scots and Englishmen were resolved not to allow union to proceed. No British state was created. The prerogative appears here as a broken reed; it could not even override the determination of Oxford and Cambridge colleges to exclude Scots. If the parliaments had been more cooperative, as they were in 1706–7, things might have been very different.[113]

So the union illustrates the limitations of personal monarchy. The legislatures and executive institutions of government were not united in 1603, and this continuing non-union was more significant than the union that *had* occurred. The change in royal style, the issuing of the 'Unite' coinage, the Union flag, and mutual naturalization of the 'post-nati' (those born after 1603) are just not as important to the theme of this book as the activities of the Scottish parliament, privy council, law courts, and church. Even in royal patronage, the quintessence of personal monarchy, James rarely pursued a fully 'British' policy. At times he showed signs of doing so: the earl of Dunbar was a patronage broker in both kingdoms between 1605 and 1611, and extended royal influence in the Borders by wielding authority on both sides of the Border.[114] But policy in England was then being made principally by Robert Cecil, earl of Salisbury, whose interest in Scotland seems to have been limited to the prospect of wealth from the Hilderstone silver mine.[115] After his death in 1612, there was briefly more union in the field of patronage-broking; in 1613–14 James tried to make his anglicized Scottish favourite, Robert Kerr, earl of Somerset, into an influential man in both kingdoms. But Somerset antagonized both English and Scots, and the project lapsed on his downfall in 1615. His successor, Buckingham, was an English (and Irish) patronage broker only.[116]

The 'personal monarchy' described in this chapter is an institutional concept; it refers to a polity in which many organs of the state operated in the name of the crown alone. This naturally gave importance to the crown's wearer, but it certainly did not mean that the individual monarch took all the decisions or exercised all the power. This point will recur in Chapter 6, which will consider the relationship between monarch and privy council; we shall

[113] Levack, *Formation of the British State*, 179–97.

[114] Wasser, 'Pacification of the Scottish Borders', 134–41, 151–3.

[115] Salisbury to Sir Roger Ashton, 18 Feb. 1608, HMC, *Salisbury*, xx. 74–5. I am grateful to Dr Pauline Croft for a discussion of Salisbury's policy-making role. For more on his involvement with Scotland, see Ch. 2 above.

[116] Cuddy, 'Anglo-Scottish Union', 107–24; V. Treadwell, *Buckingham and Ireland, 1616–1628* (Dublin, 1998).

find that practical power was usually exercised by the council, and that monarch and council normally operated by consensus. This method of government involves 'personal monarchy', but is not limited to that. And it needs to be distinguished carefully from any suggestion that royal government was 'personal' in the sense of being driven by royal whim, having no significant rules, procedures, or institutions. This would have produced a 'personal' government in which (to paraphrase a more recent prime minister) there is no such thing as the state, only individual kings and nobles and their clients.

This argument is indeed sometimes found. Perhaps it is encouraged by the low level of research on Scottish institutions compared with the excellent work that has been done in other areas, such as the nobility. One proponent of this view of 'personal' government is Keith Brown, who has made the nobility his special field. James VI, in his last seven years in Scotland, 'finally found himself able to dominate Scottish politics', but 'he did so as a personal ruler, not through the agencies of a state apparatus'. As a result, 'it could all so easily have fallen apart' with an unsatisfactory or minor ruler; the system required an able monarch at its head.[117] It certainly might have fallen apart; unfortunately, Professor Brown cites the periodic political instability of early seventeenth-century France to show what might have happened in Scotland. The logic of his case therefore seems to require France not to have had a 'state apparatus' either, a position that will find few adherents. He has helpfully warned that the existence of a state apparatus cannot be inferred every time we detect political stability, but a further warning is necessary: just as political stability can exist without the state, so too can political instability occur in a centralized state. If there are struggles (even military ones) for control of the state's apparatus, that hardly proves that the state's apparatus does not exist. Other chapters of this book present evidence that the Scotland of the 1590s and onwards did have a state apparatus. The civil wars of the early 1570s led to the formation of a breakaway administration in the north-east, with its own privy council and signet in the queen's name.[118] Nothing like that happened in the wars of the 1640s.

Nor is this all. James in the period 1595–1603 certainly worked hard— harder than he ever did before or later; and his efforts seem to have paid off (though Professor Brown is surely right that there was nothing inevitable about this). Whether James worked 'as a personal ruler' is another question, however. He was important personally, but what he was mainly doing was to attend the privy council frequently. Very likely he often took the lead there in shaping broad policy and setting priorities. Modern prime ministers, who are also important personally, presumably do much the same in their Cabinet

[117] K. M. Brown, 'From Scottish Lords to British Officers: State Building, Elite Integration and the Army in the Seventeenth Century', in N. Macdougall (ed.), *Scotland and War, AD 79–1918* (Edinburgh, 1991), 133.   [118] A. L. Murray, 'Huntly's Rebellion'.

meetings. But it is unusual for prime ministers to be better informed than their departmental heads about the challenges facing each department, so they are constrained by the options presented to them. No doubt the Cabinet's discussions on these options are also sometimes shaped by personalities. In James's privy council, which also contained the most important departmental heads, things were much the same. One may also ask what James was up to between council meetings. One of his major projects in the late 1590s was to persuade his nobles to end their feuds, but even in this task it has been convincingly argued that he did not do so just as a 'personal ruler'; he was 'surrounded by highly talented advisers and councillors who helped make his government so successful'.[119]

What difference was made by James's residence in England after 1603? It is conventional to stress the importance of the union of crowns for the practicalities of Scottish government: 'absentee monarchy', we are told, transformed the political and administrative scene. Now certainly there was some effect from the advent of a *dual* monarchy, in which the king and his advisers had to coordinate the government of two separate realms. This was indeed an issue in both realms. We should be sceptical, however, about the separate concept of '*absentee* monarchy', which is supposed to relate to Scotland alone. Let us imagine for a moment a looking-glass world in which Queen Elizabeth succeeds to the Scottish throne in 1603 and moves her court north to Holyrood. What a difference for the government of England!—for one thing, the monarch is no longer vulnerable to aristocratic conspiracies like Essex's rebellion of 1601. Absentee monarchy thus helps to enhance royal authority in England. However, although Elizabeth herself succeeds in governing England at a distance, the great queen's successors are no longer so familiar with the English political scene. By the 1620s this is leading to frequent misunderstandings and clashes with parliament. The court, remote from English affairs and ill-informed, runs into increasing difficulties, until eventually civil war breaks out . . . It seems that the political developments of early seventeenth-century England could readily be explained by 'absentee monarchy'.

Lacking, however, such a convenient portmanteau explanation, English historians have been obliged to do the hard work of developing other explanations for such early seventeenth-century eventualities as royal clashes with parliament, civil war, and so forth. We in Scotland should learn to do the same. 'Absentee monarchy' can be defined by two separate criteria, neither of which is wholly credible.

The first criterion is the supposed 'removal' of the 'Scottish' royal court, based on the assumption that the court of James VI and I was essentially English and not Scottish. By this criterion, the *composition* and not the physical location of his court was what mattered; consisting largely of

---

[119] Brown, *Bloodfeud*, 215.

Englishmen, it would have remained just as much an English institution if it had been removed from Whitehall and relocated in York, Dublin, or even Edinburgh.[120] The main reason this is not credible is that James's court was *not* essentially English in composition; in its upper levels it was staffed largely by Scotsmen, much to the annoyance of the English.[121]

The second criterion, focusing on distance, is a little more plausible. The road to court was certainly longer once the king moved to Whitehall. But if physical distance is to be the criterion, then 'absentee monarchy' must have existed in Caithness and Sutherland long before 1603. A physical-distance model of 'absentee monarchy', which would be relative rather than absolute, has yet to be demonstrated by research. A comparative study of sixteenth-century political society in northern Scotland, northern England, and southern France might well reveal some distinctive common patterns caused by royal remoteness; however, it is unlikely that anyone would wish to label these patterns 'absentee monarchy'. Even within England, the king and his court moved around on summer progresses, but a well-organized communications network took care to keep them in touch with events.[122] Perhaps from a Scottish point of view James and his court were on permanent progress after 1603. But that does not make them 'absentee'.[123]

So monarchy was scarcely less 'absentee' in Lancashire (where the king paid a quite unprecedented visit in 1617) than in Lanarkshire; the term is simply not a helpful one in understanding the royal court's relationship with political society. What mainly mattered in both counties was not the physical distance to the court, but the nature of the political connections between the court and the other institutions of central and local government. These connections did alter slightly in Scotland in 1603, though the change was less important than earlier shifts between royal minorities and majorities. But the connections remained firmly in place. Dual monarchy became an issue, but 'absentee monarchy' did not. Whitehall was bombarded with letters from Scottish officials assuring James that they regretted his 'absence'; this should be recognized as the routine flattery that it was. Such correspondence itself shows how closely James and the people around him kept in touch with Scottish affairs. The royal court was not in the least 'absent' from Scotland after 1603; it was very much present, and indeed a power in the land.

Scottish government became more personal and monarchical in the period covered by this book; it is time to ask why. The powers of the crown under

---

[120] James in 1607 did offer (or rather threaten) to move his court to York: Wormald, 'Creation of Britain', 175–6.   [121] Cuddy, 'Anglo-Scottish Union'.

[122] P. Harrison and M. Brayshay, 'Post-Horse Routes, Royal Progresses and Government Communications in the Reign of James I', *Journal of Transport History*, 18 (1997), 116–33.

[123] There is also the issue of *ceremonial* distance between monarch and subjects, concerning which it has been intriguingly suggested that Charles I 'managed even to create absentee monarchy in England by distancing himself from his subjects': D. Stevenson, 'The English Devil of Keeping State: Élite Manners and the Downfall of Charles I in Scotland', in R. Mason and N. Macdougall (eds.), *People and Power in Scotland* (Edinburgh, 1992), 139.

James rested not only on his personal right to issue legal commands, but also on his ability in practice to attract men to his service, and to reward those who served him. This was partly a matter of the glamour of life at the royal court, and the honour to be derived from an association with the court, but the most attractive rewards came in the form of hard cash and broad acres. Even a glamorous court itself meant expense. The increase in the king's power thus depended ultimately on access to resources—his own, or those of his subjects. Disposable royal revenues expanded greatly in the years after 1603, and the projectors and patent hunters who swarmed round the court were hoping for a share. These were the years of a slight but palpable curtailing of the influence of parliament. Parliament itself, by passing so many penal statutes over the years, had put weapons into the hands of the crown. The expansion of administration, regulated by proclamation, offered another field of opportunity to the projector. Meanwhile, the fact that parliament *had* passed all those statutes might mean that it was no longer needed. There was no automatic reason why government should continue to require a large legislative programme, and indeed the volume of legislation was more than halved in the early seventeenth century.[124] There was still a great deal of important parliamentary legislation, but it was confined to a narrower range of issues by the crown.

And yet, for all this successful royal activity, parliament still had reserves of strength. Some of its powers had been nibbled round the edges, but they remained substantially intact. James's claim to be sole legislator, quoted in part above, was an aspiration rather than an established fact. 'We dayly see', he wrote, 'that in the parliament (which is nothing else but the head courte of the king, and his vassals) the lawes are but craved by his subjects, and onely made by him at their rogation, and with their advice'.[125] What James omitted to mention was firstly, the formal point that laws were made (in the words of the standard enacting clause of a statute) 'by the advice *and consent*' of parliament, and secondly, the real point that he did not control parliament, but had to reach an agreement with its members—in fact, *he* had to ask *them*, rather than the other way round as he boasted. In the early seventeenth century he would build a court party which would indeed give him a measure of political leverage in parliament; this never amounted to complete control, although it might eventually have done so. In the meantime, parliament's basic ability to pass laws remained. Its exclusive power to authorize direct taxation was unchallenged—and this was revenue on which the crown had come increasingly to depend. Whether these powers would be enough to ensure parliament's long-term survival was an open question at the end of James VI's long reign.

---

[124] Rough figures for acts of parliament: 1581–90, 410; 1591–1600, 493; 1601–10, 209; 1611–20, 137; 1621–30, 114.

[125] James VI, *Trew Law*, in *Political Writings*, 74.

Such a question focuses attention squarely on a vital issue: the potential for conflict between crown and parliament. This book cannot pursue all the political ramifications of this topic, but a few observations may be made. In his early parliaments, James VI seemed no more likely to come into conflict with the institution than Henry VIII did in England. But the rise of a more powerful royal prerogative, of the kind that might exclude parliament from decision-making, did create the potential for conflict. This should not be surprising, once it is accepted that the prerogative did indeed expand in the way set out above. Of course, 'parliament' itself is to some extent a shorthand expression, since it was not a thing but a meeting place; power was held not by 'parliament' but by the people who had the right to attend it (see above, Chapter 2). Many important people wielded power both in parliament and out of it. But parliament tended to broaden the matrix of governmental authority, giving more scope for influence to the minor estates—burgh and shire commissioners. In a personal monarchy they tended to be kept at arm's length.

It has often been noted that Scottish parliaments never suffered, as English ones did, a complete breakdown in their relations with the crown in the early seventeenth century. There were no 'addled parliaments' in Scotland, and a parliament was held (in 1633) even after the suspension of the English institution in 1629. This, it is sometimes suggested, was either because there were no serious political problems in Scotland, or because the Scottish parliament was subservient to royal control. Neither of these ideas is true; the Scottish pattern looks far more like the English one than has been supposed.[126] After 1621, James and Charles were to hold four more parliaments in England: one more, plus two conventions of estates, in Scotland. The Scottish parliaments of 1621 and 1633, and the convention of 1625, would prove fully as restive and intractable as their English counterparts. If, therefore, there was a similar tendency for the crown to do things on its own authority, cutting out the need for parliament in those areas, it need occasion no surprise. It should also be recalled just what it was that was so controversial in 1633: it was an act on the royal prerogative.[127] In 1637, 'the poynt of the kings praerogative' was still 'the kitlest point eyther *in jure* or *facto*, in kirk or staite disputes'.[128]

---

[126] On political divisions, see Goodare, 'Scottish Politics in the Reign of James VI'; on parliament and the crown, see Goodare, 'Scottish Parliament of 1621'.

[127] On the 1633 parliament, see Lee, *Road to Revolution*, 131–3. The objection was to the combination of an act recognizing the royal prerogative with an act allowing the king to regulate clerical dress by decree: in the vote, the opposition almost defeated the combined act.

[128] Sir Archibald Johnston of Wariston, *Diary, 1632–1639*, ed. G. M. Paul (SHS, 1911), 275. 'Kitlest' = trickiest.

CHAPTER FIVE

Executive Government

It is unproffitable and inutile to mak lawis and statutis for polecy to be
had, without the samyn be kepit.

APS ii. 344, c. 14

A curious proposal landed on the desk of John Murray of Lochmaben, a gentleman of the bedchamber and prominent court patronage broker, in 1614.
The Scottish bishops had been approached by a gentleman offering to arrest
three Catholic priests known to him if he were given a fixed reward beforehand for this service. At first the bishops had told him: service first, reward
afterwards. But he would cooperate only on his terms, so they decided to
support his scheme. In fact we hear no more of it; perhaps Murray or the king
decided not to pursue it.[1] But it sheds an intriguing sidelight on the
administrative procedures of the Scottish state. The saying and hearing of
mass had been a serious statutory offence for two generations; whose job was
it to ensure that this law was implemented? Who made the decisions on this,
and who carried them out? In Chapters 6 and 7, we will examine the main
central institutions that implemented the law, before moving on in Chapters
8 and 9 to look at local institutions. We may also learn why the business of
law enforcement was not exclusively in the hands of institutions, and what
roles might be played by people like the anonymous anti-Catholic gentleman
and the court patronage broker.

First, however, we need a framework to explain what the 'enforcement' or
'implementation' of law actually meant. What was the 'executive'? How was
government carried out 'in the localities', to use a favourite phrase of early
modern historians? Was law always 'enforced' in the sense of making people
do what they did not want to do? Many governmental commands do not
seem to have been fully obeyed; should this make us sceptical about the power
of government? Or should we look more carefully at what government was
trying to achieve when it issued the commands?

'Executive' authority can be simply defined, but some aspects of it need
careful attention. A law has been passed: now it has to be put into effect. One
thread running through this book so far has been the issue of the initial

---

[1] Bishops to Murray, 23 June 1614, *Eccles. Letters*, i. 343–4. The 'gentleman' was not named.
Possibly he was connected with the arrest of the Jesuit John Ogilvy, on which see Pearce, 'John
Spottiswoode', 171–3.

making of law or government policy: who did it, and how? Now it makes sense to move on to how that law or policy was enforced. Laws may attract acquiescence or even enthusiastic compliance, but they also contain sanctions for non-compliance which are rarely there for decoration. But how are laws—commands issued by recognized authorities—to be enforced, other than by commands issued by recognized authorities?[2] If laws are commands, are commands also laws? How, in short, do we distinguish between a legislative and an executive act?

The basic principle here is that legislative commands apply generally—to all people in stated circumstances—while executive commands apply to particular individuals who have been found in the circumstances previously stated by the legislation. This is distinct from the often-cited doctrine of 'separation of powers' which postulates a trinity of legislative, judicial, and executive powers, separate but equal. Scotland had a single sovereign authority—the crown in parliament—which could not be split up in this way. Moreover, 'judicial' power is not conceptually distinct. The exercise of 'judicial' power involves either applying existing laws to individuals (executive power), or setting judicial precedents which create law (legislative power). Courts of law are hybrids from this point of view; most of what they do is executive power, but they can also be legislative.[3] A twofold distinction, between creating law and applying it, seems more appropriate. In addressing the question of how the law was implemented, implementation by the courts must be included.

Executive powers can be divided into 'central' and 'local'. Indeed a similar division can be made for legislative powers, since local courts often passed their own acts (the equivalent of modern by-laws) with general applicability; but the issue of 'centre and localities' relates primarily to executive powers. The question often seems to be: how well could a centrally made law be implemented in the localities?

However, this is not as helpful a question as it may seem. There is value in the concept of 'centre and localities'—but not as it seems commonly to be understood. The concept usually conjures up an image in which the locality is *here*, the centre is *there*, and interaction between them takes the form of a man on horseback who brings commands from the centre and returns with petitions from the locality. These journeyings to and fro tend to create a geographical model of centre and localities; government becomes a species of diplomacy between two homogeneous and geographically separate entities.

---

[2] Cf. John Austin, *The Province of Jurisprudence Determined*, ed. W. E. Rumble (Cambridge, 1995), 197.

[3] Goodare, *State and Society*, 17. On law and judicial precedent, see Ch. 3 above. A subordinate question seems still to be unresolved today: whether precedents create or merely discover laws. Creation seems more straightforward (where exactly were the laws before their discovery?), but the result was the same for the present purpose.

This geographical model raises the question of where on a map our horseman might find these entities, 'centre' and 'locality'. Was Carrick, for instance, a locality? We can surely agree that it was. And a horseman with petitions from Carrick would surely have to ride to Edinburgh. Did that then make Edinburgh the centre? The people in charge of the burgh, the provost and bailies, would say no; they also were governing a locality. Quite likely they would direct our horseman out of the burgh and down the Canongate, to see the privy council at the Palace of Holyroodhouse—for there, if anywhere, the centre would be found. But once there, the horseman might discover that it was not the privy council he wanted but the court of session, in which case he would have to go back up the Canongate to the Edinburgh tolbooth where it met. Or if he did want the privy council, it might be away with the king, perhaps at Falkland Palace. The search for the 'centre', it seems, might not be an easy one. Moreover, we are beginning to realize that the 'centre', wherever it might be, was also a locality. If the court of session met in the Edinburgh tolbooth, so did the burgh council. Everywhere in Scotland was a locality.

And everywhere in Scotland was also the centre. There was nothing unique about Edinburgh in this respect. The horseman from Carrick might not need to ride to Edinburgh (or Falkland) at all, for he could find a privy councillor close at hand in the form of the earl of Cassillis, the leading local magnate. The horseman himself might be a dependant of Cassillis or of one of his clients. When a parliament met, all the members of the political classes were notionally present or represented, and had accepted responsibility for obedience to the commands of the state. Parliaments usually met in Edinburgh but could also do so elsewhere.[4] The law itself did not depend on one's geographical proximity to a representative of the state. The law is the law, even if there are no police officers nearby. Some people disobey the law, but not because nobody has brought it to them from the 'centre'. If central power (including the law) did not exist at all outside the gates of Holyrood Palace, then every study of Scottish kingship needs to be rewritten. It seems more likely that central power did exist; but if so, there is no obvious a priori reason to assume that it existed in one geographical location (the 'centre') and not in another (the 'localities').

Thus, within the territory over which the state exercised its authority, geography was unimportant to the concept of 'centre and localities'. We should rather envisage a network of power woven over the entire nation, in which central and local power were warp and weft. There were certainly differences in how central government interacted with different regions; even in today's age of global communications, remote regions may suffer (or

---

[4] In our period, parliaments met in Edinburgh, Holyrood, Perth, and Stirling; additionally there were conventions of estates in Dalkeith, Dundee, Dunfermline, Falkland, Haddington, Linlithgow, and St Andrews. See Young (ed.), *Parliaments of Scotland*, ii. 753–5.

benefit) from receiving less official attention. In our period, a locality near Edinburgh would have rather more involvement with central government.[5] More research might clarify how we should disentangle this issue from questions of distinctive regional political allegiances; much discussion of the 'localities' is really about the latter question.[6] Differences in governmental treatment were probably not as great as is sometimes assumed; certainly the government increasingly aimed to treat all regions the same and to iron out local variations.[7] But that is a secondary issue. The primary point is that in any locality (that is, in any place), we can find both local and central power being exercised.

This does not mean that the concepts of 'centre' and 'localities' should be abolished: far from it. Central and local power existed in the same places, but were *conceptually* separate. Local power did things that tended to make the locality distinctive; central power did things that tended to make the locality the same as everywhere else. Both kinds of power were exercised in localities (that is, in places); but in our period, we begin to see slightly less of the former and a great deal more of the latter. This central power was central, not because it was exercised from Edinburgh (or Falkland, or London, or wherever), but because people exercising power in one locality used the same standards as those in other localities. For this to happen, they had to have an agreed common standard of reference. That standard, in many ways, was what central government consisted of.

This common standard of reference could consist of men, or bodies of men, in a single place—such as Edinburgh (or Falkland, or London, or wherever). Or it could consist of laws made or commands issued there. After the parliamentary statutes were printed in 1566, men could take them home, and read them, and use them. If they did so in Carrick, that locality was still being governed by men in Carrick, but they were now doing more of the same things that were being done in Cunningham, or in Caithness.

Meanwhile, local power also consisted of people taking a common standard—one that was unique to their locality. But here we need to put the concept of a 'locality' under the microscope; it can look quite different depending on the lens that we use. If Carrick, one of the three bailiaries of Ayrshire, was a locality, then what about Ayrshire itself? And what about Ballantrae, one of Carrick's parishes? 'Localities' existed at several levels, including parish, county, and region, all with their own 'local' elites. The 'locality' was not so much a single entity as a Russian doll, with a smaller one always concealed

---

[5] Wasser, 'Violence and the Central Criminal Courts', 12.

[6] e.g. G. Donaldson, 'Scotland's Conservative North in the Sixteenth and Seventeenth Centuries', in his *Scottish Church History*.

[7] Except in the Borders and Highlands. These were explicitly treated differently from the rest of the country, although only in the Borders was there a realistic prospect of eliminating their distinctiveness. On the Highlands, see Ch. 10 below.

inside it.[8] The geographical model of 'centre and localities' finds it almost impossible to cope with this. Ballantrae was a seat of the Kennedys of Bargany, who were frequently at odds with the earls of Cassillis, bailies of Carrick: local power versus local power.

The geographical model tends to suggest that local power and central power would be exercised by different men or bodies of men. Sometimes this might be so, but not necessarily. In his bailie court, the earl of Cassillis could exercise a slice of autonomous power in Carrick; as a privy councillor, he was expected to follow the central government's line. Which standard of reference would he take? Conflict between centre and localities, like that between court and country in England, was often experienced (when it occurred) not between two separate entities but within the minds of individuals.[9]

It remains to consider in more detail how central and local power were articulated, and how often they did, in fact, conflict. The role of the nobility was crucial here. It changed a great deal during the period with which this book is concerned, but without losing any of its importance. It was always the nobility, more than anyone, who linked centre and localities. They did so by exercising power in two modes: both local and central.

Traditionally, the local mode of noble power predominated. Keith Brown, who has done more than anyone to increase our knowledge of the nobility, has touched on the subject of centre and localities in a case study of a feud in Carrick, involving the earl of Cassillis, that took place between 1601 and 1604. It illustrates the use of local power well. Cassillis used his position as privy councillor to bolster his power, but he won the feud largely because he had more followers and firepower in the locality than his main rivals, the Kennedys of Bargany. On the other hand, there were signs that central power might also enter the locality. The feud had a dramatic coda in 1611 when two leading participants were tried in the central justiciary court and executed for murder, an almost unheard-of occurrence in earlier feuds.[10]

Professor Brown has also demonstrated that it would be hard to find a case study showing so much local autonomy twenty years later, or even ten.[11] The nobles abandoned their private armies, and with them, much of their means

---

[8] G. E. Aylmer, 'Centre and Locality: The Nature of Power Elites', in Reinhard (ed.), *Power Elites and State Building*, 60–3; M. Braddick, 'State Formation and Social Change in Early Modern England: A Problem Stated and Approaches Suggested', *Social History*, 16 (1991), 1–17 at 7–11.

[9] D. Hirst, 'Court, Country and Politics before 1629', in K. Sharpe (ed.), *Faction and Parliament: Essays on Early Stuart History* (2nd edn., London, 1985), 117; cf. L. Stone, *The Causes of the English Revolution, 1529–1642* (London, 1972), 108, and Aylmer, 'Centre and Locality', 77. For an insightful discussion of this as it relates to Carrick, see Adams, 'A Regional Road to Revolution', 8–12.

[10] K. M. Brown, 'A House Divided: Family and Feud in Carrick under John Kennedy, Fifth Earl of Cassillis', *SHR* 75 (1996), 168–96.

[11] Id., *Bloodfeud*, app. 1 and *passim*. For a regional case study sensitive to the issues raised here, see Adams, 'James VI and the Politics of South-West Scotland'.

of issuing commands without having to look over their shoulders at central government. They had to obey more of the law of the state, including even the law against murder. This was difficult for some of them, but on the whole they learned how to do it. After all, they could play the leading role in shaping that law. Those who worked actively for central government were rather more central and rather less local than nobles had traditionally been. This tendency would eventually lead to the eclipse of traditional local power, as the people in charge of central government (with or without peerage titles, and eventually with or without landed estates) found that they could govern more intensively and more bureaucratically.[12] Much of this is the story of the late seventeenth and eighteenth centuries, but its origins can be detected in our period. The nobility, or at least the leading nobility, were thus both central and local.

Territorial magnates played a dual role because they had two goals. One was to maximize their influence in their own territories, which tended to involve setting up barriers to influence from any other source—including central government. The other was to maximize their influence at the royal court, which would be more worthwhile if the court in fact exercised influence itself. In the past the first goal had usually taken priority; by the early seventeenth century it often did not. The goal of central power became more attractive because more resources were available centrally. Disposable wealth was extracted from the localities by central taxation, which could be redistributed to the nobles through their connections with government; previously wealth had been available to them mainly through the rents they received as local landlords. As time went on, fewer nobles retained local power networks of the kind that had helped to exclude central power; more of them found themselves associated rather with central than with local power. But the reason that there was so little overt conflict between centre and localities (less than has been imagined by some historians who have set the two up for such a conflict) was that the nobles usually played the role of linking the two so well.

Having clarified the question of central executive power, we can now begin to try to answer it. In some ways this is a matter of identifying executive institutions—such as privy council and court of session, or (in the localities) sheriff courts and kirk sessions. But it is better to begin with an analysis of executive *acts*.

In 1585, it was felt necessary to pass a law saying simply that the law should be enforced.[13] It saw the problem as 'misknawlege of his hienes lawes and actis of parliament' and the 'negligent executioun of the panis thairof'. But surely, especially now that the statutes were in print, the 'jugeis, officiaris and ministeris of the lawes' did know the law—or at least could find it out if it was important? And surely they were not negligent when it came to their

---

[12] For more on the changing role of the nobility, see Ch. 12 below.   [13] *APS* iii. 375, c. 2.

own interests? If they were not enforcing the law, perhaps there was some reason other than ignorant negligence for this?

Historians who have asked this question have often come up with a simple answer. Scottish government was weak and ineffective, so it is not surprising if its laws were not enforced. The evidence most often cited for this is that statutes on many subjects were repeated after a few decades—which proves that they were not being implemented. But does it prove that? Might not repetition of statutes prove rather that someone continued to think they were worthwhile, and in fact they *were* being implemented?[14] Much of the evidence for either argument can be slotted neatly into the preconceptions on which the argument is based. In 1595, Mark Acheson of Acheson's Haven (later Morison's Haven) in East Lothian was summoned for exporting grain, contrary to the 'actis of parliament and proclamatiounis for the retening of victuall within the cuntrie'. He had already been warned twice in 1594. But in 1597, he was summoned again—this time for deforcing a searcher for forbidden goods.[15] Some might treat this as evidence that the laws are being entirely disregarded. Here is someone exporting grain with impunity, even re-peating his offence—how many more must be getting away scot free! But oth-ers might argue that this case shows how *difficult* it is to export grain. Thus, it has to be done from a minor port, because the royal burghs are too well po-liced; and even here, a customs official manages to interfere, if perhaps not too successfully. The latter view is probably preferable on balance, though the truth clearly lies between two extremes; but the main point is that the repeti-tion of statutes does not in itself prove either implementation or non-implementation.

A related problem arises if we try to measure the success of statutes by their own comments on the problem in hand. In the later sixteenth century it be-came conventional for statutes to have preambles, and these have often been quoted to foster a pessimistic perception of law enforcement. For instance, there were many statutory efforts to improve the process of putting criminals to the horn (outlawry). One, in 1579, lamented that 'the disobedience of the proces of horning is sa greit and commoun that the personis denunceit rebel-lis takkis na feir thairof'. This is familiar enough. But if we accept it at face value, what are we to make of the act of 1573 which said that people had 'greit feir and terrour ... to incur the said process of horning'?[16] The answer is that the latter act was tightening up on the penalties for benefice-holders at the horn, and needed to imply in its wording that this was worth doing: they

---

[14] For a typical example of the view that repetition equals ineffectiveness, see F. J. Shaw, 'Sumptuary Legislation in Scotland', *JR*, NS 24 (1979), 81–115 at 98. One scholar more willing than some to consider both views, despite his generally dismissive attitude to parliamentary power, was Rait, *Parliaments of Scotland*, 47.

[15] NAS, treasurer's accounts, 1593–6, E21/70, fos. 163ᵛ, 97ᵛ, 127ʳ; treasurer's accounts, 1596–7, E21/71, fo. 132ᵛ. Cf. A. Graham, 'Morison's Haven', *Proceedings of the Society of Antiquaries of Scotland*, 95 (1961–2), 300–3.

[16] *APS* iii. 142–3, c. 13; 74–5, c. 8.

would have the same 'feir and terrour' as lay folk. By contrast, it would have been odd for the 1579 statute *not* to say that there were problems with horning, because it was being introduced to solve such problems.

Preambles to statutes cannot, therefore, be taken at face value. Their authors commonly put in all kinds of excited remarks to convince parliament and the public (and perhaps themselves) that the law was worth having. They exaggerated the seriousness of the disease; they claimed that all previous laws had totally failed to cure it; and they prescribed an infallible remedy: this was no more than common form. More can be learned from the substance of statutes than from their hypochondriac preambles; and in the case of horning, there is the act of 1598 which enjoined privy councillors to set a 'guid example of obedience' by not actually appearing at the council table while at the horn.[17] Even that may show only that you might evade the rigours of the law if you were well connected.

The substantive texts of statutes may tell us something about implementation, but they need careful interpretation. How many laws were passed with resounding claims to universal, complete, and permanent implementation! Many scholars have taken these claims literally, and have concluded that the aspirations of policy-makers ran well ahead of their achievements. They have brimmed with sympathy for legislators in their well-intentioned uphill struggle, or have rebuked them sternly for relying on futile scraps of paper. Both attitudes miss the point. Policy-makers, despite the formulas in their statutes, did not necessarily think in terms of full, permanent implementation.

The statutes can thus be divided up according to what kind of implementation was expected of them. These strategies of implementation are not concrete or mutually exclusive. Quite a number of statutes fall into two or more groups, while some might be implemented in different ways at different times, or in different ways in different places (the issue of local power again). Rather, they are tendencies which can be found in the statutes.

The first tendency may be called discretionary enforcement. Statutes of this kind were enforced when someone chose to do so, and only then. Parliament passed them with sweeping claims, certainly. But nobody thought that they would be implemented permanently; nobody thought that they would be observed all over the country; and nobody thought that they would be applied to everyone, even in a locality which was paying attention to them. They were enabling statutes. The government, worried about some social problem, passed a statute inviting central or local administrators to consider what, if anything, they would do about it.

To take an example: the poor law was enacted in 1575 to deal with the social threat of growing poverty and vagrancy. It required parishes to assess the level of poverty, and to impose local taxation to pay regular poor relief to all those in need. Probably not a single parish did so—at least, not

---

[17] *APS* iv. 178.

immediately or regularly. Certainly the government made no attempt to compel them. But arguably, the act did encourage thinking about how to tackle vagrancy at a local level, and it gave parishes a discretionary mechanism of which they could take advantage to cope with a temporary crisis.[18] This was as much as legislators could expect or even desire.

Some acts were worded in a general way but were clearly inspired by local initiative. The act of 1592 ordering that approach roads to burghs should not be blocked, particularly those roads leading from inland burghs to the sea, looks like the initiative of a particular burgh.[19] Some acts applied explicitly to a particular locality, like that of 1621 banning wooden or thatched roofs in Edinburgh. The penalty for non-compliance was to be put to the horn by the burgh magistrates, so the implementation of the act was firmly in their hands.[20]

Discretionary enforcement could also reinforce the discretion of central government. There were many statutes and even more proclamations against shooting wild game. This was not principled conservationism; it was about preserving the royal sport. The laws were usually proclaimed (and only enforced) at a time and place when the king was actually hunting.[21] Statutes might sound permanent, but the problem that they addressed was often intermittent. Mark Acheson, exporting grain contrary to statute, would have been less likely to get into trouble if the mid-1590s had not been years of famine. The law limiting the followers which a litigant could bring to the law courts was important only when there was a serious attempt at intimidation.[22] All these were matters in which the central government had given itself the power to crack down—not in a statute saying that it had discretion to punish the activity if it chose, but in one saying baldly that the activity was illegal. Scholars who have assumed that the state's executive machinery was inadequate have often failed to recognize that the intention was discretionary enforcement.

In general we should think of the executive as enforcing the law, but it might also be implementing an unwritten policy. Clearly this would allow it wide discretion. In the early seventeenth century, the privy council began to authorize many local bridge tolls in order to finance the construction or repair of bridges. There was no law that bridges had to be built, but there was a policy that it was desirable. Each grant of a toll was certainly a coercive order which should be regarded as the 'executive' implementing a bridge-building 'policy', even if that policy was never written down, and even if there was no single moment at which the council formally adopted it. They may

---

[18] *APS* iii. 86–9; Goodare, 'Parliament and Society', ch. 8; R. Mitchison, *The Old Poor Law in Scotland: The Experience of Poverty, 1574–1845* (Edinburgh, 2000), 10–14.

[19] *APS* iii. 579–80, c. 78.

[20] *APS* iv. 626–7, c. 26. For burgh lobbying to obtain such acts, see Ch. 2 above.

[21] e.g. *APS* ii. 541, c. 15; NAS, treasurer's accounts, 1601–4, E21/76, fo. 78ʳ; *RPC* vi. 353, 542.

[22] *APS* iii. 301, c. 17 (reissuing *APS* ii. 51, c. 29; 495, c. 15); *RPC* iv. 508.

have drifted into it, but it was still government action that definitely happened.

Some executive acts were based on formal written laws, but in practice responded to changes in public demand. The privy council authorized more bridge tolls in the early seventeenth century than before, not because they had previously had a policy of rejecting proposals for such tolls, but because more people wanted to build or repair bridges. Witch-hunting occurred in short, sharp bursts—five nationally between 1590 and 1662. These were rarely initiated by a specific decision of central government, but arose through a moral panic in which central and local authorities shared a consensus. The central policy-makers did not decree this kind of enforcement.[23]

Even if the law was being enforced, the authorities (central or local) might have discretion to ignore inconvenient aspects of it. The statute of 1563 against witchcraft was certainly used, but it actually prescribed death not just for witches, but also for consulters of witches. This clause was tacitly ignored. The earl of Orkney was accused by the privy council in 1609 of imposing exorbitant fines on consulters of witches. The earl could have cited the statute as evidence that he was actually being lenient, but instead replied that without the fines the islanders 'wald all have becommit witches and warlockis for the people ar naturally inclynit thairto'. The council did not really want to prosecute consulters of witches at all.[24]

Discretionary enforcement of statutes did not mean that unenforced statutes fell into formal desuetude. This concept would soon become familiar in Scots law: by it, where a statute was not being enforced, and a contrary practice had grown up unchallenged, the statute was held to have been permanently superseded. Thomas Craig seems to have been the first to enunciate this doctrine in a legal work, in about 1605, and he added that Scotland differed from England where statutes were always in force (at least nominally) until repealed. The doctrine was not mentioned by Sir James Balfour in the 1580s or Sir Thomas Hope in the 1630s, and seems to have entered the canon of Scots law only with Viscount Stair in 1681.[25] Moreover, the discretionary enforcement under discussion here was something that also existed in England, where there was no desuetude. In English local government (as also in Scotland), there were far more laws than could be enforced in

---

[23] J. Goodare, 'Witch-Hunting and the Scottish State', in id. (ed.), *The Scottish Witch-Hunt in Context*, 136–8.

[24] Larner, *Enemies of God*, 66–7; P. D. Anderson, *Black Patie: The Life and Times of Patrick Stewart, Earl of Orkney, Lord of Shetland* (Edinburgh, 1992), 89; M. Wasser, 'The Privy Council and the Witches: The Curtailment of Witchcraft Prosecutions in Scotland, 1597–1628', *SHR* 82 (2003), 20–46. During the panic of 1597, the council had regarded consulters as 'na lesse gilty' than witches and meriting 'indifferent and equall punishement' (*RPC* v. 410), but this view was never put into practice.

[25] Craig, *Jus Feudale*, I.8.9; Balfour, *Practicks*; Hope, *Major Practicks*; Stair, *Institutions*, I.16; *SME* xxii. paras 129–30, 364, 376. It was possible, but rare, for Scottish statutes to be repealed in our period.

full. This required justices of the peace to set priorities. They saw this as a strength, allowing them to reach consensus as to which laws were the current priorities.[26]

One category of legislation with discretionary enforcement grew to controversial prominence in the early seventeenth century: the so-called penal statutes. Here also, discretion was possessed by central rather than local government. The penal statutes were a group of laws, mostly fairly recent, creating new crimes, mostly economic, which were punishable by fines or escheats to the crown. The most important were the statutes limiting interest rates, and those banning the export of bullion. Breaches of them were prosecuted before the privy council by a royal official, usually the treasurer or king's advocate or both, sometimes together with an aggrieved subject pursuer.[27] But because they usually lacked individual victims, the crown could legitimately refrain from prosecuting them if it chose. The parliament of 1612 gave statutory backing to a commission to issue pardons (often at a price) to those in breach of the statutes, because 'the rigorus exactioun of the same [penalties] mycht turne to the overthraw of a multitude of his majesties subjectis'.[28]

In a few extreme cases of discretionary enforcement, no actual enforcement was envisaged at all. Local authorities were not being invited to enforce the statute; the subjects were being invited to comply with it. In 1579, a statute was passed requiring all members of the propertied classes to possess Bibles and psalm books. Possibly some law-abiding citizens went out and bought them as a result; but nobody could have expected punishment if they did not. A 'sercheour' was appointed in 1580 with power to enforce the statute in Edinburgh; but if this was ever widely known it was soon forgotten. In 1584, the exiled presbyterian minister James Melville was in Newcastle attending to the spiritual welfare of a group of nobles who had been forced to flee, he felt, for loyalty to their religion. He told them of the need for Bibles and psalm books, but not of the legal obligation to possess them. Indeed, he limited his advice to saying that 'everie an that can reid' should have them.[29]

Such laws were small beer. By contrast, another type of law where enforcement was discretionary was a matter of life and death: the law on treason and

---

[26] A. Fletcher, *Reform in the Provinces: The Government of Stuart England* (New Haven, 1986), ch. 6. This could have international implications. The Scots were surprised in 1602 when an English campaign against their cloth exports was launched under a statute of Edward IV: Nicolson to the English privy council, 22 May 1602, *CSP Scot.* xiii, II. 987.

[27] Cf. McNeill, 'Jurisdiction of the Scottish Privy Council', 14.

[28] *APS* iv. 473–4, c. 9, which also gives a convenient list of the penal statutes then in force. For the implementation of the penal statute against usury in the 1610s, see Goodare, *State and Society*, 209–10.

[29] *APS* iii. 139, c. 10; *RSS* vii. 2395; Melville, *Diary*, 183. For the books' voluntary acquisition see M. H. B. Sanderson, 'The Printing and Distribution of the Bible and Psalm Books in Sixteenth-Century Scotland: Some Additional Documentation', *Records of the Scottish Church History Society*, 29 (1999), 139–49 at 147–9.

related state crimes. They were reserve weapons. Treason, for instance, was what the king said it was: as James VI advised his son, 'I remit to your owne choise to punish or pardone therein'.[30] The supreme penalty was hardly ever paid. Laws on censorship were similar: there was frequent criticism of James, but he let many hostile comments pass without invoking the statutes, although a few of his critics were rigorously punished.[31] In an effort to suppress presbyteries, the Black Acts of 1584 banned all assemblies, prompting David Calderwood's complaint that 'there is no particular specificatioun of the judgments and assembleis heere called in questioun . . . commoun lawes should be cleere, to assure the subjects certanelie what sould be done or left undone'.[32] The earl of Arran, who masterminded the acts, knew that it was in his interests to leave things vague.

Discretionary enforcement went hand in hand with another executive tendency: negotiated implementation. Agencies deciding whether to enforce a statute no doubt discussed the matter beforehand; but once transgressors of the law had been identified, the question of what should be done to them could itself be negotiable. This was the reality behind the advice that a king's duty

> Is for to do everilk man justice,
> And for to mix his justice with mercie,
> But rigour, favour or parcialitie.[33]

The admixture of mercy to justice was most noticeable in the field of criminal law. The law might prescribe a specific punishment for a specific offence; but the privy councillors, to whom usually fell the thankless task of coping with feuds, were desperately willing to overlook offences if this would reduce future trouble from powerful families. Any means, coercive or conciliatory, would be adopted on a pragmatic basis.[34] In 1579, John Boswell of Auchinleck complained that he feared 'bodilie harm' from John Crawford of the Shaw and other Crawfords. Although there had already been 'divers bluidscheddis betuix thame', the privy council passed over these crimes and merely ordered the Crawfords to give lawburrows (security) that they would not harm him further.[35] In enforcing law and order, the stress was very much on achieving order. If mercy to either side was exercised without this legitimate aim it might degenerate into illegitimate 'rigour, favour or parcialitie'. This was, perhaps, class-based law: the peasant murderer could expect no mercy, whereas the noble could obtain a remission at a price. On the other hand,

---

[30] James VI, *Basilicon Doron*, in *Political Writings*, 23.
[31] Goodare, 'Parliament and Society', ch. 7.
[32] *APS* iii. 293, c. 4; Calderwood, *History*, iv. 64.
[33] Lindsay, 'Ane satyre of the thrie estaitis', in *Works*, ii. 187. 'But' = without. This idea was based on the analogy of God's justice to humankind, which was also necessarily (because of humanity's sinful nature) tempered with mercy. Cf. T. I. Rae, 'The Political Attitudes of William Drummond of Hawthornden', in G. W. S. Barrow (ed.), *The Scottish Tradition* (Edinburgh, 1974), 138.
[34] Brown, *Bloodfeud*, ch. 9.   [35] *RPC* iii. 148–9.

when such a small fraction of crimes came before the courts, perhaps a higher proportion of nobles' crimes did so. This was certainly the case during the first three decades of the seventeenth century, the period when the bloodfeud was gradually eradicated.

If remissions were available at a price, how was that price negotiated? First of all, for a case of slaughter, it had to be preceded by assythement—compensation to relatives of the victim. That required one set of negotiations. At justice ayres, further negotiations would follow with 'lords componitors' on the price of a remission.[36] Remissions were available only from the crown, but one of the administrative problems of the period was the ease of obtaining one at court by pulling the right strings—sometimes (and this was the key point) without satisfying victims. Periodic acts ordered that no remissions would be given for a year, three years, five years—these orders probably came at times when the privy council was asserting its influence.[37] An act of 1592 sought additionally to pursue holders of existing remissions, with or without the concurrence of the injured parties, to get them to find caution to pay assythements.[38] In practice it could be hard to overturn even a dubious remission, although the exchequer seems to have succeeded on one occasion in 1595. After 1603, remissions granted by the king seem usually to have been processed through the privy council, which could thus block any of which it disapproved. Moreover, the king intervened only rarely in the court of justiciary itself.[39]

The fiscal aspect of executive acts, apparent with remissions, is even clearer with 'unlaws' and 'wills' in the court of justiciary, the central criminal court. 'Unlaws' were financial penalties imposed by the court after conviction, which could be converted through negotiation into a reduced 'composition'. 'Wills' were penalties imposed on those who 'came in the will' of the monarch, submitting without a trial in the hope of more lenient treatment.[40] The merchant Edward Johnstone came in the king's will for treasonable behaviour during the Edinburgh uprising of 17 December 1596. The king's will was that since he himself owed huge sums to the financier Thomas Foulis, and since Foulis owed 8,000 merks to Johnstone, Johnstone should not pursue Foulis for the 8,000 merks (or for any interest payments) until the king

---

[36] J. Wormald, 'Bloodfeud, Kindred and Government in Early Modern Scotland', *Past and Present*, 87 (May 1980), 54–97 at 82.

[37] e.g. *TA* xii. 14; *APS* iii. 67; 298, c. 12; 426; 457, c. 54, para 4; iv. 18–19, c. 16. The problem went back to the 15th c.: e.g. *APS* ii. 104, c. 7; 118, c. 2. Royal lieutenants, who were temporary, often received the power to issue remissions, but no regular officers had it.

[38] *APS* iii. 575, c. 67.

[39] *Trials*, ed. Pitcairn, ii, I. 97; BL, 'Notes furth of the registers of exchequer, 1583–1674', Harl. MS 4628, fo. 2ᵛ; NLS, Sir Thomas Hamilton to James, 14 Jan. [1612], Denmylne MSS, Adv. MS 33.1.1, vol. iv, no. 2; Wasser, 'Violence and the Central Criminal Courts', 109–10. For the council's effort to block a remission that it had not seen in advance (perhaps because the recipient, Sir James MacDonald, lived in England), see council to James, 7 June 1621, *Melros Papers*, ii. 401–3.

[40] A. L. Murray, 'Notes on the Treasury Administration', p. xxviii.

had paid Foulis. Johnstone probably never saw his money again. Nor was that all, for his escheat was granted to a courtier, Sir George Home of Spott, who mulcted him of another 3,500 merks.[41] These complex transactions, involving four different parties, must have involved careful negotiation.

A few statutes were statements of intent—announcements that the government intended to implement a certain policy, but by negotiation rather than naked coercion. An act of 1617 established a commission to negotiate with holders of heritable offices about surrendering them for compensation.[42] Having the commission established by parliament no doubt made it look more impressive, but did not alter the law. Parliament did not give it powers of compulsory purchase, though no doubt it could have chosen to do so.

The implementation of law by negotiation reminds us that the law does not always need to be rammed down people's throats. Presented with the opportunity to use law-enforcement agencies to achieve their ends, many people do so willingly. They cooperate with the state in order to obtain justice or to do down their rivals. Many statutes thus called only for supervision, not enforcement. Although permanent, they did not require executive agencies of government to be continually vigilant over their implementation. Instead they made private law, establishing ground rules for settling disputes between individuals. State power manifested itself in people's employment of agencies of the state as tools for this purpose.

The making of private law still represented state power. Statutes allowing divorce on grounds of adultery (1563) or desertion (1573) were not going to be followed by campaigns to require all partners of adulterers to seek divorce, or to make sure that partners once divorced stayed that way.[43] Having empowered the Edinburgh commissary court to grant such divorces, the government left the individuals concerned to take advantage in their own way of the rights thus conferred. The statute on executors (1617) made it their duty to render an account to widows, children, and nearest of kin, but it was up to the latter to demand that they do so.[44] But one person's right is usually another's obligation. The courts adjudicated between one individual and another, but had machinery to ensure that their decrees were obeyed. People divorced against their wishes by the statute of 1573, or called to account by that of 1617, knew that these statutes were coercive.

The private law laid down by the state coexisted with other laws that might primarily represent moral, rather than legal, authority. Many of the conventions defining a valid marriage contract (that it be heterosexual, for example) drew their real force from tradition and consensus. Even after the nationalization of the commissary courts in 1564, the church had a closer involvement in most people's marriages than the state. But the state increasingly

---

[41] *Trials*, ed. Pitcairn, ii, I. 33–4.
[42] *APS* iv. 549–50, c. 24. For the activities of this commission, see Ch. 8 below.
[43] *APS* ii. 539, c. 10; iii. 81–2, c. 1.   [44] *APS* iv. 545, c. 14.

tended to set the rules in the difficult borderline cases. Another traditional rule for a marriage was that it be permanent—and this *was* interfered with by the statutes of 1563 and 1573. These laws (and the courts that administered them) *were* validated by the state.

Statutes could be private law, with no active official enforcement as such, and still represent a definite government policy. The series of statutes regulating the collection of teinds between 1567 and 1617 enhanced the rights of peasant tenants vis-à-vis tacksmen (lessees) of teinds, probably to benefit landlords, who were rivals of the tacksmen for the peasants' surplus product.[45] The statutes did not lead to officials going out into the fields to tell tacksmen of teinds to treat the peasants decently, or to show consideration for landlords. The legal levers placed by the state in the peasants' and landlords' hands were what made the difference.

The multiplication of laws on teinds illustrates the way in which our period saw a dramatic expansion of statute law. Not all the laws calling for implementation were statutes, but more and more of them were. Partly this legislative success was possible because the government had effective strategies for implementing the new statutes: people in government liked the statutes they saw, and wanted more of them. Some laws were fully and literally enforced, but many were not intended to be; instead they were applied using the sensitive strategies which have been defined here as discretionary enforcement and negotiated implementation. The next two chapters will discuss the central institutions whose job it was to apply these strategies.

[45] Conveniently summarized in A. A. Cormack, *Teinds and Agriculture* (Oxford, 1930), 89–97.

CHAPTER SIX

The Privy Council

The Privy Council acts generally as his [the king's] deputy: it is easily accessible to the complaints of suitors, and is as fair and impartial in its decisions as when the king was present in person. It must be borne in mind also that the intervention of courtiers not infrequently diverts the ends of justice.

Craig, *De Unione*, 451

Most questions about how Scotland was governed tend sooner or later to lead back to the privy council. Below the crown, the council was the supreme executive authority, with a general political competence that allowed it to intervene in almost any area of government. This was partly because the privy council had a closer connection to the monarch than any other executive body. Much of what appears on casual inspection to have been done by the monarch was in fact done by the monarch advised by the council. In reality, the council could often act in the monarch's name after consultation that need only have been a formality, or even with no consultation at all. The monarch could be involved, and often was, but such involvement should not be inferred without specific evidence. The privy council was a corporate body, with its own administrative structure and traditions, able to run the daily central government by itself.

The council's effectiveness did not derive simply from assembling a dozen 'councillors' round a table. Many of the councillors were also officers of state, with departmental responsibilities in the administration. The council's power derived from the officers' recognition that it should coordinate their departments. This chapter discusses the council itself, while the departments that answered to it are dealt with in Chapter 7.

The privy council was so vital to government in the late sixteenth century that it is possible to forget how new it was. In the form which it eventually took, it began in 1545. Its prehistory is one of administrative flux.[1] Fifteenth-century Scotland had 'lords of council', individuals appointed by the crown, whose main function was to hold judicial 'sessions' offering adjudications on

---

[1] What follows is a brief summary of a complex topic, at present best elucidated by the following: Chalmers, 'King's Council', ch. 1 and *passim*; A. L. Murray, 'Exchequer, Council and Session'; the introduction by A. L. Murray to *Acts of the Lords of Council*, iii (Edinburgh, 1993); and M. Godfrey, 'The Assumption of Jurisdiction: Parliament, the King's Council and the College of Justice in Sixteenth-Century Scotland', *Journal of Legal History*, 22 (2001), 21–36.

civil litigation. Certain of the 'lords of council' could also be designated as 'lords of exchequer', whose duties were to carry out an annual audit of royal accounts in the exchequer and to adjudicate on any resulting legal disputes. In 1532, fifteen of the 'lords of council' became a president and fourteen senators of the new college of justice, a corporate body endowed with former church revenues. The 'sessions' that they held became more formal and regular. The jurisdiction of what became known as the 'lords of session' (more formally, 'lords of council and session') expanded rapidly, as did the amount of business that they handled. The 'lords of council and session' retained and continued the archival records, the 'acts of the lords of council'.[2] The old, undifferentiated 'lords of council' were now a residual group with few functions of their own, though the lords of exchequer were still drawn from them. Between about 1488 and 1545, therefore, there was some administrative differentiation, though with much overlap in personnel.

The lords of council could also advise the king. In this capacity they, or some of them, could be described as a 'secret council', a term synonymous with 'privy council'.[3] In the late fifteenth century this was a collection of individual sworn councillors, who were not a corporate body and did not meet regularly. There was also a small inner group, described by Trevor Chalmers as the 'daily council'. The 'daily council' met regularly, but was not a corporate body either—it kept no records. Its main function was to advise the king on the distribution of patronage.[4] As for the 'secret council', it had never been constantly in being, even on paper, and after 1532 it faded away. Most orders were issued by the king alone, and it was up to him what advice he took, if any. It has even been argued that there was 'no clearly identifiable royal council' for the remainder of James V's personal reign.[5] This is probably exaggerated, since some administrative rather than judicial initiatives were still taken by 'the lordis', like a proclamation of 1538 against corrupt or mixed wine.[6] But such examples are rare, and the absence of any *corporate* council for James's political affairs seems clear. His councillors did not usually do things themselves.

Thus we have an oscillating pattern of political councils, as government itself oscillated between royal majorities and minorities. In the majorities the king governed personally, taking such advice (from the magnates or others) as

---

[2] 'Court of session' is a convenient modern term for the court held by the 'lords of council and session', as they were called. The court of session was never described at the time as a court, since it lacked standard attributes of a feudal court like suitors, assize, and dempster, but this should not prevent us from recognizing it as one. The 'college of justice' created in 1532 was the corporate body within which the court was held.

[3] The Scottish privy council throughout our period referred to itself in its registers as the 'secret council', though other official documents often called it the 'privy council' and it was probably spoken of by that name. Both terms meant that the 'counsel' being offered was confidential, in contrast to bodies like parliament or general council which offered public counsel to the monarch.

[4] Chalmers, 'King's Council', 90–7.   [5] Cameron, *James V*, 334–5.
[6] *Acts of the Lords of Council in Public Affairs, 1501–1554*, ed. R. K. Hannay (Edinburgh, 1932), 475.

he pleased; the men formally designated his 'councillors' or 'lords of council' were his appointees. In the minorities, there was a more collective style of government by the magnates, with a more active role for parliaments and councils. During James IV's early years, in 1490, a 'secret council' was appointed by parliament, its power enhanced by the fact that there was no formal regency.[7] A 'secret council', poorly documented but evidently wielding political authority, resurfaced in the minority of James V, its beginnings perhaps coming when in 1513 two dozen lords were 'ordanit to remane daily with the quenys graice to gif hir consell in all materis concerning the wele of the realme', in rotation.[8] The records of the 'lords of council' in the pre-1545 period contain a good deal of public business in the early years of James IV and minority of James V, but much less during their adult reigns.[9]

The privy council began during the minority of Mary, when a return to conciliar government was to be expected. Some kind of privy council had come into existence by March 1543.[10] The early regency of the earl of Arran was tossed in the storm of international warfare and domestic faction, exacerbated by the regent's own indecisiveness. The government found it useful to establish formal collective responsibility for its decisions. The essence of the decision taken in 1545 was not to create a new body to coordinate the government, but to keep a record of administrative decisions. It was not a deliberate innovation, but the latest oscillation of a pendulum that had been swinging for some time.[11]

However, the pendulum did not swing back again in subsequent royal majorities—those of Mary or James VI. Earlier 'secret councils' had been temporary stopgaps for lack of an adult monarch, but from Mary onwards it was the norm that an adult monarch governed with a council. This cannot be explained all at once; aspects of it will be discussed later, in Chapter 12. The remainder of this chapter, meanwhile, shows how the privy council worked, which may also help to explain why it was so successful. Government was becoming more elaborate, and that meant more paperwork, more departmental specialization, and more consultation by policy-makers. The privy council proved to be a good vehicle for combining these; it succeeded because it was well adapted to changing needs.

The privy council was a corporate body that kept records. Medieval government was often a matter of the king deciding that something should be done and telling a man to do it, which the man then did. There was often no need to write down that the decision had been taken, or that someone had

---

[7] *APS* ii. 220, c. 11.

[8] Murray, 'Exchequer, Council and Session', 108; *Acts of the Lords of Council in Public Affairs*, 4. The 'quenys graice' was the regent, Margaret Tudor.

[9] *Acts of the Lords of Council*, iii, p. xxiii.   [10] Merriman, *Rough Wooings*, 121.

[11] Arran's successor as regent, Mary of Guise, also had a privy council, though its records have disappeared. For an attempt to reconstruct its membership see Ritchie, *Mary of Guise*, 126.

advised the king in taking it, or that the man had been told to do it, or that he had done it. A decision in a law court would have to be minuted, and resources (unless disbursed by the king personally) might have to be accounted for; but otherwise governmental decisions and commands, and their execution, could be entirely oral. A corporate decision-making body operated differently. Colleagues who were formally equal had to reach a single decision, by consensus or by majority vote, to which all then had to adhere. There was a clear incentive to write the decision down: it might prevent arguments among them later.

Writing decisions down also allowed the enforcement of larger numbers of more detailed and sophisticated decisions, forestalling objections by those on the receiving end of the policy. This also implied keeping copies of documents issued to the subjects. Traditionally the document was handed out and no copy was kept; this still happened for many documents in our period. But increasingly, governmental action involved a combination of paperwork in official files and in the hands of the subjects. James Hall of Foulbar and his brother had in 1596 killed David Montgomery and two children by burning his house, whereupon they were warded, gave assythement (compensation) to Montgomery's kin, and received a royal remission. In 1612, John Montgomery of Scotstoun revived the case, but the Halls escaped prosecution after producing to the privy council a letter and two warrants relating to their warding and release, and obtaining 'the extract of an act of adjournall' under the subscription of the justice clerk, confirming that they had found surety to underly the law on their release. The Halls had the first three documents themselves, but the fourth came from the files of the court of justiciary.[12]

The privy council, then, successfully established itself as the central executive organ of government. It was a body which, unlike its predecessors, did things itself. And during our period it did more and more things. The volume of its recorded business steadily increased, more than quadrupling between 1560 and 1625.[13] Moreover, the upward trend continued throughout— unlike with parliament, where the volume of its output peaked in the 1590s and then declined. The government of Scotland did not always need more laws, but it did always seem to need more active implementation of the laws.

The importance of the privy council can also be charted in the pattern of its frequency of meeting. Important public business often cannot wait; thus the privy council never had the 'vacance' periods observed by most courts including the court of session.[14] In frequency of meeting, instead of steady

[12] *RPC* ix. 442–3. For assythement see K. M. Brown, *Bloodfeud*, ch. 2.
[13] This point, and the following points about frequency of meetings, are based on *RPC*, *passim*. The records are more or less complete for this period. They are missing for most of the 1550s, so comparisons with the council's earlier years are difficult.
[14] The court of session's vacances varied, but generally totalled about four months of the year. See *APS* iii. 32, c. 29; 104, c. 16; 376, c. 4. In session, the court usually met daily, which was more

growth, there were two distinct phases. In Mary's reign there was usually less than one recorded meeting a week, and much longer intermissions were frequent. Government could thus be carried on without the council, for a month or two at any rate. This pattern continued under Moray's regency and through the civil war of the early 1570s. But in 1572–3, with the regency of Morton and the return of settled government, there was a sudden increase in the number of recorded meetings, which now took place every three days or so. This became the norm for the rest of our period, though with phases of even greater busyness. Seemingly the only thing that could halt the constant forward thrust of administrative activity was an epidemic of plague, when normal public life could be temporarily suspended.

The late sixteenth-century privy council dealt both with individual cases and with general, public ones. The historian's sense that the latter were more important was shared by some contemporaries, as when Lord Binning complained that councillors had been 'more empesched at this meiting with particular actions nor publict affaires'.[15] This may sometimes have been justified, at any rate when public business was pressing (Binning wrote with a Highland uprising on his hands). But the private business was important too. It demonstrated the state's power. And it brought concrete results to individuals, whereas 'public' decisions possibly might not.

One leading English scholar, Penry Williams, has argued that Tudor governments did not think of themselves as having 'policies', and that the word 'policy' had negative connotations. Statesmen and councillors dealt with business as it came up, with little effort to distinguish between formulating major policies and making routine decisions about individuals; there was no bureaucracy to filter out the less important decisions and take them at a lower level.[16] It is not the purpose of this chapter to start a debate about the English privy council, but one may ask whether the Scottish privy council wasted its time on minor decisions. On the whole, it did not. In making decisions on individuals, it was dealing either with *marginal* cases, in which the rule was unclear, or with *awkward* cases, in which powerful people were involved.[17]

As an example, we may take the two dozen decisions made by the council in a fairly typical month in the middle of our period, July 1594.[18] The most pressing decisions related to treason or potential treason. Seven supporters of

---

often than the privy council, but unlike the latter it was not in constant session. The pre-1545 'lords of council' had no regular pattern, but in 1501–3 they met less frequently than the later privy council and often took breaks of over a month: *Acts of the Lords of Council*, iii, *passim*.

[15] NLS, Binning to Patrick Hamilton, 15 Sept. [1614], Denmylne MSS, Adv. MS 33.1.1, vol. v, no. 83. In 1578 there was a rule that public affairs should be dealt with in the morning, and private suits in the afternoon: *APS* iii. 97, c. 4.

[16] P. Williams, *The Tudor Regime* (Oxford, 1979), 21–3.

[17] It would also be untrue to say that 'policy' had negative connotations in Scotland, where it normally meant the process of government, and indeed well-organized government. One example among many may be found in the epigraph to Ch. 5 above.

[18] *RPC* v. 149–61.

the forfeited earl of Bothwell were ordered to enter in ward, and they found caution to do so. Five more failed to find caution and were outlawed. Eight supporters of the dissident Catholic earls similarly found caution, and sixteen were outlawed. Some of Bothwell's partisans were later restored. A public appeal was issued (particularly addressed to the church) for support against the threat from Jesuits and Catholic earls. A commission of lieutenancy was issued to three nobles to raise forces against them, and a proclamation announced military musters.

Several decisions were made about the government's limited money. £4,000 was allocated to the queen's 'apparrelling', and £3,000 to the prince's forthcoming baptism. Several burghs, which had received part of the king's tocher (dowry) on loan, repaid it and were issued with discharges; the comptroller and treasurer also received certain discharges over this. A proclamation ordered people to hand in their coins to the mint in exchange for a new coinage recently authorized by parliament.

All these were public matters; there was also private, judicial business. A complicated case involving the fraudulent obtaining of an escheat was resolved by the escheat's cancellation, despite the donator's contention that the lords of session rather than the privy council should be the judges. Several people, including the earl of Orkney, were summoned for alleged spoliation of a Danzig ship. Kenneth Mackenzie of Kintail had his commission of justiciary suspended on the grounds that it had been obtained without the council's consent. Finally, George Home and others, who had violently taken a horse, were ordered to return it.

This last case looks trivial, but it may not have been. The council's increasing willingness to intervene in local feuds was one of the most important ways in which the bloodfeud was brought to an end. The early seventeenth century saw more and more such cases, as the council demonstrated that it offered quick, effective, and relatively impartial redress of wrongs—something that had never been available in the localities. Traditional dispute-settlement by local lords had had virtues, but impartiality had never been one of them. Central state power meant not only powerful offenders like Orkney and Mackenzie being brought to book, but also minor folk like George Home.

The Scottish privy council thus combined in a single body the functions exercised in England by the privy council and the court of star chamber, the latter being the councillors sitting as a court along with the judges. In our period many members of the Scottish council were also judges themselves (in the court of session), so the parallel was remarkably close. In 1610, when the council's membership was reshuffled, the two types of business acquired separate classes of records, known as *acta* and *decreta*.[19] The proclamation of

[19] In Scotland, it was the private business that was moved to the new register, whereas in England it had been the other way round: Scottish Record Office, *Guide to the National Archives*, 22; Elton (ed.), *Tudor Constitution*, 164. For the comparison with star chamber in general, see Wasser, 'Violence and the Central Criminal Courts', 29–30.

the reshuffle also empowered individual councillors to arrest people for 'ryot', which may have introduced this hitherto distinctively English term into Scottish criminal procedure.[20] By 1613, the burghs could argue that the council had no jurisdiction in a particular case, 'in respect the same is foundit upoun the payment of ane soume of money, and not upoun ane fyne for ony ryott', so that the case should be remitted to the 'juge ordinair' (the court of session).[21] As with riot, so with property: like star chamber, the Scottish privy council adjudicated on possession, but not on full legal title. Again like star chamber (but unlike any other Scottish criminal court), it did so without a jury.

One quasi-legal role which it shared with the English privy council (not star chamber) was its investigations into cases of treason. It could summon people before it, and outlaw them if they failed to come. It also interrogated suspects and prepared the crown's case. The one thing it could not do was to convict for treason. Instead it had to send the suspect for trial by jury before the justiciary court, though it could drop strong hints as to the expected verdict.[22] Since treason implied political unacceptability, this role placed the council at the centre of political life.

The large nominal membership of the Scottish privy council, typically between thirty and fifty, has led it to be thought weak or inefficient. The councillors themselves commented in 1607 on 'this kingdome, wherin thair is mo counsellouris nor in England, France, Italie and Spayne'.[23] The same phenomenon in England under Mary Tudor used to be regarded unfavourably, but English historians no longer believe that it was a problem.[24] Business in the Scottish council was usually transacted by an informal inner group consisting mainly of the officers of state, while most of the nominal members attended rarely. This could change in times of political crisis, when more nobles became involved and the council could become the nucleus of informal

---

[20] *RPC* viii. 413–15, 815–16. Riot was analogous to the traditional Scottish offence of convocation of the lieges in arms, and a parallel act of 1598 had employed the term 'convocatioun of his hienes liegis': *APS* iv. 178. Cf. Hope, *Major Practicks*, V.2.26, VI.15.10, possibly the only mentions of 'riot' in this work. It does not seem to occur in Balfour, *Practicks*.

[21] *RPC* x. 191–3, 251. The term was now being used in other courts: e.g. *Court Book of Orkney and Shetland, 1614–1615*, ed. R. S. Barclay (SHS, 1967), 11. By the later 17th c., the privy council's criminal jurisdiction was almost entirely to do with riots: Sir George Mackenzie, *Laws and Customes of Scotland in Matters Criminal* (Edinburgh, 1678), 374–84.

[22] The most famous case of such investigative interrogation is probably that of John Knox in 1563. Knox's detailed account shows that he was not facing a formal indictment for treason, for the case was abandoned before one was ever drawn up: Knox, *History of the Reformation in Scotland*, ii. 90–100. It has also been claimed that the council could impose punishment for treason if the suspect confessed: McNeill, 'The Jurisdiction of the Scottish Privy Council', 33. However, the case cited (*RPC*, 2nd ser. i. 376), does not bear this out. For English practice, see J. Bellamy, *The Tudor Law of Treason* (London, 1979), 104, 118, 122, 167–8.

[23] *RPC* vii. 530. They were arguing that councillors should not have immunity from prosecution, not that a large council was weak.

[24] D. Hoak, 'Two Revolutions in Tudor Government: The Formation and Organization of Mary I's Privy Council', in Coleman and Starkey (eds.), *Revolution Reassessed*.

conventions of the nobility. The last time this happened in earnest was in 1593–4.[25] Perhaps a large privy council was an *advantage* here, facilitating a flexible and inclusive response. In any case, we should not judge the regular structures of government primarily by what happens in a crisis.

The weightiest regular role in the council, after the monarch, was played by the officers of state. The 'quenis officiarris' were emerging as an identifiable group in parliaments by the 1560s at least.[26] The term 'his hienes ordiner officiaris of the estate' was apparently used for the first time in 1579. This did not denote a permanently fixed list, and who was or was not an officer of state remained flexible during our period.[27] The leading officers of state had specific responsibilities, which we might call departmental, for aspects of the administrative system. This is another way in which the Scottish council resembled its English counterpart: the highest executive organ consisted of a single council that coordinated the work of the administrative departments.[28] And as in England, the council was not *sovereign*; sovereignty was exercised by parliament (formally defined as the crown in parliament). It was the job of the council (formally defined as the crown and council) to implement the laws passed in parliament by applying them to individuals.

Scotland's possession of a *single* council is easily taken for granted. Yet things could have been far otherwise. In 1569, a striking programme of administrative reconstruction was set out in a memorandum commissioned by the Regent Moray from his veteran Protestant colleague, Henry Balnaves.[29] Balnaves divided the government's responsibilities into four areas: schools and church, 'the lawis and the ordinarie executioun thairof', military matters, and finance. The regent should appoint a 'minister' for each of these, and also 'cheis twa, thre or four of your previe counsale to mak continewale residence with your grace'. These men should meet every morning in the council chamber. Each of the four ministers should have one day a week to present his department's business. His proposals would be considered by the council, 'ressounit, admittit, or repellit', and if approved the regent should 'put the same be your authoritie in executioun, and that be way of provisioun, to ane parliament'. This would leave two days for 'incident effairis and particular complayntis'. It is unclear what would have happened to the remaining privy councillors. If their services were still required at all, most likely they would have formed councils for each of the ministers. A further point to note

[25] *RPC* v, p. xix (for the crisis period); pp. xix–xx, xxxvi, xlvi, lix–lx, lxxxi–lxxxiv (for frequency of attendance during the 1590s). For more on conventions of the nobility, see Ch. 2 above. For the distinction between the executive business of the council and the legislative business of parliament, see Goodare, 'The Scottish Parliament and its Early Modern "Rivals"'.

[26] Goodare, 'Scottish Political Community'.

[27] For this point and a discussion of the individual offices see *SME* vii. paras. 789–818.

[28] For the officers and departments, see Ch. 7 below.

[29] HMC, *Sixth Report, Appendix* (London, 1877), 645. The author is unnamed but was evidently one of the non-noble privy councillors at Elgin, 24 June 1569 (*RPC* i. 673), and an old associate of Moray's. This points clearly to Balnaves.

is that Balnaves envisaged a major role for parliament in ratifying the council's daily business.

This scheme would have caused fragmentation of the privy council, as departmental ministers ceased to meet regularly with one another. A greater weight of responsibility would have fallen on the regent personally (and later on the king), and the likely beneficiaries would have been courtiers outside the administration but with the regent's ear. This is more or less what happened in Spain and in several other monarchies. Philip II had separate councils, as in the Balnaves model, for each department or project, and communicated with them by letter, using the royal secretaries as intermediaries. He himself and the secretaries (who were clerical staff rather than policy-makers) were thus the only coordinating authorities for the government.[30] Philip did all his own paperwork and took his own decisions, but his successors handed these tasks over to favourites who seemed more able to handle them.

Balnaves's scheme had been commissioned by Moray himself, so why it was not implemented is unclear. One likely explanation is that Moray's regime began to come apart at the seams in late 1569, and energy for restructuring the administration was in short supply.[31] The council itself could have been altered easily enough, but Balnaves's four ministries cut completely across existing departmental boundaries, and disentangling them would have been a lengthy and complex task. So the unitary privy council survived.

Instead of the fragmentation planned in 1569, the Scottish privy council later began to sprout subcommittees (usually known as commissions) to help it deal with the increasing volume of its business. An early commission, to investigate a dispute in St Andrews, was set up in 1586.[32] The king's absence in Denmark in the winter of 1589–90 echoed the traditional pattern whereby royal minorities fostered conciliar rule, and the council set up a further such commission then.[33] The former view that a 'general commission' or 'standing commissions' were established for trying witchcraft in October 1591 has recently been modified to show that the commission established then was another such temporary body.[34]

Chancellor Maitland, whose appetite for administrative reform may lie behind much of this activity, was probably responsible for an attempt to

[30] M. J. Rodríguez-Salgado, 'The Court of Philip II of Spain', in R. G. Asch and A. M. Birke (eds.), *Princes, Patronage and the Nobility: The Court at the Beginning of the Modern Age, c.1450–1650* (Oxford, 1991), 222–6. There was a council of state, but it met rarely and was not influential. For the general European tendency towards multiplication of councils, see P. M. Ribalta, 'The Impact of Central Institutions', in Reinhard (ed.), *Power Elites and State Building*, 24.

[31] Moray to Cecil, n.d. [Oct. 1569], and Drury to Cecil, 5 Nov. 1569, *CSP Scot.* ii. 698–9.

[32] *RPC* iv. 42–4.

[33] It was issued on 11 Jan. 1590, 'gevin under our signet and subscryvit be our counsell in our name': NAS, GD149/265, part 2, fos. 1ʳ–10ʳ.

[34] J. Goodare, 'The Framework for Scottish Witch-Hunting in the 1590s', *SHR* 81 (2002), 240–50.

create a permanent council subcommittee. In June 1590, one month after the king and Maitland returned from Denmark, a commission was set up to deal with Border and Highland affairs, along the lines of a statute of 1587 which had called for special monthly meetings of the council on the matter. The commission's membership was similar to that of the full council, but took care to include those with experience of Border affairs, and had a separate register for its business. The special council itself met regularly for only six months, but continued in existence, transacting occasional business, until at least 1599. It raised official pressure on the region, and this pressure was never to be lifted. Much more Border (and some Highland) business was transacted by the regular council, and recorded (often more than once a month) in the special register.[35] A new standing commission on the Isles was established early in 1608, and continued until at least 1623.[36]

Permanent commissions never became common, but in the early seventeenth century the council began to appoint a stream of temporary commissions, usually for fact-finding and for processing the initial stages of some business or other. Thus the archbishop of St Andrews and six others (five of whom were not councillors) investigated a dispute within the university in 1607; a high-powered commission heard complaints against the earl of Orkney in 1609.[37] As the council's business swelled, it became increasingly sophisticated in delegating it.

In 1621, another form of restructuring was tried. James created a ten-member cabinet council within the privy council because of the 'exceeding grite nomber' of councillors. It was a mixture of leading officers of state and trusted courtier nobles, who were to be 'imployed in oure most weyghtie affairis' and called to a 'more strict attendance'. But the cabinet council did not take root. At most it seems to have formed a body giving informal leadership to the full council. Although the full council's effective, regular membership was not necessarily much more than ten, it was that body alone which made substantive decisions.[38]

The conclusion should be that the privy council's strength was its flexibility as a single united body—as it was in England too.[39] None of the attempts to vary the formula came to anything permanent; there was no fragmentation of councils. To speak of an *esprit de corps* might be going beyond what the records, mostly severe and formal, will allow; but the councillors certainly developed a sense of their collective responsibility for government. They did not normally disagree in public, for instance; that was part of what it meant

[35] *APS* iii. 461, c. 59, para 1; Rae, *Administration of the Scottish Frontier*, 127–9; *RPC* iv. 781–814; v. 733–48.   [36] *RPC* viii. 737–61.

[37] *RPC* vii. 332–3; viii. 299–300. Other such commissions can be traced in the indexes to *RPC*, s.v. commission (though many commissions listed there are not of this nature).

[38] Cabinet councillors to James, 29 Nov. 1621, *Melros Papers*, ii. 434–5; *RPC* xii. 604; Taylor, 'Scottish Privy Council', 10–12.

[39] There were no permanent committees of the English privy council either before the 1630s: K. Sharpe, *The Personal Rule of Charles I* (New Haven, 1992), 269.

to be a 'secret' council. Of course they argued freely around the council table, and sometimes their disagreements spilled over into the public view, becoming faction struggles. This can happen with modern Cabinets too, which also have collective responsibility. Conflict, though, was exceptional. It is cohesive cooperation which is most striking about normal relations between councillors.

As well as councillors' relationship with one another, they had a relationship with the monarch. The privy council's importance derived fundamentally from its close links with the monarch. When we speak of the powers of the crown, or of the royal prerogative, we often mean powers that were wielded by the monarch in consultation with the privy council. Sometimes, indeed, the privy council wielded the prerogative itself, taking decisions on its own authority. All government was done ultimately in the name of the crown, but the precise position of the monarch in the administrative process needs careful attention.[40]

It was absolutely essential that monarch and privy council should have a good working relationship. There were often disputes within Scottish governments, but serious disputes between monarch and entire council are conspicuous by their absence. Sir James Melville in 1588 'fand not sic ernestnes with the consaill as with the king' for a Danish marriage;[41] but no more is heard of the dispute. This contrasts strikingly with the frequently expressed royal dissatisfaction with parliaments, still more with general assemblies. The privy council, as much as the crown—together with the crown—*was* the government, or at least the daily central government. Crown and privy council had a consensual relationship. Neither Mary nor James VI ever disagreed strongly or for long with their privy councils. The one exception to this was the final six weeks of Mary's reign in June–July 1567, when after her enforced marriage to Bothwell the privy council was captured by an anti-Bothwell noble coalition. It undertook numerous proceedings (including the issue of a printed proclamation) against him and his adherents, as well as routine governmental measures.[42] Even this really represents factional struggle within the government, since Bothwell still had supporters; but the capture of the privy council represented a significant stage in the final defeat of his faction.

To say that there was consensus between monarch and privy council is not to say that the monarch controlled the privy council, so that the councillors became marionettes dancing to the royal tune, as has sometimes been argued for James VI.[43] The most obvious evidence of royal initiative and control comes after 1603, in the many royal letters instructing the council to do this or that, which the council then did. But did the king write the letters as well as

---

[40] For the powers of the crown generally, see Ch. 4 above.   [41] Melville, *Memoirs*, 365.
[42] *RPC* i. 519–31; *CSP Scot.* ii. 531–2.
[43] Notably by Taylor, 'Scottish Privy Council', 1 and *passim*.

signing them? It is often assumed that he did, and this forms the basis for many further assumptions about royal power and personal monarchy. However, it is inherently improbable that a king like James would personally have undertaken the drudgery of writing official letters, and there is evidence that he did not. We can learn much about decision-making processes from seeing how official documents were drafted.

Lord Napier, in his memoirs, gave copies of three letters from King Charles to the council in 1628, setting in motion a royal visit to Scotland and ordering the council to entrust Napier with various responsibilities. Had we merely had these letters in the council register, we might have agreed that the initiative came from the king: it would have seemed that he issued the orders, and the council implemented them. But Napier also related that the project was *his* idea, and that the king rejected it. The letters, drafted by Napier, were neither signed nor sent; they never reached the council register. The king decided not to embark on a visit. Even that decision was not an autonomous royal initiative; Charles acted on the advice of the treasurer, the earl of Mar, which he preferred to Napier's.[44]

To take the example of some letters that *were* sent: Chancellor Dunfermline, receiving two royal letters to the council in 1614, protested that

I am certane thir lettirs has neiver bein directed be his majestie as thay ar wrettin, nor his majestie wald neiver have signed thame, gif thay had bein red to his majestie . . . for thay ar direct aganist our law, forme and practic, and by all rason and in greate pairt foundit upon ontreuth.[45]

The suggestion that James was likely to sign documents without reading them at all may have been tendentious—Dunfermline would otherwise have had to imply that the king knew that he was signing letters 'direct against our law, forme and practic'. But Dunfermline clearly thought that the suggestion carried credibility. Once the question is agreed to be whether James routinely *read* his official correspondence or not, the question of whether he routinely *wrote* it is less likely to arise.[46]

So routine government was carried out in the king's name by his councillors. One of them, Sir Thomas Hamilton, made a revealing emendation in a letter to James in 1615. He first wrote, 'I have caused set downe ane act of counsall of the declaration of your majesties counsall . . .', but then changed the last phrase to 'your majesties will'.[47] Whether James knew that the act was his will before he read this seems unlikely. The appearance of personal

[44] *Memorials of Montrose and his Times*, 2 vols., ed. M. Napier (Maitland Club, 1848), i. 37–8.

[45] Dunfermline to Lord Burntisland, 21 June 1614, W. Fraser, *The Melvilles, Earls of Melville, and the Leslies, Earls of Leven*, 3 vols. (Edinburgh, 1890), ii. 75.

[46] For the letters that James did write, see G. G. Simpson, 'The Personal Letters of James VI: A Short Commentary', in Goodare and Lynch (eds.), *The Reign of James VI*.

[47] NLS, Hamilton to James, 6 Apr. [1615], Denmylne MSS, Adv. MS 33.1.1, vol. vi, no. 27.

government by the king had to be preserved, but the king operated within the options set by his ministers.

One of the reasons for this was that so much governmental activity required legal expertise. James knew some law, but he had no reason to become involved in the details; that was one of the things that councillors were for. His naive fondness for Danish legal procedure, in which he believed that 'a man stands up and reads the law, and there is an end, for the very law-booke it selfe is their onely judge', would not have been shared by trained lawyers.[48] In 1617, Hamilton (now Lord Binning) advised James delicately that a draft proclamation imposing the death penalty on those interceding on behalf of forfeited traitors might be unwise (he meant illegal). He returned it to the king and 'framed the substance of ane proclamation which I send heirwith to your majestie to be sene at your gude laiser and directed to be amended whair your majestie findis any thing to be added, paired or altered'. Instead of death, the penalty of 'incurring his heyghnes heigh and havye displeasour' was substituted.[49] James was not the puppeteer in this case: Hamilton was.

The privy council could do things on its own account, without the monarch; it needed only to be able to use the monarch's name. In 1586, the council struck down a royal letter allowing the resetting of certain outlawed persons. The letter had been 'purchest outwith counsall . . . to stop the ordinare forme of executioun of the lawis', and lacked the subscription of the 'ordinare officiar to quhome sic thingis propirlie appertenis'.[50] The king was not present to approve this overruling of his authority. Of course, both Mary and James attended their councils periodically, probably when more important decisions were needed—although King James's remarkably assiduous attendance between 1595 and 1603 should not be taken as a norm. Before 1603, the council's private acts usually ran in its name alone. Public acts might be by council alone, monarch alone, or occasionally monarch with council's advice; usually, however, the act was silent as to whose authority was being deployed. The monarch's presence or absence made no difference to this. Government by a unitary privy council was government that could use, but did not require, the active participation of the monarch.

After 1603, the council had to do things without the monarch all the time. When the king went south, he left the council with powers to do a number of extra things: to appoint a lieutenant to command armed forces; to order the treasurer to pay out money; to receive resignations of royal lands and offices, and make new grants of them; and to issue commissions to exchequer auditors. These had hitherto been matters 'to the quhilk our awin authoritie and command wes requisite, the counsall haveing na farder thairin bot to obey our will'.[51] This was true in theory but not in practice, which is

---

[48] James VI & I, speech in star chamber, 1616, in *Political Writings*, 212.
[49] NLS, Binning to James, 1 and 6 May 1617, Denmylne MSS, Adv. MS 33.1.1, vol. viii, nos. 18, 20; *RPC* xi. 122.
[50] *RPC* iv. 118–19.   [51] *RPC* vi. 558–60.

why James's departure caused so little disturbance to the routine of the executive.

How did the physical location of monarch and privy council affect their relationship? Traditionally, Scottish monarchs spent part of their time in Edinburgh and Holyrood, part of it in palaces not too far away like Linlithgow and Falkland, and part of it travelling round the country. Usually they kept their council with them. The council may thus have been away from its records and some of its staff, and a royal progress typically reduced the quantity of council business. However, much of that business would relate to the royal errand to the region concerned, so it was probably worth doing. Sixteenth-century Scotland was a decentralized place, and some governing had to be done on the spot.[52] As well as these official progresses, there were royal holidays and hunting trips, in which the council was not involved; it remained in session in Edinburgh.

On at least one occasion the privy council divided itself, amoeba-like, into two separate organisms. In 1598, the king went on a military expedition to the west and took the privy council with him. Lord Seton, meanwhile, was deputed to remain in Edinburgh with whatever councillors and lords of session and exchequer he could collect, for the purpose of dealing with the private (but not public) business of the council.[53]

The arrangements made in 1589 for the king's absence in Denmark can be seen with hindsight as a trial run for what happened after 1603.[54] James committed the government to the privy council, and gave it a president, because the chancellor was going with him. In case that was not enough, he charged the 'baronis and landitmen' of Lothian, Fife, Stirlingshire, and Strathearn to take turns attending in Edinburgh to assist the council. Lord Hamilton was put in charge of the Borders and given a separate council, which could also combine with the privy council if major decisions were needed. James took the signet and great seal with him to Denmark, so temporary duplicates were made (an arrangement not repeated after 1603,

---

[52] e.g. *RPC* i. 216–23 (Mary's progress to Aberdeen and Inverness in 1562); *RPC* vi. 292–300 (James's progress to Brechin in 1600). Most of what is said here about monarchs applies also to the regents who governed during James's minority.

[53] *RPC* v. 477–86. For what may have been a similar arrangement in 1602, although decisions were registered only from one group of councillors, see *RPC* vi. 451–6. Something similar had been projected for Mary's progress to the north in 1562, when a rota of councillors was planned to 'mak continewale residence with hir grace', the rest presumably remaining in Edinburgh. In the event, more councillors came with her, possibly all of them, and there is no trace of a second council in Edinburgh: *RPC* i. 216–23. The registration of one meeting 'Apud Edinburgh' during this period (p. 220) is probably an error for Aberdeen. In Dec.–Jan. 1581–2 there was a temporary schism in the council between the supporters of the duke of Lennox, meeting in Dalkeith, and those of the earl of Arran, meeting in Edinburgh and Holyrood. Although the king joined Lennox's group, it was Arran's which had the registers and got its decisions (or at least some of them) recorded: *RPC* iii. 435–9.

[54] It would be interesting to know whether they were so seen at the time, but James and his councillors had to be discreet on the subject during Elizabeth's lifetime.

when the seals remained in Edinburgh). Documents concerning the revenue that normally needed the king's signature could be signed by the treasurer and treasurer depute.[55] Some of these arrangements may have been unnecessarily elaborate; there is no evidence of attendance by regional 'baronis and landitmen', and Hamilton's council was not invited to join the privy council. Conciliar administration worked, and was seen to have done so.[56]

The advantages of a known, fixed residence and ready access to records and staff began gradually to outweigh the advantages of presence at a trouble spot. This may explain why the restless wanderings of medieval monarchs ground to a halt all over Europe in the sixteenth and seventeenth centuries, as their successors immured themselves in vast central palaces like the Escorial or Versailles. The Scottish privy council's wanderings ceased in 1603, when it no longer had to attend on the king and so fixed itself permanently in Edinburgh. It did not relocate itself to Wick to deal with the Orkney rebellion of 1614, although that might have been a likely sixteenth-century thing to do. Instead it remained in the capital and generated an avalanche of paperwork to suppress the rebellion.[57] This, not the council's correspondence with the king, was the real 'government by pen'.

And there was still only one privy council. Not only did it not move to London, but no second council for Scottish affairs was established there. If either of these things had happened, the logical next step would have been to send a viceroy to Scotland to supervise the daily administration, breaking the direct link between council and monarch. This might well have worked, and indeed was more common in a European context than the Scottish arrangement. Barcelona was about the same distance from Madrid by post (four days) as Edinburgh was from London. But Catalonia had a viceroy, so that the government on the spot was kept at arm's length from decision-making by the Council of Aragon in Madrid. The viceroy played a dual role, being the government's representative in the province and the province's representative at the centre, and trying to juggle Madrid's desire for more government and Barcelona's desire for less.[58] Scotland's government by a unitary king-and-council prevented this, as the Scots were well aware. A 'conquered and slavishe province to be governed by a viceroy or deputye, lyke

---

[55] *RPC* iv. 422–30.

[56] In 1536–7, by contrast, James V's nine-month absence in France had led to the appointment of six 'vicegerents and lieutenants', who were not designated as a council or as councillors: *RMS* iii. 1618; Cameron, *James V*, 133.

[57] See some of it in NLS, Denmylne MSS, Adv. MS 33.1.1, vol. v.

[58] J. H. Elliott, *The Revolt of the Catalans: A Study in the Decline of Spain, 1598–1640* (Cambridge, 1963), 12, ch. 4. Not only were there no Spanish-style viceroys, there were not even any French-style provincial governors. Such a governor was not in charge of a fully autonomous province, but he can be described as 'the king's alter ego, replacing the person of the king in his absence'. He also had to maintain his own representatives at the royal court in order to keep up channels of communication. D. Potter, *War and Government in the French Provinces: Picardy, 1470–1560* (Cambridge, 1993), 97, 107–8.

suche of the king of Spaynes provinceis' was what they did not want to become.[59]

Scotland's unusual position was not established deliberately in 1603. The king expected a rapid move towards complete union with England. In the meantime, several other possible configurations of authority could have been established, most involving the bicephalous solution of a council for Scottish affairs in England alongside the council in Edinburgh. James in July 1603 took formal advice from 'sik of our privie counsall of Scotland as ar heir resident with us'. Sir John Skene in about 1608–10 thought that 'sick counsellours (Scottishmen) as shall happen to be with his majestie present in England' could and perhaps should advise the king on Scottish patronage grants. In 1619 the Scottish privy council was said to be seeking information from 'the lords of his majesties Scottis counsell in England'.[60] None of these configurations was adopted for regular use.

One of the reasons why a Scottish council in London never became formalized may have been that there were alternatives, involving members of the English privy council. The English council contained several Scotsmen, and on occasion they met separately to discuss Scottish business. In 1607, they interrogated some of the supporters of the unauthorized Aberdeen general assembly.[61] A yet more striking alternative surfaced briefly in 1609, when the king wanted an offence by a Scottish courtier in England investigated by 'my lords of his privy council mixed of both nations'.[62] All these episodes, like much else to do with the union of crowns, have an ad hoc quality to them. The arrangement that endured was the one that happened to work; the alternatives offered fewer benefits and were not pursued.

If we insist on locating the 'centre' of power geographically—a project of limited value, as was argued in the previous chapter—then this suggests that power remained in Edinburgh, subject to constant correspondence with a king who was elsewhere. This has often been described as 'absentee monarchy', but that is misleading. The expression 'absentee monarchy' conflates two separate issues: that of *dual* monarchy, and that of the internal government of Scotland when the king was living elsewhere. Dual monarchy was an issue because James had to juggle two separate countries and make sure they did not conflict or diverge. He periodically did things in Scotland because of what the English wanted, and occasionally succeeded in creating 'British' structures to transcend the separation of the two polities. This was sometimes important—indeed, it could be important to both polities. James's choice to

---

[59] Parliament to James, Aug. 1607, *RPC* vii. 536. The Scots probably had Ireland in mind here, but it would not have been tactful to say so. Cf. Goodare, 'Scotland's Parliament in its British Context', 25–30.

[60] *RPC* vi. 582; A. L. Murray, 'Sir John Skene and the Exchequer', 152; *RCRB* iii. 75.

[61] J. Morrill, 'The Formation of Britain', in S. G. Ellis and S. Barber (eds.), *Conquest and Union: Fashioning a British State, 1485–1725* (London, 1995), 24–5.

[62] Sir Thomas Lake to Salisbury, 18 Nov. 1609, HMC, *Salisbury*, xxi. 159. Whether the investigation took place is unclear. I am grateful to Professor Conrad Russell for this reference.

live in the southernmost of the polities was sometimes relevant to this, although perhaps not as vital as is sometimes assumed. But dual monarchy is not the subject of the present chapter.[63]

What matters here is how the daily executive government of Scotland was configured. Here, much less changed in 1603. King and privy council still took, and issued, consensual decisions. They no longer reached those decisions through discussions round the same council table, but they had not always done so before 1603; even then, James never attended *all* council meetings. They had had other media for those discussions: informal conversations with individual councillors in other places, or sometimes correspondence. Those media—established media, it must be noted—were the ones that came to dominate after 1603. Because the king was four hundred miles away, it is sometimes assumed that he was impossibly remote, but the post took only four days as a rule. Very few issues were so pressing that they could not wait a week and a half for an exchange of letters; the council itself met only every three days or so. While most of James's communication with his privy councillors was by post, he sometimes used councillors like the earl of Dunbar who were prepared to travel regularly between England and Scotland—what Maurice Lee has called 'government by visitation'.[64] Even Dunbar took royal letters with him, so this was still to some extent communication by post. It was certainly still government by the privy council.

In short, it is not clear that a king who communicates regularly with his councillors by post is ever truly 'absent'. Philip II did so even in governing Castile, from which he is not usually described as an 'absentee'; even in the Escorial his effective communications with ministers were by letter, not in person. He was also away from the Escorial for about half the year on average, but he was still not an 'absentee'—because his paperwork went with him. He even claimed to do more work when away, because he had to give fewer audiences.[65] If James VI in about 1603 had taken up residence in Inverness or Dumbarton, keeping the seat of government in Edinburgh and corresponding regularly with his council, historians might have thought it an unusual arrangement but they would probably not have labelled it 'absentee monarchy'. Perhaps we should write less about absentee monarchy and more about postal monarchy.

One aspect of the council's relationship with the monarch was its relationship with the people around the monarch. The system of personal monarchy,

---

[63] The effect of England and of 'Britain' on Scottish government is discussed in Ch. 2 above, in Goodare, *State and Society*, 242–9, and in id., 'Scotland's Parliament in its British context'.

[64] Lee, *Government by Pen*, 62. James's phrase 'government by pen' did not mean correspondence between Edinburgh and London; he was drawing a contrast with government by the sword. For the postal system see W. Taylor, 'The King's Mails, 1603–1625', *SHR* 42 (1963), 143–7.

[65] Rodríguez-Salgado, 'Court of Philip II', 216–19, 225–6.

discussed in Chapter 4 above, did not mean that the king did everything himself; it implied a political system in which those who governed did so with royal sanction alone. Conciliar government could be as much part of this system as government through the royal household. Nevertheless, we need to consider the role of the household, from which the council was kept—or kept itself—at arm's length. This role might be important in any area where the monarch was personally important, and in practice the influence of the household was probably greatest when it came to the royal signature.

'Signatures' were documents that were authorized to pass the privy seal or great seal or both.[66] These included grants of lands, offices, and money, commissions of justiciary and lieutenancy, and licences to do various normally forbidden things (from eating meat in Lent to exporting prohibited goods). 'Signatures' meant what they said: the monarch had to sign them. Since Mary or James could not know the detailed circumstances of each signature, they had to have good advice. Privy councillors and officers of state tended to think that the most trustworthy advice was available from them, but they were not constantly around to give it. The people who *were* around the monarch were the members of the royal household. James VI spent a lot of time with the gentlemen of his chamber, and thought himself able to judge whether they were trustworthy.[67] If one of them gave him a piece of paper and asked him to sign it, it is understandable that he often did so. Equally understandable is the sometimes adverse reaction of the officer of state on whose desk the paper landed next.

There were two ways in which signatures could be controversial. Was it appropriate that this person should receive the grant at all? And if so, had they paid a suitable fee for it? The grant of royal lands might not be a problem to anyone if the crown received value for money, while most licences to export prohibited goods were simply a means of regulating trade. The important question was how much the crown received for them in 'composition', or agreed fee.[68] On the other hand, the questions with a commission of justiciary were not fiscal ones: they were whether a crime had in fact been committed, whether there was a case against the suspect, and whether the commission's recipient was a fit person to convene a criminal court to try the suspect.

There were also two ways for an officer of state to block an inappropriate signature: before it had been signed, or after. The seals existed partly to provide a check on what the monarch had signed. Probably an officer could always object to a signature, though evidence is available mainly for the period after 1603 when the objection had to be made by post.[69] But it was obviously

---

[66] Certain documents (notably infeftments of heirs in lands) could pass the seals without a signature.

[67] Cf. Juhala, 'Household and Court of James VI', 32–5 and ch. 3.

[68] This is discussed in detail by Murray, 'Treasury Administration', pp. xxiii–xxiv.

[69] See Dunfermline's letter of 21 June 1614, quoted above. An objection by the treasurer in 1580 was heard by the privy council, which decided in favour of the grantee—but at least the

preferable to intercept signatures before they had been signed, which meant making the officers of state the sole channel by which signatures could reach the monarch.

Such a position was achieved, at least in theory, at the outset of our period. In 1561, in one of its earliest acts under Mary's personal rule, the privy council ordained that all signatures should be presented to the queen by the treasurer, a rule which seems tacitly to have been modified to require presentation by the officer of state to whom the business appertained (usually treasurer, comptroller, or secretary).[70] Thereafter, this rule was probably adhered to— as a rule. But there were exceptions, sometimes frequent exceptions, and it was these which the privy council sought periodically to eliminate. It took the view that there was something inherently surreptitious, and thus probably scandalous, about a signature that bypassed the normal channels. This may have been unfair to some recipients, who may have fully deserved their grant but who saw no reason not to take advantage of a court connection that would help to ensure that they received it. With other grants the council's view was probably only too accurate. At any rate, the conflict of interest between council and household periodically erupted into bitter struggles for the royal signature.[71]

After 1598, and still more after 1603, the struggles between council and household faded. The king could not take a regular part in the administration after he left for England, and a cashet was made—a metal stamp with his signature. This was committed to one of the leading councillors, the future Chancellor Dunfermline, with instructions to use it only under the council's supervision.[72] An elaborate procedure developed, firmly under the control of treasurer and exchequer, for preparing documents to be casheted.[73] James could still sign things himself, but this caused fewer controversies. The political system was becoming more stable after about 1598, so there were fewer struggles over *anything*. James probably signed fewer Scottish documents after 1603, and the council was probably in a better position to block inappropriate grants even after he had signed them. Conflict between

council was able to discuss the matter: *RPC* iii. 312–13. It was important to keep the course of the seals functioning, so that grants would not pass unexamined. In 1566, the court of session ordered a writer to the chancery not to pass royal signatures through the great seal unless they had previously passed the signet and privy seal: *Acts of Sederunt*, 9.

[70] *RPC* i. 160. This may perhaps explain why registers of signatures are extant for the comptroller from 1561, and for the treasurer from 1563: Scottish Record Office, *Guide*, 31. However, Murray, 'Treasury Administration', p. xxi, suggests that such registers could have existed earlier.

[71] Goodare, *State and Society*, 110–13.

[72] The cashet was initially held by a courtier, Sir Patrick Murray, but it was taken from him after only three months: *RPC* vi. 560, 579. Cf. *APS* iv. 440, c. 21, for a ratification of the council's control in 1609. Dunfermline kept the cashet until his death: NLS, Melrose to Murray of Lochmaben, 19 June [1622], Denmylne MSS, Adv. MS 33.1.1, vol. ix, no. 9. Some kind of cashet existed before 1603, though the circumstances of its use are unclear: for forgery of a 'kingis stamp' in 1587, see *Trials*, ed. Pitcairn, i, II. 157–8.

[73] Sir Thomas Hope, *Minor Practicks*, ed. J. Spotiswood (Edinburgh, 1734), 290–5.

household and council also lessened when, after the chamber politicians ousted the Octavians in 1598, they came *out* of the chamber. Sir George Home of Spott and Sir David Murray of Gospertie, who became treasurer and comptroller at this time, are prominent examples of this trend.[74] Instead of frustrating the administrators behind the scenes, they became administrators themselves.

So far we have considered the privy council's relationship with the monarch, and with the royal household. Its relationship with the nobility is also relevant. If behind the influence of the monarch might stand the gentlemen of the chamber, then behind *them* might stand the magnates whose relatives they often were. After 1603, when the bonanza of pensions and other patronage for nobles got under way, the quest for largesse had to begin at the royal court and not with the privy council, despite the latter's role in coordinating fiscal policy.[75]

The magnates also had direct influence, notably in the way that the council was appointed. In England, the 1530s saw a transition from a council broadly representative of the political nation to one created by the monarch alone.[76] The older representative tradition continued longer in Scotland, displayed in the repeated need for the council's membership to be established or confirmed in parliament. Conceivably the statutes on the subject might have been rubber stamps for decisions taken elsewhere. But when parliament did not *generally* act as a rubber stamp for the government, there is no direct reason to infer that it would have done so when it came to appointing the council. Parliament continued periodically to endorse the privy council up to 1598.[77] The council after that looked similar, and only minute inspection of its membership could establish conclusively how much had changed; no doubt the monarch always played an important role in the council's appointment. Still, it is unlikely that if James had had a completely free hand before 1598 he would have tolerated the presence of the master of Glamis, who remained on the council until he was elbowed aside by the Octavians in 1596. He had been *persona non grata* with the king since the Ruthven Raid, fourteen years before, but had a strikingly active parliamentary record, serving on many parliamentary commissions.[78]

After 1598, noble privy councillors had to be committed royal supporters, trusted by James personally. They did not disappear; the Scottish privy council was never whittled down to the tiny core of dedicated administrators

[74] Goodare, 'Scottish Politics in the Reign of James VI', 42.
[75] Goodare, 'The Nobility and the Absolutist State', 170–4; Cuddy, 'Revival of the Entourage'. The Scottish chamber was transmuted in 1603 into the English bedchamber, staffed largely by Scots.
[76] J. Guy, 'The King's Council and Political Participation', in A. Fox and J. Guy (eds.), *Reassessing the Henrician Age* (Oxford, 1986).
[77] For this and other points about royal and parliamentary power, see Ch. 4 above.
[78] Nicolson to Bowes, 14 June 1595, *CSP Scot.* xi. 609; James to Sir Thomas Hamilton, 6 May 1599, *Melros Papers*, i. 1.

seen in England in the later years of Elizabeth.[79] Instead the nobles continued to attend infrequently, while the dedicated Scottish administrators got on with the work. The only nobles to be found as working councillors were recently created lords of erection.[80] The boundaries of the privy council nevertheless remained permeable, so that the leading nobles could feel that they were able to penetrate into it. One commentator in 1610 thought that 'the haill nobillittie . . . had ever beine borne counsallouris'.[81] This, although not strictly correct, was plausible. The absolutist state was always an aristocratic one. But like the king himself, the nobility now had to work with and through an established executive organ of central government supervising a range of administrative departments. Those departments call for their own investigation.

[79] L. L. Peck, 'Peers, Patronage and the Politics of History', in J. Guy (ed.), *The Reign of Elizabeth I: Court and Culture in the Last Decade* (Cambridge, 1995), 92–3.

[80] *RPC* v, pp. lxxxi–lxxxiv; Taylor, 'Scottish Privy Council', 13. The 'lords of erection' were new peers whose titles and estates were based ('erected') upon secularized monasteries.

[81] *A Chronicle of the Kings of Scotland*, ed. J. W. Mackenzie (Maitland Club, 1830), 179.

CHAPTER SEVEN

Officers and Departments

The quyet, happie and weill governed estait of this your majesteis native and ancient kingdome: the caussis quhairoff, nixt your majesteis most rair and princelie wisdome in directing so wyslie everie thing tending to the wniversall weill of ws all, I can not in my simpill judgment bot ascrybe the same to the fidelitie and cair of your majesteis principall officiaris and servandis in quhome so vorthely ye haif satlit the burdene of the affairis.[1]

This chapter explores the administrative structure of central government. Without some understanding of this, we will never grasp how early modern Scotland was governed. The last chapter showed the privy council developing in the later sixteenth century into a body with a general executive competence from which no area of government was excluded. Much of the council's importance derived from the fact that its core membership, like the modern Cabinet, comprised the officers of state, who supervised the departments that actually delivered the governing. This chapter discusses those departments, how they were governed, and how they governed.

Today, not all Cabinet ministers are in charge of major departments; nor are all large government offices headed by a minister of Cabinet rank. So we must not expect things to be any tidier in early modern times. There was often a link between important ministers and important departments, but not always. Some of the important officers of state lacked a 'department' and instead functioned interdepartmentally, either because they were basically political leaders rather than specialized administrators, or else because their administrative duties required them to work with more than one department.

The term 'department' itself has to be construed broadly, and includes some bodies over which the control of the privy council and officers of state was indirect. There were indeed straightforward executive departments with officers of state in charge, like the treasury. But we will also encounter less obviously council-driven bodies like the court of session—which administered private law rather than executing official policy—and the general assembly—which certainly made and executed policy, but which had a more distant and sometimes difficult relationship with the crown. Yet the court of session, if not directly council-driven, operated very much in tandem with the council

---

[1] NLS, Sir Robert Melville of Murdochcairny to James, n.d. [c.1609], Denmylne MSS, Adv. MS 33.1.1, vol. iii, no. 44.

simply because their memberships overlapped, in the later part of the reign of James VI becoming almost the same. As for the general assembly: parliament laid down a framework of ecclesiastical law within which it had to operate, and the crown, via the council, did supervise the assembly and exercise influence in it which usually prevailed. The theory of 'two kingdoms', with assembly and parliament as independent and parallel bodies, was an aspiration by the opposition rather than a reality practised by those actually in power in the church.

Because bodies like the court of session and general assembly had a degree of autonomy, they could formulate their own policy proposals and put them before parliament. They have been seen doing so in Chapter 2, when they were considered as lobbyists seeking to influence the policy of central government. The role of the court of session in lobbying for legislative change is an important aspect of the way it functioned in governing. Here, however, another side of these bodies' work is considered: their executive role, in which they implemented the policies once made. In doing so they coercively influenced aspects of the lives of those subordinate to them.

The link between government ministers and departments can immediately be qualified so far as concerns the first minister, the chancellor. He had formal precedence over all other officers of state, and his post was in practice one of the three most important ones in our period.[2] His department, the chancery, was responsible for the great seal. Its main function was to process the inheritance of land titles and the confirmation of land transfers between subjects, an important but largely mechanical task. New royal grants (many of which were in practice sales) of land and of some other rights also had to pass the seal. Even here, most chancery business was routine, since the real decision to make a grant was taken elsewhere. In medieval times, some important judicial procedures had been initiated by brieves from chancery, but these were superseded when the court of session rose to dominance in the early sixteenth century.[3] Important great seal documents first had to pass the privy seal, the keeper of which was usually a privy councillor, though the privy seal office was in itself even more humdrum.[4] The chancery's administration was managed by the director of chancery, a lesser official, who rarely made news unless he or his subordinates were accused of charging inordinate fees. Little responsibility seems to have been borne by the chancellor.[5]

---

[2] To some extent, offices were what their holders made of them, but the lists of chancellors, secretaries, and treasurers do contain almost all the top-ranking politicians of our period. For lists of officers of state see E. B. Fryde et al. (eds.), *Handbook of British Chronology* (3rd edn., Royal Historical Society, 1986), 179–204. The main scholarly account of them is in *SME* vii. paras. 789–800. Some scattered further information, including officers less important than those discussed here, is gathered by Walker, *A Legal History of Scotland*, iii: *The Sixteenth Century*, 126–38.

[3] A. L. Murray, 'Scottish Chancery'.

[4] For the keepership of the privy seal when the office was at the height of its influence, see Sanderson, *Cardinal of Scotland*, 51–3.

[5] Balfour, *Practicks*, ii. 644–55. The director of chancery was appointed by the crown, not the chancellor: Chalmers, 'King's Council', 33–5. For a complaint against him see *Aberdeen Letters*,

The chancellor himself was important in roles that were basically political rather than administrative. His key responsibility was to preside at meetings of the privy council. He could also preside at meetings of the court of session if he chose to attend, but he rarely if ever did, and the chair was taken by the lord president.[6] Some chancellors in our period had legal training enabling them to act as judges, but most did not. King James even left the chancellorship vacant between 1595 and 1599, showing that the office was not administratively vital. In England the chancellor was becoming the head of the judiciary (and thus losing some political significance), but this did not happen in Scotland, perhaps for lack of a court of chancery. The chancellor also took the chair in parliament, but most parliamentary debates were held outside the chamber, often in meetings of individual estates, rather than under his formal supervision.[7]

The secretary was the second of the really prestigious officers. He too was intimately connected with the privy council: he was responsible for its records, and was expected to be present at all meetings if possible. His duties were comparable to those of his English counterpart—a comparison that was drawn at the time between William Maitland of Lethington and Sir William Cecil.[8] The secretary had to be well educated, a requirement not applied to all officers of state. He probably prepared the council's agenda before meetings, and supervised most of the subsequent paperwork. From time to time there was also a secretary depute.[9] The council's own records were dealt with by the council clerk. Administrative orders of the council were issued either (in the form of warrants) by the keeper of the signet, or (in the form of signed extracts from the register) by the council clerk—both of whom the secretary supervised. The signet, the first of the three seals, had grown in importance during the early sixteenth century, at the expense of the privy seal.[10]

The sixteenth-century secretary's main responsibility was foreign affairs, which could include the handling of Border policy. This makes it remarkable that the office retained its prominence after 1603, when such affairs were no longer managed from Edinburgh, and when Border policy first became an internal police matter and then faded from significance. The secretary's remaining duties were all connected with the privy council, which he continued to attend after the departure of the king; the secretary's continued importance is another measure of the council's own significance. From 1626 onwards there would usually be a secretary or joint secretary at the royal court, often

---

ii. 142. For his unsuccessful attempt to obtain precedence over other royal officers in 1633 see *RMS* viii. 2190.

[6] Hannay, *College of Justice*, 103–7.

[7] Rait, *Parliaments of Scotland*, 508–10; A. R. MacDonald, 'Deliberative Processes in Parliament'.

[8] For an account of the secretary see Loughlin, 'Maitland of Lethington', ch. 1.

[9] *ER* xxii. 63.

[10] The privy council used what was usually called the 'court signet', while a 'common signet' (or more than one) was used to initiate cases in the central courts: R. K. Hannay, 'The Early History of the Scottish Signet', in his *College of Justice*, 317–20.

acting as the formal channel of communication between the king and the Scottish administration; but under James VI the secretary was simply the most responsible privy councillor.

The clerk register's functions were interdepartmental. He was responsible for a wide range of governmental records. He played an important role in organizing exchequer audits, appointed exchequer clerks, and had custody of the exchequer rolls. He had ultimate custody of the registers of the great seal, although no function in their creation. More influential was his custody of the parliamentary registers and the records of the court of session; he appointed the clerks of session, who doubled as clerks of parliament when that met. In the early years of the privy council he also claimed responsibility for its records, but here he was elbowed aside by the rise of the secretary. The secretary appointed some council clerks after 1564, and gained full control of the council registers in the mid-1590s. The secretary also supervised the first register of sasines, a new government department created in 1599, but that register was discontinued in 1609. When it restarted, in 1617, it was run by the clerk register.[11]

Finance was crucial to government. There were several financial departments, which until 1610 operated separately. Their basic role was to collect royal revenues and to spend them. The treasurer and comptroller had offices handling most of the royal money, and the treasurership was one of the three most prestigious offices with the comptrollership not far behind. The treasurer collected feudal casualties, compositions for crown charters and other grants, profits of justice, and revenues from the coinage; the comptroller collected the rents of crown lands and the customs. Treasurer and comptroller handled comparable amounts of money in the sixteenth century. In the early seventeenth century the treasurer's revenues declined while the comptroller's, which included the customs, expanded hugely. The two offices were combined in the same person, thereafter called the treasurer, from 1610.[12]

The treasurer's income from feudal casualties, although fiscally modest, was collected from the most prestigious people and sometimes affected them deeply. If the heir to a landed estate was a minor, the wardship would fall to the crown; the decision as to who should control the estates during the minority, and on what terms, could be crucial. It was the treasurer, or his officials under his supervision, who made that decision, often after delicate negotiations with the heirs' families and bidders for the wardship.[13]

---

[11] A. L. Murray, 'Lord Clerk Register', 129–39.

[12] See in general A. L. Murray, 'Notes on the Treasury Administration'; NAS, id., 'The Comptroller, 1425–1610' (David Berry prize essay, 1970), GA355.93; id., 'The Comptroller, 1425–1488', 1–29. There is an important account of the financial archives: Scottish Record Office, *Guide*, 27–81.

[13] J. Goodare (ed.), 'Fiscal Feudalism in Early Seventeenth-Century Scotland', *SHS Miscellany*, xiii (forthcoming, 2004).

The treasurer's responsibility for profits of justice meant that his office was not solely financial. When unlaws (financial penalties) were imposed on criminals by the court of justiciary or by justice ayres, these were usually 'composed for', an agreed proportion being paid in lieu of the total sum. That proportion had to be agreed between the treasury officials—often specially appointed 'compositors'—and the criminals. The latter were also expected to satisfy any injured parties or find surety to do so. The negotiations here were a law and order issue as well as a fiscal one. The treasurer in the early seventeenth century was periodically involved in campaigns to enforce the penal statutes.[14]

The comptroller was politically important because of his responsibility for supplying the royal household (on which more shortly). Problems with this would be taken seriously by those who mattered. However, his administrative importance begins with his role in revenue collection. His landed income was gathered from a network of variously named local officials collectively called *ballivi ad extra* (bailies outside burghs) who collected rents and other dues from crown lands. The comptroller could appoint some of the *ballivi ad extra* himself, though others were either hereditary or effectively monopolized by local landed families.[15] When the crown lands were directly managed, the comptroller wielded a good deal of patronage through his right to set tacks (leases). In the later sixteenth century, however, the lands were gradually feued out—alienated to proprietors ('feuars') in return for annual feu duties fixed in perpetuity. These dues were usually similar to the previous rents, and there could be short-term gain from entry payments. In the long run, income from crown lands would diminish, and so would the comptroller's control over them.

The customers collected customs in the royal burghs. They were either appointed directly by the comptroller, or by the crown under the privy seal with his consent. The latter arrangement, which was more common, allowed the customer to continue in office if there was a change of comptroller, but the comptroller evidently had a large measure of practical control over these officials.[16]

Both the treasurership and the comptrollership called for a combination of administrative ability, wealth, and social eminence. Both posts saw the rise of a humble administrator: Robert Richardson from treasurer clerk to treasurer (1561), and John Fenton from comptroller clerk to comptroller (1582, though returning to the clerkship next year). On the other hand, the offices could be exercised by depute, which sometimes led to treasurers, especially, having little connection with their office. Most treasurers and comptrollers were nobles or leading lairds who were personally active even when a depute was in post.

---

[14] For these, see Ch. 5 above.
[15] NAS, Murray, 'The Comptroller', GA355.93, pp. 26–7. [16] Ibid. 31–2.

Two other revenue-handling offices were created as indirect results of the Reformation. The thirds of benefices, a tax on church benefices for the benefit of the crown and the Protestant church, were administered initially by the comptroller (1562–8) and then, less successfully, by the church (1568–73). The thirds then returned to royal administration, and a separate post of collector general was established for them in 1574. The collector general was never politically vital, but the post was important enough to be held in the 1570s by an influential peer, Lord Boyd. He supervised a large network of regional subcollectors, and could influence ministers whose stipends were assigned ('modified') by his office rather than being raised locally. As parish benefices were gradually assigned directly to ministers, thirds were collected in fewer benefices and the work declined.[17]

The treasurer of new augmentations was a post created in 1587 to administer the revenues accruing to the crown from the act of annexation of 1587. This act had transferred the superiority of episcopal lands from bishops to crown, and the treasurer of new augmentations thus collected the revenues from these lands—mainly feu duties. The post was held concurrently with that of collector general. Both posts, like that of the comptroller, were combined with the treasurership in 1610.

Temporary financial departments were constituted whenever there was a parliamentary tax. Collectors of these taxes were not usually privy councillors before 1596, but thereafter they almost always were, demonstrating their increasing importance. Taxes were traditionally granted for a specific purpose, but the purposes stated in the acts gradually became vague. It was increasingly clear that taxes were really going towards the general expenses of government; the accounts of tax expenditure confirm this. In the early seventeenth century taxation came to be voted every few years and collected every year, so that one tax began as the last one ended. In theory the outgoing collector of taxation would make his final accounts to the exchequer, his department would be dissolved, and a new one constituted by the new collector. In practice, administrative continuity was achieved because although the official collector of each tax was different, each collector from the 1580s until the late 1620s appointed Archibald Primrose as clerk of taxations. Primrose thus fashioned a semi-permanent department out of a series of nominally temporary ones. This continuity was particularly helpful because not everybody paid taxes promptly, and at any one time the collectors could be pursuing arrears of two, three, or four previous taxes.[18]

---

[17] *Accounts of the Collectors of Thirds of Benefices, 1561–1572*, ed. G. Donaldson (SHS, 1949); G. Donaldson, 'The "new enterit benefices", 1573–1586', *SHR* 32 (1953), 93–8. For the initial rentals collected see *The Books of Assumption of Thirds of Benefices: Scottish Ecclesiastical Rentals at the Reformation*, ed. J. Kirk (British Academy, Records of Social and Economic History, 1995). [18] Goodare, 'Parliamentary Taxation'.

The mint was a financial department in its own right, which in the later six-teenth century provided significant revenues through currency debasement. Two officials were in charge of it. The master of the mint had managerial and financial responsibility for its operations; the general of the mint had a more honorific role and was responsible for the assays which gauged the quality of the coins produced. Policy on the mint was closely supervised not only by the treasurer (to whom the master of the mint accounted) but also by the monarch and privy council.[19]

All the departments discussed so far were both revenue and spending departments, with revenues being disbursed directly from the offices that collected them. Some of these disbursements were regular, like the monthly pay received from the treasurer by the gunners in Edinburgh Castle, while ad hoc expenses were paid by means of royal warrants to treasurer or comptroller. One partial exception to this was the royal household, which collected no money of its own but was to some extent a spending department managed by the masters of the household.[20] They would make payments, accounted for in the 'bukis of houshald' or 'bukis of the equurie' (stables), which the comptroller (or sometimes treasurer) would reimburse in bulk.[21] Occasionally a master of the household would make a contract with the comptroller to supply the household for a fixed sum payable by the latter.[22] However, the household was not financially autonomous and many of its costs were paid directly by the comptroller or the treasurer. Typically the comptroller covered general household expenses while the treasurer paid for the wardrobe. There was sometimes friction over this demarcation, especially when money was short, as it increasingly and chronically was during James VI's personal reign.

There thus developed a pressing need for a body to coordinate financial decision-making. The traditional system of separate financial officers, each dealing with their own branches of revenue and expenditure, was breaking down under the pressure of financial stringency. Early modern European states saw a general trend towards the creation of unified institutions for financial management; Scotland was no exception.[23]

Attention here falls initially upon the growth of the exchequer. At the outset of our period, the exchequer was a largely passive body, convoked once a year to receive and audit financial accounts from central and local

[19] J. E. L. Murray, 'The Organisation and Work of the Scottish Mint, 1358–1603', in D. M. Metcalf (ed.), *Coinage in Medieval Scotland, 1100–1600* (British Archaeological Reports, no. 45, 1977).

[20] Juhala, 'Household and Court of James VI', *passim*, and App. 1 for lists of masters of the household (of whom there were usually two or more in office at one time). For a detailed study of an earlier period see A. L. Murray, 'Financing the Royal Household: James V and his Comp-trollers, 1513–1543', in I. B. Cowan and D. Shaw (eds.), *The Renaissance and Reformation in Scotland* (Edinburgh, 1983).   [21] *ER* xxii. 30–1.

[22] NAS, Murray, 'The Comptroller', GA355.93, p. 67.

[23] Ribalta, 'Impact of Central Institutions', 31–2.

financial officers none of whom had responsibilities outside their own departments. It spent more time adding up figures than it did making policy decisions. As an auditing body its initiatives were limited to inducing financial officers to submit accounts promptly (a challenging but routine task). It was also a court; the exchequer auditors were lords of council, and there was sometimes overlap between the exchequer and what would become the court of session. Judicial cases concerning the revenue were brought either by financial officers attempting to enforce a payment, or by subjects attempting to establish that they were not liable to make a payment.[24]

A statute of 1584 marked a new departure, the beginning of a permanent exchequer commission which would supervise and coordinate the individual financial officers. The transition to a permanent exchequer was gradual: meetings were at first concentrated in a few months of the year as before, and they were largely confined to adjudicating on the complaints that an increasingly intrusive fiscal policy was generating. These complaints chiefly related to church revenues in government hands, the main new source of landed revenue at this period. But the foundations of a distinct and more active exchequer had been laid.[25] In 1587, the ordinary exchequer (the body receiving the financial officers' accounts) was statutorily limited to the months of July and August, much as it had been before 1584.[26] However, the exchequer could meet as a court of law or as a conciliar body at any time, making an important decree in February 1588.[27]

A revived and resurgent permanent exchequer was established in 1590, and for the next eight years it was at the centre of financial management. Its prominence was such that the exchequer was said to have been the 'only consell' for a while in 1590, and even a move to have 'na prevy consaill bot the chekker' was considered.[28] This was not a move hostile to the council, however, since their memberships overlapped; both king and privy council sought to expand the exchequer's jurisdiction. Among their proposals was one that would have allowed the exchequer to take over all criminal cases on the grounds that they concerned crown revenue. The court of session joined the chamber faction (who were unhappy that the scheme would restrict access to the king) to defeat the plan.[29] The continuing council–exchequer link is illustrated by an order of 1594 that the 'lordis of . . . secreit counsale and chekker' should meet twice weekly for council business and twice weekly

---

[24] A. L. Murray, 'Procedure of the Scottish Exchequer'; id., 'Exchequer, Council and Session'.

[25] *APS* iii. 309, c. 26; A. L. Murray, 'Sir John Skene and the Exchequer', 126; NAS, exchequer auditors' act book, 1584–6, E4/1.

[26] It was to meet on Tuesday afternoons during the sitting of the court of session (in 1584 it had been Tuesday and Thursday afternoons): *APS* iii. 455, c. 49.

[27] There is reference to 'the act of secret counsell, session, and exchecker, upon the 14 of Februar 1587[/88]', relating to teinds and benefices: *BUK* iii. 886. This implies that some form of exchequer commission existed then. The decision is not recorded in the surviving (though damaged) privy council register: *RPC* iv. 251–2.

[28] Melville, *Memoirs*, 373, 391.

[29] Bowes to Burghley, 7 Nov. 1590, *CSP Scot.* x. 416.

for exchequer business.[30] But while the privy council was never wholly hostile to the nobility, the exchequer in the 1590s was sometimes seen that way; it was a smaller body and included few or no nobles among its commissioners.

The exchequer by this time had three functions, sometimes four or five. Its traditional auditing task continued.[31] It continued to be a court for hearing many legal cases relating to the royal revenues, exercising a branch of the conciliar jurisdiction along with the privy council and court of session. It made strategic decisions on revenue management, such as the campaign to increase blench fermes during the 1590s. And it sometimes exercised a measure of control over expenditure.

The fifth function was added with the appointment of the Octavians in January 1596. This eight-man commission gained additional powers for the exchequer, and placed it at the centre of Scottish government for the next two and a half years. One new thing they did was to take over the financial offices themselves.[32] Previous exchequer commissioners had supervised the treasurer, comptroller, and other financial officers, but only the latter had actually handled money.[33] Now the two functions were combined.

The Octavians made the exchequer into a powerhouse, stepping up the pace of change with initiatives on customs, crown lands, and other matters.[34] In June 1596, apparently, the exchequer was discussing public business on Mondays, Tuesdays, and Fridays, and private suits on Wednesdays; the privy council met only on Thursdays.[35] This is not surprising when the exchequer's remit is considered. One of the Octavians (or someone associated with them) saw the privy council as responsible for 'peace and war, the Borders and the Highlands, and other weighty matters'. The list he made for the king of the exchequer's responsibilities was rather longer:

the compts of your hienes rents, propertie, casualitie and collectorie, the coine, wynes and taxations, your wardrobe, the reparation of your houses and castells, the furnishing and expences of your house and stable and other charges, the compts of the colledge rents and how the foundations are observed, the modifying of the ministers stipends, the compt of the common good of burrows and of the anuales disponed for hospitals, to hear the dilligence of sherriffs and others in matters wherein they are appointed judges, and executors, to take order with the number and names of the officers of arms and of the dilligence done for the escheats of persons being at the horne.[36]

---

[30] *RPC* v. 118.

[31] A. L. Murray, 'Dirty Work at the Exchequer: Inverness's Charter and Accounts, 1592–1594', *Scottish Archives*, 4 (1998), 85–90, describes a remarkable episode in this work.

[32] This was reputedly a lucrative move, on which Sir James Melville blamed their unpopularity: Melville, *Memoirs*, 390. But the financial offices were not always profitable at this time: Goodare, *State and Society*, 120–9.

[33] The distinction is not absolute as the comptroller was always himself an exchequer auditor, and the treasurer often was too.

[34] Murray, 'Sir John Skene and the Exchequer', 127–31.

[35] BL, 'Ordor of the Exchequer House', in 'Copies of documents relating to the revenues of Scotland', Add. MS 24275, fo. 11ʳ.

[36] BL, 'Proposalls for reformation of certain abuses in the state', in Harl. MS 4612, fo. 48ᵛ.

The exchequer had not been regarded as a full conciliar authority in 1588, when the general assembly asked the king 'to grant to the act devised by the lords of the exchecker, of the third in favours of planting of the kirks, and to establish the same by act of secret counsell'. But in 1596 it was to the exchequer, not the privy council, that the general assembly brought its proposals for teind reform.[37] Although the Octavians resigned in January 1597, they were reappointed to a similar, enlarged exchequer commission, and more initiatives continued to be taken until a reaction took place in June 1598. The old system of separate financial officers was restored, and there were to be no more permanent exchequer commissions. This was no doubt a manoeuvre by courtiers, angry at the Octavians' squeeze on patronage.[38] The result lacked the kind of tidiness that the Octavians had promoted, although it had a certain logic. Revenue was to be maximized, and James's final years in Scotland saw reckless promotion of fiscal schemes, some of which yielded nothing but recriminations and embarrassment. With the removal of the royal court in 1603, fiscal pressure was eased, and royal giving continued unchecked.[39]

In 1610, however, the outline of a weighty new financial department was created by combining all four regular financial offices (treasurer, comptroller, collector general, and treasurer of new augmentations) in one person, the earl of Dunbar. The accounts for the two major offices (treasurer and comptroller) continued to be kept separately, by separate clerks, but policy for them could now be coordinated.[40] In 1611, after Dunbar's death, the treasurership was left vacant for two years, and then in 1613–16 held nominally by the earl of Somerset, royal favourite. The treasurer depute, who did the work, was first subsumed in an eight-man treasury commission—dubbed the 'New Octavians'—which may have continued until 1613, and then assisted by two receivers of rents (who were formally his subordinates, but sometimes rendered the treasurer's accounts themselves). The foundations of the later system, whereby the finances would be coordinated by the treasury through a corporate treasury commission, had been laid.[41]

However, in the meantime there was some experimentation. A new conciliar body, the commissioners of rents, paralleled the 'New Octavians'. Both bodies were first appointed on the same day, 15 October 1610, a time when the exchequer was temporarily in abeyance. The commissioners of rents were

---

[37] *BUK* ii. 707; Calderwood, *History*, v. 421–33.

[38] *APS* iv. 165; Murray, 'Sir John Skene and the Exchequer', 131. Cf. Goodare, 'Thomas Foulis'.   [39] Goodare, 'The Nobility and the Absolutist State', 169–70.

[40] The lesser offices of collector general and treasurer of new augmentations lost their administrative identity in 1611 when their accounts were engrossed with the comptroller's accounts: Scottish Record Office, *Guide*, 49. In the 16th c., treasurer and comptroller had sometimes shared the services of some administrative staff: NAS, Murray, 'The Comptroller', GA355.93, pp. 59–60.

[41] *RPC* ix. 594–5; HMC, *Mar & Kellie*, i. 65–6; Calderwood, *History*, vii. 158. Cf. A. L. Murray, 'Scottish Treasury'.

commissioned to supervise receiving officers and to direct letters to enforce payments to the king; in 1612 they were described as 'the commissionaris who hes the charge and handling of his majesties rentis'.[42] They have left few records separate from those of the privy council, and seem in fact to have been the members of the council, or most of them, commissioned to act as revenue administrators. Since the commissioners of rents were not a court, perhaps the exchequer now concentrated on its judicial role and left the commissioners of rents to take administrative decisions. Like the council, but since 1598 unlike the exchequer, the commissioners of rents were probably in constant session. They could even encroach on the council's remit, since they were the same people. On 1 February 1614 it was the commissioners of rents who discussed a possible resignation of the reversion of the earldom of Orkney, not a purely fiscal matter. On 1 March, the next instalment of the question was discussed by the privy council.[43] In 1615, royal creditors were to apply to the commissioners of rents and not the king. They were to inform him whether the debt was genuine, so that he could decide whether to pay it.[44] These seem administrative rather than judicial matters. Eventually, however, the commissioners of rents became commissioners of exchequer. This seems to have occurred by February 1626, when Charles I mentioned the 'commissioners to concurr with our thesaurair and deputie thesaurair for manageing of our rentis and reulling of our exchecker'.[45] Later that year, a new commission of exchequer seems to have subsumed the commissioners of rents, and the two terms were treated as synonymous by 1628.[46]

Meanwhile, as a court, the exchequer was now more like the court of session, but its authority was less. In 1614, faced with a dispute between the customs tacksmen and the earl of Moray about the customs of the waters of Spey, Findhorn, and Lossie, 'the excheker thoght the mater controverted and the parties securities produced to be of such qualitie and consequence as thay wald not tak upon thame the decision thairof, bot remitted the mater to the session'.[47] And all these fiscal bodies, like the privy council, depended on clientage exercised at the royal court. A gentleman of the bedchamber could be told in 1629 of a 'signature by the lordis of the excheckeris and ordinance' which 'lyeth unpast the seales till your mynde be knowen'.[48] The nobles in the

---

[42] *RPC* ix. 85–6, 334. The archive of royal letters to the commissioners of rents begins in 1613: NAS, E17/2.

[43] NLS, Denmylne MSS, Adv. MS 33.1.1, vol. v, nos. 11, 15. The distinction is obscured because both these discussions were minuted by the council: *RPC* x. 206, 215.

[44] *RPC* x. 408. For an example of this in action, see James to treasurer depute, 3 Dec. 1615, *Earl of Stirling's Register of Royal Letters, 1615–1635*, 2 vols., ed. C. Rogers (Grampian Club, 1885), i. 7.

[45] *RPC* 2nd ser. i. 231.   [46] Ibid. 265–7; *Earl of Stirling's Register*, i. 323, 342.

[47] NLS, Sir Thomas Hamilton to James, 4 Feb. [1614], Denmylne MSS, Adv. MS 33.1.1, vol. v, no. 10.

[48] Lord Balmerino to Sir Robert Kerr of Ancram, 13 Apr. 1629, *Correspondence of Sir Robert Kerr, First Earl of Ancram, and his Son William, Third Earl of Lothian*, 2 vols., ed. D. Laing (Bannatyne Club, 1875), i. 48–9.

1590s had felt threatened by the permanent exchequer, but that was now long in the past.

The executive agencies considered so far were all directly coercive: they ordered people about against their will. That was not all they did, of course. The privy council heard individual cases, in which wronged parties benefited from the remedies it offered. Financial agencies reallocated money rather than just extracting it from people's pockets. Royal creditors could approach the exchequer and even attempt to sue the financial officers. On the whole, though, the heavy hand of state power is manifest both in the council register and in the tax rolls. Where it is much less manifest is in the next executive agency we have to consider: the court of session. Yet the court of session did implement the law by applying it to individuals who presented themselves before it seeking 'justice', and those who lost their cases were experiencing the coercive power of an institution that may legitimately be regarded as a department of government.

There was no single departmental head for the court. The president of the court of session, usually known simply as the lord president, was sometimes a link between the session and privy council. He was not head of a department, partly because the chancellor retained a more than nominal role in the court of session, but mainly because the court of session (in its institutional guise of the college of justice) was a corporate body in which all the judges were important collectively. Sixteenth-century lord presidents were not usually politicians; the near-continuous tenure of the post by William Baillie of Provand through successive changes of regime from 1566 to 1593 illustrates this. His successor, Alexander Seton, later earl of Dunfermline, was lord president before he became a politician (as one of the Octavians, in 1596). Thereafter, lord presidents were always politicians because the session judges became privy councillors, but they were mainly politicians *as* privy councillors. When Charles I ordered in 1626 that privy councillors could not also be session judges, the officers of state and leading politicians resigned their judgeships, while the new judges were lawyers and not politicians.[49]

The court of session provided a service to people by resolving their disputes for them. It was a service they very much welcomed, and made more and more use of. The court's origins lay in the fifteenth century, but its formal institution as a 'college of justice' in 1532 enabled it to acquire jurisdiction over landed property—thus assuring it a flood of business—and also gave it the personnel and resources to meet that demand. The court's records demonstrate this growth vividly. For the 1560s, 1580s, 1600s, and 1620s respectively, there are 24, 41, 55, and 87 volumes of 'acts and decrees'.[50] It is hardly

---

[49] *RPC* 2nd ser. i. pp. xxxiii–xxxviii; Brunton and Haig, *Senators of the College of Justice*, 273–5.

[50] NAS, CS7/21–44 (1560s), CS7/81–121 (1580s), CS7/189–243 (1600s), CS7/340–426 (1620s). The growth was partly due to increasing prolixity in minuting cases; on the other hand, records in the 1560s also contain other material, particularly deeds.

likely that people had four times as many disputes at the end of our period as at the beginning; clearly, they were taking more of their disputes to law, or at least to the central courts.

How these disputes would have been settled in the past is an open question: probably some of them had been dealt with by local courts, some by arbitration, and some by the extra-judicial mechanism of the bloodfeud, while some would have remained unresolved. The precise relationship of these mechanisms is unclear, and more than one mechanism was needed for some disputes (as when arbitration followed a feud). The rise of the court of session looks as if it was filling a gap left by the decline of the bloodfeud, but this is probably too simple. There was a large increase in litigation in the English central courts too between 1560 and 1640, exactly contemporary with the Scottish trend although England had abandoned bloodfeud some time earlier.[51] The rise in Scottish litigation if anything *antedated* the decline of the bloodfeud, which did not begin in earnest until about 1600. But whatever the reason for its rise, the court of session became a flagship institution of central government.

The successful launch of this flagship brought several new developments in its wake. One was a newly professional approach to the business of government. The professional ethos of the court of session depended not only on the fifteen trained and salaried judges, but also on the lesser members of the college of justice: the advocates and writers to the signet. The advocates conducted clients' cases in the court, and provided legal advice; there were at least fifty-two advocates in 1586. The writers to the signet acted for clients in a wider field, writing the documents that passed the signet to initiate many legal cases, and also other documents. There were thirty-eight writers to the signet in 1586.[52] Advocates and writers had their own rivalries with one another and with the senators, but they would close ranks against any outsider in true professional style. There was an attempt in 1587, apparently by Maitland, to improve the training of writers to the signet and other seals, and (what upset the clerk register) removing existing writers who did not meet the new standards. This last aspect of the plan seems not to have been implemented.[53] The numbers of writers to the signet and advocates increased throughout our period, as did their wealth. Professional justice did not come cheap—though no doubt the most prominent alternative, bloodfeud, had its costs too, including the maintenance of military retinues.

So demand for the court's justice was keen, and one result was predictable: there was jostling in the queue outside the Edinburgh tolbooth. Here, as in other aspects of a hierarchical society, one was expected to know one's place. In 1583, the privy council ordered that the backlog of poor people's cases

---

[51] C. W. Brooks, *Pettyfoggers and Vipers of the Commonwealth: The 'Lower Branch' of the Legal Profession in Early Modern England* (Cambridge, 1986), ch. 4.

[52] Hannay, 'Early History of the Scottish Signet', 322.

[53] NAS, GD149/265, part 2, fos. 41ʳ–44ᵛ.

should be cleared. The clerk register's new system in 1585, calling cases by region and lot rather than influence, provoked some bitter memoranda.[54] As well as having one's case heard, such influence could also mean *not* having one's case heard. The burgh of Forfar in 1613, attempting to suppress traders in nearby unfree Kirriemuir, purchased letters charging them to desist, but was soon lamenting that 'the erll of Angus thair superior hes suspendit the saids chairges, quhilk suspensione lyis as yitt undiscussit in respect that the erll of Angus has gritt moyane'.[55]

The desire of Forfar, Angus, and the other litigants in the queue was for 'justice'. On the whole, and accepting a certain amount of wire-pulling by powerful people, it seems clear that this is what they felt they got, otherwise they would not have flocked to the court in ever-increasing numbers. But 'justice' does not exist in a vacuum: it follows rules. What the court administered was the *law*. And the law that it administered was the law of the state. This clearly included statutes, but the court's own judicial precedents were also part of the same legal structure, and so even were customs (as interpreted by the judges) and the principles of Roman law (used, selectively, as a guide towards the setting of precedents).[56] Much of this structure consisted of private law, which (as discussed in Chapter 5 above) did not need to be enforced directly. People came to the court voluntarily to demand 'justice' as parliament had defined it. In administering 'justice', the court was adjudicating between competing claims to it, and sometimes the losing parties did need to be coerced.[57] But the general acceptance of its legitimacy meant that the court of session encountered few difficulties here.

This point—that the court administered the law of the state—is underlined by comparing it with alternative models of dispute-settlement. The bloodfeud used not law, but traditional codes of honour. Local courts used written laws, but their lack of professionally trained judges limited their ability to compete with the court of session. One of the ways in which the court of session consolidated its influence was by exercising its power to remove selected cases from them.[58] The contrast with the early sixteenth century, when local courts had had priority in hearing property cases, could not have been greater. Moreover, in this age of expanding lay literacy, written documents possessed a growing attraction as means of dispute-settlement. Written evidence was best, and litigants went to great lengths to obtain it.[59] The session judges'

---

[54] *RPC* iii. 610–11; BL, Add. MS 33531, fos. 195ʳ–206ʳ.

[55] *RCRB* ii. 401–2. For Angus's view, that Forfar's action was 'prejudiciall to my preivilege and libertie of my regalities', see Angus to Sir John Ogilvie of Inverquharity, 21 May [1613?], W. Fraser, *The Douglas Book*, 4 vols. (Edinburgh, 1875), iv. 248–9. But he seems to have been reluctant to let the court decide.

[56] See Ch. 3 above; also Ch. 2 for the court's role in lobbying parliament for legislative change.

[57] For the messengers of arms, whose task this was, see Ch. 8 below.

[58] For the conflict between law and codes of honour, see K. M. Brown, *Bloodfeud*, ch. 7; for local courts see Ch. 8 below.   [59] Finlay, *Men of Law*, 111–12.

professional training gave them the best claim to sophisticated understanding of such evidence.

However, the court of session gained some of its legitimacy by being seen to be pragmatic, concentrating on the need to settle the dispute rather than scoring points about particular forms of 'justice'. Instead of proceeding to the issue of decrees, the court could encourage litigants to submit to arbitration, which was quicker, cheaper, and more flexible. The evidence so far studied comes from the court's own records, but if examined in conjunction with privately sponsored arbitration agreements, the procedure of arbitration might be found straddling a divide between publicly provided and privately provided justice.[60] A good way of looking at this would be to see the court's formal adjudications as the core of the government's dispute-settlement service, surrounded by a periphery of arbitrations provided by nobles. This is comparable to the 'aristocratic penumbra' of government discussed in Chapter 1 above.

The court of justiciary might be regarded as complementing the court of session, having jurisdiction over criminal cases as the latter did over civil. But the parallel would be inexact, and the court of justiciary remained a modest institution in size. Still, its activities were a matter of life and death, and sometimes politically important when trials for treason were held. Local courts suffered less diminution of their criminal jurisdiction than they did of their civil, and when cases did reach the notice of central government there were other ways of dealing with them: notably by justice ayres and commissions of justiciary.[61] Moreover, the demand for central 'justice', in the form of a dispute-settlement service, came largely in the field of civil law.[62] So the court remained with just one or two justice deputes to convene it; they often doubled as advocates in the court of session.

The court's administrative head was the justice clerk. He was responsible for the paperwork, not only of the court of justiciary itself, but also of justice ayres when these were held. The routine work was done by a clerk depute, and in the late sixteenth century clerks depute began to be appointed by the crown, showing that their status was growing. Far from harming the status of the justice clerk himself, this seems to have helped him to assert his position as an 'assessor' (adviser) to the justice deputes. These were often junior advocates whose social status was modest compared with the justice clerk, who was an officer of state and usually a senator of the college of

---

[60] M. Godfrey, 'Arbitration and Dispute Resolution in Sixteenth-Century Scotland', *Tijdschrift voor Rechtsgeschiedenis*, 70 (2002), 109–35. Baron courts could use arbitration: *Carnwath Court Book*, p. ci. It was important to English justices of the peace: Fletcher, *Reform in the Provinces*, 79–81. [61] See Ch. 8 below for these.

[62] As it did elsewhere in Europe: B. Lenman and G. Parker, 'The State, the Community and the Criminal Law in Early Modern Europe', in V. A. C. Gatrell et al. (eds.), *Crime and the Law: The Social History of Crime in Western Europe since 1500* (London, 1980), 16. The records of the justiciary court are incomplete, but what survives shows no clear trend towards expansion of its business, unlike for the court of session: NAS, JC1, JC2.

justice.[63] The post of justice general, held by successive earls of Argyll, should also be mentioned, although it was more honorific than administrative. It was not entirely a sinecure, as the earls could appoint justice deputes and even preside in person over important political trials, but the justice general did not routinely supervise the justice clerk.[64]

Institutional continuity in the court was impeded by the treatment of a 'justice court' as a one-off event to try a particular case. Commissions of justiciary, which were mainly used to enable crimes to be tried locally, could also be issued for trials in the tolbooth of Edinburgh if the crown wanted to constitute the court in a particular way.[65] Indeed, the court of justiciary may not always have been conceived as an institution fixed in Edinburgh; rather it could be seen as a body that was supposed to perambulate the localities but had unfortunately got out of the habit of doing so.[66] Trials in Edinburgh often had to involve the burgh magistrates, as they possessed the only prison. Before it was upgraded early in the seventeenth century, this could be a problem.[67] Still, in practice there came to be a court of justiciary in being, more or less constantly, in Edinburgh—certainly by the early seventeenth century. The law encouraging public prosecutions was a potentially far-reaching development.[68]

This brings us to the king's advocate, the crown's legal counsel. The story of this office's development is closely connected with several other governmental developments. It has recently been studied in detail for the early sixteenth century by John Finlay. The office emerged in the 1490s, largely in order to pursue the king's patrimonial land rights more actively.[69] The king's advocate did not run a fully independent department, but cooperated with other royal officers in pursuing legal cases in which they were interested. These were usually the financial officers, though a wide variety of types of case were involved. The king's advocate could appoint deputies to deal with particular cases, or the king could employ other advocates to represent him, in a flexible series of ad hoc arrangements. From 1555 there were usually two queen's advocates, indicating that business had increased.[70]

Once established, the office underwent two qualitative developments in the late sixteenth century. The king's advocate had long brought some criminal

---

[63] R. K. Hannay, 'The Office of the Justice Clerk', *JR* 47 (1935), 311–29.

[64] For the fifth earl of Argyll as justice general see Dawson, *The Politics of Religion*, 57–8. It is often stated that the earls held the post hereditarily, but no 16th-c. evidence for this can be found. The appointment of the fifth earl in 1562 was clearly not hereditary: HMC, *Fourth Report, Appendix* (London, 1874), 485. There eventually emerged an assumption that the post was hereditary, because the future eighth earl resigned as hereditary justice general in 1628.

[65] e.g. *HP* i. 157–9.   [66] Willock, *Jury in Scotland*, 43–5.

[67] NLS, Robert Colville of Cleish to Sir John Bellenden of Auchnoule, justice clerk, 20 Oct. [1560s?], Adv. MS 22.3.14, fo. 56^r. For more on prisons, see Ch. 9 below.

[68] Wasser, 'Violence and the Central Criminal Courts', 408.

[69] J. Finlay, 'James Henryson and the Origins of the Office of King's Advocate', *SHR* 79 (2000), 17–38. The office eventually became known as 'lord advocate', but this term was not used in our period.   [70] Finlay, *Men of Law*, ch. 7.

actions, particularly on deforcement of royal messengers. From 1579 the advocate increasingly became a public prosecutor, leading prosecutions for serious crimes in the court of justiciary and playing the primary role in trials before the privy council itself. He often prosecuted alongside an injured party, and now could do so alone if the latter declined to act—a key innovation that marked a move away from the idea that justice was a matter of restoring equilibrium between criminal and victim. More and more, crime would now be punished primarily by the state.

The second development was an administrative reconfiguration of the office. Sir Thomas Hamilton, one of the Octavians, was appointed one of the two king's advocates in 1596 and became the sole holder of the post the next year. This reduction to a single advocate gave him increased status; he did not act personally in such a high proportion of cases as his predecessors, but appointed a series of regular deputies to deal with routine cases. They came to form an embryonic judicial department.[71] By the reign of Charles I, Sir Thomas Hope as king's advocate was simply the government's law expert, and played a leading role in political debates that touched on law—which meant, in practice, almost all political debates.[72]

Public prosecution was important because the authorities were increasingly pursuing a variety of offences which might not have a traditional injured party to act as prosecutor. These included adultery, incest, witchcraft, hearing of mass, harbouring Jesuits, usury, and forestalling of markets. Most of these were also ecclesiastical offences which presbyteries were trying to prosecute. A conflict of jurisdiction tended to emerge between them and the secular criminal courts in prosecuting the new victimless crimes. The ultimate ecclesiastical sanction was excommunication, while several of the secular crimes carried the death penalty. Should a conviction in a church court lead to automatic criminal conviction, as some in the church argued? And what of the presbyteries' demand that defenders testify on oath, which was against the criminal courts' practice, appearing to force defenders to incriminate themselves? As king's advocate, Hamilton guided the privy council in the late 1590s and 1600s in bringing a series of test cases that restricted ecclesiastical jurisdiction and established the primacy of the criminal courts.[73]

The admiral's court was a lesser jurisdiction, but there was a period when it could have become a greater one. It had emerged in the fifteenth century, deriving originally from military responsibilities. While the admirals' judicial powers focused on crimes committed at sea, their court was also theoretically competent to decide all maritime cases 'tuiching the carrying, lousing, and

[71] G. W. T. Omond, *The Lord Advocates of Scotland*, 2 vols. (Edinburgh, 1883), i. 42–51; Paton (ed.), *Introduction to Scottish Legal History*, 39–40; Wasser, 'Violence and the Central Criminal Courts', 83, 177–9.

[72] Cf. his apparent dominance of debate in a convention of estates: 'Diary of the convention of estates, 1630', ed. Goodare.   [73] Goodare, *State and Society*, 186–92.

away taking of merchandice be sea'. This was potentially a powerful weapon for centralization, as many cases in burgh courts might have been claimed for it. A session case of 1533 held that debt cases between a Scottish and a foreign merchant fell under the jurisdiction of the burgh court, not the admiral.[74] Could this area of jurisdiction be claimed for the centre? The office of admiral was held in the 1570s by the Regent Morton, and in 1581, following the latter's execution, an article was submitted to parliament on the 'ordoure betuix the merchandis and marrinaris for pilleit guidis'.[75]

This suggests that the burghs wanted a redefinition of jurisdiction in maritime causes; but when they got one, in 1587, it was quite the opposite of their hopes. Francis Stewart, fifth earl of Bothwell, received a new charter of the admiral's office, allowing him to hold

civil and criminal courts . . . in all actions committed at sea, between native and foreign merchants or between foreign and foreign, concerning merchandise, fishings, materials of war, piracies, contracts, pledges and agreements . . . and on violators of the laws of the realm concerning exporters and regraters of victual, flesh, corn and other prohibited and uncustomed goods, as freely as any admiral of the realms of France, Spain, England, Denmark or other foreign nations.[76]

Here was a brand new central jurisdiction, professedly based on foreign example, with a widely extensive remit. The powers to enforce the law on contracts and to regulate exports were particularly significant.[77] The initiative was probably connected with the appointment of an active vice-admiral, David Collace, in 1586, and was also a reward to the recently appointed hereditary admiral, the earl of Bothwell.[78]

It took some time to establish the new system. William Welwood, in his brief summary of maritime law published in 1590, commented that 'the place ordinair for this jurisdiction is not as yit constitut', and hoped for at least one admiral's court 'in ilk seaward shire'. He was unsure about the admiral's jurisdiction; traditionally it was mainly criminal, but this limitation might not continue. 'Civil debaits' should be 'decydit be the judge of the brough quhairunto the schip is frauchtit, quha is, according to the common custome, the deane of gyld'. The admiral was 'also be the custome of uther nations quhom we follow in that erectioun, judge to the civil causis, bot without prejudice of the lawis and consuetud foresaid'. The convention of royal burghs was less hesitant about the court, and was stung into forthright

---

[74] Balfour, *Practicks*, ii. 630, 635. Under this system there were, or could be, local admirals depute in coastal districts: for the appointment of one in 1533, see W. Fraser, *Memorials of the Montgomeries, Earls of Eglinton*, 2 vols. (Edinburgh, 1859), ii. 120–1.

[75] *APS* iii. 214, c. 9. [76] *RMS* v. 1316.

[77] The admiral hitherto had had some civil jurisdiction, but not in these matters: *Acts of the Admiral's Court of Scotland (Acta Curiae Admirallatus Scotiae), 1557–1562*, ed. T. C. Wade (Stair Society, 1937), pp. xvii–xviii and *passim*.

[78] R. G. Macpherson, 'Francis Stewart, 5th Earl Bothwell, c.1562–1612: Lordship and Politics in Jacobean Scotland' (Ph.D. thesis, Edinburgh, 1998), 161–3, 259.

protest at the admiral's 'new exactiounis'.[79] The project might have succeeded if the unrelated political antics of the hereditary admiral had not brought ruin on his court. In 1592, on Bothwell's forfeiture, the burghs were able to hit back, securing a statute limiting the admiral's jurisdiction to what it had been under James V.[80]

It was some years before the admiral's jurisdiction showed any signs of recovering from this setback. Bothwell's successor as admiral, the duke of Lennox, had his subordinates repeatedly criticized for exceeding their authority in the 1600s, and had to appoint a new set of deputes in 1608–10.[81] The court was flatteringly described as a 'soverane judicatorie' in 1609, in an act allowing it to issue its own hornings instead of relying on the court of session.[82] This phrase may well have derived from the French concept of 'sovereign courts', distinguished by exercising final and plenary justice derived directly from the crown.[83] In 1611, Lennox apparently received 'the same infeftment' that Bothwell had had in 1587, prompting a protest from Edinburgh based on the 1592 statute. This may have been successful, since no more is heard of it.[84]

The admiral's court seems to have attained some stability during the 1610s, to judge by a later abstract of its decisions which begins in 1613. The court was now exercising jurisdiction in both civil and criminal causes, operating with an assize for the latter. In 1617, the court fined the magistrates of Crail for having 'usurped the admirals jurisdictione' by adjudicating on an assault committed on shipboard. It also executed someone for piracy. But its civil jurisdiction was meagre by comparison—and it was there where the real possibilities for growth had lain in the 1580s.[85] Its power was at a low ebb in 1630, at least according to the burgh of Leith. Eleven of Leith's eighty-four complaints against the overweening power of Edinburgh related to the way in which Edinburgh's magistrates and water bailies had allegedly usurped the admiral's jurisdiction. This complaint, incidentally, illustrates a common process of centralization, by which one subordinate local

---

[79] William Welwood, 'The Sea Law of Scotland', ed. T. C. Wade, *STS Miscellany* (1933), 77–9; *RCRB* i. 339–40. There had been admiral deputes in the localities before, but their jurisdiction had been limited. See a reference to an admiral depute in Kirkcudbright in 1578: *RSS* viii. 471.

[80] *APS* iii. 580, c. 79. Next year, another statute reaffirmed the principles of standardization and foreign example, but ceded control to the burghs. Cases between merchant and merchant were once more to be tried by the local dean of guild court: *APS* iv. 30, c. 38.

[81] Goodare, *State and Society*, 82–3.

[82] *APS* iv. 440–1, c. 22. A similar phrase had been used of the exchequer in 1597: Skene, *DVS*, s.v. scaccarium.

[83] R. Doucet, *Les Institutions de la France au XVIᵉ siècle*, 2 vols. (Paris, 1948), i, chs. 6–8.

[84] *Edin. Recs.* vii. 296–8.

[85] NLS, 'Ane abbreviat of the registers of the high court of admiralitie', 1613–73, in Adv. MS 6.2.1, fos. 23ʳ–23ᵛ and *passim*. This volume records only three or four cases per year in our period; presumably more were heard, but how many more is unclear. The court's own registers are not extant for this period. Cf. S. Mowat, 'Shipping and Trade in Scotland, 1556–1830: The Records of the Scottish Admiralty Court', *Mariners' Mirror*, 83 (1997), 14–20.

power centre appeals to the central government to support it against a local rival.[86]

How far does the general assembly of the church belong in this analysis of executive agencies of government? It was obviously a governmental body, in the basic sense that it regulated people's lives. In that respect, it was functionally no different from the convention of royal burghs. The fact that the king and privy council sometimes argued with the general assembly does not prove that the general assembly was independent of 'state' control, any more than the fact that king and council sometimes argued with the convention of royal burghs proves that the burghs were independent. The assembly was even less independent of parliament; its own records show repeatedly that it recognized the supremacy of statute. It could argue vigorously, but it rarely issued a direct challenge even to the most obnoxious laws.[87]

Accounts of the general assembly have usually emphasized its political roles. These were certainly vital. It organized a movement for religious change, lobbying the monarch, privy council, and parliament for support, and agitating publicly when thwarted. Of course the general assembly, like parliament, was not a homogeneous thing; it was a forum containing diverse and shifting views, so that when we speak of 'the general assembly' we are really speaking of a majority among its members. The progress of the Protestant movement can be charted by investigating both the interactions of the assembly with the civil powers, and the shifting of views within the assembly itself.[88]

However, when the actual business of the general assembly is examined, it is revealed as spending most of its time as an executive body.[89] It issued streams of orders to synods, bishops, superintendents, commissioners, presbyteries, and parish ministers. It initially saw its main subordinate bodies as the synods, but when presbyteries started to be established in the 1580s they overtook the synods in importance.[90] Its shifting attitude to bishops, superintendents, and commissioners has furnished much material for the political history of the church, but they were important because they were the church's local executive authorities, admitting and supervising parish ministers, arranging for them to be financed, and settling cases of church discipline. The general assembly examined the performance of these local executive authorities, sometimes minutely, both by conducting general enquiries and by calling for reports from them on specific topics. It disciplined them for lapses. And it established commissions to transact specific business, which in turn could be supervised in the same way as its regular subordinates.

---

[86] *RPC*, 2nd ser. iii. 659–61. Leith seems to have been unsuccessful, since Edinburgh's privileges were confirmed in 1636: *RMS* ix. 605.   [87] See also Ch. 3 above.

[88] A. R. MacDonald, *Jacobean Kirk*; id., 'James VI and the General Assembly'.

[89] See *BUK, passim*. Aspects of this are discussed in Shaw, *General Assemblies*, chs. 19–24.

[90] MacDonald, *Jacobean Kirk*, 38.

The general assembly was not routinely required to execute royal proclamations or parliamentary legislation directly. Still, in 1581, after the issue of a proclamation against Catholicism, the assembly 'injoynit and concludit, that all ministers and pastours . . . execute the tenour of his majesties proclamatioun', making provision for them to report their 'duetifull diligence' and stipulating deprivation for failure.[91]

General assemblies met frequently in the period 1560–1600 but became slowly less common thereafter, eclipsed by bishops and archbishops acting as leaders of synods and provincial assemblies. These were manifestly executive bodies, with the initiative in ecclesiastical legislation having passed to the crown. The crown acted via a combination of parliamentary statutes, acts of rare and sometimes nominated general assemblies, and the royal prerogative.[92] The Jacobean bishops may have helped to formulate the details of policy, but the broad outlines were established by the king himself.

To give the bishops additional executive power, a new institution was established in 1610: the court of high commission.[93] Although the court had a large membership, it was controlled by the bishops. It was established as part of the programme of restoring full diocesan episcopacy, but while the rest of this was enacted by the general assembly in 1610 and ratified by parliament in 1612, high commission was established by the royal prerogative alone. This was evidently deliberate, and presumably connected with the contemporary struggle over the prerogative powers of the English high commission. By establishing the Scottish court as he did, James was displaying his powers.[94]

The court's own records are no longer extant. If we had half a dozen fat printed volumes of its business to consult, it would surely occupy a less marginal place in our perceptions. We can of course answer only questions for which evidence is available, but it seems better to proceed on the assumption, clearly shared by contemporary members and victims of the court, that it was a weighty organ of government. It was empowered to punish any breaches of ecclesiastical order, using fines and imprisonment (powers impugned by critics of the English court) and excommunication. In practice, while it dealt with some breaches of godly discipline (such as adultery), most of its business was with religious dissidents—Catholics and presbyterians. This placed the court in the front line of political controversy. From an

[91] *BUK* ii. 526–7.
[92] For the administration of the church in this period see Foster, *The Church before the Covenants*, ch. 6.
[93] What follows owes much to G. I. R. McMahon, 'The Scottish Courts of High Commission, 1610–1638', *Records of the Scottish Church History Society*, 15 (1963–5), 193–209. There were initially separate courts for the archdioceses of St Andrews and Glasgow; they were united in 1615.
[94] R. G. Usher, *The Rise and Fall of the High Commission* (2nd edn., Oxford, 1968), chs. 8–10.

institutional view it was a successful addition to the armoury of the central executive.

Parliamentary legislators generally expected other bodies to implement their laws, but parliament could also create its own bodies directly. In the late sixteenth century, several parliamentary statutes set up special commissions to carry out their work. Parliaments in the 1580s and 1590s established commissions to reform hospitals, to issue a new coinage, to implement the royal revocation of thirds of benefices, and for numerous other purposes. The commissioners were usually officers of state and others active in the administration.[95] But commissions eventually went into relative decline; they failed to match the enormous expansion of other forms of executive action. Probably the government had developed more effective administrative machinery. Not that much is known about the achievements of parliamentary commissions: most have left no trace of their successes or their failures. Occasionally we are told that 'na thing is yit performit' by a commission. Commissions' ad hoc nature, which has preserved few written records, probably hampered them. Although a hospitals commission was invited to 'creat clarkis' and no doubt others did, they lacked the continuous momentum which only a permanent bureaucracy could provide.[96] Executive parliamentary commissions eventually faded from the scene—although one late commission, that for the revaluation of stipends in 1617–18, had an immense impact throughout the country.[97]

If anything replaced the executive parliamentary commission in the early seventeenth century, it was the executive royal commission. The privy council or its own commissions could also do a similar job; but it is probably no coincidence that parliamentary commissions finally faded out in the 1610s just as the crown was creating new forums to pursue its more interventionist economic policy.

One such forum was the commission on manufactures. It was set up in July 1623, initially to promote cloth manufacture though with a much broader long-term remit. It has been described as an 'industrial parliament', with a membership of sixty-nine nobles, lairds, and burgesses, organized into three estate-like groups although nominated by the crown. It was partly prompted by the failure of a scheme to have Scottish wool sent to England to be woven. Its planning must also have drawn on an English commission on trade, with over fifty members representing official and commercial interests, set up in October 1622 for the same purpose as the Scottish body. The Scottish commission was charged to consider the organization of manufacturing, how to promote new industries, and whether existing industries might be 'reformed and reduceit to a more perfyte and proffitable forme of workeing', by

---

[95] *APS* iii. 219–20, c. 17; 437, c. 9; 545–7, c. 15. Goodare, 'Parliament and Society', app. C, gives an analytical list of parliamentary commissions.
[96] *RPC* iii. 199.   [97] Foster, *Church Before the Covenants*, 161–4.

creating chartered or regulated companies of manufacturers. There seems to be no evidence, however, that it acted for any length of time.[98]

The commission for grievances, established in the previous month, was more active. Its authority also rested on the great seal, but its purpose was quite different. Although it did not last, it achieved at least a few of its aims.[99] It was more like an alternative privy council, with a remit to review the workings of the government itself, partly to redress actual grievances but also (and perhaps primarily) to tighten up on administrative procedures. It was explicitly based on an English model.[100] It invited complaints of harm done by 'certane projectis made by particular persouns for their privat gaine'—mainly monopolies, against which a political tide was running in England. It also announced its intention to enforce the penal statutes more strictly. Complex and long-drawn-out negotiations followed with complainers, mainly the royal burghs. Two monopolies were cancelled, but the burghs clearly thought this a meagre harvest for their efforts, especially when it was accompanied by renewed harassment of usurers and bullion exporters.[101] The commission, 'much repynned' against, petered out in 1626.[102]

By the end of the reign of James VI, the departmental structure of Scottish government had developed so far that it would have been barely recognizable to the administrators of James IV or even James V. This was partly because of the creation of the privy council, though that has not been the subject of the present chapter. What we have seen here is that some more specialist institutions had been given new functions, and some of the most important had been created from scratch.

Nor had many institutions *lost* functions. This was not a matter of *plus ça change, plus c'est la même chose*. The institutions familiar under James IV were usually still active under James VI; the new ones were simply added to the old, resulting in an intensification of government. True, one or two old ones declined in political significance—notably chancery, which lost some decision-making functions; but the basic administrative functions even of chancery continued.

---

[98] *RPC* xiii. 290–1, 293, 298–302, 811–13; S. G. E. Lythe, *The Economy of Scotland in its European Setting, 1550–1625* (Edinburgh, 1960), 94–5. For the English commission on trade, few records of which survive, see B. E. Supple, *Commercial Crisis and Change in England, 1600–1642* (Cambridge, 1959), 66–7, and *Stuart Royal Proclamations*, i, no. 229. For a parallel and exactly contemporary Spanish body, the 'Junta de comercio', see Elliott, *The Count-Duke of Olivares*, 144–5.

[99] *RPC* xiii. 219–22. It does not seem to have been a subcommittee of the privy council, as stated by Macinnes, *Charles I and the Making of the Covenanting Movement*, 41; but some at least of its proceedings were recorded in the council register, and the members were all councillors. [100] For which see *Stuart Royal Proclamations*, i, nos. 217, 239.

[101] *RCRB* iii. 168–73; *RPC* xiii. 436, 438; Calderwood, *History*, vii. 575–6.

[102] Sir James Balfour of Denmilne, *Historical Works*, 4 vols., ed. J. Haig (Edinburgh, 1824–5), ii. 131–2; HMC, *Mar & Kellie*, i. 141; Macinnes, *Charles I and the Making of the Covenanting Movement*, 51. The burghs, however, still believed that it might meet in July 1627: *RCRB* iii. 246.

The momentum for change had begun in the 1530s, with the establishment of the court of session as a college of justice. It was in the later sixteenth century that the potential of this development was realized with the dramatic growth of central litigation. Similarly, the privy council itself first took the form in which it would rise to dominance in 1545, but only in the personal reigns of Mary and James VI did it first become clear that a privy council was now something more than an alternative to an adult monarch.

The exchequer grew dramatically in scope during the 1580s and 1590s. This was particularly remarkable because its new activities involved the coordination of financial policy, something in which the privy council was also involved. Yet there was no reported rivalry between council and exchequer, no doubt because of the overlap in their membership. On the contrary, both council and exchequer had conflicts with the king's chamber. After the abolition of the permanent exchequer in 1598, the way was clear for the merger of the four financial departments as a single treasury in 1610. This did not handle all the government's money—one new source of revenue, parliamentary taxation, remained separate—but the treasury did allow more coordination of financial policy than had usually been possible in the sixteenth century.

The general assembly, and later the court of high commission, were completely new. The pre-Reformation church had obviously been governed, but this governing did not occur particularly at a national level or by institutions closely bound up with the state; rather power had been exercised within individual archdioceses and dioceses, with ultimate authority deriving from the pope.[103] The Reformation was very much a national event, and after 1560 the church was governed intensively at a national level.

A few of these developments represented a transfer of power from localities to centre, but in general this is not how they should be viewed. Just as the old central institutions continued alongside the new ones, so the local institutions continued to exercise real power. The potential of the admiral's court, revealed in the new charter of 1587, was never fully realized because of successful pressure from the royal burghs. What was more common was for local institutions to adapt to more regular central supervision. The next two chapters will discuss local executive power in more detail, focusing first on the traditional institutions of local government, and then on new ones created in our period. For the new institutions, we will again find the Reformation exercising a powerful influence for change. First, however, we will look at the traditional institutions. Even there, although continuity is often evident, stagnation is not.

---

[103] Possibly the Scottish national level of authority had been stronger before 1472, when instead of archbishops there were regular 'provincial' councils covering most of Scotland: D. E. R. Watt, *Medieval Church Councils in Scotland* (Edinburgh, 2000).

CHAPTER EIGHT

Traditional Local Government

Quhere can there be a smaller thing that concernis the majestie of a prince nor a seall, for the substance of it is but wax? yit, gif thou disdainfully use that seall, and contemne it, and stampe it under thy feet, thou art compted als guiltie of his bodie and blood, as he that puttis hand on him, and thou wilt be handled after ea way.

Robert Bruce, Sermons, ed. Cunningham, 51–2

Royal authority pervaded the localities of the kingdom. Most Scots were not told what to do by Queen Mary or King James or their regents or councillors personally, but by people acting in their name and carrying symbols of royal authority, such as letters under the royal signet. Robert Bruce, who in the sermon quoted above was expounding the respect due to the sacraments, may have misled his congregation slightly about royal officers: deforcement of an officer was not normally treason.[1] But it was certainly a serious offence, and if respect for the representatives of the law had been lacking, Scotland could not have been governed by the law.

At the sharp end of law enforcement we find the messengers at arms and local courts' officers. They, if anyone, carried the authority of the crown into the localities, as the executive officers of the courts. There were various types of officers. The most prestigious were the royal heralds and pursuivants. Below them, more numerous and accessible for ordinary duties, were the messengers at arms. All these were supervised by the lyon king of arms, wore the royal livery, and were collectively known as officers of arms. Below them were further officers attached to sheriff, baron, burgh, and other local courts, bearing various titles—officers, mairs, messengers, serjeants—and wearing the livery of that court. Messengers at arms did indeed carry letters under the royal signet, and did risk being 'disdainfully used' by those who did not wish to receive them.[2]

---

[1] Hope, *Major Practicks*, VI.31.1–22; Finlay, *Men of Law*, 189.

[2] M. H. B. Sanderson, *Mary Stewart's People* (Edinburgh, 1987), ch. 9, dissects one messenger's duties; see also C. J. Burnett, 'Early Officers of Arms in Scotland', *Review of Scottish Culture*, 9 (1995–6), 3–13; Willock, *The Origins and Development of the Jury*, 150–1; and (on messengers in criminal cases) Wasser, 'Violence and the Central Criminal Courts', 188–93. It may be helpful to think of messengers at arms as self-employed, licensed to act for the courts on a case-by-case basis. Present-day sheriff officers are comparable.

The messengers at arms and local courts' officers had various coercive duties. They summoned the accused, the assize, and the witnesses; they collected debts and court fines; messengers at arms outlawed people, 'putting them to the horn', for wilful disobedience (such as not paying debts and court fines); and if horning did not bring offenders to heel, they followed it up by seizing the moveable goods or arresting the persons of those at the horn. Putting to the horn in debt cases was typically initiated by a creditor who would employ a writer to the signet to draw up the necessary documents. These would be validated by having the royal signet applied by the keeper of the signet or his deputy, and were addressed to the messenger at arms who implemented them.[3] Local courts did not have the direct authority to put people to the horn, and sheriff courts' first sanction tended to be poinding (seizure of goods), implemented by the sheriff's own officer. If this failed then the court could seek royal letters to put the defaulter to the horn.

Some of this work can be illustrated from the stewart court of Annandale. One of the clerks of court sat every Friday in the tolbooth of Lochmaben, 'accompaniet with tuo or thrie officeris of the said stewartrie, for directing of preceptis upone complaintis'. The clerk granted precepts to complainers who appeared to have a case; the officer then had to summon the offender, and to appear in court to testify that this had been done.[4] Annandale was in the Borders, and some of the court regulations themselves show that many of the local folk were supremely uninterested in what happened in the tolbooth of Lochmaben; that was not where real authority lay. The Borders were unusual in some ways, but were still part of the structure of the state in a way that the Highlands hardly were.[5] Much of the present chapter will ask how far public authority could be made answerable to the central authorities, particularly as it intersected with more private, more local, and less accountable forms of power.

Messengers at arms, although essential to the workings of government, had a reputation for corruption—they might, for instance, take bribes to omit names from summonses to assizes, or to deliver a summons in the wrong form (the charges might later have to be dropped when this was discovered).[6] The parliament of 1579 legislated against the issue of general criminal summonses, without named defenders, as it gave too much scope for messengers to insert or delete names unduly.[7] Sheriffs were ordered in 1586 to supply the names of their officers, along with their registers of hornings.[8]

---

[3] Hannay, 'Early History of the Scottish Signet', 303–5; *RPC* vii. 171–2. There were several signets for this routine work. A writer to the signet was equivalent to a modern solicitor.

[4] NLS, 'Ordour to be observit in the stewart court of Annandaill', in MS copy of Balfour's 'Practicks', Adv. MS 24.6.3 (3), fo. 244ʳ. This passage does not occur in the published version.

[5] Goodare, *State and Society*, 218–28.   [6] *RPC* xiii. 380–1.

[7] *APS* iii. 143–4, c. 14. The same parliament referred a further article on abuses by messengers at arms to the privy council: ibid. 152, c. 36.

[8] NAS, treasurer's accounts, 1586–7, E21/65, fos. 72ᵛ, 78ᵛ, 79ᵛ.

The royal burghs complained to parliament of the 'inordinat gredynes' of messengers at arms in 1587, and a thorough shake-up was attempted. Messengers' numbers were to be restricted, with just two hundred for the whole of Scotland, between two and twelve for each sheriffdom. They were to be men of substantial property and were to find cautioners to guarantee responsible behaviour. The lord lyon was to supervise them, holding a court twice a year to deal with complaints against them.[9] But attempts to implement this met with local resistance at justice ayres the following year. The assizes, who were usually alleged to suffer from messengers' extortion, were willing to get rid of a corrupt individual but refused to give names for a general purge.[10] No revised list of messengers was ever 'publist and imprentit' as the statute had required. In 1592, another set of injunctions by the lord lyon again attempted to reduce the numbers of messengers, and ordered 'that they shall not be bound feed houshold servants to any particulare master, but common and indifferent and ready to serve the king and all his lieges'.[11]

Messengers and other court officers were vital, but more significant on the whole were the courts to which they were responsible. Courts were administrative as well as judicial. Local judges and local administrators tended to be the same people, as they were in England, though a separation was often made between judicial and administrative office on the Continent. The heads of local courts thus had responsibility for implementing governmental initiatives.[12]

Many local courts were thoroughly traditional, having established their authority in the days before statute came to dominate the law; they were often reluctant to adapt to an environment of flux, driven by the constant evolution of government policy. Other courts, although locally based, possessed authority deriving more directly from the crown or some other national source. They might be agents of centralization—but they might also be drawn by their local connections into cooperating with the traditional regime. How did each fare, and how successful were they in maintaining control over how, when, and whether they would administer the law?

The main rural administrators were the sheriffs. They were all local nobles or lairds, with lands, kinsfolk, and clients within their sheriffdom, which they were expected to use in keeping up their authority. An earl at the royal court was a suitable sheriff, for he would both have a sheriff depute and maintain a client network in his locality, but a merchant of Edinburgh was 'a persone

---

[9] *RCRB* i. 240–1; *APS* iii. 449–50, c. 30; 456–7, c. 54. The number of 200 applied to the whole category of 'officers of arms'; seventeen of them were the lord lyon himself and his heralds and pursuivants, with the rest being messengers at arms. Most large sheriffdoms were allocated twelve messengers but Edinburgh had twenty-four. A further act in 1592 tightened up aspects of this as part of regularizing the jurisdiction of the lord lyon, who had disputed with the burgh of Edinburgh over the right to supervise the messengers: ibid. 554–5, c. 29; 586, c. 88.

[10] BL, questions at a justice court, 17 Apr. 1588, Add. MS 33531, fos. 217ʳ–218ᵛ.

[11] NAS, Leven and Melville muniments, GD26/7/393, fos. 51ᵛ–53ʳ.

[12] Cf. Hindle, *The State and Social Change*, 30; Fletcher, *Reform in the Provinces*, 88–9.

altogidder unfitt and uncapable of suche a charge and burdyne'.[13] The thrice-yearly head court of the sheriffdom was supposed to be an assembly of all the landed proprietors; if they 'compeiris nocht in sufficient number, or sendis nocht their attournayes ... thereby the schireff-court is weake, and nocht weill stuffed'.[14] Sheriffs and their courts were very much a part of local landed society, rather than something imposed from outside.

The executive powers and responsibilities of sheriffs were multifarious: they had fiscal, judicial, administrative, and even military tasks to perform. One of the rubrics in Balfour's 'Practicks' read simply: 'The schiref sould cause the lawis be kepit.'[15] The staple diet of sheriff courts was judging crime—particularly slaughter and theft—and administering land titles, particularly entering heirs to their lands.[16] Much of this was uncontroversial, but a few duties of sheriffs attracted detailed attention.

Sheriffs' activities might be divided for the present purposes into those responding to local demand, and those prompted by central government. Of course there was much overlap between the two, especially in terms of broad principles—but just because everyone agreed that crime should be punished, that did not mean that consensus prevailed as to how to do it. The punishment of routine crime had traditionally been of little interest to central government (though this was beginning to change); it was unlikely to escalate into the kind of regional disorder that affected political stability. On the other hand, the holding of wapinshawings (military musters) was traditionally the sheriffs' job, and military forces were of much concern in Edinburgh. Then, one of the most vital tasks that sheriffs performed for James VI was to collect his taxes; it is hard to imagine that the localities would have minded if their sheriff had neglected this responsibility.[17]

Sheriffs were in one sense well placed to ignore royal demands. In the sixteenth century, they all held their offices heritably, except in Orkney and Shetland, where the crown's influence was as yet indirect. King James saw 'no present remedie' for heritable jurisdictions, which were 'the greatest hinderance to the execution of our lawes'.[18] But in what way? Were they amateur?

---

[13] *RPC* xii. 615–16, 624–5.   [14] Skene, *DVS*, s.v. schireff.

[15] Balfour, *Practicks*, i. 17. Skene had a similar rubric.

[16] This is a heavily abbreviated summary. See the valuable overview of sheriffs' duties by W. C. Dickinson in *Fife Court Book*, app. B. Robbery and murder—more serious than theft and slaughter—were two of the 'four pleas of the crown', and competent only to a justice court. Cf. Skene, *DVS*, s.v. schireff, and the list of duties in a sheriff's commission, 1622: *RPC* xii. 624–5.

[17] They collected taxes on lay lands, but not on ecclesiastical benefices or on burghs: Goodare, 'Parliamentary Taxation', 36–40. For wapinshawings, see Goodare, *State and Society*, 136–40, 150–4, 157–8.

[18] James MacGill and John Bellenden, 'Discours particulier d'Escosse', ed. P. G. B. McNeill, *Stair Society Miscellany*, ii (1984), 108–9; James VI, *Basilicon Doron*, in *Political Writings*, 29. Some mairs, the most traditional sheriffs' officers, were also heritable. Skene thought that such mairs 'knawis nocht their office, bot ar idle persones, and onely dois diligence in taking up of their fees', but it has been suggested that this was too pessimistic: Skene, *DVS*, s.v. marus; *Fife Court Book*, pp. lxii–lxvi.

But at least their justice was comprehensible to non-literate people, in contrast to the arcane jargon of Edinburgh professionals. Were they partisan? But in a feuding and locally oriented age this was easy to understand, and it was even possible to develop mechanisms to counteract it. The idea that justice could be abstract was a hard one to grasp.

The sheriff courts' popularity may have been declining, and some sheriffs lacked the 'strang hand'—the network of kinsfolk and clients—necessary to do the job.[19] More people were going to Edinburgh to seek law. This is a trend that antedates government interest in administrative centralization: there was a demand for central justice throughout the fifteenth century, and often the council was not at all pleased at litigants coming to bother it. Perhaps the council was in an impossible position. In 1487, it announced that it would no longer act as a court of first instance, leading to protests from litigants; in 1488, James III reversed this, only to be seen as autocratic for undermining the jurisdiction of the local courts.[20] By the mid-sixteenth century, this had changed: a professional court of session was actively seeking to extend its influence over the localities, for instance by advocating cases from the sheriffs' courts, and this was generally accepted.[21] The eclipse of the brieve of right in the early sixteenth century, and the related transfer of cases on fee and heritage to the session after 1532, also removed an important responsibility from sheriffs.[22]

On the other hand, sheriffs were gaining new tasks as well as losing old ones. The immunity of churchmen from the secular courts was removed in 1560, which extended the sheriffs' jurisdiction in one area, though it may not have brought in much extra business.[23] The expansion of statute made more work for sheriffs. This was not qualitatively new in our period; in fact, probably a larger proportion of fifteenth-century statutes had called for implementation by sheriffs. But now the quantity of statutes multiplied. The Reformation made saying of mass a crime which it was sheriffs' responsibility to punish; notaries were to be supervised by the court of session, and sheriffs had to present them for examination; intervention in the economy grew apace, and it was sheriffs who were told to enforce fishing regulations or stop unlicensed export of sheep and cattle.[24] Finally, the establishment of regular parliamentary taxation in the 1580s required sheriffs, as key local collectors, to till this thankless field almost continually.

---

[19] *APS* iv. 145, c. 48.   [20] Chalmers, 'The King's Council', 252.

[21] Balfour, *Practicks*, ii. 340–2.

[22] MacQueen, *Common Law and Feudal Society*, 209–10.

[23] Balfour, *Practicks*, i. 18; *APS* iii. 221–2, c. 20; G. Donaldson, 'The Church Courts', in his *Scottish Church History*, 44.

[24] *APS* iii. 22–3, c. 5 (mass); ii. 487, c. 19, and iii. 448–9, c. 29 (notaries); iii. 146–7, cc. 24, 27 (fishing); iii. 226, c. 31 (sheep and cattle). For a fuller conspectus of such statutes up to 1597, see Skene, *D VS*, s.v. schireff. For sheriffs' statutory responsibilities in the 15th and early 16th cc., see also *Fife Court Book*, pp. xliv–xlvi.

One of the major duties of sheriffs, and one in which they found themselves under close scrutiny from the privy council, was to enforce hornings.[25] Being 'put to the horn' was the dreadful fate of those who did not obey the decreet of a royal court—or a royal summons: it was a favourite weapon against political undesirables, who, if they failed to answer the summons within six days, might be put to the horn. Of course, the local cattle thief, or local debtor (for not all hornings were for criminal offences), was a vastly more common type of outlaw; but people at the horn were all 'rebels', and collectively they represented an aspect of Scottish society that the privy council came in our period to regard with deep detestation and distrust. Remaining at the horn— that is, ignoring the fact that one had been outlawed—had to be stamped out; and it was the job of the sheriffs to do it.

In theory, the solution was clear. Those who remained at the horn had to get themselves 'relaxed' from it—which basically meant (in the examples above) paying the debt, offering compensation for the stolen cattle, or rehabilitating themselves politically with the king, and then having the sheriff court register this. Failure to do so would lead to their property being 'escheated'—confiscated for the benefit of the crown, or of their feudal superior. But here we come back to the messengers at arms. The process of poinding and distraint, which put the confiscation into effect, was not one of their favourite tasks—they risked being deforced, assaulted, or even killed. Without a 'strang hand' from the sheriff to back them up, they were helpless against the more powerful offenders (who were the ones that the government was most concerned about). Discretion may well be the better part of valour, but sixteenth-century Scottish sheriffs brought discretion to a fine art.

So it was up to central government to intervene. This was first done in 1579, with a statute requiring sheriffs to keep registers of hornings and relaxations from the horn. They were to report names of those at the horn to the treasurer three times a year, so that the treasurer could arrange for them to be escheated.[26] Sheriffs were regularly prodded thereafter to produce their registers of hornings: most sheriffs (sometimes sheriff clerks) were asked for them six times between 1585 and 1602.[27] Once, perhaps despairing of the sheriffs, the order went out that those obtaining letters of horning should themselves give in the names to the treasurer.[28] In 1587, sheriffs were to give in names of their deputes and clerks, and find caution to render annual accounts; in 1592,

---

[25] For procedure on hornings in general, see Balfour, *Practicks*, ii. 557–61; Hope, *Major Practicks*, VI.27.1–126; *Fife Court Book*, pp. xxxix–xl. It was normally the sheriff clerk's job to authorize hornings: Gordon, *Sutherland*, 368.

[26] *APS* iii. 142–3, c. 13, which followed on an act of session. Cf. Hope, *Major Practicks*, VI.27.37–43.

[27] NAS, treasurer's accounts, 1585–6, E21/64, fo. 93ʳ; treasurer's accounts, 1586–7, E21/65, fos. 72ᵛ, 78ᵛ, 79ᵛ; treasurer's accounts, 1589–90, E21/67, fo. 211ᵛ; treasurer's accounts, 1593–6, E21/70, fos. 141ᵛ, 181ᵛ; treasurer's accounts, 1598–9, E21/72, fos. 91ᵛ–92ʳ.; treasurer's accounts, 1601–4, E21/76, fos. 91ᵛ, 104ʳ. Cf. James to Sir John Gordon of Pitlurg, 19 Dec. 1585, 'The Straloch Papers', *Miscellany of the Spalding Club*, i (1841), 3.

[28] NAS, treasurer's accounts, 1593–6, E21/70, fo. 184ʳ.

the deputes and clerks were to be admitted to their offices by the court of session; in 1597, copies of inhibitions, interdictions, and hornings registered in sheriffs' books were to be deposited annually with the clerk register.[29]

As well as supervising sheriffs, the central authorities could take their own initiatives. The king himself did so in 1596, calling for those who held decreets of horning to bring them to him for action; one correspondent thought that by the end of the month there would not be a single person left at the horn.[30] That was unrealistic. But there was more and more central action to deal with hornings. From 1597 onwards, hornings could be registered either in the books of the sheriff clerk or in those of the court of session, at the option of the party obtaining the horning. From 1606, the court of session could grant letters of horning upon decreets of poinding obtained before sheriffs or bailies of regality. From 1610, a 'general register' of hornings, supplementing the 'particular' registers of each sheriffdom, was established.[31]

Pressure on sheriffs themselves also continued. In 1598, all sheriffs were summoned personally to explain why they were not enforcing hornings; if they came, there is no record of it.[32] Four Border sheriffs and their deputes came to the brink of dismissal on the issue in 1600, while a commission was set up to discuss how sheriffs could obtain the 'moyene and concurrence' of the local elite in order to enforce the law—lack of this was sheriffs' normal excuse when charged with negligence.[33] A sheriffship should be an onerous duty and not a privilege, thought the king, who assumed that a working sheriff would be out of pocket (and should be rewarded) in 1606.[34]

Horning was something of a blunt instrument, and one way of sharpening it was to draw a distinction between civil and criminal hornings. The local commission of 1588 (of which more in Chapter 9) was to enforce criminal hornings only, as was the Border commission of 1605. In 1608 the king was reluctant to grant a military commission to arrest the recalcitrant earl of Orkney, because the hornings from which the earl had failed to get himself relaxed were purely civil. When it was found legal to kill someone at the horn for debt in 1611–12, the law was rapidly changed to protect those at the horn for civil causes.[35]

From 1615 to 1620, the royal guard undertook a major centrally directed campaign to eradicate remaining at the horn. Making a catalogue of everyone

[29] *APS* iii. 457, c. 52, para 15; 554, c. 28; iv. 140–1, c. 42.
[30] Richard Douglas to Archibald Douglas, 8 Jan. 1596, HMC, *Salisbury*, vi. 7–9. This was just as the Octavians were being appointed.
[31] Hope, *Major Practicks*, VI.27.45; *RPC* ix. 443–5; *APS* iv. 286, c. 9; Scottish Record Office, *Guide to the National Archives*, 215–20, which also records the dates of the earliest surviving 'particular registers'. These dates are before 1625 in about half the sheriffdoms; probably there were further records which have perished.
[32] *RPC* v. 440; cf. NAS, treasurer's accounts, 1599–1600, E21/73, fos. 79ᵛ, 100ᵛ; treasurer's accounts, 1600–1, E21/74, fos. 44ʳ, 55ᵛ; Rae, *Administration of the Scottish Frontier*, 14.
[33] *RPC* vi. 68–9.
[34] Sir Thomas Lake to Salisbury, 10 Oct. 1606, HMC, *Salisbury*, xviii. 319.
[35] *RPC* iv. 300; vii. 705; P. D. Anderson, *Black Patie*, 86; *RPC* vi. 730–1; *APS* iv. 471, c. 3.

at the horn in Scotland was seen as a complex, but seemingly not impossible, administrative task.[36] The king's advocate's clerks, accompanied by the guard, worked their way steadily northwards from East Lothian (no doubt the Borders were felt to have received sufficient recent attention), moving through the eastern and central sheriffdoms of Scotland as far as Caithness. They interviewed those at the horn, and if possible imprisoned those who failed to get themselves relaxed from it. So many of the hornings were for debt that the government sometimes appears to have been acting as a debt-collecting agency. But it certainly reminded the localities of the power of the state.[37] The sheriffs seem to have welcomed this campaign, and regretted the disbanding of the guard on its completion in 1621. Sir Patrick Home of Polwarth in 1626 was 'much empesched with a trublesome office of sheref-schip, espectiallie about captiones, quherwith the guarde wes wont to take ordour, and now bund on the baks of schereffs'.[38] By this time, the self-sufficiency of the sixteenth-century sheriff had been broken down.

Sheriff courts were coming to be more regularly functioning, bureaucratic institutions. Much of the responsibility for keeping them going fell to sheriff clerks. The statute of 1579 on registration of hornings required sheriff clerks to be constantly on duty (and to be 'honest famous men').[39] This became more important once the crown succeeded, during the early seventeenth century, in dislodging many heritable sheriffs and instituting an annual turnover in the post. The crown usually appointed clerks to non-heritable sheriffs, although the sheriffs themselves might claim a right to this. Lord Binning in 1617 thought that the best sheriff clerk would be an advocate; he would normally live in Edinburgh, but would be able to appoint and supervise a legally trained clerk depute. Indeed, with more expertise in the law than either the clerk depute or the sheriff himself, such a clerk would be able to guide both.[40] New-style legal professionalism was being carried into the localities.

Sheriffdoms sometimes contained devolved royal jurisdictions. To take two examples, Ayrshire was divided into three bailiaries with their own courts, while Dumfriesshire contained the stewartry of Annandale. At least one sheriff devolved his jurisdiction to a number of bailies at parish level, in a move that forms a fascinating semi-private parallel to the introduction of justices of the peace. The acting heritable sheriff of Sutherland in 1619, Sir Robert Gordon, tutor of Sutherland, deputed his brother Sir Alexander to act in his place when he left for England; 'and becaus it wes too much trouble for

---

[36] *RPC* x. 376–7.
[37] *RPC* x. 425–6, 511; xi. 560–1, 565, 573–5, 583–4; xii. 24–5, 38–9, 176–7.
[38] Home to Sir Robert Kerr of Ancram, 22 Mar. 1626, *Correspondence of Sir Robert Kerr*, i. 41–3. 'Captiones' = arrests.
[39] They also had to keep registers of inhibitions and interdictions by an act of 1581: *APS* iii. 223–4, c. 24.
[40] Binning to James, 14 Mar. [1617], *Melros Papers*, i. 282–3. Cf. Hope, *Major Practicks*, V.7.4; and *RPC* x. 233–4, for the privy council's supervision of a clerk in 1614.

Sir Alexander to discharge that burthen [of the tutorship], and also the office of shirrefship, he therfor appoynted severall baillies, in all the parishes of Southerland, who would be continually among them, to minister justice, and to decyde all controversies'.[41] This was meant to be temporary, and was probably unusual.

Below the sheriff was the private jurisdiction of the baron court. All important landlords (and some less important ones) held their lands in the form of baronies, with the right to hold baron courts for the tenants of their lands. The baron court was thus a court close to the ordinary people. Courts could also be held for estates outwith baronies, if their lords' charters included the phrase 'cum curiis'. They lacked jurisdiction over life and limb, but since baron courts rarely exercised this by our period, non-baronial courts were similar in practice.[42]

The baron court administered the law of the land (the law itself was not private), and in this sense at least it was open to government influence. But it was relatively unimportant to central government. Its jurisdiction usually included a vestigial right to try the crimes of theft and slaughter, but only when the criminal was taken 'with the fang' or 'red-handed'; most cases of theft and slaughter went to sheriff courts.[43] Much of its business concerned the regulation of farming, where common fields and grazings required careful cooperation by the community.[44] Apart from this, most cases in baron courts concerned minor offences such as assault and petty debt—particularly unpaid rents:

> *Chamberlain:*
> The roomes are rental'd to so high avail,
> The tenants termly cannot pay their hail,
> The bygone years (you know, sir), have been ill.
> *Bailie:*
> They do not so (you'll grant), continue still.
> *Chamberlain:*
> I cannot help't, I poind, arrest, remove,
> And all I do is for the laird's behoove.[45]

The double act of bailie and chamberlain—the former in charge of a court which was supposed to be for the general good, the latter simply the laird's

---

[41] Gordon, *Sutherland*, 362. For justices of the peace, see Ch. 9 below.

[42] *Court Minutes of Balgair, 1706–1736*, ed. J. Dunlop (Scottish Record Society, 1957), is the earliest surviving set of records of such a court. Baron courts were held by those whose charters contained the phrase 'in liberam baroniam' (in free barony).

[43] *Carnwath Court Book*, pp. cvii–cviii.

[44] A. J. L. Winchester, *The Harvest of the Hills: Rural Life in Northern England and the Scottish Borders, 1400–1700* (Edinburgh, 2000), ch. 2.

[45] [Patrick Anderson,] *The Copie of a Baron's Court, Newly Translated by What's-you-call-him, Clerk to the Same*, ed. D. Webster (Edinburgh, 1821), 17. 'Roomes' = landholdings. On jurisdiction over assault see R. A. Mactaggart, 'Assault in the Later Baron Courts', *JR*, NS 7 (1962), 99–126.

estate agent—emerges clearly from this contemporary comic verse-drama. In fact our period probably saw some decline for the baron court, as feuing weakened traditional rural ties between laird and tenant, before it was revived as an engine of seigneurial control in a modernizing agrarian regime from the late seventeenth century.[46] It had been more important in the past: in the fourteenth and fifteenth centuries it had been an arbiter of the land-holding of the lord's vassals, and it had registered some land titles until the late fifteenth century, when this was taken over by notaries. Fifteenth-century statutes, too, had often called upon the baron court to implement various aspects of social, economic, and military policy—setting prices, enforcing tree-planting, regulating begging, and holding wapinshawings, for example.[47]

But by now, parliament and privy council usually ignored baron courts. James VI would probably have endorsed the later complaint that in these courts 'it is very well known that persons of very little integrity sit as judges', and that they bent the law to convict, seeking escheats.[48] Like sheriffs, baron courts were increasingly suffering incursions by the court of session into their jurisdiction, using advocation—a procedure ordering the removal of complex or serious cases from them.[49] Skene seems to have wanted to promote baron courts in 1597, arguing that fines for absence from them should be revived;[50] but this in itself may indicate decline.

The executive officer of a baron court was not dignified enough to be called an officer of arms, but he usually had to be literate and preferably had some acquaintance with the law. He was usually a tenant of the baron himself, although his job involved disciplining the other tenants. He stood therefore at the interface between the governor and the governed, and would have to exercise a mediating influence. The 'order' sought by the state and the 'order' sought by the local community could be two different things.[51]

And yet the baron court was not the court closest to the people, for two other institutions could claim that status. Within baronies there were often burghs of barony—small towns that lacked the status and privileged trading rights of the royal burghs, being restricted to local trade. But they did have government, in fact more intensive government than the countryside. A

---

[46] M. H. B. Sanderson, *Scottish Rural Society in the Sixteenth Century* (Edinburgh, 1982), 18; I. D. Whyte, *Agriculture and Society in Seventeenth-Century Scotland* (Edinburgh, 1979), 44–5; R. Mitchison, *Lordship to Patronage: Scotland, 1603–1745* (London, 1983), 81.

[47] MacQueen, *Common Law and Feudal Society*, 117–19 and *passim*; L. Ockrent, *Land Rights: An Enquiry into the History of Registration for Publication in Scotland* (London, 1942), 57. Statutes on these and many other matters are listed in *Carnwath Court Book*, pp. lxviii, lxix, lxxii.

[48] Mackenzie, *Laws Criminal*, 515. Cf. *Carnwath Court Book*, p. lxxix.

[49] *Carnwath Court Book*, p. xlvi.   [50] Skene, *DVS*, s.v. amerciamentum.

[51] Whyte, *Agriculture and Society*, 48; cf. K. Wrightson, 'Two Concepts of Order: Justices, Constables and Jurymen in Seventeenth-Century England', in J. Brewer and J. Styles (eds.), *An Ungovernable People: The English and their Law in the Seventeenth and Eighteenth Centuries* (London, 1980), and J. A. Sharpe, *Crime in Early Modern England, 1550–1750* (London, 1983), 34, 77.

community of a few hundred people might have two bailies, a clerk, and an officer or serjeant, as well as specialist officials like an ale-taster or a herdsman. Usually their administration was more or less closely supervised by the proprietor, the baron, but they can also be seen as in some ways self-governing.[52] New burghs of barony were regularly being created for lords throughout our period, so they seem to have possessed a dynamism lacking in some other traditional jurisdictions.[53]

A comparable jurisdiction for rural areas—very possibly the most popular jurisdiction for ordinary people, although little is known of it—was the birlaw court. It was linked with the baron court but adjudicated on disputes between neighbour and neighbour, often about farming. The birlawmen or bailies were the judges: they, as well as the clerks and officers of the court, were drawn from among the ordinary folk themselves. Some birlaw courts may have operated in a smaller locality than the barony, even a single farm-ing settlement. The birlawmen were either appointed by the baron or elected under his supervision. In some cases they acted as police officers for the baron court itself.[54] Birlawmen are found in the non-baronial court of Balgair. The birlawmen of Falkirk seemingly could not impose fines of £10, but had to get the regality court to do this for them.[55] Nobody concerned themselves greatly with government in burghs of barony, or birlaw courts, except the common people.

By contrast, one of the most significant, and most problematic, institu-tions—at least for central government—was the privileged type of baronial jurisdiction known as a regality. Regalities covered about half the country— much the same as in Spain.[56] They accounted for less than half of the popula-tion, and many regalities were in crown hands; but private regalities were still extensive. They possessed an exclusive right to try serious crime. Often this theoretically included the four pleas of the crown (robbery, murder, rape, and fire-raising, over which sheriffs had no jurisdiction), but whether regalities actually exercised their theoretical powers is less clear, and no legal writer of

[52] *Court Book of the Burgh of Kirkintilloch*, pp. lii–liii; I. D. Whyte, 'The Function and Social Structure of Scottish Burghs of Barony in the Seventeenth and Eighteenth Centuries', in A. Mączak and C. Smout (eds.), *Gründung und Bedeutung kleinerer Städte in nördlichen Europa der frühen Neuzeit* (Wiesbaden, 1991).

[53] e.g. E. P. Dennison and R. Coleman, *Historic Coupar Angus* (Scottish Burgh Survey series, Edinburgh, 1997), 24.

[54] No birlaw court records survive from before the 18th c.; information on them has to be gleaned from the records of baron courts. See R. A. Dodgshon, *Land and Society in Early Scotland* (Oxford, 1981), 166–7; *Carnwath Court Book*, pp. cxiii–cxvi; D. Robertson, 'The Burlaw Court of Leith', *Book of the Old Edinburgh Club*, 15 (1927), 165–205; 'Extracts from the baron court books of Menzies', ed. W. A. Gillies, *TGSI* 39/40 (1942–50), 103–17 at 112–13. For an overview of the socio-economic context in which birlaw and baron courts functioned see Smout, 'Peasant and Lord'. There were birlaw courts in northern England too: Winchester, *Harvest of the Hills*, 43–8.

[55] *Court Minutes of Balgair*, 5–6, 8; *Falkirk Court Book*, i. no. 22.10.

[56] B. Lenman and G. Parker, 'Crime and Control in Scotland, 1500–1800', *History Today*, 30/1 (Jan. 1980), 13–17 at 13; Kiernan, *State and Society*, 26–7.

our period said that they did.[57] If a tenant of a regality was accused of a crime in another court, the regality court could claim the right to remove the case to itself, a procedure known as 'repledging'. Deciding who was, or was not, a tenant of a regality could lead to complicated disputes.[58] Because regalities were held by landlords, their authority was always heritable (though heritability might diffuse the lords' power in cases where the office of bailie of the regality was held heritably by someone other than the lord). They usually enhanced the general authority of the lord, who could use his control over justice to bolster his following. The earl of Angus advised his brother-in-law, William Forbes of Monymusk, to buy himself out of the regality of Alexander Gordon of Cluny and set up one of his own, 'for the baillierie of regalitie will make yow to have a dependence of the hale cuntrey'.[59] A remote lord of regality could influence his vassals' land tenure, and even demand military service:

The Tutor [of Lovat], calling a regality court at Beuly, charged all the possessors within the lordship to compeare there, and gave each a 7 yeares tack without grassum or entry mony, oblidging them . . . that, besids their bowes, every tennant should have a gun, and be ready whenever called to give attendance at randivouzes (when called) and exercise of arms.[60]

Authority was thus parcellized and massively delegated. Regalities often excluded the crown's brieves and justice ayres, and the judicial authority of the sheriff. The exceptions were the crimes of treason and witchcraft; witchcraft was a new statutory crime, created in 1563, and it is noteworthy that it was retained in central hands rather than being devolved to regalities (not to mention other local courts). When witches were tried in their own localities this was usually by special commissions of justiciary granted by the privy council.[61] Sheriffs could enter regalities to collect taxes, as they probably could on other non-judicial matters like the implementation of the poor law.[62] This, rather than the provision of justice, was becoming relatively more important to central government. Replegiations to regalities were rare in the early seventeenth century, and lords of regality seem to have had only limited scope in their courts for bending the law in their kinsfolk's favour.[63] The criminal

[57] MacGill and Bellenden, 'Discours particulier', 90–3 (where Balfour, Skene, and Hope are also cited by the editor), 110–13, 116–17.

[58] NLS, Robert Colville of Cleish to Sir John Bellenden of Auchnoule, justice clerk, 20 Oct. [c.1565 × 1575], Adv. MS 22.3.14, fo. 56ʳ.

[59] Angus to Forbes, 15 June 1610, Fraser, *Douglas Book*, iv. 246.

[60] Fraser, *Chronicles of the Frasers*, 184. This is an account of the 1580s. Wapinshawings were held separately in regalities: *APS* ii. 362, c. 21.

[61] J. Goodare, 'Witch-Hunting and the Scottish State', in id. (ed.), *The Scottish Witch-Hunt in Context*, 125–6, 129–30.

[62] No lord of regality is mentioned as a tax collector in the decreets of the commissioners appointed to hear disputes over the taxes of 1594 and 1597: NAS, decreets on the taxations, 1594, 1597, E62/1–2. A handful of regalities collected the tax on annual rents, introduced in 1621: NAS, extraordinary taxation accounts, E65/9.

[63] Wasser, 'Violence and the Central Criminal Courts', 107, 263.

jurisdiction of regalities was probably more modest in practice than in theory. The mid-seventeenth-century regality court of Falkirk never exacted the death penalty—something that a sheriff court could not have done without.[64] In most respects it acted as an ordinary baron court.

Still, regalities were bitterly criticized by James VI, and clearly hampered the enforcement of the government's will. In 1609, parliament passed a tough statute to prevent excommunicated Catholics from succeeding to lands: the director of chancery was not to give out brieves or accept retours on their behalf. However, since regalities usually issued their own brieves, the act had to draw back from enforcing the policy on them, stating merely that 'it shall be lauchfull' for lords of regalities to do it.[65] Justices of the peace were told in 1612 that they could proceed against offenders in regalities if they cited the offender first, and if there was no counter-citation by the lord of regality within fifteen days. The JPs protested that this would 'mak thame to be bot as serjandis and officiaris to the uther judgeis', but it was as far as the privy council dared to go.[66] A well-established regality could defend itself against frontal attack. When the king's lieutenant, the duke of Lennox, took over Spynie regality in 1594, 'verray few comperit' and he was obliged to preside over a spate of acquittals.[67]

So the usual approach to the issue of regalities was indirect. The crown exploited its established right to take treason cases out of regalities' hands, having a new series of 'statutory treasons' created in parliament: theft or reiving by landowners; murder under trust; saying mass; fire-raising in coal workings; resetting Catholic priests; brawls in law courts; and refusing a new alloy coinage.[68] Spynie regality illustrates awareness of the possibilities here. An acquittal was granted in a case of slaughter, and the pursuer protested that 'the dome forsaid suld be nul, in respect that the alledgit deid forsaid is ane foule murthour, committit under clud of nycht, and consequentlie ane caus of tressone, upone the quhilk na judge may sit without ane commissioun, except the gustice'.[69]

The act of annexation of 1587, by which ecclesiastical superiorities were annexed to the crown, did not abolish the regalities connected with these superiorities—this would have been difficult for several reasons, including the fact that while the jurisdiction belonged to the lord, someone else could possess the heritable office of bailie. However, it curtailed these regalities in two

---

[64] *Falkirk Court Book*, i. p. xii.   [65] *APS* iv. 429, c. 6.

[66] *RPC*, 2nd ser. viii. 329. This paper speaks of a 'magistrat haveing heritable previledge of jurisdictioun', which might imply heritable sheriffs also, but lords of regality seem to be meant.

[67] *The Warrender Papers*, 2 vols., ed. A. I. Cameron (SHS, 1931–2), ii. 270; 'Extracts from the Register of the Regality Court of Spynie, 1592–1601', ed. J. Stuart, *Miscellany of the Spalding Club*, ii (1842), 122–6.

[68] *APS* iii. 451, c. 34; 545, c. 14; 575, c. 68; iv. 17, c. 11; 22, c. 22; 48–9. Cf. Stair, *Institutions*, III.3.29; Mackenzie, *Laws Criminal*, 403–4.

[69] 'Regality Court of Spynie', 119–21. 'Dome' (doom) = verdict; 'the gustice' = the judge in the central court of justiciary. It was a good try, but this was not in fact one of the statutory treasons.

ways. They lost the right to issue their own brieves of succession.[70] Their criminal jurisdiction was limited to cases in which the regality's stewart or bailie had actually arrested the offender, or had anticipated the (royal) criminal justice or commissioner in summoning him. Otherwise he had only the right to sit with the commissioner in the royal court.[71]

There was particular attention to regalities in the Borders, where some of their privileges were whittled away or rendered innocuous. In the last two decades of the sixteenth century, holders of regalities were successfully pressured to allow royal lieutenants to hold regality courts jointly with them. Border regalities were not allowed to repledge their tenants from justice ayres held in Peebles in 1603.[72] The privy council in 1602 looked into alleged irregularities in the regality of Sir James Douglas of Drumlanrig, ordering him to produce the court books (he complied, and they were found to be in order). But the complainer against Douglas could not have his case heard by the council directly, for 'it wes found be his majestie and counsale that he sould not be redressit ... be ressoun he wes the laird of Drumlangrigis vassall and held his landis of him'.[73] This had changed by 1623; Douglas's successor wanted to repledge someone to his regality court, but the Border commissioners claimed that before 1603, and 'in the tyme of the lait earle of Dunbar' (the leading Border commissioner in 1605–11), he was entitled only to have his bailie hold a court jointly with the king's justice depute.[74]

One statute of 1587 actually gave, or perhaps returned, a responsibility to regalities. Actions on molestation in property had been coming to the court of session, but because they were holding up 'wechtie causis of heretage', they were to be heard instead in the local courts—sheriff and regality courts. However, parliament did not just leave it at that, but laid down a series of procedural regulations on matters like selection of the assize.[75]

Central government, then, generally regarded regalities as distempered members of the body politic, but on the whole could manage to live with them. It certainly did not want to supersede baron courts as such. On the contrary, they would be maintained as essential aspects of landlords' seigneurial power. Few or no new regalities were being granted, but new grants of

---

[70] *APS* iii. 434, c. 8. This probably continued even after the superiorities were granted away—the monasteries to secular 'lords of erection', and the bishoprics to the renovated episcopate. The act of 1606 restoring bishops' temporalities, although repealing the act of annexation, said nothing about bishops' rights in regalities, and they are unlikely to have regained the right to issue brieves: *APS* iv. 281–4, c. 2. An official memorandum at the time of the parliament of 1612 proposed cryptically 'whan prelacies vaikes, to tak ordour with the regalities': *RPC* xiv. 570.

[71] Mackenzie, *Laws Criminal*, 405–6.

[72] Rae, *Administration of the Scottish Frontier*, 78–9; Lord Home to earl of Morton, 11 Dec. 1603, *Registrum Honoris de Morton*, 2 vols., ed. H. Cockburn (Bannatyne Club, 1853), i. 191.

[73] *RPC* vi. 472–3, 481.

[74] *RPC* xiii. 368. For similar encroachments in the regality of Lennox, see *RPC* viii. 263–4, 309–10; xiii. 505–6.　　　　　　[75] *APS* iii. 445–7, c. 23.

baronial jurisdiction were still occasionally being made.[76] The power of lords in local society can be illustrated by the earl of Callendar's regality court of Falkirk. In 1642 it banished five women for being 'unlawfull persones' and warning them that if they returned they would be scourged through the town and branded with 'his lordschips burning irne of Falkirk'.[77] There was nothing here that undermined the jurisdiction of central government. It was probably assumed that baron courts, and perhaps even regality courts, would be integrated into a national structure as their holders, the nobility, themselves came to be domesticated.

One of the biggest difficulties for the crown, both with the sheriffs and with the regalities, was that they were held heritably. As such they were 'the greatest hinderance to the execution of our lawes' and 'do wracke the whole countrie', as King James wrote extravagantly in *Basilicon Doron*. There were, however, advantages to heritability of judicial office. It provided, first of all, stability. The sixteenth-century Ayrshire magnates, the earls of Eglinton, Glencairn, and Cassillis, feuded murderously with one another about a number of issues (particularly possession of church benefices and offices), and it was perhaps just as well that they could not fight over the sheriffship of Ayr, which was held heritably by the Campbells of Loudoun.[78] Secondly, it offered legitimacy. Political power had to retain its link with landed estates—that was a point on which old-style regional magnates and new-style courtier earls agreed—and since the land was heritable, surely the jurisdiction that went with it should be heritable too? Holders of regalities who read *Basilicon Doron*'s animadversions on their iniquities may well have wondered why, if heritability was so bad in their case, it was good for the *crown* to be heritable.

But they would have been unwise to express such thoughts at the court of James VI. Official papers and correspondence, when they mentioned heritable jurisdictions, always did so on the assumption that they were a problem. The case in their favour was largely unheard, or at least unwritten.[79] But courtiers, councillors, and officials must have been aware of the advantages of heritable jurisdictions—especially since, of the eighty-odd heritable

---

[76] e.g. *RMS* vii. 35 (1609), a grant to a gentleman of the bedchamber. Within regalities there were still new creations of burghs of regality—the equivalent of burghs of barony within ordinary baronies. Two examples are Dunfermline in 1562 and Melrose in 1621: E. P. Dennison and R. Coleman, *Historic Dunfermline* (Scottish Burgh Survey series, 1996), 27; eid., *Historic Melrose* (Scottish Burgh Survey series, 1998), 35.

[77] *Falkirk Court Book*, i. no. 53.1.

[78] K. M. Brown, *Bloodfeud in Scotland*, ch. 4. Hugh Campbell of Loudoun did feud with the fourth earl of Cassillis—see Donaldson, *All the Queen's Men*, 103–4. Sheriffs, as members of local landed society, were inevitably drawn into its disputes. The point is that Campbell's possession of office was not disputed. The same goes for the subordinate offices of Ayrshire, the three bailiaries, which were also heritable: MacGill and Bellenden, 'Discours particulier d'Escosse', 109.

[79] A debate held by the university of Edinburgh in the king's presence in 1617 touched on the subject, apparently inconclusively: *The Muses Welcome to the High and Mighty Prince James* (Edinburgh, 1618), 226.

regalities and sheriffships in late sixteenth-century Scotland, a number were held by courtiers, councillors, and officials.

There was, in fact, no intrinsic reason why heritable officers should not abandon their local roots to become components of an absolutist administrative system focused on the royal court. Such systems were usually marked by bureaucracies in which many of the offices were a species of personal property—often heritable property. On the other hand, the crown in an absolutist state also sought to gather patronage into its hands, and to draw lesser jurisdictions into a direct dependence on itself. Confronted with judges and officials holding heritable or life tenures, the instinct of Charles I and his policy-makers was always to wish that they might be reduced to holding office at the royal pleasure.[80] The tension between these two tendencies—both bureaucratizing, both centralizing, and both inextricably entwined with traditional values and practices about patronage, clientage, and noble privilege—played itself out in the attempts of the Scottish government to shape for itself a policy on the heritable jurisdictions.

One aspect of the policy had been shaped long before, at least in general terms. A statute of 1455 had banned the granting of any more offices heritably.[81] This was not always observed, since the causes which had moved previous kings to make such grants—the need to empower a trusted royal servant to impose some kind of authority on a disaffected and perhaps distant region, not to mention the desire to reward a courtier or buy a magnate's support—had not disappeared. The earl of Caithness was granted a heritable justiciarship in 1566, which gave him even more rights of justice than a regality, and which covered the entire diocese of Caithness rather than being confined to his own lands as a regality would have been. But this was annulled by the court of session in 1584, on the grounds (*inter alia*) that the crown had no right to make the grant: 'the saidis priviledgis being sa annexit to his hienes awin persoun . . . that his hienes can not be the lawis and consuetude of this realme transsumit the samin in the persoun of ony our soverane lordis subjectis'.[82] On the whole, the age of new grants of heritable office was long past by 1560.

Still, there was as yet no general wish to reverse the process and place the heritable jurisdictions under systematic pressure. The parliament of December 1567 had the opportunity to consider some radical ideas, several of which emerged via the commission set up to draft legislation for it. The commission

---

[80] P. Anderson, *Lineages of the Absolutist State*, 33; G. E. Aylmer, *The King's Servants: The Civil Service of Charles I, 1625–1642* (London, 1961), 123–5.   [81] *APS* ii. 43, c. 5.

[82] *RMS* iv. 1726; *APS* iii. 357–60, c. 24. Sir Robert Gordon related that Caithness's office gave him 'a power to banish and kill such as he should think expedient, with power also to give pardons for any maner of cryme, except treason': Gordon, *Sutherland*, 145; cf. 152. Caithness's justiciarship was unusual, but there were also occasional grants of heritable justiciarships of regalities, which may or may not have included greater powers than the regality already possessed: e.g. *RMS* iv. 2305; v. 1914. Caithness's son regained the justiciarship in 1592, but it was not stated to be hereditary: *RMS* v. 2078.

drafted an act to require holders of public office to accept Protestantism; parliament inserted an exception clause for heritable office-holders. The commission considered an act banning the heritable regranting of any judicial office that came into crown hands; it was abandoned.[83]

Statutory action against the heritable jurisdictions was certainly possible in theory. English franchises had been abolished in all but name by the Franchises Act of 1536.[84] The new regime of James IV, in 1488, had suspended the jurisdictions of its defeated opponents for three years.[85] James VI, however, had no idea what to do about the major heritable jurisdictions—sheriffships and regalities—when he wrote *Basilicon Doron* in 1598. He would very much have liked to abolish them, but he knew that parliament would never agree.

However, an active and systematic policy on heritable jurisdictions emerged in 1613, shaped by several converging tendencies. The traditional nobility, who held most of the sheriffships, were feeling a need for infusions of cash. They were also being encouraged to attend the royal court and to work for the crown. Meanwhile, the crown had overcome its most serious financial problems, and was showing itself willing to subsidize the nobility.[86] The nature of the deal, to a courtier like the duke of Lennox, became clear. Lennox had the heritable sheriffship of Dumbarton: the king had money. The king wanted to recover the sheriffships: Lennox wanted to demonstrate his loyalty and zeal for royal service, and also to be rewarded for it. That the sheriffship of Dumbarton would change hands for cash seemed clear; the only question would be, for how much?

In fact there were several other questions. Even a courtier noble would hesitate before surrendering an important traditional privilege in his locality.[87] Even in its palmy years between about 1606 and 1620, the crown's coffers were not bottomless. And even though James wanted to pay his courtiers money for their jurisdictions, he also wanted to pay them money simply for being courtiers—so why should they rush to hand over their privileges when they could keep them and still be subsidized? Finally, factional politics impeded the policy. It was promoted by Archbishop Spottiswoode, a rival of Chancellor Dunfermline—who opposed it. Nevertheless, in 1613, a reluctant duke of Lennox and earl of Abercorn were persuaded by the king to

[83] *APS* iii. 38; 24, c. 9; 39; Goodare, 'Scottish Parliamentary Records', 256–8.

[84] Elton (ed.), *Tudor Constitution*, 37–9. The two 'Acts of Union' of 1536 and 1543 deprived the Welsh Marcher lordships of most of their rights of jurisdiction, especially over pleas of the crown: P. Williams, *The Council in the Marches of Wales under Elizabeth I* (Cardiff, 1958), 24–5.

[85] *APS* ii. 207, c. 6; for the act's implementation, see S. I. Boardman, 'Politics and the Feud in Late Medieval Scotland' (Ph.D. thesis, St Andrews, 1990), 170–1, 191. The act applied to sheriffships and bailiaries, but probably not to baronies or regalities.

[86] K. M. Brown, 'Noble Indebtedness in Scotland'; id., *Noble Society in Scotland*, ch. 4; Goodare, 'The Nobility and the Absolutist State', 170–2.

[87] Cf. Adams, 'James VI and the Politics of South-West Scotland', 239–40.

surrender their heritable sheriffships: 'therfor, you sheirreifs, stand to your taikling', advised Viscount Fenton.[88] Many of them did not, and the royal campaign made slow but steady progress. The king was planning a parliament to deal with 'sherrefshepes of inheritance' in December 1616, and the Venetian ambassador listed heritable jurisdictions as one of four items on James's agenda for his visit to Scotland in 1617. A parliamentary commission was set up to negotiate surrenders of heritable jurisdictions on payment of compensation.[89] By the end of James's reign, eight sheriffships had come into crown hands, mostly in the south-eastern heartland of the Scottish state.[90]

Less was done about recovering regalities, because the government made the sheriffships a higher priority. Revocations may have regained some regalities for the royalty; that of 1587 revoked all grants of heritable office made in James VI's minority.[91] However, such revocations were not intended to be enforced in full, and only detailed local research could find out exactly what was surrendered. Charles I's council took a high theoretical line on his revocation, and advised him in 1626 that 'all or the most pairt of heretable offices . . . may be lawfullie recovered by your majestie'; this was proclaimed publicly next year. However, heritable sheriffships and regalities continued to be purchased, rather than confiscated.[92]

Moving now to the towns: much of what has been said about sheriffs could be said again about the courts of the royal burghs. They represented localism at its most entrenched, having gained considerable autonomy. They taxed themselves and collected their own burgh fermes, accounting to the government merely for a fixed sum. Their officers were all locally chosen, and the only significant royal official in a burgh was the customer (of whom more in Chapter 9). Their courts were quite like sheriff courts, with annual (or more frequent) head courts which all burgesses were expected to attend, and with similar criminal jurisdiction.[93]

But there were two differences. One was that burghs and their courts also had special concerns relating to their trading function; the other was that their courts were better staffed and more effective. Instead of a sheriff, a sheriff depute or two, a sheriff clerk, and their personal servants, there were

---

[88] Fenton to Mar, 27 Jan. 1613, HMC, *Mar & Kellie*, ii. 48; *RPC* x. 20–1. For a good account of the political background to the campaign (perhaps underestimating its achievements), see Lee, *Government by Pen*, 123–5. For details of the campaign, see C. A. Malcolm, 'The Office of Sheriff in Scotland: Its Origin and Early Development', *SHR* 20 (1923), 129–41, 222–37, 290–311 at 303–6.

[89] Fenton to Mar [Dec. 1616], HMC, *Mar & Kellie*, ii. 72; *CSP Venetian*, xiv. 477 (the others related to religion, wardship, and finance); *APS* iv. 549–50, c. 24.

[90] *RPC*, 2nd ser. i. 658–60. The sheriffships were Edinburgh, Haddington, Berwick, Linlithgow, Selkirk, Dumfries, Dumbarton, and Forfar. Recovery of heritable jurisdictions continued throughout the reign of Charles I.   [91] *APS* iii. 441, c. 14.

[92] *Earl of Stirling's Register*, i. 39–40; Row, *History*, 345; BL, 'Notes furth of the registers of exchequer, 1583–1674', Harl. MS 4628, fos. 7ʳ⁻ᵛ, 14ᵛ.

[93] H. L. MacQueen and W. J. Windram, 'Laws and Courts in the Burghs', in M. Lynch et al. (eds.), *Scottish Medieval Town*, 212–22.

typically from two to four bailies and a provost (the magistrates who held the burgh court), plus a council of twelve burgesses, a treasurer, and a dean of guild who represented the corporate interests of the merchants. Council and guild acted with the magistrates in making and implementing trading policy. In sixteenth-century Dunfermline, with a population of a little over a thousand, that would make one official for every seventy people.[94] In comparison with the countryside, the towns were intensively and minutely governed.

Statutes calling for implementation by sheriffs usually also called for implementation by burgh magistrates in towns, but unlike with the sheriffs it seems to have been taken for granted that this would probably happen. As for burghs' concerns over local trading privileges, burgess-ship, apprentices, and the like, they were rarely concerns of royal government. If laws were passed on these subjects, they were usually initiated and supervised by the convention of royal burghs. The convention ordered its members in 1580 to enforce eight statutes passed in the previous year's parliament.[95]

Much burgh administration was carried out by guilds, corporate bodies controlled by their members. They worked in tandem with the publicly elected burgh councils, in a way that resembles the interface between seigneurial and royal courts in the countryside. But in contrast to the regalities, nobody ever suggested abolishing the jurisdictional privileges of the guilds. So long as burgh self-management remained stable, central government left well enough alone. Here was where permissive legislation, discussed in Chapter 5 above, was at its most successful. Because burgh magistrates could, when they chose, govern intensively, parliament was happy to furnish the tools, and let them decide whether, when, and how to get on with the job. The Dundee magistrates were worrying about incest in 1583, and about regulation of their maltsters in 1588: they had no difficulty in obtaining commissions of justiciary to enforce the relevant laws.[96] But if they ignored these laws in other years, nobody outside Dundee was bothered by it. The process of bringing new powers to the localities, to which we now turn, did affect the towns, but it affected the countryside far more.

---

[94] E. P. D. Torrie, 'The Guild in Fifteenth-Century Dunfermline', in Lynch et al. (eds.), *Scottish Medieval Town*, 246. Burgh 'setts' (constitutions) varied. Dunfermline in 1618 had a provost and two bailies as magistrates, plus a council of sixteen (nine merchants and seven artisans), a treasurer, and a dean of guild: 'Setts of the Royal Burghs of Scotland', ed. J. D. Marwick, *Scottish Burgh Records Society Miscellany* (1881), 201. Many burghs also had craft incorporations, often seven or fourteen in number; otherwise artisans might join the merchant guild. There were also numerous subordinate burgh officers, those for Glasgow being listed in J. McGrath, 'The Medieval and Early Modern Burgh', in T. M. Devine and G. Jackson (eds.), *Glasgow*, i: *Beginnings to 1830* (Manchester, 1995), 31.

[95] *RCRB* i. 102–3.

[96] Dundee City Archive and Record Centre, miscellaneous burgh papers, nos. 66, 70.

CHAPTER NINE

New Powers in the Localities

To inquire diligentlie of nauchtie and unrewlie personis and travell to bring thame in the way agane, ather be admonitioun or threitning of Goddis judgementis or be correctioun.

The Second Book of Discipline, ed. Kirk, 200

While traditional local courts either continued unchanged or experienced quiet restructuring to increase central influence over them, new powers were emerging alongside them. The Reformation was new, dynamic, and powerful. The power that it wielded was not just a matter of evangelical zeal, though that came into it; it was also directly coercive. The 'correctioun' of 'nauchtie and unrewlie personis' became a central concern of the new courts of the Protestant church, a prominent example of the expansion of authority into new areas of social life. The extension of early modern European state authority into the field of moral regulation has been called 'creating culprits'.[1] English studies have also noted an intensification of government in this period, with more prosecution for moral offences. The relationship between this trend and religious developments is complicated, but the trend itself seems to be well established.[2] The suppression of unruly behaviour was, however, only one aspect of the Scottish church courts' business; and the church courts themselves were only one example of the new powers that were spreading in the localities of late sixteenth- and early seventeenth-century Scotland. Some of those powers arose autonomously, while others were created and supervised by central government.

The prominence of the church courts is a good reason for beginning this chapter with them. Kirk sessions were established gradually after 1560 in each Lowland parish, and presbyteries followed after 1581 in groups of parishes to coordinate their work. Kirk sessions set their own course, leaving the legislators struggling in their wake: the reverse of the traditional view of statutes as the beacons of progress which hidebound local authorities followed only reluctantly. They had potentially a wide area of competence: even the grain exporter Mark Acheson, mentioned in Chapter 5 above,

---

[1] M.-S. Dupont-Bouchat, 'Guilt and Individual Consciousness: The Individual, the Church and the State in the Early Modern Era, Sixteenth–Seventeenth Centuries', in J. Coleman (ed.), *The Individual in Political Theory and Practice* (Oxford, 1996), 125–38.

[2] K. Wrightson and D. Levine, *Poverty and Piety in an English Village: Terling, 1525–1700* (2nd edn., Oxford, 1995), 200–5.

may have felt the impact of the Edinburgh kirk session when in 1594 it was asking the presbytery of Haddington to stop grain exports from East Lothian.[3] Their main governmental concern was in moral discipline, especially the punishment of fornication and adultery, to which were usually added other offences such as breach of the sabbath. The impact of this programme on the common people is discussed in Chapter 11 below; here we shall examine kirk sessions' place in the broader matrix of central and local power.

One conceptual approach that has been tried for England is to treat the clergy themselves as an autonomous professional group providing services to the state, while recognizing the interpenetration of civil and religious ideology in the central aspirations of the state.[4] Whether or not this works for England, it is largely unhelpful in Scotland because the clergy worked with the laity in the church courts themselves. If you were summoned before the kirk session you were being governed directly, just as you would be if you were in trouble before the baron court. The public penances imposed by the session were fearsome sanctions in themselves, and could be backed up directly by fines or imprisonment. In mixed civil and ecclesiastical offences like incest, adultery, or witchcraft, the church courts could also play a decisive role in bringing criminal prosecutions on a capital charge.

In moral discipline, kirk sessions acted primarily on their own initiative. A parliamentary statute was passed against fornication as early as 1567, but it was not followed up centrally, and the sessions themselves seem largely to have ignored it. St Andrews kirk session had been punishing fornicators on its own authority for more than a generation when, in 1593, it finally decided to make its penalties 'aggreabill with the act of parliament'. In Aberdeen, fornicators were still being fined £5 into the seventeenth century, though the statute had specified £40. In many parishes, the fine would be related to the offender's resources.[5] With their own momentum and their own wellsprings of authority, kirk sessions had little need of statutes. Their authority was effective, and accepted as legitimate, because the parish elders were local men who personally knew the people whom they governed. Kirk sessions were 'an idea whose time, in Scotland, had come', because there was a demand for 'order' in local communities, especially among the smaller proprietors who had become more numerous with the feuing movement of the mid-sixteenth century.[6]

[3] E. E. MacQueen, 'The General Assembly of the Kirk as a Rival of the Scottish Parliament, 1560–1618' (Ph.D. thesis, St Andrews, 1927), 186.

[4] Braddick, *State Formation*, 44–5 and pt. 4.

[5] *APS* iii. 25–6, c. 14; *St Andrews Kirk Session Register*, 2 vols., ed. D. H. Fleming (SHS, 1889–90), ii. 767; Aberdeen City Archives, kirk session accounts, 1617–18; Foster, *The Church before the Covenants*, 79.

[6] Todd, *Culture of Protestantism*, 8–16, 403–9. Cf. the support of the 'middling sort' as crucial to any success achieved by comparable policies in England: Hindle, *The State and Social Change*, ch. 7.

Kirk sessions did not always have full autonomy from the traditional local courts in rural areas. This is an under-researched subject, but some recent studies bear on it. Frank Bardgett, in a detailed study of the early kirk session register of Monifieth, has noted the church's success in bringing perhaps half the population to its communion services, and in instituting a system of discipline. Dr Bardgett also feels that the growth of parish discipline reinvigorated the parish as a unit of government, possibly at the expense of the barony. This is important, but Michael Graham has pointed out that the disciplinary success rate in Monifieth was a good deal lower than in the towns. He has also drawn attention to the fact that in another mainly rural parish, Anstruther Wester, the baronies were so strong that the minister was obliged to hold different sessions with different elders for each landed estate.[7] As Margo Todd observes, civil and church courts did usually cooperate in the localities, more than they did in England.[8]

But perhaps this is because the church courts were not wholly separate from the civil courts? They certainly were not separate in towns, where the kirk session was usually linked closely to the burgh council, and indeed supervised by the council.[9] It is no surprise to come across something similar in the countryside too. The session of Innerwick sat together with the lord's bailie or officer in disciplinary cases.[10] David Leslie was tried in the Shetland lawting, or criminal court, in 1603, for having kept his cows in the church of Cunningsburgh: he was 'decernit to mak his repentance in presence of the minister and haill congregatioun on Sonday nixt in sackclayth' and to pay 40s. to the crown.[11] At least one regality court seems to have regarded itself as virtually overlapping in membership and function with the kirk session. When Elspeth Monteith 'confessit certaine poyntis of thift and adulterie' and was 'ordanit to be banyschit' from the regality of Falkirk, it is not clear that she was receiving a criminal sentence or that her crimes were ever put to an assize. Instead she was being treated much as a kirk session might have treated her. The same court regarded the 'bailies or kirksessioune' as equivalent in the licensing of incomers to the district.[12]

It seems likely, therefore, that the church's distance from secular authorities at the lowest levels was limited.[13] There were evidently distinctions at work, since the traditional local courts remained relatively static while kirk sessions

---

[7] F. D. Bardgett, 'The Monifieth Kirk Register', *Records of the Scottish Church History Society*, 23 (1987–9), 175–95; Graham, *Uses of Reform*, 125–9.

[8] Todd, *Culture of Protestantism*, 262.

[9] Lynch, *Edinburgh and the Reformation*, 39–41; Leneman and Mitchison, *Sin in the City*, ch. 2.   [10] Todd, *Culture of Protestantism*, 369.

[11] 'Acts and statutes of the lawting, sheriff and justice courts within Orkney and Shetland, 1602–1644', *Maitland Miscellany*, ii (1840), 149.

[12] *Falkirk Court Book*, i. nos. 1.16, 117.3.

[13] A related issue is how many levels of authority were needed to accomplish any given governmental task. In England, it has been suggested that the concurrence of two or more authorities was needed for many, perhaps most, tasks: Fletcher, *Reform in the Provinces*, 94.

grew steadily in numbers and effectiveness during our period; but the idea of the church courts as self-contained should be treated with caution. The parish elders who constituted the sessions were basically lay people who could play other roles in other areas of government. What was new was to some extent not the church courts as such, but the new governmental functions that they made their own.

One new area of governmental activity was poor relief. Kirk sessions were the only bodies to take this at all seriously in the countryside, but their activities differed substantially from what statute required.[14] It should be stressed that kirk sessions were the only bodies regularly *interested* in poor relief, not the only bodies capable of undertaking it. The misleading claim has been made that the church administered the poor law 'because no other body had an effective system of local government'.[15] Yet even as late as the 1650s, Yester kirk session could raise funds only by working separately with the three baronies within the parish. Landlords were willing to contribute to poor relief, but only if they controlled it, so that 'for practical purposes the unit that mattered was still the barony, not the parish'.[16]

The prosecution of witches was another new area of governmental activity in which the church took the lead. The kirk session was not a criminal court, however, so its control of witch-hunting extended only to the pre-trial stages of interrogation and collecting witness testimony. To hold a criminal trial the next stage was usually to petition the privy council for a commission of justiciary, which would be granted to a minimum of three lairds or people of equivalent status. For this purpose the kirk session (or presbytery, if it was coordinating the prosecution) seems to have sought the cooperation of the highest-status people it could mobilize—even peers if they were available. Further research will be needed to determine how many of those petitioning for commissions of justiciary were in fact parish elders, but probably many were not. Witch-hunting, therefore, was another area in which the kirk session had to work together with others outside it—in this case, the leading landlords of the parish or presbytery.[17]

As committees of ministers with no lay membership, presbyteries seem to have been more autonomous than kirk sessions. They were closer to the general assembly; in 1583, the presbytery of Stirling acknowledged that its acts had to be in line with the assembly's policy.[18] At this early period, the civil authorities were suspicious of them and so were unable to supervise them effectively, but over the next two decades or so the right of crown,

[14] Goodare, 'Parliament and Society', ch. 8.

[15] Mitchison, *The Old Poor Law in Scotland*, 1.

[16] R. Mitchison, 'A Parish and its Poor: Yester in the Second Half of the Seventeenth Century', *Transactions of the East Lothian Antiquarian and Field Naturalists' Society*, 14 (1974), 15–28 at 17–18.

[17] Macdonald, *Witches of Fife*, ch. 10; J. Goodare, 'Witch-Hunting and the Scottish State', in id. (ed.), *The Scottish Witch-Hunt in Context*.

[18] *Stirling Presbytery Records, 1581–1587*, ed. J. Kirk (SHS, 1981), 113.

parliament, and privy council to supervise their work was gradually established (notably by subjecting their powers of excommunication to review).
The re-establishment of episcopacy further eroded their autonomy.[19]

Once the Golden Act had recognized them in 1592, there was a period in
which presbyteries' cooperation in civil government was actively sought. The
court of session was ordered to back up their decisions in 1593, and they were
authorized to punish Catholic recusants in 1594.[20] In 1594 and 1599 they
were asked to report names of adulterous and incestuous persons to the treasurer: this would have been a significant first step towards integration of
church and state social control, since such cases formed the largest single element in presbyteries' business.[21]

The relationship between presbyteries and central government was potentially fruitful. But the breakdown of that relationship after 1596 tended to
return presbyteries to the status of pariahs of local government, usable only
in carefully delimited ways. The government hoped by 1610 (when diocesan
episcopacy was fully restored) that presbyteries would simply fade away—
'cutt tham schort of thair power, and leave tham a bare name, quhiche for the
present may please, but in a litle tyme sal evanische'.[22] Their obstinate refusal
to do so, and the emergence of an organized party of presbyterian dissidents,
kept alive the vision of a fully godly state. The survival of that vision, coupled
with inability to share it on the part of king and bishops (all pious individuals
no doubt), was one of the most corrosive political weaknesses of the early
seventeenth-century Scottish state in the localities.

Still, central government had a number of other paths to the localities
either actually or nominally in its control, and it showed increasing skill and
determination in navigating them. If some of these paths were indirect or
proved to be dead ends, the Scottish government was not alone with this
problem. When Philip II wanted to stop the export of horses from Spain, he
had to turn to the Spanish Inquisition to organize border patrols.[23] It is now
time, therefore, to examine some of the newer, or more flexible, institutions
and procedures which could enable authority to be exercised in a more
integrated way.

To be a credible force in the localities, the government had to show itself
able to do justice. Despite the growth of court of session, it was still important
to bring the courts to the litigants. Many must have thought of the central
courts the way we think of the European Court—important, but would
we ever take a case there? For serious criminal justice, there were periodic
travelling courts: the justice ayres. These had been normally held twice yearly
in each sheriffdom in the fourteenth and fifteenth centuries. They possessed

---

[19] Goodare, *State and Society*, ch. 8.   [20] *APS* iv. 16–17, c. 7; 62–3, c. 4.
[21] NAS, treasurer's accounts, 1593–6, E21/70, fos. 118ᵛ, 119ᵛ, 123ʳ; treasurer's accounts,
1599–1600, E21/73, fos. 74ᵛ, 87ʳ; *Stirling Presbytery Recs., passim.*
[22] Archbishop Spottiswoode to James, 12 Mar. 1610, *Eccles. Letters*, i. 235.
[23] Kiernan, *State and Society in Europe*, 30.

jurisdiction to punish the most serious crimes, the four pleas of the crown. They were major events, mobilizing the existing local machinery of the sheriffdom to try all such crimes committed since the previous ayre.[24] The conventional wisdom has been that they were eclipsed after the death of James IV in 1513 and the appointment of the earl of Argyll as hereditary justice general: in their place emerged a rudimentary central criminal court. Justice ayres were then revived after a statute of 1587.[25] In fact the story was quite different.[26]

It is easy to show that reports of the death of justice ayres after 1513 were exaggerated. James V, Mary of Guise, and Queen Mary all held them personally, at least occasionally. The Regent Moray made them a priority.[27] The *coup d'état* of the Ruthven Raiders was made easier in 1582 because 'many of the consaill' were away 'to hald justice aires in dyvers schyres of the contre', according to Sir James Melville, whose job it was to hold the West Lothian court.[28] The best source for justice ayres is the treasurer's accounts, which record fines collected from major ones.[29] Justice ayres were an established component of central justice throughout the sixteenth century—until they fizzled out almost completely in the 1590s.[30] The question is not whether the 1587 act was successful in reviving justice ayres, but why they declined.[31]

Justice ayres, even at their best, hardly offered regular criminal justice for ordinary people. Even if, as seems likely, only the major ayres were recorded in the treasurer's accounts, there would still have been several years between courts in any one sheriffdom. They were held in order to assert political control by the central government, and to raise money:

> For the pure peopill cryis with cairis,
> The misusing of justice airis,
> Exercit mair for covetice,
> Then for the punisching of vyce.[32]

---

[24] MacQueen, *Common Law and Feudal Society*, 59; on sheriffs' involvement, see *Fife Court Book*, pp. xlv–xlvi.

[25] Paton (ed.), *Introduction to Scottish Legal History*, 39; Willock, *Jury in Scotland*, 44; Walker, *Legal History of Scotland*, iii. 228. The statute is at *APS* iii. 458–61, c. 57.

[26] There is also no evidence that the 16th-c. earls of Argyll held the post of justice general heritably, though they did hold it successively from 1515. See Ch. 7 above.

[27] G. Donaldson, *Scotland: James V–James VII* (Edinburgh, 1965), 52, 123; Ritchie, *Mary of Guise*, 166; Melville, *Memoirs*, 198.

[28] Melville, *Memoirs*, 276–7; cf. Henry Widdrington to Sir Francis Walsingham, 19 July 1582, *CSP Scot.* vi. 143.

[29] There are also numerous references in *Trials*, ed. Pitcairn, to cases that were continued to justice ayres, though such a reference does not prove that the ayre took place.

[30] Goodare, 'Parliament and Society', app. B.

[31] The English agent reported the holding of a series of justice ayres in 1602, but if they had been regular events they would not have been news: Nicolson to Cecil, 28 Nov. 1602, *CSP Scot.* xiii, II. 1085.

[32] Lindsay, 'Ane satyre of the thrie estaitis', in *Works*, ii. 253.

It was the civil wars of 1567–73 and their aftermath that saw the most political dissent—and the most judicial activity. The Regent Moray in 1569 extracted £27,168 from the citizens of Aberdeenshire, and in a series of courts
in the west in 1574 the earl of Argyll hanged eight score people, 'although
hempe and towe were scant'. Between 1573 and 1576 the Regent Morton
held a series of justice ayres in the south-east, in which hundreds were fined
for a range of socio-economic crimes (like salmon fishing out of season, or
cutting green wood) which just happened to have been combined with support for the queen's party.[33] Robert Lindsay of Pitscottie had supported the
king, but his distaste swamped his syntax in his chronicle: 'thair was no thing
at that tyme bot haulding of justice airis from schyre to schyre and the puir
men war hereit and Goddis plaigue rang at this tyme quhat of derth and quhat
of evill weathir and falsit invy and malice and na creddit all rang at this tyme
in Scotland'.[34]

By 1628–9, when justice ayres were briefly revived, they had long sunk
into disuse and had virtually to be reinvented. They emerged under a new
name, 'circuit courts', borrowed from England. The initiative was probably
connected with Argyll's resignation as hereditary justice general in 1628, but
it had been announced the year before. The new justice general, the earl of
Menteith, had his duties separated from the holding of circuit courts,
although he was also one of the commissioners to hold them. The judges held
their courts in groups of sheriffdoms. Dumbarton had to repair its tolbooth
when a circuit court arrived there in October 1628.[35] Assistance in presenting
offenders was sought from justices of the peace and sheriffs. In regalities,
they were to hold courts jointly with the lords of regality—a characteristic
encroachment into regalian privilege.[36] When the time came for the following
year's 'circuit courts' in 1629, Edinburgh made urgent approaches to the
royal court to try to get them discharged, at least as far as penal statutes went;
such a discharge was given for penal statutes infringed before August 1628.[37]
It was already 'dowted' in November 1629 whether the programme would be
repeated. The reasons for the circuit courts' abandonment are still unclear,
but the unpopularity of the penal statutes is a likely reason.[38]

---

[33] *TA* xii. 198; BL, Killigrew to [. . .], July 1574, Cotton MSS, Caligula, C.iv, fos. 271ᵛ–272ʳ;
TA xiii. app. 2.   [34] Pitscottie, *Historie*, ii. 312. 'Rang' = reigned.
[35] *Dumbarton Common Good Accounts, 1614–1660*, ed. F. Roberts and I. M. Macphail
(Dumbarton, 1972), 60. The resignation was by Lord Lorne, future eighth earl of Argyll, who
had been infefted in his father's estates.
[36] Charles to council, 7 Mar. 1627, *RPC*, 2nd ser. i. 538. For the implementation of the
scheme, see *RPC*, 2nd ser. ii. 345–7, 373–4, 420–2, 434–9. Menteith's commission is at *RPC*,
2nd ser. viii. 364. For regalities, see Ch. 8 above.
[37] *Edin. Recs.* vii. 59; William Maxwell to Sir John Maxwell of Pollok, 20 Sept. 1629; W.
Fraser, *Memoirs of the Maxwells of Pollok*, ii. 204. Edinburgh had earlier tried to get the burghs
exempted from the courts' jurisdiction: *Edin. Recs.* vii. 48. There are fewer records of the circuit
of 1629, but see *RPC*, 2nd ser. iii. 111, 391, 406, 441, 466–8.
[38] MacQueen (ed.), 'Two Visitors in the Session, 1629 and 1636', 165. Cf. Hannay, 'The
Office of the Justice Clerk'.

An easy alternative to the justice ayre was the issue of a commission of justiciary to some private individual, to deal with a specified local crime.[39] Sometimes similar were commissions as 'sheriffs in that part': these could give authority to act as sheriff to try a specified case in which the regular sheriff was held to have a personal interest, though such commissions were usually issued for administrative rather than judicial purposes (such as the holding of inquests for service of heirs). These commissions were hardly accountable centrally, and were if anything a surrender to local pressure. When this type of commission was used in England, it was found to be less effective and more partisan than the earlier general eyre. It is true that there are no recorded protests such as those quoted above against justice ayres. But effectiveness is a matter of perspective; one person's effectiveness may be another's oppression. The general eyre had indeed been seen as oppressive and arbitrary. Its replacement by local commissions of various kinds was a response to the local demand for agencies and powers to deal with crime and public order.[40]

Commissions could be abused in two ways—either to pursue an innocent person unjustly, or to procure a collusive acquittal of a criminal. There were clear signs in the late 1580s and 1590s that commissions of justiciary were getting out of hand. The gentlemen of the chamber found it easy to persuade the king to sign them, and could not see why they should take responsibility for deciding whether their friends' friends would really be as trustworthy agents of royal justice as they claimed. The privy council tended to take a more impartial view of what constituted justice, but was only periodically able to win the king to this viewpoint. It was a classic instance of the difficulties faced by a personal monarchy.

The struggle was played out behind the scenes, but sometimes emerged into public view. The council clashed with the chamber, who were 'causing his majeste subscryve sindre hurtfull signatours and commissions', in 1590.[41] Under the Octavians, the council in February 1596 ordered that it must consider all requests for commissions. By April this had to be supplemented by an order that commissions must also pass the quarter seal; probably the alternative seal authorizing commissions, the signet, was proving harder to control.[42] Orders were issued discharging all current commissions in 1587, 1594, and 1598—a clear sign that injustice was being done and being seen to be done—while all commissions empowering the commissioner to bear firearms were cancelled in 1608.[43] A statute of 1592, as well as discharging all

---

[39] Willock, *Jury in Scotland*, 44–5, 155.

[40] J. Bellamy, *Crime and Public Order in England in the Later Middle Ages* (London, 1973), 2–3; G. L. Harriss, 'Introduction' to K. B. McFarlane, *England in the Fifteenth Century* (London, 1981), p. xxii. [41] Melville, *Memoirs*, 375.

[42] *RPC* v. 268–9; BL, 'Notes furth of the registers of exchequer, 1583–1674', Harl. MS 4628, fo. 4ʳ. For more on the royal signature and the struggle to control it, see Goodare, *State and Society*, 110–13.

[43] NAS, treasurer's accounts, 1587–8, E21/66, fo. 93ᵛ; *RPC* v. 130–1; NAS, treasurer's accounts, 1598, E21/72, fo. 47ʳ; *RPC* viii. 195–6.

current commissions of justiciary, announced that no more were to be granted 'generallie' (that is, for all instances of the crime rather than for the trial of named individuals).[44] The act (a brief clause in a bulky package of measures) failed to restrain general commissions entirely, but complainers against one such commission in 1612 cited the act, commenting that 'all suche generall commissiounis ar dischargit be act of parliament, and his majestie hes not bene in use to grant ony of thame bot sometymes, and that verie sindle, in materis of thift'.[45] It seems to have been around this time that a register of signet commissions was established, evidently as a means of monitoring them.[46]

By the seventeenth century the council had succeeded in staunching the flow of commissions of justiciary, probably aided by the departure of the royal court. There were still various general commissions on matters the government thought were important, such as one to punish Catholic ritual celebrations in the diocese of Moray in 1616; but they came via the council.[47] This continued to provoke debate, and a newly appointed justice clerk in 1623 found 'great confusion and disordour in the place; and next, many principall parts of that office exerced by commissions, and by other judges not competent'.[48] However, the struggle of the 1590s was over. No more orders needed to be issued discharging the current commissions. Commissions of justiciary had been used for want of anything better at a time when the demand for justice was heavy. When they threatened to get out of control, the government failed to steer them in the direction it wanted—but it was eventually able to apply the brakes.

One important class of commissions of justiciary—those for trying witchcraft—continued to be granted regularly for most of the seventeenth century. After 1598 they were usually in the hands of the privy council alone, and no disputes with the chamber are reported. Such disputes were less likely concerning witches, who rarely had personal connections at the royal court. The central authorities had little control over the final outcome of witchcraft trials by commission, but they did not need to, so long as they retained the power to grant, or withhold, the commission; this made the council effectively the place at which the decision on the suspect's guilt or innocence was made. The decision was based on evidence collected beforehand in the locality and presented to the council by the leaders of the prosecution—usually a small group of local lairds in consultation with a presbytery or kirk session.

---

[44] *APS* iii. 556, c. 30.   [45] *RPC* ix. 389–91. 'Sindle' = seldom.

[46] A commission signed by the king but 'not registered or signetted, nor yet subscribed by the ordinary officers of estate', was quashed in 1602: *RPC* vi. 445. The first extant register is NAS, register of commissions, 1607–16, PC7/1.

[47] *RPC* x. 650–1. The commissioners were the bishop and the bailie of the regality of Spynie, the latter presumably because it would allow entry to the regality.

[48] Sir Archibald Napier of Merchiston to James, 11 Dec. 1623, *Memorials of Montrose*, ed. Napier, i. 19.

The commission, which was often for 'trying and burning' the witch, was merely the last stage of a process of smooth and efficient cooperation between centre and locality.[49]

Mention of kirk sessions leads back to the church, and to parish-level administration. Kirk sessions were flourishing there as new and effective agents of government, and it was perhaps for that reason that central government began to try to insert its own representatives into parishes alongside them. Kirk sessions were not directly amenable to central direction, and parish commissioners might be able to do other things unconnected with their remit. The civil parish began to emerge in England in this period, driven partly by the need to administer the Elizabethan poor laws.[50] There was already such a system in Orkney and Shetland, where the bailie was a public parish official, appointed by crown or bishop, who held courts, collected rents, and headed local military musters.[51] A similar network of administrators, answerable to Edinburgh, could bypass the more intractable sheriffs and bring central government into closer contact with the people.

Administrative experimentation characterized the Reformation's early years. The privy council, charged in 1563 with implementing an act of parliament on repairing parish churches, sought to construct a hybrid institutional structure involving four different sources of authority. A secular, centrally appointed 'sheriff in that part' (probably covering a group of parishes) was to organize the election of assessors by the parishioners who were to pay two-thirds of the tax. The rest was to be paid by the pre-Reformation benefice-holder, and the receiver of the tax was to be the parish minister. However, this never established itself on a regular basis.[52]

A more straightforward scheme, to establish crown judicial commissioners in each parish, was launched in 1579. They were to implement laws on poor relief, sabbath enforcement, and Bible possession.[53] No doubt they were intended (when and if appointed) to work with kirk sessions, but they were to derive their authority directly from the crown—or from the bishops, which amounted to almost the same thing in 1585 when Archbishop Adamson was wanting to appoint parish 'censors of maners'.[54] It is unlikely that many commissioners were appointed, though there was one in Edinburgh in 1585, and a poor relief act of 1588 kept a place for them.[55] By 1592 the idea was being merged with the presbyterian church structure. The general assembly, having appointed ministers as commissioners to plant churches, assign stipends, and

---

[49] Goodare, 'Witch-Hunting and the Scottish State'. The much-discussed cancellation of witchcraft commissions in 1597 is dealt with by id., 'Framework for Scottish Witch-Hunting'.

[50] Hindle, *The State and Social Change*, ch. 8.

[51] F. J. Shaw, *The Northern and Western Islands of Scotland: Their Economy and Society in the Seventeenth Century* (Edinburgh, 1980), 61.

[52] *APS* ii. 539–40, c. 12; *RPC* i. 247–8; *APS* iii. 76*–77, c. 15.

[53] *APS* iii. 138–42, cc. 8, 10, 12.   [54] Calderwood, *History*, iv. 267.

[55] *Edin. Recs.* iv. 421; *RPC* iv. 302–3.

prosecute Catholics, persuaded the privy council to issue them with blank signet commissions for them to give to nobles and burgh magistrates to support them. Presbyteries were offered their own commissioners in 1594, and ministers were invited to nominate commissioners in 1595. None of these schemes got far.[56] Since both privy council and general assembly supported them, their failure is probably to be attributed to the indifference of parish elders. Their own authority sufficed for their usual work, and when they needed to call in the existing civil magistrates they generally received their cooperation.

The 1590s saw at least one scheme to create civil administrators at presbytery level. In 1592 there was an order to compile rentals of annexed temporalities of church lands. 'Certane weill affected gentilmen in everie presbiterie' were nominated as commissioners, but this was 'randerit ineffectuall be the refusall of the saidis commissionaris to accept that burding upoun thame'.[57] This failure should probably be ascribed to the nature of the commission—a basically fiscal one—rather than to hostility to civil commissions as such.

There were fewer schemes for parish commissioners after that, but the idea did not disappear entirely. There were echoes of the English civil parish in 1616, when the general assembly, backed by the privy council, ordered parish ministers to keep registers of baptisms, marriages, and burials. This scheme took only fitful effect, and there was little or no effort to enforce it. At best it may have encouraged kirk sessions to persevere if they were already keeping such records.[58] It certainly did not create an alternative power network to the kirk session.

The next local authorities to be considered are the commissary courts. These replaced the pre-Reformation church courts, principally the courts of the bishop's officials. They were launched as secular bodies in 1564. There were something over twenty commissaries, one in each of the smaller dioceses and several in the larger ones.[59] The officials' courts had been answerable mainly to the bishop, with appeals lying to the official principal of St Andrews (and probably Glasgow for that archdiocese) and then ultimately to Rome. Now appeals lay from 'inferiour commissaris' to the central commissary court of Edinburgh and thence to the court of session. The session issued hornings on commissaries' decrees. The Edinburgh commissaries collected the local commissaries' registers, appointed substitutes for them, and themselves dealt with all testaments over £50. Each local commissary also had a 'procuratour-fiscal' with extensive responsibilities,

[56] RPC iv. 753–4; APS iv. 63, c. 8; RPC v. 200; Goodare, 'Framework for Scottish Witch-Hunting', 244–7.   [57] RPC iv. 744–5.

[58] RPC x. 669–70; M. Flinn (ed.), Scottish Population History (Cambridge, 1977), 45–51.

[59] D. B. Smith, 'The Spiritual Jurisdiction, 1560–1564', Records of the Scottish Church History Society, 25 (1993–5), 1–18; Ollivant, The Court of the Official, 163–5; P. G. B. McNeill and H. L. MacQueen (eds.), Atlas of Scottish History, to 1707 (Edinburgh, 1996), 381.

himself becoming executor to all testaments where the nearest of kin failed to do so.[60]

The court of session could regulate the commissary courts, but the general assembly, to its annoyance, could not. When in 1595 the general assembly was wanting to restrict the remarriage of adulterers, it had to 'travell with the commissars'.[61] In 1609, the courts were partially subjected to the bishops, who gained power to appoint the commissaries and took over much of the supervisory role of the Edinburgh commissary court. The court of session retained its appellate jurisdiction and even gained the right to advocate cases to itself from any local commissary court.[62] The commissaries, neither fully secular nor fully ecclesiastical, illustrate the fruitlessness of trying to divide early modern government into 'church' and 'state'.

The most successful civil scheme to increase the density of the matrix of local power operated not at the level of the parish, which the church had made its own, but at that of the sheriffdom. This was the introduction of justices of the peace. Following a statute of 1609, JPs were first appointed in 1610. They were mainly the leading lairds of each sheriffdom, backed by the local nobles and any privy councillors who were around. Detailed articles setting out their authority were issued in 1611, and ratified (slightly modified) by statute in 1617.[63] The JPs had constables, also an innovation, as their executive officers. The statute of 1609 envisaged them mainly as suppressing feuds, but this proved not to be their main area of work; instead, they were to extend the authority of the state further down the social scale, to regulate those who previously had been ruled by the authority of their landlords. Of course JPs were landlords too, but they were now acting by virtue of state authority as well as their own; and the rules were more detailed than before. There were about four hundred JPs, a dramatic expansion of the number of local administrators.[64]

The JPs' oath bound them to do equal justice to rich and poor.[65] But it was unlikely that they would often confront the rich, since most of the offences with which they dealt were committed mainly by the poor, or at least by the not-rich—offences like vagrancy, resetting of gypsies, and cutting green wood. Their jurisdiction over other offences, especially riots and breaches of the peace, covered only offenders of 'meaner degrie' than landed gentlemen. The latter were instead to be reported to the privy council. Many offences could be punished only if the regular courts—sheriff or regality—failed to act within fifteen days; here the JPs had the opportunity to become a second line

---

[60] Balfour, *Practicks*, ii. 655–63.
[61] *Acts of Sederunt*, 6, 16–17; *BUK* ii. 543 (cf. 540–1); Calderwood, *History*, v. 370–1.
[62] *APS* iv. 430–1, c. 8; Balfour, *Practicks*, ii. 664–8.
[63] *RPC* ix. 75–80, 220–6; *APS* iv. 434, c. 14; 535–41, c. 8. The bishops had asked the king in Jan. 1609 to get the treasurer to appoint 'searchers' in each sheriffdom to report those carrying firearms to the privy council: *BUK* iii. 1068–9. This became one of the JPs' tasks.
[64] McNeill and MacQueen (eds.), *Atlas*, 222.   [65] *RPC*, 2nd ser. viii. 297–305.

of attack against disorder and insubordination. They also received exclusive powers to fix wages and prices.[66] It was this aspect of their work—regulation of the local economy—that would eventually give them their importance.

It was in the countryside that JPs made most difference, but they also existed in towns. The privy council had to sort out the powers of shire JPs in burghs.[67] Burgh councils themselves gained the powers of JPs within their burgh, and were able if they wished to appoint constables, as they did in Edinburgh. The magistrates of Edinburgh used the opportunity of the introduction of constables to draw up, and print, their own regulations for their conduct, more detailed than those called for by the statute; constables were elected regularly thereafter.[68] Constables acting for the justice of the peace court in late seventeenth-century Aberdeen have been described as 'moral traffic wardens'.[69] A study of policing in the later seventeenth century has found the constables to be functioning regularly and playing a key role both in town and countryside.[70]

King James remarked to the English in 1616: 'Government by justices is so laudable and so highly esteemed by mee, that I have made Scotland to bee governed by justices and constables, as England is.'[71] These officers obviously derived in some sense from England, but they did not have the opportunity— nor were they ever intended—to build up a comparable position as the primary agents of local government. There were already sheriffs in that position. There was potential for conflict with sheriffs, for instance in the 1617 regulation that JPs were to report to the privy council any sheriff imposing an inadequate penalty for assault.[72] The impression given by the sources, however, is that there was little such conflict, and that the JPs carved themselves out a niche in local government. By 1629, it was taken for granted that 'generall justice' in the localities was to be had from JPs in their quarter sessions and from sheriffs. What this commentator thought more noteworthy was that 'the judges of the [court of] session beare such a hande over them as they will call in question allmost every thing they do, let them doe the best they have'.[73] Probably there was less central intervention than this would suggest, but it still indicates a fairly stable and well-integrated system. Stability may not have been enhanced by the characteristic clericalism of Charles I: in 1635, a royal warrant to the privy council ordered that they should choose some ministers from every presbytery to be JPs. Many ministers refused, while some accepted.[74] But there seems to be no doubt that JPs had been successfully established. The statement that 'less than half of the Scottish shires had

---

[66] RPC ix. 409–11.   [67] RPC ix. 525–6.   [68] Edin. Recs. vi, pp. xxxvii, 77–8, 108.
[69] Lynch and Dingwall, 'Elite Society in Town and Country', 182.
[70] J. G. Harrison, '"Policing" the Stirling Area, 1660–1706', Scottish Archives, 7 (2001), 16–24.
[71] James VI & I, speech in star chamber, 1616, in Political Writings, 221.
[72] This regulation did not however give JPs 'the authority to amend or annul obviously bad decisions of the sheriff's court', as stated by Lee, Government by Pen, 128.
[73] 'Two Visitors in the Session', 165.   [74] Row, History, 388.

commissions [of the peace] still functioning by 1625' is based on a misreading of the evidence.[75]

It is hard to gauge the reaction of JPs themselves. There are no surviving quarter sessions records from this period, but much of the JPs' work, perhaps most, was done individually, and did not require formal record-keeping. We have an enthusiastic paper from the Aberdeenshire JPs, delighted to have the opportunity to tackle offences that they felt were neglected by the sheriff, and the case in 1613 where the Berwickshire JPs imprisoned a suspected thief and complained successfully to the privy council when the sheriff refused to try him.[76] The JPs of the south-western counties seem successfully to have carried out the privy council's order to regulate freight charges on voyages to Ulster.[77] The shire commissioners in the convention of estates of 1630 (many doubtless JPs themselves) wanted JPs' powers extended.[78]

The main evidence of reluctance consists of an obstructive paper from the East Lothian JPs, written at the height of the famine of 1623 when they were supposed to be organizing poor relief. They complained that poor-rates were 'odious', wilfully misconstrued their powers, and summed up their responsibilities as 'ane service toylsome and trublesome unto us, importing nathair credit nor benefit, bot ane schadowing appeirance of ane commoun weill as we apprehend'.[79] This is the authentic voice of property-owners who intend to stay that way and who see government as undermining rather than buttressing their position; it should be taken seriously. Much less weight should be attached to the too often quoted outburst of Archbishop Gledstanes in 1611 that 'the realme had many hundreth yeares bene weill governed without justices of peace'; Gledstanes was an ineffective politician who was neither trusted by the king nor respected by his colleagues.[80]

Gledstanes's remark may at least serve to introduce the question of how innovative the creation of JPs was. Although introduced on an English model,

[75] Macinnes, *Charles I and the Making of the Covenanting Movement*, 10. The main evidence cited is a list of JPs of eight sheriffdoms, but this is simply a list of the sheriffdoms without heritable sheriffs, where the crown normally appointed a sheriff annually from among the serving JPs: *RPC*, 2nd ser. i. 658–60. We should treat this evidence as a *sample* of the sheriffdoms, suggesting that JPs were established in *all* of them. Also cited is a collection of reports from JPs on local prices, where only a minority of sheriffdoms' replies are recorded: ibid. 670–5, 677–8. But this hardly proves that the JPs in all other sheriffdoms were inactive locally, and the index to this volume of *RPC* alone attests to activity by other JPs that was noted by the privy council. Failure to examine such evidence has led to excessive scepticism about JPs, such as the recent (unreferenced) statement that 'JPs were established in Scotland in 1609 but were not effectively in place until the end of the century': Todd, *Culture of Protestantism*, 409.

[76] *LP James VI*, 300–2; *RPC* x. 57.

[77] M. Perceval-Maxwell, *The Scottish Migration to Ulster in the Reign of James I* (London, 1973), 147. For more on south-western JPs see Adams, 'A Regional Road to Revolution', 56–7.

[78] *APS* v. 219.

[79] *RPC* xiii. 834–8. For an example of their interpretation of the law, they complained that 'no certane number' of JPs was designated as having power to act between quarter sessions; in fact the statute said that three JPs were to act.

[80] *RPC* xiv. 621–2; Lee, *Government by Pen*, 96, 147–8.

they had a native prehistory, for the government had long sought to introduce some kind of royal commissioners into the localities. It was always intended that such commissioners would be local landed men, rather than visiting *intendants*. The story begins in 1575, when a national network of fifty-four local commissioners was appointed to hold regular wapinshawings. Their reports were to be 'rollit in bukis' and sent to the regent.[81] In 1581, parliament created a network of rural justices—mainly, but not entirely, sheriffs and burgh magistrates—to enforce river-fishing regulations.[82] The general assembly asked in 1586 'that judges may be appointit in all shyres for executioun of the acts of parliament made against the breakers of the sabbath day, adulterers, and such oppin transgressours of Gods law'.[83] The statute of 1587 to reorganize justice ayres envisaged over three hundred local commissioners to arrest criminals. This scheme bears the closest resemblance to what happened after 1609; however, the resounding tinkle it produced at the time is better attested than usual, and next year another idea was tried: the issue of high-powered commissions to fifty-eight individuals to implement a number of laws in each sheriffdom.[84] Included in their remit was the enforcement of criminal hornings, normally the sheriffs' job. They also had to implement the poor law (by appointing parish commissioners), banish Jesuits, mediate in local feuds, and hold wapinshawings—most of these being tasks on which statutes had recently been passed. No more is heard of these commissions either, but they would not be likely to have left much trace except in family papers. Quite possibly they had some impact: they were, after all, similar to the justiciary commissions which were undoubtedly popular with local elites; on the other hand, they did not offer the unique combination of power and irresponsibility that was the hallmark of the commission of justiciary.

The trouble with all these sixteenth-century commissions was that they appeared to be rivals of the sheriffs, and this was not a role that people were queueing to adopt. Even in 1610, when JPs were being introduced, the aim was for them to tackle 'licht insolencyes' which 'did verry oft kendle suche flames of disordour and feid as hardlie thairefter culd be quenched'.[85] Instead, however, they found their role in regulating the local economy—weights and measures, roads and bridges, price-fixing, poor relief—rather than trying to compete directly with the sheriffs. As the economy expanded, and as the state's desire to intervene to regulate trade increased, so new local institutions

---

[81] *APS* iii. 91–2.

[82] Ibid. 217–18, c. 15. Another act of this parliament empowered baron courts to set prices 'on all stuf'—one of the few statutes of this period to involve baron courts: ibid. 225, c. 28. This later became the responsibility of JPs.

[83] *BUK* ii. 659. Cf. the request of 1574 for commissions to 'gentlemen' in each sheriffdom to deal with incest, adultery, and witchcraft: *BUK* i. 305. This was not the same project as the one that emerged in 1575, but it shows that the idea of local commissions was widely circulated.

[84] McNeill and MacQueen (eds.), *Atlas*, 222; *RPC* iv. 300–2.

[85] *RPC*, 2nd ser. viii. 297.

would emerge to fulfil that function. This is the true measure—modest, but palpable—of the JPs' success.[86]

A coda to the story of the JPs may be offered—one that sums up several aspects of the increasing pressure of government on the localities. Increasing numbers of people were being identified or labelled as offenders, and agents of the state were actually managing to come into contact with many of them: so suitable accommodation had to be found for them. Dundee decided to build a new prison in 1589 for adulterers and fornicators, apparently on its own initiative.[87] Urban kirk sessions increasingly used brief periods of imprisonment as a punishment, as well as imprisoning suspects while their cases were investigated, and demanded that the prisons should be up to standard.[88] Central government also began to show concern that burghs should possess prisons: the new royal guard started to arrest people in the early seventeenth century, and prisons were particularly needed for tax defaulters. Imprisonment was regularly used, not as a punishment directly, but as a weapon to extract payment of fines or compensation.[89] Localities were expected to pay for prisons, by taxation if necessary; from 1597 it was a statutory requirement that all royal burghs should have them. When Stonehaven was made the administrative centre for Kincardineshire it was charged to have a prison. Special attention was paid to prison accommodation in Edinburgh: new prison regulations were drawn up in 1606, and a new prison wing was added to the tolbooth in 1610. In 1614, poor people who had been imprisoned there by order of the privy council were to receive a maintenance allowance. From 1617, burghs had by statute to imprison anyone on a warrant from a single JP.[90] The development of prisons, central regulation of them, and the increased responsibility they gave to burghs as the nerve centres of local power, are all characteristic of the period's burgeoning administrative sophistication, or at least complexity.

It remains to examine an area of local administration which was more directly controlled from the centre: the customs collection service. In the late Middle Ages the burghs had gained control of their local fermes and taxation, but had left the collection of the great customs (duties on overseas exports, and from 1597 on imports) untouched in crown hands. Local influence over the customer's office was found in some burghs, such as Kirkcudbright, where the sixteenth century saw a dynasty of Maclellans as customers. When in 1602 the current incumbent arrested a ship to collect unpaid customs, no

---

[86] Cf. S. J. Davies, 'The Courts and the Scottish Legal System, 1600–1747: The Case of Stirlingshire', in Gatrell et al. (eds.), *Crime and the Law*, 134.

[87] Dundee City Archive and Record Centre, Dundee council minutes, vol. ii, p. 20.

[88] Graham, *Uses of Reform*, 50, 54, 95–6.

[89] *RPC* vii. 59; x. 224, 580; xii. 307–8; Wasser, 'Violence and the Central Criminal Courts', 156–7.

[90] *APS* iv. 141, c. 44; *RPC* ix. 114; *Edin. Recs.* vi. 21–2, 55; *RPC* x. 287; *APS* iv. 538, c. 8, para 17. Cf. J. Cameron, *Prisons and Punishment in Scotland* (Edinburgh, 1983), 27–34.

customs had been paid into the exchequer for twenty years.[91] Yet this pattern was not repeated, it seems, in the most important burghs—and over 80 per cent of customs revenue came from just four burghs.[92] Nor were the burghs able to determine the customs rates. They were reduced to lobbying to influence customs policy: one angel noble was paid to the advocate John Sharp to draft Edinburgh's successful protest against new customs rates in 1582. Shortly after, the crown set the customs in tack (i.e. lease) to the burghs; but the very fact that it was able to do so (and later to terminate the contract) shows that it was maintaining central control over the customs bureaucracy.[93]

The customs tack to the burghs was an example of administrative privatization. Others are not far to seek. Piecemeal tacks of local customs were quite common in the sixteenth century, presumably in response to local initiative, though the national tack of 1586 was a failure. A new age of centralized customs farming began in 1598 and continued for most of the next forty years, perhaps buoyed up by the return of trading prosperity in the early seventeenth century.[94] The government supervised the tacksmen in some detail, directing them on how to do their jobs rather than simply collecting the money. Meanwhile, the existence of the tack could allow the government to shelter from criticism. In 1613 the burghs' complaints about the customs were regarded as criticisms of the tacksmen, and the government could pose as an arbitrator.[95]

As governmental aspirations expanded, resources did not always keep pace. Machinery was not available to enforce all the new legislation. Yet the new areas of official concern represented potentially lucrative pickings for anyone willing to risk the opprobrium of their neighbours, for the legislation often imposed financial penalties for disobedience. The early seventeenth century was the great age of the patentee and the private informer.

Patentees and informers were multifarious, but their activities followed identifiable patterns. Informers provided information. The pure informer pointed out to a court that the law was being broken, and then left it to the

[91] A. L. Murray, 'Customs Accounts of Dumfries and Kirkcudbright', 121–2. For details of local customs administration see id., 'Customs Accounts of Kirkcudbright, Wigtown, and Dumfries', 136–46.

[92] I. Guy, 'The Scottish Export Trade, 1460–1599', in Smout (ed.), *Scotland and Europe*, 62. They were Edinburgh, Aberdeen, Dundee, and Perth.

[93] *Edin. Recs.* iv. 232.

[94] For the beginning of customs farming, see *ER* xxiii. 237–46, 334–5. For key negotiations between government and customs tacksmen, see *RPC* ix. 262–71, 625–6, 715–24; x. 598–602, 620–1; xi. 214–15, 249, 266. Direct collection resumed in 1617, because no tacksmen put in a high enough bid: Binning to James, 7 Nov. 1617, *Eccles. Letters*, ii. 516–17. However, farming began again in 1628: NAS, comptroller's accounts, 1628–9, E24/46. The general farming of the Scottish customs antedates the 1605 'great farm' of the English customs: F. C. Dietz, *English Public Finance, 1558–1641* (2nd edn., London, 1964), ch. 15.

[95] *RCRB* ii. 425–6; *Edin. Recs.* vi. 101–4. For some administrative requirements on the tacksmen see James to Salisbury, 29 Sept. 1611, HMC, *Salisbury*, xxi. 313–14.

court to enforce the law. A more active informer would also assist by gathering information or by arresting the lawbreaker. Such responsible activity might well be rewarded. The informer really arrived as a private agent of government when he was rewarded systematically for a series of informations, receiving either a fee, or a proportion of the financial penalties. At this stage, such rewards would be open to anyone, but active informers would make them a regular business.

The informer would be transformed into a patentee if he then negotiated a special deal for himself—perhaps he alone would be entitled to a reward for informing, although others could also do so. An informer with monopolistic tendencies would receive the sole right to bring informations about the offence concerned. Finally, the patentee could also receive further rights, including the ability to intervene actively in the business being regulated. Instead of simply reporting faulty products, he would certify the quality of unfaulty ones. This could in theory be a voluntary system, but patentees in practice would have it made compulsory: all producers would have to have their goods certified, and pay a fee to the patentee's agents. The patentee would now be a monopolist.

Informers were used in the field of criminal law, particularly in the penal statutes. Traditional crimes had individual victims, who could be relied on to report them to the authorities. Saying mass or exporting bullion did not harm individuals, so incentives might be needed if prosecutions were to be obtained. These incentives usually took the form of a share in the fines, compositions, or escheats falling to the crown from convictions. Such rewards could be given at any time, but the government increasingly tended to publicize what the reward would be.[96] Informers in 1599 were to have half the escheats of those convicted for deforcing officers of arms or breaking arrest. In 1610, an attempt to enforce the law against eating meat on Wednesdays, Fridays, and Saturdays offered informers half the fines, while in 1614, informers were to get one-third of the fines or compositions for criminal prosecutions of adultery.[97] Local courts could do something similar. The regality court of Falkirk ordered that fines for allowing cattle to stray should be divided equally between the lord and the 'delaitter'.[98] Increasingly, informers were expected not just to inform, but to bring prosecutions themselves. They became, in effect, executive agents of the government.

A few examples may be given of informers becoming patentees. In 1619, three minor courtiers formed a syndicate to search for resetters (i.e. harbourers) of gypsies, on the promise of receiving half the resulting compositions and escheats for five years. This was not an actual monopoly (though it seems

[96] For a negotiated reward see BL, 'Notes furth of the registers of exchequer, 1583–1674', Harl. MS 4628, fo. 2ʳ.

[97] *APS* iv. 186; *RPC* ix. 55–6; x. 283. Cf. a local commission active on adultery in 1620: *RPC* xii. 293. Most adultery was prosecuted non-criminally by kirk sessions, however.

[98] *Falkirk Court Book*, i. no. 1.13.

that they originally wanted one), since anyone could report resetters of gypsies and have them punished; but only the syndicate could do so and make
money.[99] This project did not threaten powerful vested interests, but a patent
granted in 1610 to Lord Balfour of Burleigh certainly did. He was to enforce
the law on usury, prompting a protest from the burghs.[100] In 1619 a commission to Jerome Lindsay empowered him to bring criminal prosecutions for
adultery throughout Scotland, and to keep half the fines and compositions,
until he had received the sum of £3,000 due to him by the crown.[101] The
organizers of such projects no doubt used them to create networks of local
clients who would carry out the actual work of detecting and prosecuting
offenders. Networks of patentees' agents were hardly state officials, but they
did a good deal of the state's work for it.

Two schemes, although seemingly stillborn, illustrate aspects of the thinking of the government at this time. An obscure East Lothian laird, William
Ogill of Popplehill, received a wide-ranging commission in 1607 to enforce
the poor laws and other statutes, appointing deputes in each parish for such
tasks as arresting vagrants. The commission also gave him responsibility
for implementing the statutes against fornicators, sabbath-breakers, and
blasphemers. This project, extraordinarily extensive on paper, was probably
intended to empower Ogill to supervise those whose responsibility it was to
enforce these acts—in practice, kirk sessions—or, more likely, to charge them
fees for making enquiries into their activities. It was never heard of again.[102]
In 1622, the bishops were empowered to appoint judicial commissioners in
every parish to implement a number of statutes on matters of concern to kirk
sessions—fornication, drunkenness, sabbath breach, and the poor law, for
instance. The commissions, to last for one year, were perhaps experimental.
They would presumably have operated in conjunction with kirk sessions, and
might have pointed towards a merger of civil and ecclesiastical authority at
parish level. Again, nothing further is heard of the scheme.[103] Bishops controlled the church at the centre, but seem not to have put down deep roots in
the localities.

In the early 1630s the sudden demise of the circuit courts left a gap for
entrepreneurs wishing to enforce the penal statutes. One such was Captain
Edward Maxwell, who was commissioned to identify and fine transgressors
of these statutes in the south-west. Commissions of justiciary were issued to

---

[99] RPC xii. 152; LP James VI, 319–20. For more on this syndicate, and other matters concerning gypsies, see Ch. 11 below.
[100] RCRB ii. 329. Usury was defined as taking higher interest than the statutory 10 per cent
maximum.   [101] RPC xi. 498–9.
[102] RPC vii. 544, 748–9. For Ogill see RMS vii. 1234: he may have been a writer to the signet.
[103] RPC xii. 646–7. In what seems to have been another such scheme, Archbishop Gledstanes
referred in 1610 to parish commissioners against 'scoffers', whose jurisdiction he thought would
conflict with the newly established high commission. There is no other reference to these commissioners, and whether they were even officially approved, let alone established, is unclear.
Gledstanes to James, 17 Oct. 1610, Eccles. Letters, i. 262.

local sheriffs and others to hold courts in which Maxwell would prosecute those who 'may pretend innocencie', as well as 'the guiltie quho will rather chuse to stand out than to pay the small and moderat fynes imposit upoun thame'. The transgressors were expected to come in the king's will and to pay a composition for their fine, which did not actually require them to appear in court. The procedure thus resembled a rough and ready tax on adultery, usury, and suchlike offences. The surviving record shows Maxwell accusing about a thousand south-western delinquents in 1631–2, and if the compositions he negotiated were collected in full it would have been very lucrative both for him and for the treasury.[104]

These examples illustrate the range of patentees' activities in the early seventeenth century. A full study of them would be desirable. A final example may be mentioned, both because of its own high-profile and controversial nature, and because it shows the patentee's activities as linked with the expanding commercial economy. Lord Erskine, son of the treasurer, headed a project to regulate tanning in the 1620s and 1630s. Claiming defects in traditionally tanned leather, he and the privy council devised a scheme to enforce a new method of tanning. It was launched in 1620 with the announcement that the new method would become mandatory in 1622. Erskine would have a thirty-one-year patent to enforce it, with his agents inspecting the leather, sealing it, and collecting a fee of 4s. per hide. Leather could not be sold without the seal, on pain of confiscation.[105] Erskine brought in Englishmen to instruct the Scots in the new method, and appointed ninety-five seal-holders. His stated hope that no tanners would be more than four miles from a seal-holder sounds like bureaucratic planning.[106]

The project attracted vigorous opposition from tanners themselves, from cordiners (i.e. shoemakers, their main customers), and from the royal burghs. Although the project's stated rationale was to remedy a cordiners' complaint made in 1617 about leather quality, the cordiners 'combyned and resolvit' to 'croce and hinder' Erskine's scheme, and to 'mak this intendit reformatioun seame distaistfull to the people, as carying with it a havie burdyne to the whole land, and sua to steir the people up to exclame aganis it'. They increased their prices. Sheriffs and burgh magistrates would not 'concur and assist' the seal-holders in confiscating concealed leather.[107] The tanners complained that the seal-holders did not usually collect a fee per hide, but instead demanded 'ane yeirlie dewtie and taxatioun' from each tanner; Erskine denied this.[108] One seal-holder contracted to pay Erskine £300 per

---

[104] NAS, JC10/29, is a list of those fined within the sheriffdoms of Wigtown, Dumfries, and Roxburgh, and stewartries of Kirkcudbright and Annandale, with notes of the compositions negotiated and copies of the commissions of justiciary. I am grateful to Dr Michael Wasser for drawing it to my attention. Maxwell's own commission has not been found. For a dispute he had with the treasurer depute see *RPC*, 2nd ser. iv. 574–5.

[105] *RPC* xii. 160–79, 182–3, 189–93.   [106] *RPC* xiii. 634–46.

[107] *RPC* xii. 424, 642.   [108] *RPC* xiii. 242–8.

year, plus two-thirds of all confiscated leather; if this was standard, it hardly indicates close supervision by Erskine.[109] Complaints continued for years, and shire and burgh commissioners were still protesting in 1639.[110]

Despite commercial growth, most property in early modern Scotland was landed property, and regulating the possession and transmission of land was one of the most vital tasks that a government could perform. It is appropriate to conclude this survey of the localities with a look inside the charter chests of the local landed elite, to see how their contents were being shaped by the demands of the state.

The sixteenth century was the age of the notary, a period when more conveyancing than ever before or since was in the hands of these versatile professionals. Notaries registered all kinds of documents, but the crucial ones for land titles were instruments of sasine—documents recording that a title had been formally transferred, either by sale or by succession.[111] Most notaries were self-employed, but they owed their creation to public authority, and they were supposed to be supervised by some form of public authority. The story thus had four diverse characters: the landed proprietor, the notary, the instrument of sasine, and the state.

From some points of view, the last character might have been unnecessary. Proprietors had a choice of which notary to employ, so could market choice not eliminate fraudulent or incompetent notaries? The answer was no; rightly or wrongly, proprietors were convinced (in the words of a 1504 statute) that 'thair is sa mony fals notaris in the realme that it is dred throu thair falset that trew men sall nocht be sicker of thair heretage'.[112] Before 1560 there was the additional problem that notaries were often priests, and it was not always clear whether their derelictions should be punished by the secular courts or those of the church.[113]

So efforts were begun to get the notary, and the instrument of sasine, under control. The court of session gained authority over the admission of new notaries in 1563, when a statutory register of notaries was begun.[114] Many existing notaries derived their authority from the pope, and this was an example of the state stepping into the pope's shoes after the Reformation. A statute of 1587 aimed to tighten up on notaries' qualifications: it ordered a five-year moratorium on new admissions and a seven-year apprenticeship as a condition of admission, while requiring existing notaries to bring

---

[109] *RPC* xiii. 352–3.   [110] *Aberdeen Letters*, ii. 143, 145–8.

[111] J. Durkan, 'The Early Scottish Notary', in Cowan and Shaw (eds.), *The Renaissance and Reformation in Scotland*. Notaries' growing importance in 16th-c. burgh life is discussed by J. E. Thomas, 'Elgin Notaries in Burgh Society and Government, 1540–1660', *Northern Scotland*, 13 (1993), 21–30. The forms of the instruments of sasine are given in P. Gouldesbrough (ed.), *Formulary of Old Scots Legal Documents* (Stair Society, 1985), 66–7 (sale), 84–5 (succession).

[112] *APS* ii. 250, c. 8. 'Sicker' = secure. For conveyancing fraud, see 'Not Improven: Advocate and Leslie *v*. Brown and Johnston, 1582', ed. I. D. Grant, *Stair Society Miscellany*, i (1971).

[113] Durkan, 'Early Scottish Notary', 36.

[114] *APS* ii. 542, c. 17; NAS, register of admissions of notaries, 1563–7, NP2/1.

their cautioners up to date and to hand in their books for checking.[115] It was probably ineffective. Local authorities cooperated in the battle against fraud, sometimes enthusiastically, as when corrupt notaries had their hands 'striken of' in Edinburgh in 1563.[116]

Meanwhile, central government was experimenting with another aspect of regulation: collecting copies of instruments of sasine, 'sua that the kingis grace may knaw his tenentis, and all uthcris haifand interes may haif recours thairto', in the words of a statute of 1540.[117] The copies of the instruments of sasine would form a kind of central land register. Parliament attempted to transfer the recording of many sasines—those on succession, following on brieves from chancery—from notaries to sheriff clerks, who would present to the exchequer annually 'ane buk contenand all sesingis gevin be thame'. Sheriff clerks may have been thought more amenable to central influence; notaries were not government officials at all. The scheme would effectively have extended to the countryside the urban system whereby burgh clerks registered sasines. It 'tuk not than dew executioun'; in 1563 it was abandoned, and notaries continued freely to record the giving of sasine.[118] However, their protocol books, in which they did so, were in a sense public documents, and this led the legislators to try another approach. In 1587 it was ordered that protocol books of dead notaries were to be handed in to the clerk register, who would 'mak the samen patent and furth cumand to all our soverane lordis lieges'. This too would eventually have formed a land register; again, it was later regarded as not having been 'pute to dew executioun', although quite a few protocol books were collected.[119]

However, within a few years the law on land registration had been transformed, in a *démarche* which has shaped Scots law ever since. In the words of Scotland's most eminent lawyer: 'For the further securing of infeftments and land-rights, that excellent statute which before was attempted, was at last perfected, Parl. 1617, cap. 16'. The introduction of the register of sasines was controversial, but by the time Stair wrote, the outcome was clear: the register had been established, and 'no nation hath so much security of irredeemable land rights as we have'.[120]

Why had the introduction of such a manifest benefit been so fractiously disputed? On the other hand, why should landed proprietors have dreamed of inviting bureaucrats to interfere in the cherished contents of their charter

---

[115] *APS* iii. 448–9, c. 29.

[116] *Edin. Recs.* iii. 165–6. See Ockrent, *Land Rights*, 56–65, and Durkan, 'Early Scottish Notary', 35–7, for further government regulation of notaries at this time.

[117] *APS* ii. 360, c. 14; cf. ibid., 492, c. 2, for a revision of this in 1555. A statute of 1504 had ordered something similar, but not for publication as a register of land titles: ibid. 253, c. 35.

[118] *APS* ii. 542–3, c. 16.

[119] *APS* iii. 448–9, c. 29; iv. 549, c. 22. The legislative commission of Dec. 1567 had considered a similar measure, but parliament did not enact it: *APS* iii. 44. Many of the protocol books collected in the NAS, NP1 series may well have been deposited under the 1587 act.

[120] Stair, *Institutions*, II.3.20–2; cf. II.10.5, IV.35.12.

chests? The first proposal for a register of sasines, more or less on the form adopted in 1617, was apparently made in the parliament of 1592. But that parliament proved intractable, and the proposal was either defeated or withdrawn.[121] A register of sasines, known as the 'secretary's register' because of its supervision by the secretary, was introduced in 1599. Local registers were established, where sasines were to be registered within forty days of being given or else be null and void. There was a good deal of early effort put into this scheme—and there had to be, since notaries were hostile and apparently tried to boycott the register.[122] In 1609 it was abolished, with every appearance of finality, as 'serveing for litle or na uther use then to acquyre gayne and commoditie to the clerkis keiparis thairof, and to draw his majesties good subjectis to neidles extraordinarie and maist unnecessair trouble, tormoyle, fascherie and expenssis'.[123]

However, the register of sasines returned permanently in 1617—in much the same form as in 1599, although now under the charge of the clerk register.[124] Proprietors had two alternatives: registration locally, in one of seventeen local registers, or in a central one (useful if the lands lay in more than one district). The registration districts rationalized the sheriffdoms, so that, for example, Fife and Kinross formed a single district. There was provision for further adjustment of the districts in an almost Weberian rational-bureaucratic spirit. The local registers ignored the traditional local administrators, and were very much part of an integrated central system. Notaries continued in business after 1617, for the new system just as much as the old required professional people to operate it, but their protocol books lost all independent authority. The one exception from the register was for sasines of burgh property. This was because burghs already had registration systems functioning, either by having an official register or (as in Dundee) by giving the burgh clerk a monopoly, to exclude 'unkenth notaris'. Burgh registers of sasines became statutory in 1681.[125]

The register of sasines may not quite have been Domesday Book, but it was certainly a striking instance of the state's willingness and ability to intervene in the possession and transmission of property. One form of property that soon became of even greater interest to the state was annualrents (interest

[121] NAS, draft act for registration of sasines, probably 1592, PA7/1/39–40. The presbyterian 'Golden Act', and the act restricting royal power to appoint senators to the college of justice, exemplify the kind of measure this parliament preferred: *APS* iii. 541–2, 569, cc. 8, 50.

[122] *APS* iv. 184–5; 237–8, c. 36 (ratification and amendment in 1600); Ockrent, *Land Rights*, 69–71.

[123] *APS* iv. 407; 449, c. 40. There had been a charge of 13s. 4d. per folio for registering sasines. Likely English influences on the 1599 act, and on that of 1555, are noted by W. D. H. Sellar, 'The Common Law of Scotland and the Common Law of England', in R. R. Davies (ed.), *The British Isles, 1100–1500* (Edinburgh, 1988), 92.

[124] *APS* iv. 545–7, c. 16. For the act's implementation, see Ockrent, *Land Rights*, ch. 3.

[125] D. Murray, *Early Burgh Organization*, ii. 88–90; Dundee City Archive and Record Centre, Dundee council minutes, vol. i, p. 122; *APS* viii. 248, c. 13. Burgh clerks were themselves notaries.

payments and annuities), which were often granted by heritable bond upon which sasine was given. So it may not be entirely coincidence that four years after the establishment of the register of sasines, a remarkable tax was introduced on annualrents. Assessment and collection of the tax did not explicitly involve a search of the register—it was based on an inventory given up by creditors, attested by their oath. But the knowledge that the government had details of their property in its files may have dissuaded some people from making false returns. The 'inquisition in men's estates' and 'commissions for concealled annuells' that the tax entailed were particularly resented. Most of the major burghs chose to compound for the tax (raising the money through ordinary local taxation) rather than paying it.[126]

Much of this chapter appears on the face of it to be a story of failure, as a restless central state tried one half-baked scheme after another in order to create new networks of accountable local authority. Parish commissioners, circuit courts, and other schemes either broke down in action or never left the paper on which they were written. But this would be the wrong way to regard these schemes. Footballers do not expect every shot to land in the back of the net; they know that they have to miss sometimes in order to score. The point is that it was a new thing for central government to want to create such networks at all: earlier generations had usually left well—or ill—alone in the localities. It should be asked why so many people were so dissatisfied with the traditional local institutions as to be prepared to cooperate with the attempts, discussed in the previous chapter, to undermine their autonomy and to make them operate in new ways. This is a question that this chapter has not attempted to answer by itself, focused as it has had to be on specific innovations; some answers may emerge when it is considered in the context of other parts of this book.

Moreover, it is clear that even in its quest to create completely new institutions—one of the hardest things for a government to do—the Scottish state sometimes achieved a respectable scoring rate. The introduction and permanent establishment of justices of the peace surely counts as a success. The local sasines offices were strikingly new features of the official and administrative landscape, which could hardly have been established before our period, and had been unwelcome as late as 1609. That they eventually succeeded indicates that the state, for all its intrusiveness, had discovered a way to provide a service that actually worked, and that was useful to the propertied classes. That service was more valuable at a time of increasing central legislation, central litigation, and administrative complexity than it would have been when title to land depended more on one's reputation with the local courts. If land titles were ever registered in the fifteenth century this was done by the baron court—characteristic repository of local, seigneurial power. Power to register

---

[126] *APS* iv. 598–600, c. 2; Row, *History*, 365–6, 380; for compositions (which raised about one-third of the total sum), see NAS, extraordinary taxation accounts, 1621, E65/9.

land titles moved in the sixteenth century to the notary—more professional but still with deep local roots—and then in 1617 to a bureaucratic system controlled directly by the central state. That system worked so well that it is still in place today.

To conclude our tour of local administrators, we can gain a perspective on their relationship with the people by glancing at their numbers and distribution. James remarked in England in 1604: 'As for the execution of good lawes, it hath bene very wisely and honourably foreseene and ordered by my predecessours in this kingdome, in planting such a number of judges, and all sorts of magistrates in convenient places for the execution of the same.'[127] Was his ancient kingdom furnished with judges and magistrates in similarly convenient quantity?

Precise statistics are too much to hope for. Most of the figures that follow are estimates, and one or two are wholly conjectural. There is also the question of who to count. Administrators have been counted if they could act on their own initiative, which is sometimes difficult to gauge. Burgh magistrates have been counted individually, as have sheriffs and sheriff deputes; kirk session elders and burgh councillors have not. This makes clear that it is administrators who have been counted, not units of jurisdiction. Their jurisdictional power varied: one appearance before the sheriff might have more impact on someone's life than twenty encounters with the bailie of a non-baronial court. The administrators being counted usually had subordinates, like the baron court's officer, the constable for the JP, or the clerk for most courts. The parish minister with a dozen elders on whom to call had exceptional power here. This forms a notable contrast to pre-Reformation times, when clergy were numerous but most of them, including parish priests, had no actual jurisdiction at all. Thus the figures themselves cannot measure how actively individual administrators were supported by subordinates, though they could provide the basis for a more detailed study of that topic. As Steve Hindle has observed, 'A working definition of the early modern English state would have to stretch not only as far as individual magistrates, but beyond: to head constables, petty constables, churchwardens and overseers.'[128] In Scotland one might similarly 'stretch' to notaries and messengers at arms, both nominally self-employed but supervised by authority and surely helping the business of government. For present purposes it seems best to concentrate on the authority-bearing people, those in charge of the courts and administrative offices. So long as the limitations of this counting exercise are recognized, it can give a useful impression of the changing intensity of local government.

---

[127] James VI & I, speech to parliament, 1604, in *Political Writings*, 142.
[128] Hindle, *The State and Social Change*, 21.

Public local administrators in 1560

64	sheriffs and deputes
176	royal burgh magistrates
42	customs officials
83	bishops' officials, commissaries, and deans of Christianity
365	TOTAL (= 1 per 2,192 people)[129]

Private local administrators in 1560

1,040	bailies of barony and regality courts
500	bailies of non-baronial courts
115	bailies of burghs of barony and regality
1,655	TOTAL (= 1 per 482 people)[130]

Public local administrators in 1625

400	justices of the peace
800	parish ministers
64	magistrates of new royal burghs
50	new customs officials
25	commissaries
18	sasines registrars
20	collectors of parliamentary taxes
282	CONTINUING FROM 1560
1,659	TOTAL (= 1 per 603 people)[131]

[129] There were twenty-eight effective sheriffdoms in 1587 (*APS* iii. 459, c. 57), to which should be added the free-standing stewartry of Kirkcudbright; this figure is doubled to take account of deputes, and then the subordinate stewartries of Annandale, Strathearn, and Menteith and the three bailiaries of Ayrshire are added as their jurisdiction was quasi-shrieval. It is assumed that there were four burgh magistrates on average for each of forty-four royal burghs. Customers were active in about twenty-one of these burghs (*ER* xix, *passim*); they were assisted by cocket clerks. Diocesan administrators before the Reformation consisted of about eighteen bishops' officials (with five of the thirteen dioceses having two), and perhaps about twenty-five commissaries with independent jurisdiction and forty deans of Christianity: Ollivant, *Court of the Official*, 31–9. All these ceased at the Reformation; the commissaries should not be confused with the post-Reformation administrators with that title, although their number was about the same. In addition, sheriffdoms were supposed to have coroners, but they are omitted because of lack of evidence that they were important or even necessarily active. Population ratios are calculated on the assumption that the population was 800,000 in 1560 and 1 million in 1625.

[130] There are no statistics on non-baronial courts, so the figure given here is wholly conjectural (though one can say with more confidence that it did not change much between 1560 and 1625). For barony and regality courts, and burghs of barony and regality, see George Pryde's figures in *Court Book of the Burgh of Kirkintilloch*, pp. xlii, xlv. These are minimum figures, especially for the baronies, but they are probably in the right range. Local research can be more confident that it approaches completeness, and the ninety-five baronies and nine regalities found in the sheriffdoms of Berwick, Roxburgh, and Dumfries are much what one would expect from Professor Pryde's figures: Rae, *Administration of the Scottish Frontier*, 16.

[131] New customers have been estimated to include both those in new royal burghs and those established for the first time in existing burghs and other customs districts. The tax collectors were for benefice-holders, as taxes on other estates were collected by sheriffs and burgh magistrates; their number was not fixed precisely. All the administrators of 1560 were still continuing except the eighty-three diocesan administrators.

Private local administrators in 1625
  70   bailies of new burghs of barony and regality
  200 patentees' agents
1,655 CONTINUING FROM 1560
1,925 TOTAL (= 1 per 521 people)[132]

These overall figures are startling. They show that the public administrators increased almost fourfold relative to the population, while the private ones declined slightly. The private ones remained in the majority, but most of them had only modest authority, while some of the new public administrators (especially the parish ministers) wielded extensive powers of coercion. Meanwhile central administrators, such as executive parliamentary commissioners, were extending their own activities deeper into the localities than before (see above, Chapter 7). It is hard to think of any period of Scottish history before very recent times which saw such a large increase in the density of local administration.

How were the administrators distributed, both as between town and country and as between Highlands and Lowlands? The jurisdiction of some of them—sheriffs, baron bailies, burgh magistrates, customers—can be assigned clearly to country or to town; others, like the commissaries, served both town and country. Some burghs of barony were real towns, while others were rural settlements. So while it is clear that towns were more intensively governed, it is hard to express this in figures.

The Highland–Lowland divide, on the other hand, is quite clear: the vast majority of the administrators, both old and new, were in the Lowlands.[133] Sheriff courts operated in Argyll, where the earls were sheriffs, but probably not elsewhere.[134] Although less is known about traditional Highland administrators, they were few and probably in decline in our period. The Gaelic office of toiseachdeor (a species of coroner) may already have become obsolescent in late medieval times.[135] If this is taken into account, then the administrators–population ratios have to be reduced by about one-third to be meaningful for the Lowlands. Thus there was one local administrator for about every 186 people in the Lowlands by 1625.

These developments can be compared with parallels in English local administration. Scotland had a wider variety of public administrators than England, where the justice of the peace was so central to county government. Actual numbers of JPs at any given date are not easily compared with

---

[132] New burghs of barony and regality have been estimated with reference to McNeill and MacQueen (eds.), *Atlas*, 233. Patentees' agents are conjectural but include Lord Erskine's ninety-five seal-holders.   [133] Goodare, *State and Society*, ch. 7.

[134] Ibid. 222–33; Dawson, *Politics of Religion*, 58. In Argyll there seems to have been only one baron court, that of Lorn: ibid. 59.

[135] W. Gillies, 'Some Thoughts on the Toschederache', *Scottish Gaelic Studies*, 17 (1996), 128–42.

anything in Scotland, nor are administrators–population ratios; but the trends over time are worth pondering. It has been suggested that the numbers of JPs quadrupled between 1562 and 1714, a substantial but much slower rate of increase than in Scotland.[136] However, the rate of increase seems to have been greatest in the late sixteenth century. In six representative English counties, numbers of JPs more than doubled between 1562 and 1608.[137] This is more like what happened in Scotland, though still not as dramatic.

Scottish government was evidently becoming a powerful force in the localities. In Chapter 11, we will examine some of the things that government did with its power—policies that affected the lives of ordinary people in the Lowlands. Before then, however, it must be asked how the Highlands were governed if there were so few agents of government there. Evidently the central government of Scotland could affect ordinary highlanders only indirectly, if at all. It could, however, have a forceful and far-reaching impact on the political elite of the Highlands, as we shall now see.

[136] Fletcher, *Reform in the Provinces*, 31, 39.
[137] J. H. Gleason, *The Justices of the Peace in England, 1558–1640* (Oxford, 1969), 49. The figures were 143 in 1562 and 313 in 1608; these exclude 'dignitaries' whose presence on the commission was nominal.

CHAPTER TEN

Government and Highland Elites

They [the gentlemen adventurers of Lewis] sensyne with infinit travell, excessive paneis and exhorbitant expenssis, besydis the great loiss of thair blude and pairt of thair awin and thair cumpanies lyveis and the hasart of all the rest, have reduceit the saidis iyllis (inhabite of befoir be barbarous and evill disposit pepill as said is) to his majesties obedience.

APS iv. 248, c. 55

Governing the Highlands was very different from governing the rest of Scotland. The 'barbarous and evill disposit pepill' who lived there—the political elites of the Highlands—barely recognized state authority, and had few connections to regular institutions of government. The internal government of the Highlands was in the hands of clan chiefs who did not routinely answer to any higher authority. Clans were ruling families whose aim was to raise the largest possible number of fighting men; this in turn enabled them to dominate and extend their territories. They subsisted on the tribute they gathered from the working folk of the Highlands, and protected them from the raids of other clans. Clan power was an autonomous system, hard to influence from outside without 'infinit travell, excessive paneis and exhorbitant expenssis'.[1]

This chapter takes the power of the clans as a starting point for an investigation into central government's treatment of the region. It does not aim to provide an analysis of each individual governmental initiative; recent accounts of these are available elsewhere.[2] Instead it attempts to sketch some broader patterns in policy towards the Highlands, and to identify the motives behind each phase. One of the most prominent phases, accompanied by sharply etched attitudes towards Highland elites, came around 1600. The statute quoted above was passed then, in support of a scheme to colonize the island of Lewis with lowlanders as a prelude to conquest of the rest of the Isles. This phase of government policy dominated much of the early

---

[1] For the structure of clan society see Dodgshon, *From Chiefs to Landlords*, chs. 2–4, and Macinnes, *Clanship*, chs. 1–2. Although what follows will make frequent reference to 'chiefs', it should be borne in mind that clan leadership was exercised not just by individuals but by the leading kinsmen of the clan.

[2] Goodare, *State and Society*, 255–8, 263–85; Macinnes, *Clanship*, ch. 3; M. Lynch, 'James VI and the "Highland Problem" ', in Goodare and Lynch (eds.), *The Reign of James VI*. An analysis of the crucial period 1607–17 is offered by Goodare, 'Statutes of Iona'.

seventeenth century. As it was the most active yet seen in the Highlands, it requires careful scrutiny; but it needs to be set in context of what had gone before, and of what came afterwards.

Scottish kings had long claimed the Highlands to be part of their kingdom, and nobody had any reason to contradict them. No other state had a claim to the Highlands. The chiefs themselves had no objection to recognizing the king, since the king did not usually interfere with their lives. There were occasions, of course, when he did. This was particularly so after 1493, when the autonomous but troubled lordship of the Isles was finally forfeited—though nothing was put in its place that might have established direct royal authority. James V undertook an expedition to the Isles in 1540, which prompted the payment of royal rents in the next two years.[3] But invading the Highlands every generation or two did not amount to *government* there, any more than Scottish raids into Northumberland amounted to government of Northumberland. On the contrary, military invasions indicate that government was not occurring. Regular state structures were largely absent from the Highlands, and the members of the Highland elite were largely absent from 'Scottish' political society.[4]

Some of the appearance of what 'Scottish' political society recognized as government was kept up by the Campbell earls of Argyll. The Campbells were a Highland clan, but their leaders also participated regularly in Lowland politics. They could often obtain the trappings of Lowland authority to use in their own domains—charters, commissions of justiciary, and commissions of lieutenancy. But the grant of a royal commission to an earl of Argyll did not usually represent a royal policy for the Highlands as such. It was a reward for Campbell service in the Lowlands. In return for this, Argyll could obtain royal backing for *Campbell* policy—the aggrandizement of the clan at the expense of its neighbours, principally the MacDonalds. This could seem on paper like the crown using the Campbells to keep the MacDonalds in order, but it was not—as can be seen from an episode in the early 1530s when the tables were turned. James V was disenchanted with the fourth earl of Argyll, and wanted fighting Islesmen to stir up trouble for Henry VIII in Ireland. Argyll was removed as chamberlain of Kintyre and replaced by James MacDonald of Dunyveg. On paper this looked like the crown using the *MacDonalds* to keep the *Campbells* in order.[5] The Highland reality was that neither Campbells nor MacDonalds needed the other to keep them in order, and their relationship was simply one of two neighbouring and often rival clans. The 'government' was an external factor in this; it did not actually govern.

[3] J. Munro, 'The Lordship of the Isles', in L. Maclean (ed.), *The Middle Ages in the Highlands* (Inverness Field Club, 1981), 31–3; Macdougall, *James IV*, 100–1, 116; Cameron, *James V*, 239–40.
[4] For the clans' aloofness from regular governmental institutions see Goodare, *State and Society*, 221–33.   [5] Cameron, *James V*, 232–9.

For most of the sixteenth century, lowlanders' attitudes to highlanders were twofold. On the one hand, highlanders had long been seen in certain contexts as 'barbarous and evill disposit pepill' (the phrase of the statute of 1600, quoted above). On the other hand, there could be grudging admiration for the highlanders' primitive simplicity and martial valour, these being qualities that Renaissance thinkers were inclined to value. George Buchanan in 1582 noted the 'native simple hardiness' with which the highlanders kept up their fighting spirit. He also commented of North Rona, Scotland's most remote inhabited island:

Here alone in the universe, I imagine, are to be found a people who know no want, among whom every necessary of life abounds even to satiety. Unacquainted alike with luxury and avarice, they find in their ignorance of vice, that innocence and tranquillity of mind, which others laboriously search for in the discipline and the precepts of wisdom.[6]

The attitudes of Robert Lindsay of Pitscottie, a Fife chronicler writing in the 1570s, are clearest in the way that he ignored the Highlands almost completely. On the rare occasions when he mentioned any highlanders as taking part in his history of 'Scotland', he recognized their martial valour but refrained from praising it. Relating an episode in 1439 when 'the men of the Yllis invaidit syndrie pairts in Scotland baith be fyre and sword', he described them as 'crewell murtheraris and traitouris'. Lindsay's assumption that the Isles were not part of Scotland is remarkable, but we shall see that others shared it. He also told how, in 1513, 'Mackleine ane gret man of the Yleis of Scotland' missed the battle of Flodden through being 'intill ane strang cuntrie . . . nor wist nocht quha was his freind nor his foe for he dred Scoittsmen als mekill as Inglismen becaus he undirstwd nocht thair leid nor thay his'. Although Maclean did not count as a Scotsman, he and his men 'faucht verie crwellie' against a detachment of Englishmen.[7] So at best the Highland elite deserved respect for its values, even if these were different from those of the Lowlands. At worst, the highlanders were savage barbarians. Usually they could be ignored; but when the state was trying to achieve more than before, it would want to fashion some kind of policy towards the Highlands.

That policy's genesis can be compared, in broad terms, with the earliest phase of active Tudor policy in Ireland, between about 1534 and 1594. Most Irish elites had similar attitudes to government as Scottish highlanders. The act of 1541 making Henry VIII king of Ireland was part of a programme of incorporation of these elites as members of a newly constructed body politic under the crown. This programme had its coercive elements, but English 'reformers' believed that the innate superiority of their law and political

---

[6] Buchanan, *The History of Scotland*, i. 41, 55. North Rona was more remote than St Kilda, and much smaller. Cf. M. Robson, *Rona: The Distant Island* (Stornoway, 1991), 20–8.

[7] Pitscottie, *Historie*, i. 29, 274–6. 'Intill' = in; 'strang' = strange; 'wist' = knew; 'leid' = speech. Both these tales may well be apocryphal, but they illustrate attitudes in the 1570s.

culture had the potential to regenerate Ireland as a second England. The implementation of 'reform' focused on viceroys who were expected to implement increasingly detailed programmes with carefully specified costs and timetable. The repeated failure of these programmes was an important element in the late Elizabethan drift towards uncompromisingly coercive and colonial policies.[8]

The Scottish state seems to have passed through a similar phase in the 1580s, aspiring to civilize the Highlands through incorporation, and not as yet aiming directly towards colonization. But the phase was shallower and briefer. There was little or no literary discussion of how the Highlands could be 'reformed', in contrast to the debate on Ireland. There were no viceroys or political managers staking their careers on the implementation of reform programmes. Still, the early Scottish statutes on the Highlands can themselves be seen as setting out an agenda for 'reform'.

The most important of these statutes, passed in 1587, launched a programme of Lowland-style law enforcement for both Highlands and Borders. Since local landlords and chiefs could not be trusted to hand over criminals voluntarily, it required them to find caution that they would answer for any criminals on their lands. In the Borders this codified existing practice, but it was new to the Highlands. Still, it is possible that the government hoped that chiefs would cooperate with it. Careful implementation was envisaged, and there was a detailed census of individual landlords and chiefs. The statute was intended as a framework for Highland policy, and in 1590 was transcribed into the opening folios of the minute-book of a new council committee for Highland and Border affairs. It was then that active pressure on Highland chiefs to cooperate began. The centrepiece of the programme, the requirement for landlords and chiefs to find caution, was coercive, but it did work through established elites rather than mounting a frontal attack on them.[9] To the extent that it was legal and administrative rather than military or expropriatory, the programme certainly had a strong 'reforming' element.

In 1594, statutory pressure was stepped up. Parliament ordered a census of suspected individual criminals belonging to a long list of clans, and announced that the chiefs of these clans 'may be estemit the verie authoris, fosteraris and mantenaris of the wickit deidis' they committed. Few major clans

---

[8] B. Bradshaw, *The Irish Constitutional Revolution of the Sixteenth Century* (Cambridge, 1979); C. Brady, 'The Decline of the Irish Kingdom', in M. Greengrass (ed.), *Conquest and Coalescence: The Shaping of the State in Early Modern Europe* (London, 1991); C. Brady, *The Chief Governors: The Rise and Fall of Reform Government in Tudor Ireland, 1536–1588* (Cambridge, 1994).

[9] *APS* iii. 461–7, c. 59; *RPC* iv. 781–3; Goodare, *State and Society*, 266–7. The political elites of the Borders are not discussed here, although they received a great deal of governmental attention, because they were not excluded from the Scottish body politic in the way that most Highland chiefs were. For policies towards the Borders see Rae, *Administration of the Scottish Frontier*, chs. 8–9, and Wasser, 'Pacification of the Scottish Borders'; for the parallels between these and early Highland policies see Goodare, *State and Society*, 254–8.

escaped inclusion on the list. The intention of the census was to distinguish 'betuix thame that ar and desiris to be estemit honest and trew men, and thame that ar and escheamis nocht to be estemit thevis, reifaris, sorneris, and resettaris and sustenaris of thift and thevis'. Chiefs who failed the relevant tests were to be held responsible for their followers' misdeeds, being ordered to finding cautions and surrendering hostages for good behaviour.[10] The key word was 'sorneris'. These were fighting clansmen, the basis of the clans' military power, for whom the common folk of the Highlands were obliged to provide free board and lodging. There was an established tradition of parliamentary attempts to punish the extension to the Lowlands of sorners' exactions, but no serious attempt had hitherto been made to treat sorners as thieves in their own territory.[11] To do so might possibly have been seen in Edinburgh as 'reforming'; but it would have undermined the basis of clanship, and no chief could have cooperated at all willingly with it. The statute was not, in the event, implemented.

In 1595, the government shifted from demanding law enforcement towards demanding money. Hitherto the chiefs had been told to accept the central courts' power to punish crime, because the government was extending to the Highlands a system developed in the Borders. Payment of royal rents, which was not an issue in the Borders, had not been mentioned. But in 1595, a report was produced on the crown's landed property by Sir John Skene of Curriehill, recently appointed as clerk register. Skene announced that large tracts of the Isles should pertain by right to the crown as a result of the forfeiture of the lordship of the Isles in 1493, and that the chiefs of the Isles were obstructing this. After naming most of the chiefs, he concluded: 'Giff thir menis libertie micht other be force or industrie be restranit, thir ilis and landis befoir specifiet and the pepill wald be als obedient as the duellaris in Fyiff or Lowthiane.'[12]

This novel idea was immediately adopted, and the demand for royal rents was at or near the heart of almost every official initiative on the Highlands for the next generation. Skene's proposal to enforce it by 'force or industrie' was a natural prologue to a direct attack on some of the island clans. This soon happened, perhaps connected with Skene's own appointment in January 1596 as one of the Octavians, eight exchequer commissioners with extensive powers. A military expedition was mounted to Islay, heartland of the powerful but disorganized MacDonalds of Dunyveg, in October–November 1596. The expedition procured a humble submission from the clan's chief, Angus:

---

[10] *APS* iv. 71–3, c. 37.

[11] Goodare, *State and Society*, 256. The idea of punishing sorning only in the Lowlands survived in the statute of 1587: *APS* iii. 464, c. 59, para 11.

[12] A. L. Murray, 'Sir John Skene and the Exchequer', 129, 139–41. 'Other' = either; 'thir' = these. Further study of the subject of Highland rents before 1595 would be desirable, but they seem to have been demanded only fitfully even under James IV and James V, and less thereafter.

he would, for instance, surrender his son as a hostage, remove the clan from Kintyre, and accept the intrusion of new crown tenants in Islay.[13] It is unlikely that much of this was implemented, but such military action, if repeated, had the potential to effect drastic change in the Highlands. The launch of the demand for royal rents marks the end of the period in which the government could reasonably expect that Highland elites would wish to cooperate with its programme. From 1595 onwards, the programme was unambiguously coercive.

The parliament of 1597 introduced a further novel element into government policy. It ordained that chiefs' land titles would be invalidated unless they registered them within a six-month deadline—assuming, rightly, that they would not comply. The rationale for the act was partly stated to be the payment of rents, since the Isles were 'for the maist pairt of his hienes annext propertie'. But official concern had now broadened further. The act complained that highlanders' 'barbarus' behaviour 'makis the saidis Hielandis and Iles, quhilkis are maist commodious in thame selwes, alsueill be the ferteillitie of the ground as be riche fischeingis be sey, altogidder unproffitabill baithe to thame selffis and to all uthuris his hienes lieges within this realme'. These lieges were unable to 'traffique' in the region. In order to introduce 'civilitie and polecie', three towns were also to be built in the Highlands— and probably not by highlanders.[14]

Behind the enactments of 1597 lies the desire of lowlanders to open up the Highlands to economic development or exploitation. This is something that must be treated under the heading of colonialism, because colonialism is bound up with economics. With the launch of the privately sponsored Lowland colonization of Lewis in 1598, all pretence of conciliation of local elites was cast off, at least in the Western Isles. The colony itself will be discussed shortly; it serves as a reminder that colonization is only partly planned by governments, being also driven forward by entrepreneurs. The Highlands were thought to possess economic potential in grain, fish, cattle, and precious metals. Not all these would prove viable, but desire for them was behind many public and private initiatives. Taking a broad view of those who fostered colonization, they extend well beyond just those who went to the Highlands, or who organized expeditions there. They include those who invested in trading ventures involving the Highlands, or courtiers who procured grants of privileges allowing them to broker such investment. They also include foreign entrepreneurs, notably English cattle-traders and Dutch fishermen.

Grain was initially seen as the most likely resource to be extracted from Lewis. The colonists' first contract with the government, in 1598, included an

---

[13] *APS* iv. 97–8; *RPC* v. 296–7, 306–10, 312–14, 321, 324. Lachlan Maclean of Duart paid his rents to avoid being attacked: N. Maclean-Bristol, *Murder under Trust: Sir Lachlan Mor Maclean of Duart, 1558–1598* (East Linton, 1999), ch. 18.

[14] *APS* iv. 138–9, cc. 33–4.

obligation to pay 140 chalders of bere as part of the annual feu duty to the crown. In 1600, on better acquaintance with the island, this was replaced by 3,600 fish.[15] Official policy on cattle usually focused on banning or restricting their export from Scotland rather than promoting the droving trade from the Highlands, but the shire commissioners in 1639 took a different view, complaining about fiscal exactions on 'bestiall that comes from the Hielandis and Yles', many of which were exported to England.[16] As for precious metals, the prospect was eagerly noted in 1604 of 'sylver, iron and lead in Argyll and Loghquhaber'.[17] People believed that there were riches in the Highlands to be exploited. But first, access to them needed to be controlled by the right people—the present highlanders being undoubtedly the wrong people.

The reason the highlanders were the wrong people was partly that they did not obey the government, but also that their cultural values were seen to have only a subordinate place for commerce.[18] This anti-commercialism was not ascribed to them just because they were uncivilized and remote. The Shetlanders, equally uncivilized and remote, were different; they did not resist their economy being taken over by German fishermen in the sixteenth and seventeenth centuries. Instead they welcomed the Germans for bringing them a range of commodities in exchange for the fish that formed their principal export.[19] But, as John Leslie wrote, the 'rude pepill' of the Highlands 'admitt na man thair with thame to the fisheing willinglie excepte thair awne nychtbouris and cuntrey men. Nathir ony maner of way gif thay labour to fishing bot sa mekle as serves to thair awne use for the tyme, nocht kairing as it war for the morne.'[20] Bishop Leslie will have recalled that it was Christ who had exhorted his disciples to take no thought for the morrow, but it was not an attitude likely to encourage economic development.

There were several ways of solving this problem. Some historians have assumed that only one colonial policy was possible: a policy of dispossession and large-scale settlement on the North American model. Having decided that such a policy was not followed, or was followed only to fail, they dismiss the issue of colonialism altogether.[21] But even in the eighteenth- and

---

[15] *APS* v. 248, c. 55.   [16] *APS* iii. 226, c. 31; *Aberdeen Letters*, ii. 144.

[17] 'A treatise about the union of England and Scotland', in *The Jacobean Union: Six Tracts of 1604*, ed. B. R. Galloway and B. P. Levack (SHS, 1985), 54. Sir Robert Gordon heard that gold had been found in a remote part of Sutherland, only for knowledge of the site's location to disappear with the discoverer's death: Gordon, *Sutherland*, 6. This may well have originated as miners' folklore.

[18] It is Lowland perceptions rather than Highland realities that mattered here. Highlanders seem to have had unauthorized trading links with Ulster, at least during the 1590s: M. Lynch, 'National Identity in Ireland and Scotland, 1500–1640', in C. Bjørn et al. (eds.), *Nations, Nationalism and Patriotism in the European Past* (Copenhagen, 1994), 113. But Highland chiefs' elaborate patterns of tribute-taking, distribution, and display certainly were not 'commercial': Dodgshon, *From Chiefs to Landlords*, ch. 3.

[19] H. D. Smith, *Shetland Life and Trade, 1550–1914* (Edinburgh, 1984), ch. 2. There were also some Dutch, English, and Scottish fishermen.

[20] Leslie, *Historie*, i. 38.   [21] e.g. Lee, *Great Britain's Solomon*, 199–202.

nineteenth-century heyday of European colonization this was just one of several models, and not the most common. One alternative was military occupation and limited settlement (as in British India, or in our period Spanish America), where the native populations were subjugated and exploited rather than dispossessed. A third model was penetration by traders (as in China). This, in its early stages, could develop without the establishment of political supremacy, though eventually force might be deployed to crush resistance to the traders. A fourth was co-option of local elites (as in Africa), where favoured chiefs received military backing in return for supplying the resources (slaves) that the Europeans wanted. In this model, the Europeans needed only to sit in coastal forts and hand out guns and alcohol to their native allies. Direct military intervention was necessary only when one of the co-opted chiefs joined the native resistance or was overthrown by it. These models sometimes overlapped, or one could evolve into another over time, but they were all colonial.[22]

If we now ask which of these four models—dispossession and settlement, military occupation, trading penetration, or co-option of local elites—can be found in the Highlands under James VI, the answer is: all of them. We also find anti-colonial native resistance. The government pursued a range of different policies for different clans at different times; it was, in fact, supremely opportunist. It is a mistake to think of Highland policies as uniform: either there would be dispossession-and-settlement colonies, or there would not. Dispossession and settlement were always possibilities—but they would be initiated for a particular region only when the circumstances were right, which they rarely were. If a clan were to delegitimize itself by acts of open resistance, or were to be weakened by internal struggles, or both, then the state might move in and try to take over. By contrast, a strong and stable clan would not be threatened with outright dispossession; instead, pressure could be brought to bear on the chief to cooperate with the government. If he complied, well and good; if he dragged his feet, more pressure might be applied; if he refused, he could be attacked outright (if resources were available). Again, if the chief became cooperative, this might lead to dissension within the clan, which might cause difficulties but which might also give the government further leverage. For a colonial power, the oldest trick in the book is to divide and rule.

Colonization, in one or more of its diverse forms, was in evidence throughout the period from 1595 to the 1630s at least. This statement may seem at odds with a widely held view that the so-called Statutes of Iona of 1609 represented a turning point. But no contemporary commentators thought

---

[22] This brief and schematic analysis does scant justice to the subtlety and detail of works such as E. R. Wolf, *Europe and the People without History* (Berkeley, Calif., 1982), but it may serve to introduce the issues relevant to the Highlands. The typology of colonies is adapted from D. K. Fieldhouse, *The Colonial Empires: A Comparative Survey from the Eighteenth Century* (2nd edn., London, 1982), 11–13.

that the Statutes were significant at all, let alone that they represented a shift in policy—and in any case they were never implemented. They were merely one among several governmental initiatives of the period, and not the most important.[23] It will be argued below that processes connected with colonization can be seen in action more or less continuously. This argument cannot be refuted simply by producing evidence of 'cooperation with the highland chiefs', because there was always cooperation with *some* chiefs—and again, this occurred both before and after 1609. That is part of how colonization operates. European colonists attacked some American Indian chiefs directly, but cooperated with others who were not in the settlers' immediate path. They even made formal agreements with such chiefs—agreements that were often broken once the frontier of settlement moved forward. In British India, where there was no large-scale European settlement, the East India Company cooperated with some of the Indian princely states, some of the time, and that is no reason to deny that colonization took place. In the Highlands, different policies were always pursued for different chiefs; the cutting edge of policy was colonial, even though we could hardly expect to find colonization being actively pursued against all chiefs simultaneously. We shall, however, find similarly cavalier attitudes towards the agreements that were sometimes made with the chiefs.

At this point, we need to investigate the four colonial models in more detail. To take the story of dispossession-and-settlement colonies first: this is largely the story of the plantation of Lewis. A syndicate of 'Adventurers', mainly lairds from Fife, attempted to colonize the island, exploiting divisions among the island's traditional ruling family, the Macleods. They made three expeditions, aiming to settle lowlanders to exploit the fishing and agricultural resources of the island. The Fife Adventurers' settlements lasted from October 1598 to December 1601, from August 1605 to October 1606, and briefly in late 1609, but each settlement was eventually ousted by resistance from the Macleods. Still, when the syndicate eventually sold out, it was not to the traditional rulers of the island, the Macleods, but to a client clan of the government, the Mackenzies. Colonization had succeeded, at least negatively, in destroying an intractable bastion of clan power. It was a lesson for other clan chiefs to ponder.[24]

The Lewis scheme's difficulties meant that it remained unique, but while it lasted, projects were regularly devised to extend it. It had originally been planned, in 1598, in tandem with a Lothian lairds' syndicate to colonize Skye. In 1600, when it looked as if the Lewis colony would succeed, conquest of 'the remanent of his hienes Iyllis' was envisaged.[25] In the end the Lewis

---

[23] Goodare, 'Statutes of Iona'.

[24] W. C. Mackenzie, *History of the Outer Hebrides* (Paisley, 1903), chs. 7–8; D. Macdonald, *Lewis: A History of the Island* (Edinburgh, 1983), 25–32; Goodare, 'Statutes of Iona', 32–3, 44–5. For the scheme's context see Lynch, 'James VI and the "Highland Problem"', 211–12, 217–18, 223–4.   [25] *CSP Scot.* xiii, I. 221; *APS* iv. 248, c. 55.

plantation was the only one to be implemented in the Scottish Highlands, but it was paralleled by the Elizabethan state's sponsorship of numerous colonial plantations in Ireland. The larger-scale plantation of Ulster in the 1610s also reminded everyone—chiefs and government—of the possibilities.[26] The Ulster plantation drew on existing Scottish, as well as English, experience, and the Scots were keener on it than the English.[27]

How much actual dispossession was involved in these schemes? Evidence is scanty, especially because all schemes except that for Lewis remained paper ones. Few seem to have envisaged the mass expulsion of the population; generally the political elite were targeted. Probably, as in Ulster, mass expulsion was seen as most desirable if it could be achieved, but policy-makers were prepared to settle for something less than the *tabula rasa* of their dreams. Elizabethan colonization theory was already well developed in Ireland. It included awareness that English settlement might be total or partial, drew on classical models, and employed a law of *res nullia*, or 'empty land', to justify itself.[28] The ordinary working folk were less of a problem than the political elite, and even in Ulster there were not always enough colonists to do the actual work. So there was some overlap between the first two colonial models, dispossession-and-settlement and military occupation (North America and British India, in nineteenth-century terms); the first was simply the second writ large.

Even the Ulster plantation represented a more drastic attack on the structure of Gaelic society than any previously known; in the past, a clan defeated in warfare had merely been replaced by another similar one. The Fife Adventurers conformed to the Ulster pattern; they seem to have employed some of the local people, but agreements with Macleod leaders they regarded only as temporary (and could be broken). The Macleods *were* to be dispossessed, their tenants to be ruled henceforth in Lowland fashion. Then the marquis of Huntly's projected colonization scheme for Uist in 1607 was explicitly to proceed 'not . . . be aggreement with the cuntrey people, but be extirpatioun of thame'.[29] This probably meant merely permanent exile, and probably for the clan elite only, but such 'extirpatioun' would still have made a *tabula rasa* of Uist political society.[30]

The third colonial model, trading penetration, was active from the early seventeenth century. The scattered economic evidence suggests that

---

[26] Cf. R. Gillespie, *Colonial Ulster: The Settlement of East Ulster, 1600–1641* (Cork, 1985), especially the discussion on pp. 219–22 (where the Ulster situation is shown clearly to be colonial, although differentiated from that of New England); P. S. Robinson, *The Plantation of Ulster* (Dublin, 1984).

[27] N. Canny, *Making Ireland British, 1580–1650* (Oxford, 2001), 196–8, 226–32.

[28] Ibid. 121–34.   [29] *RPC* vii. 361.

[30] This is a cautious interpretation of difficult evidence, and it remains possible that Huntly's project would have led to a horrific massacre. Donald Gregory, whose views on Highland history still command respect, thought so: D. Gregory, *History of the Western Highlands and Isles of Scotland, 1493–1625* (2nd edn., London, 1881), 315.

exports from the Highlands grew markedly. In the southern Highlands, the Campbells fostered trade in herring and (especially) live cattle. They did not themselves engage in more than estate management; most of the actual trade was conducted by lowlanders, and much of the investment came from England.[31] The cattle-droving routes are a good example of the way in which colonial communications networks are created to transfer economic resources to the colonizing state.[32] The Mackenzies, meanwhile, opened up the Lewis fishing grounds to development: not by the local people or even by their own clients, but by the Dutch—much to the annoyance of the convention of royal burghs. Highlanders were still resisting encroachments by non-native fishermen in 1622, but the privy council was better able to get their chiefs to answer for them than it had been in Bishop Leslie's time.[33] The Mackenzies also promoted the iron industry. By 1612, Sir George Hay, the former Fife Adventurer in Lewis and future chancellor of Scotland, had established an ironworks at Letterewe in Mackenzie territory; it operated for the remainder of the reign at least.[34]

The prominence of the names Campbell and Mackenzie among clans fostering economic development was, of course, no coincidence. The fourth colonial model involved the co-option by the colonial power of sections of the native elite (Africa, in eighteenth- and nineteenth-century terms). Colonial regimes in Africa searched for native chiefs with whom to work, even creating chiefs for tribes who had previously lived without them.[35] This worked because collaboration with colonists is often attractive. The colonists have wealth, prestige, firepower; if you can't beat them, why not join them? Actually, for most members of the African elite, there were several reasons why not, one being that the colonial power required only a limited number of collaborators. When the colonists demanded slaves, the client chiefs had to obtain these by making war on other chiefs; if all had been clients, the supply would have ceased. Although there was no slave trade in the Highlands, there was a similar structural issue. Campbells collaborated with the state because of what they could get out of it, and what they could get was mainly the lands of clans hostile to the state. If the MacDonalds of Dunyveg had also become clients, the Campbells would not have had state support in annexing their lands, and the prime incentive for collaboration would have been lost.

[31] J. E. A. Dawson, 'The Origins of the "Road to the Isles": Trade, Communications and Campbell Power in Early Modern Scotland', in Mason and Macdougall (eds.), *People and Power in Scotland*, 80–3, 92–3; D. Woodward, 'A Comparative Study of the Irish and Scottish Livestock Trades in the Seventeenth Century', in L. M. Cullen and T. C. Smout (eds.), *Comparative Aspects of Scottish and Irish Economic and Social History* (Edinburgh, n.d. [1977]), 149–50; A. R. B. Haldane, *The Drove Roads of Scotland* (Edinburgh, 1952), chs. 2–3.

[32] M. Hechter, *Internal Colonialism: The Celtic Fringe in British National Development, 1536–1966* (London, 1975), 30–1.

[33] *RCRB* iii. 257–63; *RPC* xiii. 740–1, 37.

[34] *RPC* ix. 351; x. 22–3; xiv. 567; earl of Seaforth to Hay, 4 July [1624?], *LP James VI*, 365–6; J. Turnbull, *The Scottish Glass Industry, 1610–1750* (Edinburgh, 2001), 63–8.

[35] L. Mair, *Primitive Government* (Harmondsworth, 1962), 256–9.

The fostering of client clans was an easy option for the state, because it exploited traditional clan rivalries. Several vulnerable clans had internal difficulties: the MacGregors in Rannoch, after they fell out with their former allies, the Campbells of Glenorchy; the MacDonalds of Dunyveg, beset by internal dissension and the secession of the Antrim branch of the clan; and the Macleods of Lewis, locked in a fratricidal succession dispute.[36] Some clans had always faced such difficulties from time to time, and had usually been left to cope with them with help or hindrance from their neighbours alone. Now, the state itself was intervening to influence the outcome, using the legal system to tip the scales in favour of its clients. Sir Robert Gordon's comment on one such episode was: 'Thus doe the tryb of Clankeinzie become great in these pairts, still incroaching upon ther nighbours, who are unacquented with the lawes of this kingdome.'[37]

The Mackenzies' most spectacular success came in the 1610s, when the defeat of the Fife Adventurers in Lewis gave them the chance to oust the Macleods. A Highland writer later commented:

This turned to the ruin of diverse of the undertakers [i.e. the Adventurers], being exhausted in means, not haveing the language, wanting power to manage such an enterprise in a strange place farr off; so that highlanders were fittest to grapple with highlanders, and one divil, as the proverb is, to ding out another, the M'klouds in the end expired.[38]

This was achieved by Kenneth Mackenzie of Kintail, who became Lord Kintail, one of the few Highland peers. The tradition of having the government on his side had been begun by his father, Colin:

This Collin McKenzie of Kintail was a tender feeblie man but wise and judicious and had much trowble in his tyme with the feud of neighbours, against quhom he had alwayes the lawes of the countrey, and his brother Rorie Moire still acted in the feilds and putt the law in execution.[39]

The last point here—that action was needed 'in the feilds' as well as in the law courts—is a reminder that the policy of using client clans was also one of accepting the continuance of the clans' autonomous military power. This was not ideal for the state, but it was not prepared to undertake a full military conquest using Lowland forces. Client clans represented the extension of state power on the cheap; in colonization, as elsewhere, you get what you pay for.

---

[36] MacGregor, 'A Political History of the MacGregors'; J. M. Hill, 'The Rift within Clan Ian Mor: The Antrim and Dunyveg MacDonnells, 1590–1603', *Sixteenth Century Journal*, 24 (1993), 865–79. [37] Gordon, *Sutherland*, 248.
[38] Fraser, *Chronicles of the Frasers*, 241.
[39] John McKenzie, 'The genealogie of the surname of McKenzie since ther coming into Scotland', *HP* ii. 36. For the privy council's sceptical view of Kenneth Mackenzie's use of the law in 1594, shortly after he succeeded his father, see the cancellation of his commission of justiciary: *RPC* v. 161. However, he soon became a councillor himself: ibid. 273.

The main client clan in our period was, of course, the Campbells. Since the late fifteenth century they had sought a dual role. Their chief was very much a Highland chief—even claiming to be 'king of the Gael' by the mid-sixteenth century—but he was also earl of Argyll with an established place among the Lowland nobility and at the royal court.[40] The earls were unusual in constantly seeking bits of paper from the crown to enhance their Highland authority. The acceptance of the earldom itself (1457) is noteworthy, as in traditional terms it might seem like a demotion. Rulers of the medieval province had been known as *Rí Airir Goídel* ('king of Argyll'), a title conferred by no one but themselves.[41] Just as the crown could use the statute of 1597 against many land titles in the Highlands, the Campbells had their own habit of acquiring formal titles to lands, which they would file away to be produced at the right moment.[42] They also maintained a united front against their rivals. The sprawling MacDonald clan fragmented through internal conflict, while the Campbells successfully surmounted a difficult period—the minority of the seventh earl of Argyll in the 1590s—to emerge, reunited and triumphantly expansionist, in the decades after 1600.[43]

The seventh earl's achievements were striking. He exploited his indispensability to the government while at the same time accepting rather more of its supervision than he perhaps would ideally have chosen. A traditional note was struck by Lord Binning when faced with the renewed MacDonald uprising in Islay in 1615—'how necessar it is that the erle of Argyle haist thither', he fretted. But he also summoned a meeting of the 'commissionaris of the Iles', so that Argyll could be 'advysed and authorysed be thame'. It was indeed they who issued Argyll's instructions when he did eventually turn up to be appointed lieutenant.[44] In 1633, Argyll's son demonstrated both his commitment to territorial expansion and his acceptance of state supervision for this: he sponsored a voyage of exploration to an unknown Hebridean island, and had the voyage licensed by the crown.[45]

Campbell expansion illustrates a recurrent theme in colonial history: the tension between colonists on the spot, seeking tough measures to establish or maintain their position, and the metropolitan government, worried about costs or justice. The suppression of the MacDonalds' uprising in Islay in 1614 revealed exactly this tension. A commission of lieutenancy was granted to Sir John Campbell of Cawdor, but he and the privy council disagreed about what

[40] Dawson, *Politics of Religion*, ch. 2; quotation at p. 48. In Gaelic, the word '*Rí*' meant both 'king' and 'lord', indicating the lack of need to distinguish between different levels of power.

[41] MacGregor, 'MacGregors', 70–1.

[42] E. J. Cowan, 'Fishers in Drumlie Waters: Clanship and Campbell Expansion in the Time of Gilleasbuig Gruamach', *TGSI* 54 (1984–6), 269–312 at 291–2.

[43] Id., 'Clanship, Kinship and the Campbell Acquisition of Islay', *SHR* 58 (1979), 132–57.

[44] NLS, Binning to James, 16 Aug. [1615], Denmylne MSS, Adv. MS 33.1.1, vol. viii, no. 25; *RPC* x. 746.

[45] J. Willcock, *The Great Marquess: Life and Times of Archibald, 8th Earl and 1st (and Only) Marquess of Argyll, 1607–1661* (Edinburgh, 1903), 24–5.

his powers should be. Campbell wanted to ban the Islay people from possessing 'galayes and birlingis'; this was rejected because many of their infeftments required them to do so. He wanted a prohibition on their goods being 'resett' by any other subjects; it was answered that this would be 'to prejudge theme of the comon benefite of free subjectes and to hauld thame under . . . a thraldome and bondage'. He wanted to transport the leading landlords temporarily to the 'incuntrey'; it was replied that they were already under bonds to appear there once a year. The military musters were restricted to the sheriffdoms of Argyll and Tarbert; he wanted to recruit also in Dumbarton, Ayr, and Irvine, but this was rejected as 'neidles' and a 'vexatioun'.[46] The bishop of the Isles, meanwhile, warned that captured rebels should 'thoill a jurei', so that 'the inhabitants may sei that all is done legally'.[47] The uprising was suppressed, though with difficulty.

Colonization was legitimized by the development of colonialist attitudes. The highlanders were fitted early into a colonial stereotype that would later become familiar all over the world. Colonized peoples have generally been seen by their colonizers as congenitally lazy (a stereotype that never seems to be undermined by the simultaneous or subsequent discovery that they can readily perform unlimited quantities of unskilled manual labour); they are wild and unpredictable; they are savage and ignorant; they may be in need of protection (from themselves if from nobody else); and they are always 'they', seen ever in a generalized plural rather than as individuals with their own personalities.[48]

These stereotypes could be illustrated from copious sources, many of which have been explored by Arthur Williamson. He has shown that Lowland Scottish political thinkers had long denigrated and marginalized the Highlands, although hampered by having to struggle against the common European intellectual perception of *all* northern lands as barbarous.[49] For internal consumption, it is doubtful whether the issue of 'northern lands' was so important as it was to a Continental audience. Lowlanders may have worried that *Frenchmen* would confuse them with highlanders and would thus think that they were cannibals (for this was a widely circulated belief about highlanders); but within Scotland nobody was likely to make that mistake.

To take the stereotype of laziness first: among those hostile to union in 1604, Robert Pont counted 'the wild and savadg Irish of the English dominion, and of the Scottish ilands the Hebridiani, or Æbudiani, who for the

---

[46] *RPC* x. 716–22; *HP* iii. 166–8.

[47] NLS, 'Articles given to his majestie by the byshop of the Iles', n.d. (*c*.1614–15), Denmylne MSS, Adv. MS 33.1.15, no. 10.

[48] A. Memmi, *The Colonizer and the Colonized*, trans. H. Greenfeld, introductions by J.-P. Sartre and L. O'Dowd (2nd edn., London, 1990).

[49] Williamson, 'Scots, Indians and Empire'; id., 'George Buchanan, Civic Virtue and Commerce: European Imperialism and its Sixteenth-Century Critics', *SHR* 75 (1996), 20–37; id., *Scottish National Consciousness*, 117–32.

most part are enemies also to tillage, and weare out their dayes in hunting and idleness after the maner of beasts'.[50] The reference to 'tillage' illustrates one way in which the highlanders fell short of Pont's industrious ideal.

On Highland untrustworthiness, Bishop Andrew Knox exclaimed in 1614: 'becauss it is to[o] difficill to belewe thais pipill, I wold hawe a sycht of forces wiche wolde effray tham', and 'far beit from me ewer to entir undir condition or trust with that falss generatioun and bludie pepill'.[51] The labelling of highlanders as untrustworthy had a further implication: promises made to them did not have to be kept. Lord Ochiltree, in his military expedition to the Isles in 1608, invited leading chiefs on board his ship to hear a sermon by Bishop Knox—and then kidnapped them. The Fife Adventurers in Lewis repeatedly broke the agreements they made with the Macleods; this would have been regarded as dishonourable if done between social equals.[52]

The stereotype of highlanders as savage and ignorant was especially pervasive. We are likely to feel today that the sixteenth-century Gaelic world had a literature and culture at least as sophisticated as its Lowland Scottish counterpart.[53] In the eyes of the state, however, this culture was either not recognizable as culture at all, or existed only as a hindrance to the inculcation of Lowland practices. Highly educated Gaelic poets were not civilized; they were merely potential propagandists of resistance. An early modern state did not need a unified language, but it did need to denigrate and marginalize the languages that impeded it—and Gaelic was definitely such a language.

Thus, in July 1616, the privy council ordained that no heir to lands in the Isles should be allowed to inherit unless they could write, read, and speak English. The act was soon followed (in December) by a scheme for parish schools, projected to contribute towards the extirpation of Gaelic. The preamble to the July act was eloquent about Lowland attitudes to Gaelic culture:

The cheif and principall caus quhilk hes procurit and procuris the continewance of barbaritie, impietie, and incivilitie within the Yllis of this kingdome hes proceidit from the small cair that the chiftanes and principall clannis of the Yllis hes haid of the educatioun and upbringing of thair childrene in vertew and learning,—who being cairles of thair dewteis in that point, and keeping thair childrene still at home with thame, whair thay sie nothing in thair tendar yeiris bot the barbarous and incivile formes of the countrie, thay ar thereby maid to apprehend that thair is no uther formes and dewteis of civilitie keept in ony uther pairt of the countrie; sua that quhen thay

---

[50] *Jacobean Union*, 22.

[51] Knox to John Murray of Lochmaben, 11 Oct. and 23 Oct. 1614, *HP* iii. 162, 164.

[52] The breaking of promises made to highlanders was not new in our period: cf. Stewart, 'The Clan Ranald', 39.

[53] W. Gillies, 'Gaelic: The Classical Tradition', in R. D. S. Jack (ed.), *The History of Scottish Literature*, i: *Origins to 1660* (Aberdeen, 1988). One of the region's most noted artistic traditions was curtailed at the Reformation: K. A. Steer and J. W. M. Bannerman, *Late Medieval Monumental Sculpture in the West Highlands* (Royal Commission on the Ancient and Historical Monuments of Scotland, 1977), 82.

come to the yeiris of majoritie, hardlie can thay be reclamed from these barbarous and incivile formes quhilkis for laik of instructioun wer bred and satled in thame in thair youth; whereas, yf thay had bene send to the Inland in thair youthe and traynit up in vertew, learning, and the Inglis tung, thay wald haif bene the better preparit to reforme thair countreis and to reduce the same to godlines, obedience, and civilitie.[54]

These attitudes are worth quoting at length because some historians have been reluctant to give full weight to repeated official pronouncements of this kind.[55] Hostility to Highland culture was just as manifest at the Highland edge as in Edinburgh. The presbytery of Inverness, dominated by lowlanders, objected to ministers wearing 'uncomely habits such as bonnets and plaids'.[56] The first half of the seventeenth century may have been the most repressive phase of state policy towards the Gaelic language. By the 1640s, the language was less politically threatening because the old-style bardic schools, which had eulogized and sustained the traditional clan ethos for so long, had gone into terminal decline.[57]

The highlanders' need of protection was less prominent in Lowland statements than their barbarity, but it was present. The landmark statute of 1587 said that the clans were 'waistand, slayand, heryand and distroyand thair awin nychtbouris and native cuntrie people', before going on to complain that they were doing the same in the Lowlands. A commission on the Isles in 1608 noted in its instructions that the chiefs were 'useing that tyrannicall forme over thair tennentis as it maid the cuntrey to be almost unhabited'.[58]

Highlanders' status as an anonymous 'they', and lack of official interest in them as individual people, was also evident. Local church records almost always named the lowlanders who appeared before them, but a highlander would usually be recorded anonymously as 'ane hieland man'. Informing the king that the earl of Argyll had 'caused present the heades of twa notable malefactours in the Hielands', Chancellor Dunfermline added: 'I spair to truble your highnes with onpleasand, onworthie and ongodlie naymes'.[59]

That lowlanders regarded the Highlands as 'other' is strikingly evident in their repeated assumption that the Western Isles were actually separate from the country of Scotland. We have already seen the chronicler Lindsay

---

[54] *RPC* x. 777–8, 671–2.

[55] One scholar who is alert to the issues, and who draws some telling parallels with educational systems for other subordinate peoples, is K. M. MacKinnon, 'The School in Gaelic Scotland', *TGSI* 47 (1971–2), 374–91 at 379–80.

[56] Quoted in Todd, *Culture of Protestantism*, 58.

[57] Lynch, 'National identity', 130–1; A. I. Macinnes, 'Scottish Gaeldom, 1638–1651: The Vernacular Response to the Covenanting Dynamic', in J. Dwyer et al. (eds.), *New Perspectives on the Politics and Culture of Early Modern Scotland* (Edinburgh, n.d. [1982]), 59–60, 67–8; D. Withrington, 'Education in the 17th Century Highlands', in L. Maclean (ed.), *The Seventeenth Century in the Highlands* (Inverness Field Club, 1986).

[58] *APS* iii. 461, c. 59; *RPC* viii. 742–7.

[59] Graham, *Uses of Reform*, 33; Dunfermline to James, 8 July 1609, *HP* iii. 117.

of Pitscottie making this assumption, and it was shared by many others, sometimes including the government. Grain exports from Scotland were banned and an exception was made allowing exports to the Isles; the fugitive earl of Arran was said to have left the country and gone to Kintyre; the general assembly complained that over four hundred parishes in Scotland were vacant, as well as those in Argyll and the Isles.[60] Neither fully Scots nor fully anything else, the highlanders became, for the first time, aliens in their own country.

One common fate of such aliens is that they may not receive the full protection of the law. This brings us to the MacGregor clan. In 1603 the privy council ordered that the surname MacGregor should be abolished, under pain of death for all refusing to change their name. After 1611, MacGregors could be killed out of hand for being MacGregors, and the killer would be rewarded; they themselves could earn pardon only by killing other MacGregors.[61] The 'act aboleissing the sirname of Ruthven', after the so-called Gowrie conspiracy of 1600, was similar in some ways, but did not permit Ruthvens to be killed out of hand in order to achieve its aims; the family remained members of the Scottish political community.[62]

The separate nature of the Highlands meant that the government could even ponder whether the region was worth governing at all. Governments usually see their own existence as a worthwhile end in itself; they may debate what policies to pursue, but they do not ask themselves whether they should pack up and go home. But when it comes to colonies, governments can and do ask themselves just that. Colonies are expensive; they do not have to be conquered or occupied unless the returns justify it. Sir Alexander Hay, clerk register, saw Highland policy in 1615 very much in these cost–benefit terms. The expense of suppressing the MacDonalds' recent uprising in Islay, he thought, would come to ten years of 'the rent of our whole Iyles'. Since it was mainly the earl of Argyll who stood to benefit, he argued that Argyll should bear all future costs 'and disburdyne his majesties cofferis of furder chairge'.[63] This kind of cost–benefit analysis was never performed for the government of Ayrshire or Fife.

During the early seventeenth century, the state's successes caused the official rhetoric on the Highland problem to shift in tone. Instead of saying that the Highlands were incorrigibly lawless, the line now tended to be that the Highlands had been successfully pacified. Some historians have assumed that

---

[60] *APS* ii. 495, c. 14; Calderwood, *History*, iv. 547; *CSP Scot.* xii. 182–3.

[61] *APS* iv. 550–1, c. 26 (cf. *RPC* vi. 558 n.); *RPC* ix, pp. xxxiii–xlii (an important overview of the privy council's proceedings on the subject between 1610 and 1613).

[62] *APS* iv. 212, c. 2; *RPC* vi. 510–11. Cf. the measures taken against the Grahams on the English side of the Border, where also the surname was abolished, and the main effort was to banish them to colonies in Ulster and elsewhere rather than to kill them: *CSP Dom.*, 1603–10, 237. For another instance of treatment of highlanders as beyond the protection of the law, see Goodare, *State and Society*, 265–6.

[63] Hay to John Murray of Lochmaben, 21 Dec. 1615, *HP* iii. 302.

this reflected an objective diminution of political violence in the region, but this is not necessarily so. The rhetorical shift contained a new and subtle distinction between the *Highlands* and the *highlanders*; only the former had been pacified. Donald Macleod of Assynt was in 1617 living the life of a traditional Highland chief, 'nevir acknowledgeing his majesteis auctoritie nor obedience, bot leving as one who nowther respect[s] God, his majestie, law, nor justice'; he had committed various crimes and been outlawed. But, thought the privy council, Macleod saw that things were now different in the Highlands: 'now at last persaveing, in this tyme of his majesteis most happie and blissit governament, quhen his heynes is powerfull to suppres suche wretched catives, that he is not able longer to hald foote in the wicked and un-happie course of his bypast lyff', he had handed over his estates to his son.[64] Whether the council's solution (ordering the son to find caution) made much difference is uncertain; what is interesting is its tone of confidence that the Highlands had basically been pacified, even if there was little evidence for this in Assynt. Also revealing is a legal memorandum of 1615 for Lord Gordon against Sir Lachlan Mackintosh of Dunachton. Gordon complained to the king that Mackintosh was using 'broikin heigh land men' to support his claim to the teinds of Culloden, 'and gifs it out that the most pairt of the heigh land men in Scotland will tak his pairt, becaus they say they haife not threven sence your majestee maid the cuntrey so peaceable'.[65] Before, the 'heigh land men' had been blamed because the Highland region was violent; now, they were blamed because *it* was peaceful, but *they* were not.

How did highlanders respond to all this? When they were called savages, did they return the uncompliment? Occasionally they did, but it depended on the audience they were addressing. Highlanders who wanted the attention of government in the early seventeenth century had to adopt their own version of the latter's pacified-Highlands rhetoric. The pacification had officially occurred very recently, so to be taken seriously in Edinburgh, the highlanders could not simply say that they were peaceful. What they had to say was that they had been been violent, but that this was thankfully all in the past:

We your hienes poor subjectes of your majesties west and north Islandis of Scotland, in respect of the far distance of our residence fra your hienes gratious presence, hes in certane ages bypast lewit without anie gude ordour, subject to intestin truble and dis-sensioun amangis our selfis, quhairby we ar extremlie impowerischit.[66]

This petition, from three gaoled chiefs, was the kind of thing that they thought the king would want to hear. Sir Roderick Macleod of Dunvegan

---

[64] *RPC* xi. 200–1.
[65] *HP* iii. 176. In fact the Gordons also had Highland followers, and Mackintosh himself would later 'purchase a commissioun from the councell against them': Gordon, *Sutherland*, 357.
[66] NLS, petition of Hector Maclean of Duart, Donald Gorm MacDonald of Sleat, and Donald MacDonald of Clanranald, 10 Nov. [1608], Denmylne MSS, Adv. MS 33.1.15, no. 12. 'Lewit' = lived.

successfully persuaded the king that he had 'an earnist desyre to be repute civile'.[67] He knew that he was on probation at best.

Such chiefs had a problem in proving their loyalty: they might well be loyal, but to whom, or what? In his quest to rehabilitate himself with the authorities after leading the Islay uprising, Sir James MacDonald of Dunyveg wrote obsequious but still proud letters to various courtiers. He carefully protested his loyalty, but with a revealing afterthought, to 'my cuntre, I mein his majestes dominions'.[68] Others were more straightforward. The Franciscan missionaries in the 1620s observed a 'lasting and mutual enmity' between highlanders and lowlanders, while Coll MacDonald ('Colla Ciotach', kinsman and one-time colleague of Sir James) regarded his enemies simply as 'the Scotts'.[69]

The highlanders' common identity as 'the Gaels' was traditionally reinforced by bardic praise poetry. Eulogies of the chiefs stressed their honourable descent from the 'sons of Míl', legendary progenitors of Irish Gaeldom, of which Highland chiefs considered themselves an integral part.[70] However, the common Gaelic world ceased to be a reality in our period, as the English and Scottish states attacked their Gaelic peoples and drove wedges between them. By the early seventeenth century, even those Gaels who resisted often did so in terms of 'Irish' or 'Scottish' politics.[71] This was a weakness in the ideology of resistance. In practice and in their writings, the Gaelic Irish response to colonization was complex, seeking to exploit changes rather than simply resisting them. There was some development of an anti-colonial awareness in the early seventeenth century, but opponents of colonization rarely appealed to the idea of an Irish 'kingdom' or 'nation'.[72] Scottish Gaels had even less opportunity to do so, since it would have been even harder to present the 'Scottish' kingdom as Gaelic.

What highlanders did, therefore, was to distance themselves from the 'Scottish' kingdom. Their identity as a colonized people in the early seventeenth century emerges in the history they produced. National and other political identities were generally constructed through possession of a shared past. When the highlanders in the years around 1625 considered their past, did they think of the 'national' origin-legends that had collected around the identity of the Scottish kingdom and nation? On the contrary, Gaelic poetry resolutely ignored the entire history of Scotland as it was understood and

---

[67] James to council, 1 June 1613, *The Book of Dunvegan*, 2 vols., ed. R. C. Macleod (Third Spalding Club, 1938–9), i. 141.

[68] MacDonald to the earl of Caithness, n.d. [1615], *HP* iii. 219.

[69] *The Irish Franciscan Mission to Scotland, 1619–1646: Documents from Roman Archives*, ed. C. Giblin (Dublin, 1964), 90; R. Black, 'Colla Ciotach', *TGSI* 48 (1972–4), 201–43 at 212.

[70] Gillies, 'Gaelic: The Classical Tradition', 254.

[71] S. G. Ellis, 'The Collapse of the Gaelic World, 1450–1650', *Irish Historical Studies*, 31 (1999), 449–69.

[72] N. Canny, 'The Formation of the Irish Mind: Religion, Politics and Gaelic Irish Literature, 1580–1750', *Past and Present*, 95 (May 1982), 91–116; id., *Making Ireland British*, 402, 420–2.

prized by lowlanders—including the Wars of Independence, in which many highlanders had actually fought. Instead, Highland historians considered first the history of their clan (traditional clan histories began in the seventeenth century to be written down in Scots) and then that of the lordship of the Isles.[73] Such histories brought out all too clearly the separate nature of Highland political identity, and the Highlands' position as a formerly autonomous region that had been forcibly subjugated by the Scottish state.

The Campbells formed a conspicuous exception to all this, and their success did not pass without comment from the clans at whose expense they had expanded. From at least the mid-seventeenth century, much of the Gaelic poetry hostile to the Campbells attempted to denigrate them as non-Gaelic.[74] Since the Campbells obviously were and would remain a Highland clan, this represented a *political* identification of the *true* Gaels: if you don't support the Gaelic cause, you're no true Gael, no matter what language you speak.[75]

This was possible because language was ceasing to play such a central role in identifying the Gaels. The chiefs in the seventeenth century were all adopting more Lowland ways, distancing themselves from their clansmen. This was probably related to the general 'withdrawal of the upper classes' described by Peter Burke, which in some areas of Europe created a new linguistic divide between the elite and the common folk.[76] A common Gaelic identity, if one could be maintained, now had to be based at least partly on something other than language.

Aware of their position as victims of colonization, it is not surprising that highlanders sometimes translated their knowledge into action. Resistance to the expanding presence of state authority in the Highlands showed itself in several ways. There was obvious resistance, both active and passive, to most of the military expeditions of the years 1596–1625. The island clans particularly targeted—the Macleods of Lewis, the MacDonalds of Kintyre and Islay—fought back vigorously when their lands were handed over to others. Can this be regarded as specific and deliberate anti-colonial resistance? In many cases it probably cannot. The MacDonalds who resisted the Campbells in the 1610s may not have thought they were doing anything different from those who had fought the Macleans in Islay (with success) in the 1580s and 1590s. The difference was on the other side: the Macleans were solely a

---

[73] J. MacInnes, 'The Panegyric Code in Gaelic Poetry and its Historical Background', *TGSI* 50 (1976–8), 435–98 at 442–3; an important example is the 'History of the MacDonalds', *HP*, i. 1–102.

[74] W. Gillies, 'Some Aspects of Campbell History', *TGSI* 50 (1976–8), 256–95 at 264–74.

[75] There was indeed a difference in the Campbells' literary identity. Chiefs' normal identity in Gaelic praise poetry was exclusively Irish and Scottish Gaelic. The Campbells' Gaelic bards drew extensively on this, but also included unique Scottish and British elements in the literary identity they constructed for their patrons: M. O'Mainnín, ' "The same in origin and in blood": Bardic Windows on the Relationship between Irish and Scottish Gaels, *c.*1200–1650', *Cambrian Medieval Celtic Studies*, 38 (Winter 1999), 1–51 at 33–48.

[76] P. Burke, *Popular Culture in Early Modern Europe* (London, 1978), 270–81.

traditional clan like the MacDonalds themselves, whereas the Campbells were also agents of the state.[77] The Campbells' rivals eventually came to appreciate this distinction, but because the Campbells were also a clan, it took some time.

More direct evidence of disobedience to a policy initiative comes with the reaction to the proscription of the MacGregors. As noted above, they were singled out for deliberate extermination in the years after 1603. But they remained members of the *Highland* political community, whose members rarely shared the government's view that the best MacGregor was a dead one. Having successfully reduced the clan to a fugitive band of two dozen, the government's next trouble was the 'daylie resett whiche these malefactouris haif haid in the heighlandis and countreis nixt adjacent thairunto, the gentilmen and inhabitantis thairof furnissing thame with all necessareis to supplie thair wantis'.[78] There is no direct evidence for why so many highlanders defied the proscription, sheltering and supporting the remnants of the clan. We have only the official records of the repeated prosecutions of highlanders for 're-setting' MacGregors. In their willingness to do so we may see an indication of an embryonic Highland political consciousness, in terms of which the proscription was the illegitimate act of an alien power. It would be hard to be sure about this; some chiefs who protected the MacGregors probably did so cynically, in order to get the clan—who by now lived largely by violence—to do their own dirty work for them in return. But the prosecutions certainly created a divide in Highland society, between those who supported the MacGregors and those who cooperated with their persecution.[79]

There are other indications of a resistance movement involving solidarity between clans. The Macleod resistance in Lewis was aided by the MacNeills of Barra and the MacDonalds of Clanranald, although neither of these clans was in immediate danger from the colonizers; the historian of the latter clan has seen this aid as a 'conservative island community of interest' trying to close ranks against the 'alien' invaders.[80] Malcolm Macleod, a leader of the later stages of the resistance, went on to 'associat himselfe to the McDonalds of Ila and Kintyre', joined the uprising of Sir James MacDonald in Islay in 1615, and remained with him some years in exile. When Macleod spent four months as a pirate with Colla Ciotach, they gave their booty to the

[77] For the MacDonald–Maclean feud see A. Macdonald and A. Macdonald, *Clan Donald*, 3 vols. (Inverness, 1896–1904), ii. 547–75. For a shift in the Macleans' position, often allied with the Campbells in the 16th c. but becoming generally hostile to them in the early 17th, see N. Maclean-Bristol, 'The Macleans from 1560–1707: A Reappraisal', in Maclean (ed.), *The Seventeenth Century in the Highlands*, 78–81.

[78] *RPC* x. 31; and see ibid., pp. xix–xxv, for a summary of the proceedings against resetters of the MacGregors.

[79] The persecution was described by one early 18th-c. Highland writer as 'crewell': *Memoirs of Sir Ewen Cameron of Locheill*, ed. J. Macknight (Abbotsford Club, 1842), 48. 19th-c. Highland traditions decidedly favoured the MacGregors' protectors: D. Campbell, *The Lairds of Glenlyon* (2nd edn., Strathtay, 1984), ch. 3. For more details of the persecution, see Cowan, 'Fishers in Drumlie Waters', 283–91.

[80] Stewart, 'Clan Ranald', 43–4.

inhabitants of North Uist, showing a desire to build grassroots political support. They even sent an emissary to seek Spanish assistance.[81] Macleods and MacDonalds had hitherto had little in common; what these clan leaders shared was a common experience of colonization.

There were also compliant chiefs who faced resistance from members of their own clan. Donald MacDonald of Clanranald, in 1610, and Lachlan Mackinnon of Strathordale, in 1612, were attempting to cooperate with the government and faced opposition from their clansmen as a result. Members of each clan organized a resistance movement (described as 'a detestable societie') against their chiefs' collaboration. The Clan Ranald, apparently, were 'preferring bestlie barbaritie and wickednes to godlines, obedience, and honestie'. Both chiefs received commissions of justiciary against their clansmen, empowering them to convoke the lieges in arms in order to arrest their opponents. Mackinnon's commission was 'to reduce his haill clan to obedience, and by course of law to cut af as rottin memberis suche of thame as do continew in thair evill doingis'.[82]

Despite such stirrings, however, the overall impression is that there were fewer 'rottin memberis' than there might have been. Anti-colonial resistance remained sporadic, because the clans were too divided to rally effectively against the intruder. In this, the seventeenth-century Highlands differed little from eighteenth- and nineteenth-century Africa. Even the most determined leaders of the resistance to Lowland incursions were also enmeshed in traditional patterns of Highland politics, in which the enemy who mattered was the local one—the estranged half-brother trying to capture the chiefship, the hostile clan in the next valley. For highlanders caught up in such disputes, agents of state could sometimes seem like allies—even when the state was plainly hoping to move in and take over.

The other side of this equation was the state's increasing sophistication in the arts of divide and rule. Good highlanders served the state; what better form of service could they offer than against the leaders of native resistance? Sir Roderick Macleod of Dunvegan, a man who in the 1590s had fought for the earl of Tyrone against the English in Ulster, earned his knighthood in 1614 for handing over to the authorities the leader of the Lewis resistance, Neil Macleod.[83] Sir Alexander Hay had earlier recommended that Neil Macleod be deported to Virginia and given some land: 'there, I think, our countrey heir suld be best rid of him. There wald be no suche danger there as of his being in Iyireland, for albeit bothe the speiches be barbarous yit I hope he sall neide ane interpretour betuix him and the savaiges.'[84] In other words, Macleod would be unable to stir up trouble among the American Indians, and would

[81] 'The ewill trowbles of the Lewes', *HP* ii. 279; F. A. MacDonald, 'Ireland and Scotland', 155–6. It seems to have been the previous Islay uprising, in 1614, that inspired a widespread MacDonald conspiracy for an anti-plantation uprising in Ulster: ibid. 113–15.

[82] *RPC* viii. 445; ix. 324–5.   [83] Macdonald, *Lewis*, 31.

[84] Hay to [. . .], 3 Sept. [1610], *HP* iii. 121–2. Instead Macleod was executed.

have to use his undoubted talents in other ways. Hay's assumption that Lewis and Virginia were basically similar places, inhabited by similar people, is also instructive.

In practice, then, the chiefs of the Isles found it hard to unite politically in any cause—against the crown, or for it. During the Islay uprising of 1615, Sir Roderick Macleod had delicately to explain that although the loyal chiefs were willing to serve against the rebellious MacDonalds, their forces would have to be divided 'in thrie severall armyes and companyees' because of their own mutual animosities.[85] This may have impeded the suppression of the uprising, but on the whole it was something in which the government could take satisfaction.

Between about 1595 and 1625, the political elites of the Highlands were coercively shifted from the centre of their own self-sufficient world to the fringes of a larger one—the Scottish state. They were not an integral part of the Scottish body politic, unlike Lowland elites, so the state treated them more high-handedly. The demands of the state—rents, taxes, lawsuits, paperwork—were more alien to them than to Lowland elites; and although even Lowland elites may have disliked aspects of the state system, they could at least use their recognized status within the body politic to lobby or petition for better treatment. Highland chiefs, who were not respectable, faced an uphill struggle when they tried to do the same.

Nevertheless, this is what they tried to do. They ceased to maintain their traditional aloofness from the structures of the state. They started to do their paperwork. Initially, they probably regarded the compilation of written records about them (such as the early clan censuses) as a hostile act, a mark of distrust and of shame.[86] Very few Highland chiefs in the late sixteenth century have been identified regularly employing advocates or using the central courts to settle their disputes. Most of those who did were Campbells or Mackenzies, or were from families on the edge of the Highlands who cannot be classified unambiguously as clans at all, such as Munros, Buchanans, or Menzies.[87] Campbells and Mackenzies continued to have much the most extensive relationships with their lawyers; but although the other chiefs never caught up with them, there was a slow but steady expansion in the early seventeenth century of the number and frequency of chiefs' contacts with lawyers. In the years 1610–37, the chiefs of the Isles, previously the most remote from the government, were summoned annually to Edinburgh to answer for their continued good behaviour. Initially they

---

[85] Macleod to Lord Binning, 18 June 1615, *HP* iii. 243. Highlanders' political divisions at this time are listed in I. F. Grant and H. Cheape, *Periods in Highland History* (London, 1987), 116–19.

[86] For this point in relation to the most famous such survey, Domesday Book, see M. T. Clanchy, *From Memory to Written Record: England, 1066–1307* (2nd edn., Oxford, 1993), 6–7.

[87] D. A. Watt, 'Chiefs, Lawyers and Debt', 69–81. The Highlands provided hardly any clients to two representative mid-16th-c. advocates: Finlay, *Men of Law*, 163.

were supposed to appoint agents in Inverness or Rothesay on whom summonses could be served, but in 1614 most of them appointed Edinburgh lawyers.[88]

The chiefs thus spent more time seeking incorporation within the Scottish body politic than they spent rejecting or resisting it. Their early efforts at lobbying and petitioning were unconvincing, but ultimately they had a good deal of success. During the civil wars of the 1640s, Highland chiefs were drawn more into national Scottish political life, and the quest for their military support meant that they could no longer be treated so high-handedly. This had several linked effects for the rest of the century. Chiefs crowded eagerly into Lowland political society; they adopted more aspects of Lowland culture alongside the Highland ways that they still used back home; and they sought to raise cash from their estates in order to maintain their status in Edinburgh. Local rivalries among the clans changed in character, centring more on credit, debt, and formal land title. The chiefs' primary recourse in dispute-settlement was now to the law courts, and their financial indebtedness escalated. Because fighting men from the Highlands were still valued in certain state-sponsored contexts, and because the adoption of Lowland culture was confined to the chiefs themselves and to a handful of lawyers, the clans themselves continued to be fighting forces. But actual mobilization of these forces occurred more rarely, dwindling eventually into the occasional Jacobite revolts. Even when inter-clan disputes led to fighting, this normally took place alongside political and legal struggles; the law courts were a chief's first resort.[89]

So the idea of litigation had been widely accepted in the Highlands. The MacDonald vernacular poet Iain Lom recognized in the Restoration period that chiefs had to go to law, and even created a new form of heroism to praise. Lord MacDonell had supported the Macleans of Duart against Argyll, both in military confrontations in Mull and in intrigues at the royal court:

But, Lord MacDonell, readily did you keep tryst; you engaged the Inveraray Earl [Argyll] when he thought to lord it in Mull; you were ahead of him in Edinburgh and manfully conducted that business. Trivial do I deem the expenditure involved since you won your point in London.[90]

The MacDonalds' poets of the seventeenth century refused to forget the loss of Islay and Kintyre, and continued to envisage them as the centre of the clan's

[88] Watt, 'Chiefs, Lawyers and Debt', 87–8, 98; Goodare, 'Statutes of Iona', 43.

[89] Dodgshon, *From Chiefs to Landlords*, ch. 5; P. Hopkins, *Glencoe and the End of the Highland War* (Edinburgh, 1986); Macinnes, *Clanship*, chs. 4–5; D. Stevenson, *Alasdair MacColla and the Highland Problem in the Seventeenth Century* (Edinburgh, 1980); Watt, 'Chiefs, Lawyers and Debt', 189.

[90] *Orain Iain Luim: Songs of John MacDonald, Bard of Keppoch*, ed. A. M. Mackenzie (Scottish Gaelic Texts Society, 1964), 153. For the background to this see Hopkins, *Glencoe*, 58–67.

interests.[91] But Iain Lom's pragmatic recognition that the Campbells had to be beaten at their own game represented a victory for the state.

Meanwhile, the economy of the Highlands was dramatically opened up, but it remained distinctive and was not integrated into the broader Scottish economy. The Lowland economy, by contrast, was converging with England without becoming dependent upon it. Asking the question of whether seventeenth-century Scotland was a dependent economic region tends to come up with the answer that the *Highlands* were one. Lowland Scotland was producing more manufactured goods than before, and retaining the profits; the Highlands were exporting raw materials, and the profits went elsewhere.[92]

Jane Ohlmeyer has recently explored a thought-provoking model of political processes in marginal regions, based on the concept of 'open' and 'closed' frontiers.[93] A frontier opens when people first arrive in a land into which they seek to intrude their power, and closes when the resulting struggles end with the creation of a single political authority in that land. In this view, the late sixteenth and early seventeenth centuries saw the opening of frontiers in Ireland, the Scottish Highlands and Islands, and the Anglo-Scottish Borders. Wales, although culturally distinct, had already been assimilated politically. During the period, the new frontiers closed in the Borders and in the Northern Isles, as the process of assimilation was completed. However, as she notes, there are problems in an exclusively 'frontier' analysis. The most obvious of these are that it tends to prejudge the question of whether people want to be 'assimilated', and to neglect the issues of struggle and resistance. Perhaps for this reason, Professor Ohlmeyer usually prefers to employ the more familiar concept of colonization, and for present purposes it is this aspect on which it is more helpful to focus.[94]

From the perspective of the region's elites, the early seventeenth century was the high-water mark of state-sponsored internal colonialism in the Highlands.[95] From the 1640s onwards, colonialism would be experienced mainly by highlanders lower down the social scale, with the chiefs themselves

[91] D. S. Thomson, 'Three Seventeenth-Century Bardic Poets: Niall Mór, Cathal and Niall MacMhuirich', in A. J. Aitken et al. (eds.), *Bards and Makars: Scottish Language and Literature: Medieval and Renaissance* (Glasgow, 1977), 226–8.

[92] I. Whyte, 'Is a British Socio-Economic History Possible?', in Burgess (ed.), *The New British History*, 175–6; C. Smout, 'Scotland in the 17th and 18th Centuries—A Satellite Economy?', in K. Dyrvik et al. (eds.), *The Satellite State in the 17th and 18th Centuries* (Bergen, 1979). Cf. the development of Ireland: N. Canny, *Kingdom and Colony: Ireland in the Atlantic World, 1560–1800* (Baltimore, Md., 1988), 52–3.

[93] J. H. Ohlmeyer, '"Civilizinge of those rude partes": Colonization within Britain and Ireland, 1580s–1640s', in N. Canny (ed.), *The Oxford History of the British Empire*, i: *The Origins of Empire* (Oxford, 1998).

[94] For further development of the frontier model see J. Goodare and M. Lynch, 'The Scottish State and its Borderlands, 1567–1625', in eid. (eds.), *Reign of James VI*.

[95] For a much-discussed general model of this concept see Hechter, *Internal Colonialism*, ch. 2.

cooperating in the process. Indeed this had already begun under James VI, with the issue of commissions to the chiefs of the Mackinnons of Strathordale and the Clan Ranald against their clansmen; but under James this was still unusual, and perhaps the chiefs were reluctant at first. Late seventeenth-century Highland chiefs formed a distinctive, colourful, and sometimes suspect part of Scottish political society, but they were definitely included rather than excluded. The Jacobite clan chiefs of the early eighteenth century have been characterized as 'Scottish gentlemen arguing about British politics'.[96] Highland chiefs in general had become as law-abiding as could reasonably be expected. This was what had been hoped for in the 1580s; most of the outrightly colonial policies promoted in the reign of James VI had been superseded. But those policies neverthelesss left their mark—in the political divisions between client clans and others, in the garrisons that had to be established to hold the Highlands down, and above all in the exploitative way in which the Highland economy was treated. The Highlands' experience of government changed a good deal in our period, but it remained distinctive, and it remained unhappy.

[96] B. Lenman, *The Jacobite Clans of the Great Glen, 1650–1784* (London, 1984), 84.

CHAPTER ELEVEN

Government and People

Barons, be quhom the lawes of the realme are made, sould have discretion, and mair knawledge of the lawes made be themselfes, then the laik and vulgare people sould have.[1]

It was clear, even commonplace, that the law was made by and for the landed ruling class. This gave them both responsibilities and privileges. Nobles, because they possessed honour, had to be treated with special respect by the law. 'Letteris of inhibition may not be gevin aganis ony erle, lord or baron, be the lordis [of session], without ane sufficient and just cause,' wrote Sir James Balfour, 'because the samin is hurtful to mens fame and honour.'[2]

Much of the most visible government activity affected only the men with 'fame and honour', the political elite. That elite has been estimated to comprise about 5,000 landlords (of whom 1,000 were really substantial), plus a further number of lawyers, officials, ministers, and greater burgesses.[3] Perhaps the inclusion of the latter would bring the total to 10,000, quite a large number but only about one per cent of the population. If one then multiplied the figure by about ten to take account of local elites—smaller lairds and the remaining burgesses for the most part—that would still omit 90 per cent of the Scottish people. What about them?

This chapter, then, is about how government was experienced by that 90 per cent, the 'laik and vulgare people', the ones who lacked 'fame and honour'. Just because they did not participate in the making of laws, that did not mean that the laws never affected them; some laws manifestly did, at least in the Lowlands.[4] The laws' impact may be hard to determine, since the sources are sometimes fragmentary, but the attempt must be made. We will consider the peasants in the countryside; women at all social levels (who hardly ever participated in government, though wealthier women did have 'fame and honour'); and some marginalized groups, particularly

---

[1] *Quoniam Attachiamenta*, c. 13, in John Skene (ed.), *Regiam Majestatem* (Edinburgh, 1609), 79; cf. *Quoniam Attachiamenta*, ed. Fergus, 146–7, c. 11, and an English official memorandum of 1559 proposing that none should study law 'except he be descended from a nobleman or a gentleman', quoted in Fletcher, *Reform in the Provinces*, 40.

[2] Balfour, *Practicks*, ii. 476.

[3] I. D. Whyte, *Scotland before the Industrial Revolution: An Economic and Social History, c.1050–c.1750* (London, 1995), 155.

[4] The Highlands, where the impact of government was felt mainly by the elite, are discussed in Ch. 10 above.

witches and gypsies, who were singled out for particular governmental attention.

This chapter focuses on what government did to people. This is a large topic in itself, but a full treatment of the subject would require consideration also of how people responded to government action. Although the common folk were relatively powerless, they were not entirely so. If the government was to retain its legitimacy, as observed in Chapter 1 above, it had to take account of people's responses to its actions. Any governmental initiative affecting significant numbers of the common people would require implementation by local courts or other administrators who were embedded in a network of community and neighbourly interactions. These administrators would not consider the initiative in isolation, but would add it to a list of priorities. If the initiative was likely to assist popular compliance with other locally important measures, they would enforce it actively; if it was likely to stir up trouble with the people, they would probably give it low priority. In the present state of research into early modern Scottish communities, these suggestions must remain tentative, but it should be borne in mind that the common people were probably not passive when governments tried to do things to them. At the end of this chapter there are some brief remarks on people's responses to government.[5]

How in general did central government approach these people beyond the political elite? No contemporaries produced a detailed list of excluded groups, but there were numerous comments on the issue of how the poor— the majority of the excluded—should be treated. Some of the less platitudinous comments can be revealing. James VI advised his son to 'embrace the quarrell of the poore and distressed, as your owne particular', and to 'beate downe the hornes of proude oppressours'. However, this was immediately qualified: 'when ye sit in judgement', he should 'sway neither to the right hand nor to the left; either loving the riche, or pittying the poore'.[6] From one point of view, this put government above the class structure; there may well have been 'oppressours' in class society, but there was no suggestion that the state itself could be one. It would be useful to know more about what James thought 'proude oppressours' did, or how common he thought they were. His remarks at any rate do not add up to a programme of governmental intervention in the class structure (although he did have interventionist programmes in other areas, notably the bloodfeud). If the government were to pursue policies that increased social inequality ('loving the riche'), that

---

[5] There is a large literature on the subject for England. For overviews see Braddick, *State Formation*, ch. 4; Fletcher, *Reform in the Provinces*, 62–83. For some recent case studies see M. J. Braddick and J. Walter (eds.), *Negotiating Power in Early Modern Society: Order, Hierarchy and Subordination in Britain and Ireland* (Cambridge, 2001), and T. Harris (ed.), *The Politics of the Excluded, c.1500–1850* (London, 2001). This is separate from the question of how ordinary people might influence politics at a higher level, on which see W. Te Brake, *Shaping History: Ordinary People in European Politics, 1500–1700* (Berkeley, Calif., 1998).

[6] James VI, *Basilicon Doron*, in *Political Writings*, 24.

would be illegitimate; reducing inequality ('pittying the poore') would be equally wrong.

A key desideratum under James's programme of impartial government was that justice should be made available to the poor, or at least should be seen to be so available from time to time. St Louis was said to have sat under an oak tree to administer justice to all. Queen Mary did something like this in 1564, sitting personally in the court of session to stop the cases of the rich taking priority.[7] James went through the oak-tree routine in 1602, or at least got the privy council to do so on his behalf. On two visits to Perth, the council issued proclamations inviting 'puir folkis complaintis', and three or four such complaints were heard. Anyone still unsatisfied was publicly encouraged to tell the king.[8] Such gestures were largely symbolic, but they played their part in establishing the image of a just monarch.

It was agreed, then, that 'puir folkis' might have a good deal to complain about, and that the law might be able to assist them. This could lead to the view that the law, if only it were properly enforced, could bring about social change in their favour. The leading presbyterian James Melville thought that many laws were 'weill maid' but 'wantes execution, lyke ather-cape wobbes that taks the sillie flees, bot the bumbarts braks throw tham'.[9] Slightly less radical in tone, but only because he was addressing the 'bumbarts' themselves—the nobility—rather than demanding that they be curbed, was John Knox: 'It is not ynough that you abstaine from violent wrong and oppression, which ungodlie men exercise against theyr subjectes; but ye are further bounde, to witt, that ye rule above them for theire welth.'[10] By this he meant primarily that they should promote Protestantism; but the subjects' 'welth' had wider implications, including their physical and economic well-being.

As well as his appeal on *behalf* of the common people, Knox also did something very rare: he appealed *to* them directly. 'Al man is equal', he told them, in that all had equal hopes of salvation. In this world, too, all the adult male Jews in Moses' day had been members of the body politic, paying flat-rate taxation for the building of the Tabernacle.[11] The nominal exemption of the Scottish peasantry from taxation underlines their exclusion from the political nation: they did not have to be consulted, either about taxes or anything

[7] Randolph to Cecil, 8 Mar. 1564, *CSP Scot.* ii. 51. For an example of a burgh council doing something similar, see Dundee City Archive and Record Centre, Dundee council minutes, vol. i, p. 22.

[8] NAS, treasurer's accounts, 1601–4, E21/76, fos. 158ᵛ, 175ᵛ; *RPC* vi. 407–8, 445–6. There was an officer in charge of petitions, the master of requests, but there seems to be little or no evidence of him actually dealing with requests. The office was held in the 1580s and 1590s by Mark Kerr, a gentleman of the chamber and privy councillor.

[9] Melville, *Diary*, 188. 'Sillie' = weak; 'athercape wobbes' = spider's webs; 'bumbarts' = bumble-bees. The remark seems to have been proverbial.

[10] John Knox, *Appellation . . . to the Nobilitie, Estates and Communaltie*, in his *Works*, iv. 483.

[11] Knox, *A Letter to the Commonalty of Scotland*, in *Works*, iv. 528.

else.[12] No significant writers after Knox seem to have sought to include the common people in politics.

The rulers, then, were not only rich: they were enmeshed in the property structure rather than looking down on it from above. This did not necessarily mean that they were in conflict with the poor. It was possible to think that economic policies could benefit everyone. John Mair argued that tenants should be allowed to feu their holdings, thus giving them security. They 'would grow richer, and would build fair dwellings that should be an ornament to the country'.[13] For many commentators, particularly those who made policy, the prosperity of the common people was a means to an end—typically a military end: it would allow the crown to recruit more effective and better-equipped troops. Mair was alive to these aspects of policy, but he also thought that prosperity was an end in itself.

Neither Melville, Knox, nor Mair were in government, however, and their idealism was not shared by those who were. The basis of government was landed property, and parliament made no bones about keeping this out of the hands of those who lacked it. A statute of 1579 complained that inquests of perambulation were sometimes chosen from 'men of small rent or leiving, and sum of thame haveing na heritage'. Such men claimed that it was enough to be 'honest and faythfull, haveing geir worth the kingis unlaw, and subjectis of the realme'—but if this were so, said the act, then 'men of na heritages sould be juges . . . and tak away mennis heritage and landis'. A rebuttal of the classical tradition of citizenship could hardly have been more clearly delivered.[14]

From this position of entrenched property, what the landlord-legislators were prepared to offer was a tradition of occasional statutes claiming to favour the 'pure laboreris of the ground'. In 1581, a statute against slaughter of farm animals commented that 'speciale respect is had to the lawboring of the ground in dew season'.[15] More than one scholar has argued that fifteenth-century Scottish peasants did not revolt because parliament passed laws in their favour, but this probably overestimates the influence that legislation could have as well as the goodwill of the legislators.[16] In our own period, the

---

[12] There is some evidence that landlords passed on their tax burdens to the peasants, but this seems not to have involved formal consultation or political activity: Goodare, 'Parliamentary Taxation', 27.

[13] Major (Mair), *A History of Greater Britain*, 31.

[14] *APS* iii. 144, c. 17. 'Geir' = moveable property; 'unlaw' = fine or monetary penalty. For the minutely scrutinized property qualifications of one such inquest, see 'A Banffshire Process of Perambulation, 1558', ed. D. B. Smith, *Stair Society Miscellany*, iv (2002), 89–90, 105–13. Most of the members, it was admitted, 'had na heretage', but they did all have substantial tenancies. The 1579 act excluded them.

[15] *APS* iii. 217, c. 14.

[16] Macfarlane, *William Elphinstone*, 166; Donaldson, *Scotland: James V—James VII*, 14–15. Some of the statutes cited here seem only nominally to be about the poor, if that. The only really significant 15th-c. statutes on behalf of peasants were that of 1450 on tacks (that is, leases; relevant for those, probably a minority, who held them) and that of 1469 on liability for lords' debts (important only for the monetized parts of the economy): *APS* ii. 35, c. 6; 96, c. 12. Cf. Lord Cooper, *Supra Crepidam* (Edinburgh, 1951), 3–6.

only significant statutes stated to be in favour of peasants were those regulating teinding of crops. This benefited landlords too, as one such act (in favour of 'heritoures and laboreris of the ground') acknowledged; indeed the peasants were really bystanders here, in a struggle between teind-holders and landlords who both sought to appropriate the peasants' surplus.[17]

James VI's ideal government, impartial as between rich and poor, required the poor to have access to the judicial system. They would not, by definition, be interested in legal process over substantial landed property; on the other hand, it might seem unfair if a poor person was unable in practice to obtain justice against a rich one. The pre-Reformation court of the bishop's official (the predecessor of the commissary courts) has been claimed as 'an early form of community court' in that most of the litigants before it were of only modest property—neither the 'very great' nor the 'very humble'. But only the well-off could afford to pursue a contested case to its conclusion; others could afford only to register an action. To that extent, justice in the official's court could be bought.[18] And this was a court that did not profess to be concerned primarily with matters of property.

In one important way, the law did attempt to remedy this practical exclusion of poor folk from the courts: from 1535 onwards the court of session usually had an 'advocat for the puir' (in fact usually two advocates), commissioned to act on their behalf free of charge in return for a stipend. In 1587 this was extended to criminal matters. The stipend was paid only irregularly in the late sixteenth century, however. It was a duty on the legal profession, rather than a right possessed by poor people themselves. Its extent and practical effect are unclear, though a few cases have been identified as having been brought under it.[19] Judicial concern for 'pure men' was also shown in a clause of *Quoniam Attachiamenta* limiting the requirement to find security.[20] The legislative commission of December 1567 proposed to speed up legal cases involving poor people, since 'lang proces' was 'greit hurt and heirschip to all the purell'—but nothing came of this.[21]

This certainly did not mean that the property of the less-propertied was wholly at the mercy of the elite. People of modest property were able to register their possession of it, and to enter into a variety of transactions concerning it. They could make and register contracts and testaments, and some at least could sue in several courts, particularly the commissary courts and burgh courts. This much is clear from the extensive researches of Margaret

---

[17] 'Heritor' was the emerging term for a landed proprietor. The statutes were: *APS* iii. 139, c. 11; 450, c. 32; iv. 286, c. 7; 471–2, c. 5; 541–2, c. 9; v. 34–5, c. 17. They are conveniently summarized, with commentary, in Cormack, *Teinds and Agriculture*, 89–108.

[18] Ollivant, *Court of the Official*, 146–9, 161–3.

[19] Finlay, *Men of Law*, 81–6; Hannay, *College of Justice*, 68–9; C. N. Stoddart, 'A Short History of Legal Aid in Scotland', *JR*, NS 24 (1979), 170–92 at 170–3; *TA* xiii. 104 (a rare instance of payment, in 1575).

[20] *Quoniam*, c. 34, in Skene (ed.), *Regiam*, 83; cf. *Quoniam*, ed. Fergus, 174–5, c. 22.

[21] *APS* iii. 39–40. 'Heirschip' = harrying.

Sanderson in these courts' records, though her material sheds no light on the question of judicial partiality.[22]

Once before the courts, the treatment of rich and poor may have been impartial in some senses, but there was a certain asymmetry about it—as with a justice ayre in 1574 at which 'the puir men war hangit and the richmen war hangit be the purs'. The phrase seems to have been proverbial.[23] Probably some people saw nothing unjust about this, but those who commented on it clearly did. The church had the same problem. The general assembly declared in 1573 that 'great men offending in sick crymes as deserves sackcloth, they sould receive the samein als weill as the poore'. But as the ministers sought an established place in a hierarchical society, there was something of a *trahison des clercs*. As a Catholic propagandist asked: 'Quhy punish ye onlie the pure be your stuill of repentance?'[24] The rich either escaped penance altogether or succeeded in paying a financial penalty; only a small minority were subjected to public humiliation.[25] The fact that some of them did pay fines shows that church discipline had an effect on them, but they were being offered a choice between payment and public penance that became available to other classes only in the eighteenth century.[26]

Sir Thomas Smith's famous account of English social structure ended with 'the fourth sort of men which doe not rule . . . these have no voice nor authoritie in our common wealth, and no account is made of them but onelie to be ruled'. But, as he continued,

they be not altogether neglected. For in cities and corporate townes for default of yeomen, they are faine to make their enquests of such manner of people. And in villages they be commonly made churchwardens, alecunners, and manie times constables, which office toucheth more the common wealth, and at the first was not imployed uppon such lowe and base persons.[27]

Did Scottish peasants have such a voice in neighbourhood politics? Not as constables, at least until that office was introduced, along with justices of the

---

[22] M. H. B. Sanderson, *A Kindly Place? Living in Sixteenth-Century Scotland* (East Linton, 2002).

[23] Pitscottie, *Historie*, ii. 190; cf. Lindsay, 'Ane satyre of the thrie estaitis', in *Works*, ii. 252–3.

[24] *BUK* i. 284; John Hay, in T. G. Law (ed.), *Catholic Tractates of the Sixteenth Century, 1573–1600* (STS, 1901), 63.

[25] This is the unambiguous conclusion of M. F. Graham, 'Equality before the Kirk? Church Discipline and the Elite in Reformation-Era Scotland', *Archiv für Reformationsgeschichte*, 84 (1993), 289–310. Margo Todd uses his evidence but interprets it differently, arguing that 'there are enough cases of the well-born failing to buy their way out' to suggest that the message of impartial discipline for rich and poor 'was the overriding one': *The Culture of Protestantism*, 176. This may be a matter of perspective—is it more significant that the rich were *sometimes* disciplined, or that they usually were not? The rich could also buy their way around the ban on burials in church: Lynch and Dingwall, 'Elite Society in Town and Country', 182.

[26] Mitchison and Leneman, *Girls in Trouble*, 36; Leneman and Mitchison, *Sin in the City*, 35–6.

[27] Smith, *De Republica Anglorum*, 76–7. Cf. S. Hindle, 'The Political Culture of the Middling Sort in English Rural Communities, c.1550–1700', in Harris (ed.), *The Politics of the Excluded*.

peace, in 1611. Moreover, Smith, writing in the 1560s, thought of English constables as representatives of their neighbours. By the seventeenth century, they had lost this role and were simply officers of the JPs. From the start, Scottish constables were appointed by the JPs (or by the burgh magistrates in royal burghs), and so never had the representative quality that their English forebears had once had.[28] In other courts, even those without office could not participate without property. Not just members of the assize, but even witnesses in sheriff courts had to have property—in one case, goods worth 20 merks were considered acceptable after debate.[29]

Popular participation in government, in Smith's sense, was probably found in birlaw courts and burghs of barony, the officers of which were drawn from the common folk. Even then, they were normally under the control of the baron court which appointed them, but (unlike the constables) they did not exist merely to carry out the orders of that court (see above, Chapter 8). These were exceptions; the norm, as in Elizabethan England, was that the common folk were 'onelie to be ruled'.

Burgh authorities may have been closer to the common people, and in touch with some kind of public opinion—though 'public opinion' may simply be the opinion of the articulate and influential. An Edinburgh merchant surrendered his tallow export licence in 1581, with the approval of the burgh council, because he was 'nocht willing to underly the bruitt and indignatioun of the pepill'.[30] These 'pepill', consumers of tallow candles, were probably not the very poorest, but the phraseology suggests that their influence was not being exercised through the personal connections and lobbying more likely to be used by the burgh oligarchy. But if burgh magistrates could treat lesser townsfolk with respect, central government saw less reason to do so. A proclamation of 1620 addressed maltsters, baxters, mealmakers, coupers, and traders in grain—few of whom were likely to be poverty-stricken, and in many of whose workshops tallow candles probably burned—as members of the 'rude and godles multitude'.[31]

As well as a firm determination to keep power out of the hands of the 'rude and godles multitude', one may detect a characteristic style in which policies dealing with them were carried out in practice. Jenny Wormald has commented that the violence of the bloodfeud was succeeded by a 'new violence of the state'. The state, seeking religious legitimacy, unleashed waves of repression against various groups, especially witches.[32] In his seminal study of the bloodfeud, Keith Brown also offers a comparison with state violence. He

---

[28] *APS* iv. 539, c. 8, para 1; *RPC* ix. 220–6, 409–11, 477; 2nd ser. viii. 326–9; Sharpe, *Crime in Early Modern England*, 34, 77. Constables in Edinburgh had to be burgesses: *Edin. Recs.* vi, p. xxxvii. In effect, constables were messengers at arms for the JPs. For messengers at arms, see Ch. 8 above.

[29] *Fife Court Book*, 317–18.   [30] *Edin. Recs.* iv. 216–17.   [31] *RPC* xii. 203–4.

[32] Wormald, *Lords and Men*, 165. She also cites the persecution of covenanting dissidents in the late 17th c.

describes a particularly gruesome revenge killing, commenting that 'such barbarism was not really typical of the feud, and was in fact closer to the forms of execution practised by early modern governments throughout Europe'.[33] There are two issues here: the degree of suffering caused, and the way the suffering was targeted. Comparisons between bloodfeud and state on the first issue are difficult, but the ritual disembowelling inflicted on William Buchanan by the Macfarlane family in 1619 was not in the least 'typical' of official executions; some countries practised it on traitors, but Scotland was not one of them.[34]

The striking difference, as Dr Wormald has perceived, was in the way that the state targeted its violence. The violence of the bloodfeud was directed inwards, with members of the elite killing one another. The violence of the state could have been deployed in a similar way, as in early Tudor England where factional struggle and bloodthirsty treason laws left a trail of corpses at the royal court. That never happened in Scotland, where the body politic displayed a notable capacity for rehabilitating its errant members. Even the upheavals and civil wars of 1567–73 saw only a handful of prominent figures executed; after 1584 there were virtually none.[35] Instead, the 'new violence of the state' was directed outwards and downwards. Some of the ways in which this happened will emerge as this chapter proceeds; but it also manifested itself in episodes like that of Archibald Cornwell, town officer of Edinburgh. In 1601 he was auctioning some forfeited goods at the town's gibbet, including a portrait of the king. To display the portrait better, he was about to hang it on the gibbet when passers-by protested that this would be disrespectful. The incident came to James's ears, and Cornwell was hanged for *lèse-majesté*.[36]

The broad context of governmental intervention in the lives of the common people was provided by the Reformation. This was a momentous upheaval in all sorts of ways, but one of its central features was the state's move into the territory of moral regulation. This was particularly noticeable in the establishment and spread of kirk sessions, the bodies in the front line of disciplining the common people; but most government institutions were affected by the disciplinary movement. Its growing intensity is illustrated by the increasing frequency of meetings of the St Andrews kirk session. Before the 1590s it had met once a week, or less often. This gradually increased until by 1599 there were two or three meetings per week. In the 1590s, summonses were

---

[33] K. M. Brown, *Bloodfeud*, 32–3.

[34] Two particularly heinous criminals were executed by breaking on the wheel: *Trials*, ed. Pitcairn, i, II. 241; ii, II. 448–50. They appear to be exceptional. Witches were normally strangled and their bodies burned, while other executions were by beheading or hanging.

[35] After the earls of Morton in 1581 and Gowrie in 1584, the only really prominent traitors to be executed were Hercules Stewart, brother of the earl of Bothwell, in 1595, and the earl of Orkney and his associates in 1615. The process of eradicating the bloodfeud saw a handful of executions for murder in the 1610s, and a Jesuit, John Ogilvy, was executed in 1615.

[36] *Trials*, ed. Pitcairn, ii, I. 349–52.

issued on average against one in twenty-six adults in the town every year.[37] By any standards, this was intensive government.

Historians of the Reformation in Europe often argue that the Reformation enhanced state authority. This has not always been a leading theme of Scottish studies, more of which have discussed conflicts between 'church' and 'state'. Such conflicts should not be allowed to dominate our understanding of the period, nor should they obscure the essential unity of the system of disciplinary institutions supervising people's lives. But in adopting a more mainstream European perspective on the subject, attention also needs to be paid to dissenting voices in Continental scholarship. Perhaps the role of the disciplinary system in buttressing the Scottish state should be questioned? According to Lyndal Roper, moral discipline in the German Reformation was not a one-way street leading to state authority. She sees the Protestant attack on immorality, not so much as creating a newly disciplined populace, as producing a heightened awareness of the issues surrounding such offences as street fighting, drunkenness, and sexual promiscuity. If official hostility may have discouraged some people from transgressing the new moral code, it also created a moral literature of disapproval which paradoxically underlined the attractions of the immoral life. People learned that it was bad, but they also learned more about how to do it and how exciting it was. Forbidden fruit is sweet.[38]

This argument would be hard to apply wholesale to Scotland, which did not generate the exuberant 'Devil books' and other 'literature of excess' of sixteenth-century Germany. There may be some mileage in it, to be sure. The elders of the kirk session may have achieved some temporary, local reductions in moral transgressions: they certainly fostered a cadre of committed lay folk, particularly in the middling social groups from which the elders themselves were drawn; but nobody has suggested that the Scots actually ceased to sin.[39] Rather, they continued to do so but were more often caught and punished. In these circumstances, the establishment of a thou-shalt-not official culture may well have led, as Professor Roper suggests for Germany, to a shift in participants' attitudes to the activities that the authorities were trying to suppress. Whether or not extra-marital love affairs became more exciting, they probably had to be more furtive.

So it is that official culture on which we should concentrate. Whether or not Burns's Jenny, coming thro' the rye, was caught and punished, the point is

[37] Graham, *Uses of Reform*, 219.
[38] L. Roper, *Oedipus and the Devil: Witchcraft, Sexuality and Religion in Early Modern Europe* (London, 1994), ch. 7.
[39] A possible exception is Geoffrey Parker, who has pointed to a dramatic if temporary reduction in cases of fornication and adultery before the St Andrews kirk session in the mid-1590s: 'The "Kirk by Law Established" and the Origins of the "Taming of Scotland": St Andrews, 1559–1600', in L. Leneman (ed.), *Perspectives in Scottish Social History* (Aberdeen, 1988), 17–18. This, however, probably represents not a sudden burst of sexual continence but a transfer of cases to the burgh court: Graham, *Uses of Reform*, 213.

that the authorities were on the watch, and that she knew it. There is widespread agreement among historians that the Reformation and Counter-Reformation largely failed to build the devout populace for which they strove; Scotland was no exception here.[40] But the Scottish authorities were able to establish structures—from the elders of the kirk session in the front line, to the general assembly and privy council at the centre—that could demand a measure of outward religious conformity, and could punish moral lapses where discovered. The structures operated with tolerable internal efficiency, and without generating active resistance among those subjected to discipline. That is the significance of the Scottish Reformation for state power.

The discipline system, considered as a set of moral demands rather than as institutions, might have a complex relationship to the state. In Germany, moral discipline could become a political football among different authorities—guilds, town councils, ecclesiastical discipline courts. The struggle, as in Scotland, was fought out over issues like the control of excommunication. Here, Professor Roper denies that discipline was 'a zero sum game in which, regardless of the aims of the players, the state can only win'.[41] She points out that the culture of discipline proceeded in Germany by fits and starts, and that some of its most earnest protagonists tended to succumb to temptation themselves—perhaps precisely *because* immorality had been glamorized. In Scotland, this argument should probably receive less prominence. There were few scandals, for one thing. In the late sixteenth and early seventeenth centuries at least, church discipline did grow steadily, as more ministers were planted and kirk sessions put down roots. There were bitter struggles over control of this system, but the system itself—and, with it, the state—succeeded.

Detailed reasons for this have been found by Margo Todd from her perceptive study of the kirk session records. While the kirk sessions sought to instil conformity to norms of godly behaviour, this often meant in practice providing the kind of social services that people actually wanted, or that their neighbours wanted for them. Kirk sessions punished assault, quarrelling, and slander; they intervened to restore harmony in strife-torn households; they provided poor relief. Even the campaign against fornication and adultery, the main business of all kirk sessions, was not simply coercive but had some legitimacy among the common folk. Adultery could easily be seen as undesirable; fornication, although lacking obvious victims, did transgress moral norms and produce illegitimate children whose support could become a social and financial problem. The outright attacks mounted by the sessions on popular culture, in sabbath enforcement and prosecution of popular festivity,

---

[40] G. Parker, 'Success and Failure during the First Century of the Reformation', *Past and Present*, 136 (Aug. 1992), 43–82, where it is suggested that Catholic states were somewhat less unsuccessful than Protestant ones, with the exception of Sweden.

[41] Roper, *Oedipus and the Devil*, 150.

were among the least successful aspects of the discipline programme. The godly state never became a complete reality, but it did win a good deal of popular acceptance.[42]

One unresolved question remains: the extent to which the success of the disciplinary system of the Reformation was in fact urban. Professor Todd has a great deal of evidence of kirk sessions' effectiveness, but about three-quarters of that evidence comes from towns. The question of how effective rural sessions were remains without a full answer because she mixes urban and rural evidence indiscriminately. To say that towns 'provided the model' or 'set the standard' for the countryside is no substitute for systematic analysis of the similarities and differences.[43] Rural kirk sessions were not backed by anything as powerful as the burgh council. Many rural parishes gained ministers and kirk sessions much later than the towns—often not until the early seventeenth century—and these probably were not as effective when they did arrive. Further study will be needed before the full impact of the rural Reformation can be gauged.

The extension of state authority into the field of moral regulation was also its extension to cover women. Women had not traditionally come into frequent contact with organs of the state. In dealing with a woman pursuer in 1516, the sheriff clerk of Fife forgot her name and even her sex.[44] In Peebles in 1559, two men were put in the stocks 'to underlie correctioun for thair wiffis, quha trublit the toune on the mercat day'; they were ordered to find caution that their wives would not repeat the offence.[45] Before the Reformation the main courts that dealt with women were the church courts, where they often appeared in cases of defamation—mostly involving sexual allegations.[46] Once the state began to take the initiative in regulating sexual behaviour, many more women felt its impact.

It was men alone who normally governed. A search for women holding public office will always come up with occasional names, mostly of widows in minor posts formerly held by their late husbands. Nothing came of a proposal to exclude women formally from all offices.[47] They could inherit heritable offices along with the lands to which they were attached, though it is unclear whether they could exercise the jurisdiction in person.[48] Those office-holders who married or remarried (which they may have been expected to do) had to submit their authority to that of their new husbands. Women held minor burgh offices occasionally, and a male office-holder's wife could

---

[42] Todd, *Culture of Protestantism.*   [43] Ibid. 15–16 and *passim.*
[44] *Fife Court Book*, 37.
[45] *Charters and Documents Relating to the Burgh of Peebles, with Extracts from the Records of the Burgh, 1165–1710*, ed. W. Chambers (Scottish Burgh Records Society, 1872), 257.
[46] Ollivant, *Court of the Official*, 75–6.
[47] *APS* iii. 38. This proposal, made in Dec. 1567, may well have been intended to exclude women from the throne—the only major post open to them. Cf. Goodare, 'Scottish Parliamentary Records', 256–8.   [48] e.g. *RMS* iv. 344, 2636.

sometimes act in his absence.[49] Women were sometimes procurators, usually for their husbands, in the courts.[50] But major offices, like privy councillor, were held exclusively by men; as were most minor offices, like burgh bailie or messenger at arms. There was once a rumour that a woman had become an officer of state, but this was circulated maliciously; to say that women were involved in the government was to disparage that government.[51] And for every woman who was involved in government, there were hundreds of men.

Women's economic role was normally conceived as complementary to men's, and this was enforced by a variety of formal rules. In Edinburgh, no *unmarried* master skinner could have an apprentice.[52] In medieval times, single men had been ordered to find masters, but by the seventeenth century it was just single women who were regulated in this way.[53] It has been suggested that the sixteenth century was a period of gender restructuring in the European urban labour market, with direct attacks by male-dominated guilds on women's position. Other scholars have detected more continuity than change in this area.[54] Little work has been done on this subject in Scotland, and firm conclusions would be premature, though no study has identified a shift in the policy of Scottish guilds and craft incorporations. In Edinburgh, the introduction of beer-brewing technology in the early seventeenth century was capital-intensive and forced out female brewsters,

---

[49] Marion Campbell and Janet Scott, widows, became metsters (measurers) of corn in Leith in 1607; two more women, Janet Sparrow and Janet Caldwell, were appointed in 1613: *Edin. Recs.* vi. 28, 96. Elizabeth Cant, widow of the keeper of the conciergery house at Veere, the Scottish staple port in the Netherlands, was appointed in her late husband's place in 1621, since her 'abilitie to dischairge her dewtye' had been 'fund by experience'; she later remarried: *RCRB* iii. 118–19, 166–7. Barbara Logan, wife of Bernard Lindsay, customs searcher for Leith, normally acted in his place, since Lindsay was also a groom of the royal bedchamber: *RPC* ix. 353. There is less evidence of women in rural offices, but Agnes Bannatyne, a widow, was appointed in 1609 to organize repair of the Lasswade bridge and collect a toll: *RPC* viii. 336. Helen MacGill was customer of Linlithgow in the early 1580s—an office under the crown: *RCRB* i. 193.

[50] J. Finlay, 'Women and Legal Representation in early Sixteenth-Century Scotland', in E. Ewan and M. M. Meikle (eds.), *Women in Scotland, c.1100–c.1750* (East Linton, 1999).

[51] In 1585 it was said that Elizabeth Stewart, countess of Arran, had been 'maid lady controller' (i.e. comptroller): John Colville to Walsingham, 5 Feb. 1585, *CSP Scot.* vii. 555. No such appointment took effect, and this letter is not at all reliable as evidence. Colville also said in it that John Baxter had been appointed to the court of session in place of Robert Pont, but in fact Pont had been replaced in May 1584 by John Graham of Hallyards, while Baxter was never appointed: Brunton and Haig, *An Historical Account*, 191. Cf. R. Grant, 'Politicking Jacobean Women: Lady Ferniehirst, the Countess of Arran and the Countess of Huntly, c.1580–1603', in Ewan and Meikle (eds.), *Women in Scotland*, 97–100.

[52] 'The Incorporated Trade of the Skinners of Edinburgh', 61.

[53] G. DesBrisay et al., 'Life in the Two Towns', in Dennison et al. (eds.), *Aberdeen before 1800*, 56.

[54] K. Honeyman and J. Goodman, 'Women's Work, Gender Conflict, and Labour Markets in Europe, 1500–1900', *Economic History Review*, 44 (1991), 608–28; O. Hufton, *The Prospect Before Her: A History of Women in Western Europe*, i: 1500–1800 (London, 1995), 91–5.

but this was not due to government action except through regulation of the new company.[55]

The exclusion of women from public life was a restriction on the women of the elite. These were also the women with an interest in the rules on property. Since women tended to be treated as adjuncts to men, it was their marital status that determined their position. There were effectively three kinds of elite women: unmarried women, married women, and widows.

A married woman had very few property rights. If she survived her husband she was entitled to a third part of his moveables at his death, but there her rights over moveable property began and ended. Her own moveables were under her husband's control; he could alienate them, but she could not do so without his 'avise and licence'. Any contracts she might make were null.[56]

Her landed property was better protected. A legal decision of 1506 implied that neither party could alienate it. Another of 1552 held an alienation to be invalid if the husband had obtained his wife's consent by force—which implied that her free consent would be binding. This was still more liberal than one of the 'old laws', which held that a husband could alienate even his wife's terce, 'and the wife sould frelie consent thairto, like as scho sould consent and obey him in all thingis quhilk is not aganis the law and will of God'. If they were legally separated, he would retain the property but would be obliged to maintain her 'conforme to her estait'. The corollary of the wife's lack of significant property rights was that she was unable to sue or be sued in any civil legal action without her husband's concurrence.[57]

Widows had more security in their property, though it is exaggerating to say that they were 'effectively on a par with men'—this was so for moveable property only.[58] A widow's landed property would usually be held in the form of a 'terce', a nominal third part of her husband's lands, allocated at the marriage. In fact it could be less than a third (though not more). Lands acquired since the marriage could not be taken into account, though lands alienated by the husband would be deducted. However, additional lands could be allocated for the purpose in the marriage contract, known as a conjunct-fee. The widow had only a liferent interest in her terce or conjunct-fee lands; she could draw the revenues, but not alienate the property. She might find herself under pressure from her son and heir, who had a reversionary interest in it.[59]

---

[55] M. Lynch, 'Continuity and Change in Urban Society, 1500–1700', in Houston and Whyte (eds.), *Scottish Society*, 108–9. R. A. Houston, 'Women in the Economy and Society of Scotland, 1500–1800', in the same volume, deals largely with the period after about 1650. I am grateful to Professor Michael Lynch for the point about beer-brewing.

[56] Balfour, *Practicks*, i. 93–6; Stair, *Institutions*, I.4.15–17; Sanderson, *A Kindly Place?*, 99.

[57] Balfour, *Practicks*, i. 93–6, 111, 217; cf. *Regiam Majestatem*, ed. T. M. Cooper (Stair Society, 1947), II.16.　　　　　　　　　　　　　　[58] Houston, 'Women', 131.

[59] Balfour, *Practicks*, i. 105–14; Sanderson, *A Kindly Place?*, 116–17; James VI, *Basilicon Doron*, in *Political Writings*, 47. Second wives were particularly vulnerable to pressure from sons of the first marriage.

A woman from the elite classes might be forgiven for thinking that it might be in her material interests to remain unmarried. Of course, inheritances normally went to men. Still, about one-fifth of marriages would produce daughters and no sons, and then the daughters would inherit (jointly, if there was more than one).[60] In most cases their marriage would be arranged by fathers or other male kin, and few heiresses had much say in the process beyond exercising a veto on particular individuals; they were effectively being transferred from one male protector to another.[61] Single women rarely litigated.[62] Moreover, an heiress without a male protector was traditionally a prize to be fought for—literally. Abduction of heiresses was common in the sixteenth century.[63] One reason women married, then, was to obtain a man's protection—partly his physical protection, but mainly the protection of the law. The law protected her because it protected him and his possessions, of which she was one. The decline of the bloodfeud, and the law's increasing ability to prevent abductions, probably improved an heiress's chances of being left alone with her property.[64]

A related aspect of the civilizing process was the issue of men's physical violence against women. This was not normally prosecuted in the criminal courts. However, Margo Todd has shown that kirk sessions dealt effectively with the cases of marital violence that came before them. They generally sought to achieve a reconciliation that had a chance of lasting. It would be helpful to know whether women themselves had any control over the process—whether they themselves could lodge complaints or whether these had to come from neighbours. However, their testimony was evidently taken seriously, and it seems as though the extension of government in this field brought significant official regulation into households where men had previously done as they pleased to their womenfolk.[65]

There was one major exception: the crime of rape. Here Professor Todd finds that kirk sessions 'often punished the victim as well as the perpetrator for fornication, and their usual solution to the problem was to persuade the victim to marry her attacker'.[66] Although rape was technically such a serious offence as to be one of the 'four pleas of the crown', the criminal courts did not in practice prosecute it either. A convicted rapist in Dundee in 1589 was

---

[60] W. Seccombe, *A Millennium of Family Change* (London, 1992), 106–7.

[61] K. M. Brown, *Noble Society*, 120–1. For church courts upholding young women's rights to such a veto in the face of paternal coercion, see Todd, *Culture of Protestantism*, 267–9.

[62] W. Coutts, 'Wife and Widow: The Evidence of Testaments and Marriage Contracts, c.1600', in Ewan and Meikle (eds.), *Women in Scotland*, 181.

[63] E.g. the abduction of Margaret Hamilton, daughter and heiress of John Hamilton of Auchinglen, in 1596: *RPC* v. 291–2. Abduction could be collusive, a woman's way of evading parental control, but Margaret was aged only 10 at the time. She later married someone else: *RMS* vi. 1831.

[64] Cf. R. K. Marshall, *Virgins and Viragos: A History of Women in Scotland from 1080 to 1980* (London, 1983), 63–74, suggesting that during the 17th c. women gained more individual choice and initiative in seeking a marriage partner.

[65] Todd, *Culture of Protestantism*, 284–90.   [66] Ibid. 296–7.

punished only as a fornicator.[67] The official procedure for reporting
rape could have been designed to deter a woman from doing so: she should
immediately 'pass to the nixt town, and thair schaw to honest men the injurie
done to hir, and the blude, gif ony was drawin, als weill in hir bodie under hir
claithis, as in hir face, togidder with hir revin claithis, gif ony be'. She then had
to 'pass fordwart on the king's way to the schiref of that schirefdome, or to
the coroner, gif he may be had, and schaw the samin to him in maner abone
specifyit', and then do the same for the 'cheif lord of the schirefdome'. All this
had to be done without delay, not even 'the space of ane nicht'.[68] This law,
derived from *Regiam Majestatem*, was obviously not in regular use, since the
final clause, about the 'lord of the schirefdome', was obsolete.[69] In the early
seventeenth century, there were no recorded prosecutions in the central
courts simply for rape or attempted rape—there had also to be some
aggravating factor, such as the woman concerned being pregnant or under
age.[70]

It was not that the authorities ignored the issue of rape; it was because the
lawmakers chose to have the law that way that women lacked protection. In
1609, the king proposed to reform the crime of rape. The penalties for rape
itself would be increased, and pleas of mitigation through the victim's subsequent consent would be ruled out. Two new lesser offences, 'awaytaking' and
seduction, were also to be created. A nineteen-man commission was duly set
up to consider this, but the result in 1612 was a statute dealing only with the
issue of subsequent consent, which clarified existing law rather than changing
it.[71] Parliament had the opportunity to make rape a real crime, but did not
do so.

What of women as criminals themselves? The misleading claim has been
made that 'the courts had refused to regard them [i.e. women] . . . as independent criminals' before 1690, when a new infanticide statute was passed.[72]

---

[67] Dundee City Archive and Record Centre, Dundee council minutes, vol. ii, p. 41.

[68] Balfour, *Practicks*, ii. 510; cf. *Regiam*, ed. Cooper, IV.8.

[69] For its English antecedents see K. M. Phillips, 'Written on the Body: Reading Rape from
the Twelfth to the Fifteenth Centuries', in N. J. Menuge (ed.), *Medieval Women and the Law*
(Woodbridge, 2000).

[70] Wasser, 'Violence and the Central Criminal Courts', 63–5. The same applies to domestic
violence against women, though as we have seen the church courts did deal with this. England
saw a similar pattern, with rape prosecutions mainly of attackers of girls under 18: N. Bashar,
'Rape in England between 1550 and 1700', in London Feminist History Group, *The Sexual
Dynamics of History: Men's Power, Women's Resistance* (London, 1983). Rape was never
mentioned as a crime committed by 16th-c. Border reivers, although it is unlikely that it did not
occur: M. M. Meikle, 'Victims, Viragos and Vamps: Women of the Sixteenth-Century Anglo-
Scottish Frontier', in J. C. Appleby and P. Dalton (eds.), *Government, Religion and Society in
Northern England, 1000–1700* (Stroud, 1997), 175.

[71] *APS* iv. 409–10; 454, c. 48; 471, c. 4; cf. Balfour, *Practicks*, ii. 510.

[72] Mitchison, *Lordship to Patronage*, 86–7. The 1690 act did not in any sense 'criminalize'
women—it created wider grounds of proof for an existing crime: *APS* ix. 195, c. 50. In New
England, legal practice had already assimilated itself to the similar English infanticide act of
1624, and this may have happened in Scotland also: P. C. Hoffer and N. E. H. Hull, *Murdering*

In fact, when women committed serious crimes, they were always tried and punished for them in person, as any sixteenth-century court's records will show. The exception was when a wife committed a crime in her husband's presence, when only he could be accused. Women criminals were few, but not because the law refused to recognize them.[73]

What did happen—and the key date here was 1560, not 1690—was that the state began to interest itself in a wider range of offences. As well as traditional secular crimes, a new range of moral offences was created to punish. The institutions in the front line here were kirk sessions, backed up by the higher courts of the church and by the civil authorities also. The main moral offences were fornication and adultery. Although these were committed by women and men equally, and although women and men were punished equally for them (more or less), that was still a higher proportion of women than for traditional crimes. Moreover, it was women who experienced the power of the elders more immediately. Fornication and adultery were commonly discovered when an unmarried woman was found to be pregnant, whereupon she would be hauled in and compelled to name her partner.[74] Moreover, equality of punishment meant equality of monetary fines. In towns at least, most sexual offences were committed by a female servant and a male householder. Because she was far less likely to be able to raise the money than he was, she was far more likely to be banished or sent to the house of correction.[75] Moral regulation meant unprecedented regulation of women.

The issues of women, of criminality, and of state-sponsored moral discipline came together in the witch-hunt.[76] Witch-hunting could be carried out only by a state that laid claim to godliness. That it was a government operation is plain. The map of the incidence of witch-hunting—most intense in south-eastern and central Scotland and the Aberdeen area, almost non-existent in the Highlands—could easily be a map of state influence.

The experience of witch-hunting was a divisive one for communities. Many people were willing to testify against witches, and their anger at the wrongs

Mothers: Infanticide in England and New England, 1558–1803 (New York, 1984), 19–22, 38–40.

[73] Hope, *Major Practicks*, II.17.7; H. V. McLachlan and J. K. Swales, 'Sexual Bias and the Law: The Case of Pre-industrial Scotland', *International Journal of Sociology and Social Policy*, 14 (1994), 20–43.

[74] M. F. Graham, 'Women and the Church Courts in Reformation-Era Scotland', in Ewan and Meikle (eds.), *Women in Scotland*; Mitchison and Leneman, *Girls in Trouble*; Leneman and Mitchison, *Sin in the City*.

[75] G. DesBrisay, 'Twisted by Definition: Women under Godly Discipline in Seventeenth-Century Scottish Towns', in Y. G. Brown and R. Ferguson (eds.), *Twisted Sisters: Women, Crime and Deviance in Scotland since 1400* (East Linton, 2002).

[76] For what follows, see Larner, *Enemies of God*; Goodare, 'Women and the Witch-Hunt'; id. (ed.), *The Scottish Witch-Hunt in Context*; and id. et al., 'Survey of Scottish Witchcraft'. Here I focus on the experience of the community at large, since the experience of the accused witches themselves—interrogation, pricking for the witch's mark, torture, execution—is more familiar.

they believed the witches had done them makes it easy to believe that they could have been glad to see them executed. On the other hand, while willing, they were not usually *eager* to testify. Most witches were executed during five brief periods of nationwide panic by the authorities—1590–1, 1597, 1628–30, 1649, and 1661–2. The trials of these years often show neighbours testifying about wrongs done to them ten, twenty, or even forty years earlier. It is *possible* that in launching a witch-hunt, the authorities simply lifted the lid on a permanently seething cauldron of anti-witch resentment; but is it *probable*? Clearly, Scottish peasants could identify witches in their midst, but if they really wanted them dead as soon as they were identified, it is surprising that outside the panic periods they made so little effort to achieve this. It is more likely that, left to themselves, they would have continued to cope with these witches informally, without ever demanding their execution. They had after all coped in this way for centuries, using a judicious combination of avoidance, conciliation, and counter-magic. Witch-hunting arose through a combination of state initiative and popular demand, but state initiative, be- cause it was new, was the key to it.

This interpretation is strengthened by noting that many witches (perhaps about half of all those executed, though statistics can only be tentative) had no neighbours testifying against them. These witches' route to the stake began with the testimony of another accused witch under torture; they needed no reputation for witchcraft in the community at large. There is no record of what their friends and kinsfolk thought when they were suddenly hauled in, tortured until they confessed to the demonic pact, and then ex- ecuted; but it would be rash to assume that the execution of such witches was popular in their communities. Even some of the publicly known, quarrelsome witches had friends and kinsfolk who interceded for them. And one of the few ways in which a man might find himself on a witchcraft charge was through failure to distance himself from his wife when she acquired a reputation as a witch.

In this atmosphere of distrust and fear, anyone aiming to avoid acquiring a demonic reputation had to renounce two things in particular: quarrelling (and the malevolent cursing that tended to result), and folk healing. Quar- relling was especially important, since many reputations for witchcraft began with a curse that was followed by some misfortune occurring to the person cursed. This was particularly so for women witches, who comprised 85 per cent of the total; some male witches were folk healers, but men were rarely seen as issuing malevolent curses. We may never know how many women, through fear, tried to rein in their tongues and adopt a more meek and sub- missive public persona. Perhaps some tried without success. At any rate, the possibility of a witchcraft trial must have loomed in the background of many a quarrel, sharpening awareness of the language used. Some women, perhaps mainly the poorer and more marginal ones, took the opposite course to the meek and prudent one. They took advantage of the fear-ridden atmosphere to impart a cutting edge to their curses. They cultivated a reputation for danger-ous supernatural power, rather than avoiding it, in order to gain respect and influence. This was a risky strategy, and while it may have brought benefits to an unknown number, it brought ostracism and ultimately execution to many. These contrasting strategies—to curb one's quarrelsome impulses, or to let them rip—form another way in which witch-hunting divided communities. In reordering the pattern of these intimate relationships among the common folk, the authority of the state penetrated deeply.

As well as the hunting of witches, who were almost always settled members of their communities and well known to their neighbours, the late sixteenth-century state also began to pursue an active, single-minded, and repressive policy towards a group who were noted for *not* settling in communities. These were the gypsies. Gypsies, a distinct racial and cultural group with tra-ditions of mobility and of working in trades that would preserve their inde-pendence from masters, had probably entered Scotland in the late fifteenth century. The first definite mention of gypsies in Scotland (and indeed in Britain) was in 1505, when some gypsies were patronized by James IV.[77] Of-ficial attitudes to them were ambivalent for a century or so. They gained a reputation for theft, and numerous gypsy thieves were punished; on the other hand, as entertainers they were much in demand at the royal court and in noble houses. Their wish to live in a separate community, with its own cus-toms and even laws, was recognized and respected. In 1553, royal letters were issued in favour of 'Johne Faw, lord and erle of Litill Egept', ordering local magistrates to arrest certain rebels against his authority; these rebels were to be handed over to Faw, 'to assist to him in executioun of justice upoun his cumpany and folkis conforme to the lawis of Egipt'.[78] Clearly the gypsies were not being treated as fully subject to the law of Scotland.

This began to change after the civil wars of 1567–73, when the Regent Morton's regime wished to demonstrate its concern for law and order. In 1573, the privy council ordered all gypsies either to 'settill thame selffis at cer-tane dwelling places with maisteris' or else to leave the country; those failing to do so would be punished as thieves.[79] By 1588, the punishment of gypsies had entered the government's canonical list of crimes, as shown in a list of crimes to be prosecuted by justice ayres.[80]

Executive action on this began in earnest in the early 1590s, a period when the church seems to have been particularly concerned about gypsies. This was the high point of radical presbyterianism, when the net was being cast widely against moral offenders. The general assembly asked king and council in

---

[77] On the subject of Scottish gypsies in this period, see A. Fraser, *The Gypsies* (Oxford, 1992), 112–22, 137–43, and, in more detail but less reliably, D. MacRitchie, *Scottish Gypsies under the Stewarts* (Edinburgh, 1894).   [78] *RSS* iv. 1953.

[79] *RPC* ii. 210; cf. 555–6. Gypsies were also to be punished as vagrants in the poor law acts of 1575 and 1579, being singled out as idle fortune-tellers: *APS* iii. 87; 140, c. 12.

[80] BL, king's speech at justice ayre, 1588, in Add. MS 33531, fos. 215ʳ–216ᵛ.

1591 'to take ordour with the colourit and vagabound Egyptians, quhilk de-fyles the countrey with all maner of abominatioun'. A further 'greif' in 1592 was that gypsies claimed to possess royal licences, 'and under that pretence abussis the haill countrey'. The church also acted locally. The presbytery of Glasgow in 1597 wrote to three local lairds 'for benneising of the gipseis furth of thair boundis'.[81] As for secular authority: an unusually paranoid con-vention of estates in 1593, in an act against vagrants, described gypsies as 'the counterfute idill lymmarris and harlottis falslie calling thame selffis Egiptianis, being nathing ellis bot thevis, witcheis and abusaris of the people'. This bracketing of gypsies and witches came in the wake of Scotland's first nationwide witch-panic (1590–1). The act's phraseology echoed that of the witchcraft statute of 1563.[82]

An ordinance of the privy council in 1603, ratified by statute in 1609, or-dered all gypsies to leave the country. Those found within it would be ex-ecuted if it were proved that they were 'callit, knawin, repute and haldin Egiptianis'.[83] One group of gypsies, led by Moses Faw, obtained a licence ex-empting them from the act, but this was revoked in 1611; a crackdown on the group produced a series of executions and banishments for the newly created crime of having 'presumet to remane in this kingdome'.[84] Older, more toler-ant attitudes could still be found; the burgh of St Andrews was still 'en-terteneing of the giptianes' in 1612–13. But by now this was unusual, and the 1610s saw a series of prosecutions.[85]

The campaign broadened in 1619–20 to attack not just the gypsies themselves, but their resetters, especially in the north and north-east of Scotland where gypsies seem to have been common. That there were resetters of gypsies indicates some popular support for them. A syndicate in 1619, connected with the royal court, sought to attack the resetters through that characteristic administrative device of the period—a patent. They received a five-year commission that would give them, in return for bringing prosecu-tions, half the resulting compositions and escheats. One manifest aim was to extract money from the resetters, and many prosecutions seem to have resulted.[86]

Since the gypsies suffered as they did at least in part because of their un-willingness to subject themselves to masters, it might have been appropriate

---

[81] *BUK* ii. 780; *Records of the Synod of Lothian and Tweeddale*, 42; 'Extracts from the Registers of the Presbytery of Glasgow, 1592–1601', *Miscellany of the Maitland Club*, i (1833), 87.

[82] *APS* iv. 43; cf. ii. 539, c. 9.   [83] *APS* iv. 440, c. 20.

[84] *RPC* ix. 256; xiv. 562; *Trials*, ed. Pitcairn, iii, I. 201–2.

[85] Pryde, 'Scottish Burgh Finances', 302–3; *RPC* x. 132, 556, 559, 579, 655–7, 846.

[86] *LP James VI*, 319–20; *RPC* xii. 152, 243–4, 251–3, 292, 312–15. This was not a monopoly of prosecutions; other people could bring prosecutions but would not necessarily receive the reward. For an example of the syndicate's appointment of local deputes in 1620, see W. Fraser, *The Chiefs of Grant*, 3 vols. (Edinburgh, 1883), iii. 216. The syndicate is further discussed in Ch. 9 above. The comparable commissions to punish resetters of the MacGregors are discussed in Ch. 10 above.

if the state had smiled on other groups who did so subject themselves. Alas, such smiles were rare; instead, we find a pattern of state intervention to extend the masters' authority.

A prominent feature of this pattern was the enserfment of the colliers and salters. Coal and salt exports were the country's major industrial growth point in the early seventeenth century.[87] Policy towards these two complementary industries was correspondingly new. Older ideas can be seen in a memorandum of the later 1550s. Since feuding lords destroyed one another's coal pits, these should be nationalized to stimulate production, provide employment for 'pure people', and benefit the crown.[88] No trace was left of this tradition in the policy-making of the early seventeenth century.

Serfdom in the mines and salt pans began suddenly and without warning. Thomas Craig could still celebrate the freedom of Scottish workers in 1605, drawing a favourable contrast with England: 'Our servants work for a wage, and contract freely to serve for a year or six months. Of slavery there is no trace among us therefore. Our [English] neighbours, however, still retain certain survivals of slavery in the plantations, in those whom they call natives.'[89] But that was the last year in which this could have been written. The statute that was to lead to the enserfment of the colliers and salters was passed in 1606. No employer was to hire a collier or salter without a certificate from his previous employer; otherwise the latter could demand the immediate return of his worker. The new employer would be fined £100, and the worker punished as a thief. There was an additional provision, probably not widely implemented but revealing of the legislators' attitudes, allowing coal and salt employers to apprehend vagrants and take them forcibly into service.[90] Next year the privy council extended the arrangements to other mines—the main ones being lead mines. However, the owners in the late seventeenth century repudiated this and opted to employ free labour, in an effort to attract English workers.[91] Serfdom was now characteristic of the workers in coal mines and salt pans.

The question of how workers were to *become* serfs was not explicitly addressed by parliament, but the law upheld the principle that workers were allowed to sell their children into binding serfdom, normally at baptism, by accepting a payment of 'arles' (an advance payment on a contract). Stair in 1681 said that the colliers and salters were 'astricted to these services by law,

---

[87] Lythe, *Economy of Scotland*, 239–40; I. Guy, 'The Scottish Export Trade, 1460–1599', in Smout (ed.), *Scotland and Europe*, 66.

[88] NLS, 'The wayes quhairby the rentis of the quenis grace croun may be augmentit', Adv. MS 34.2.17, fos. 124ʳ–125ᵛ.

[89] Craig, *De Unione*, 307.

[90] *APS* iv. 286–7, c. 10. The act was supplemented by another in 1641, focusing mainly on hours of work: *APS* v. 419, c. 124. This and the 1606 act were re-enacted in 1661: *APS* vii. 304, c. 333.

[91] *RPC* vii. 434; T. C. Smout, 'Lead-Mining in Scotland, 1650–1850', in P. L. Payne (ed.), *Studies in Scottish Business History* (London, 1967), 121.

[even] though there were no paction or engagement', but did not say what law he had in mind. It was, he thought, 'introduced upon the common interest'.[92]

Despite the distinctiveness of colliers and salters, the programme that led to their enserfment was part of a wider pattern of government intervention in conditions of employment. Indeed, to the extent that colliers were distinctive, this stemmed mainly from their unusually demanding and specialized work.[93] The 'country acts of Shetland' in 1615 included a stipulation 'that nane fie, hyre nor conduce ane utheris manis servand except they be dischargit be thair maister or that they have dischairgit thair maisteris law-fullie fourtie dayis befoir ane lawfull terme'.[94] This was recognizably the same approach as for the colliers and salters. As we shall see shortly, an act of 1621 pursued this for all agricultural labourers.

This, like the serfdom of colliers and salters itself, went along with a programme of coercion of unemployed people. A convention of estates in 1605 ordained that able-bodied vagrants could be apprehended by any man, and sheriffs or burgh magistrates could authorize him to retain them 'as slaves'.[95] A comprehensive scheme of serfdom for destitute children was enacted in 1617. They would be enserfed by a decision of the kirk session or burgh magistrates, with their parents' consent (or their own, if aged 14 or over). They would then be bound to their masters, to work for them for (apparently) board and lodging alone, until the age of 30. The masters would be able to inflict 'all maner and sorte of punischment (the lyiff and tortoure excepted)'.[96] There is no record of this being implemented, at least not on any scale: whether through reluctance by kirk sessions, or by poor people themselves, does not appear.

All this was very much a programme of regulation of people who, in Sir Thomas Smith's words, 'doe not rule', and 'have no voice nor authoritie'. They could be ordered about in this way because they had no rights. Rights were *property* rights, and workers do not seem to have had property in their labour. Sixteenth-century burghs had been able to fix local wage rates, which was similar to fixing prices.[97] Workers could be *ordered* to work by administrative orders, central or local, and legislation was necessary only if the property rights of their employers were being infringed.

To be sure, tradition dictated that the paramount rights in economic affairs were those of consumers. Two examples from the coal industry may suffice.

---

[92] Stair, *Institutions*, IV.45.17; cf. I.3.11. I have traced no judicial decision on the issue of heritability of serfdom earlier than 1764, though the principle then enunciated seems to have been operative for a long time: W. M. Morison (ed.), *The Dictionary of Decisions of the Court of Session*, 22 vols. (Edinburgh, 1801–11), ii. 2361–2.

[93] C. A. Whatley, 'The Dark Side of the Enlightenment? Sorting out Serfdom', in T. M. Devine and J. R. Young (eds.), *Eighteenth Century Scotland: New Perspectives* (East Linton, 1999).

[94] *Court Book of Shetland, 1615–1629*, ed. G. Donaldson (Lerwick, 1991), 163.

[95] *RPC* vii. 56–7.   [96] *APS* iv. 542–3, c. 10.

[97] A. J. S. Gibson and T. C. Smout, *Prices, Food and Wages in Scotland, 1550–1780* (Cambridge, 1995), 264–9.

The first concerns workers. In Dundee in 1589, detailed regulations were enacted for the coalmen who brought coal for sale in the burgh. They were organized and were given a deacon, appointed by the bailies; prices were fixed, and they had to give priority to selling to the poor.[98] The second example concerns employers, who equally had duties to consumers. Nine Lothian coal-owners were reprimanded by the privy council in 1620 for combining to raise prices; a maximum price was set, and they were forbidden to export coal. Assiduous lobbying soon got this mitigated, but they clearly did not have an entirely free hand.[99] The burghs counter-lobbied against the export of coal, licences for which were granted as rewards for royal service. The crown was also keenly interested in the customs revenue.[100] The era of policy-making in the primary interests of enterprise had not yet arrived.

Nevertheless, it was the workers who were regulated with a heavy hand. Forced labour, often of skilled workers, was repeatedly used for the royal works. In 1604, the secretary was authorized to take 'whatsumevir workmen fra ony uther work' in order to get Holyrood Palace repaired. George Waldie, carter, was imprisoned in 1616: he had refused to work in Edinburgh Castle 'upoun idill, impertinent and fecles excuisis'. The privy council, attempting to conscript artisans in St Andrews for work at Holyrood in 1616, met surprising opposition when the burgh's provost 'disdanefullie answerit that it wes not the custome of the cuntrey to presse ony man to serve'. He was peremptorily overruled.[101] Forced labour could also be exacted as a kind of tax on a locality. In 1616, in anticipation of a royal visit, various roads were to be improved, and the council ordered the conscription of one man, to work two days a week, from each ploughgate in the parishes concerned. This was to be organized by the local landlords, along guidelines provided by a detailed report to the council.[102]

One aspect of medieval serfdom had been the lord's exclusive judicial powers over his serfs. This had parallels in some of the state-sponsored industrial enterprises of the early seventeenth century. In 1612, at Sir George Hay's ironworks at Letterewe, he had a commission of justiciary to punish any crimes committed by 'the haill personis interteyned be him under wages, pay and allowance, at his saidis workis'. At the Hilderstone silver mine in 1614, a similar commission explicitly included the power to make regulations, and to dismiss, withhold wages, fine, imprison, scourge, or set in the stocks any worker infringing them. The employers could hold justice courts to punish capital offences by their wage-labourers. A similar commission was granted to the alum monopolist, the courtier earl of Kellie, in 1620.[103]

[98] Dundee City Archive and Record Centre, Dundee council minutes, vol. ii, pp. 39–40, 50.
[99] *RPC* xii. 387–8, 418–19, 433–5, 466–7, 474.
[100] *RCRB* iii. 132–3; *RPC* xii. 752–3; Charles to council, 2 June 1626, *Earl of Stirling's Register*, i. 41–2.
[101] *RPC* vii. 9; x. 492, 607.   [102] *RPC* x. 529–30. A ploughgate was normally 104 acres.
[103] *RPC* ix. 351; x. 221–2; xii. 231–2; cf. *RMS* vii. 2153.

Only a minority worked for wages. Most Scottish people lived on the land, as peasants—small family farmers who subsisted largely from the produce of their own holdings. That produce maintained not only the peasants themselves, but also most of the elite. The power of the nobility was so significant in early modern Scotland because the nobles had large estates with many rent-paying peasant tenants.

To be a peasant, then, was to have above all an economic status and function. In order to assess the nature of the government's effect on the peasants, it is necessary first to outline their economic experience during the second half of the sixteenth century. This was a period of inflation and population growth. Inflation would not affect those peasants who not only consumed their own produce (as all did) but also paid their rents in kind; it would tend to benefit peasants paying cash rents, but the proportion of these was small before the later seventeenth century.[104] Population growth, however, affected peasants directly, as holdings became harder to obtain; competition for holdings would tend to reduce their size, marginal land would be ploughed up—and landlords would have the opportunity to raise rents. The broad picture was one of decline in peasant living standards, beginning in the mid-sixteenth century. The food they could afford to consume deteriorated in value, with less meat and more oatmeal; there were more wandering vagrants, many of whom were doubtless men who had lost or failed to obtain peasant holdings; harvest failures periodically caused starvation; and there was mass emigration in the early seventeenth century.[105]

In this calamitous context, the main governmental issues affecting the peasants may seem like sideshows; yet they were significant enough. Government action was connected with the great sixteenth-century restructuring of landholding among the elite. There were traditionally four types of landed estate: the estates of the crown, the church, the nobility, and the lairds. All were landlords of peasants, collecting rent. Intricate restructuring of this fourfold pattern of rural landholding, affecting both peasants and landlords, occurred through the slow disintegration of the estates of church and crown. As part of this process, the law faced the challenge of regulating the contractual relationship between landlords and tenants, in four broad areas: feuing, kindly tenancy, evictions, and farming practice and organization.

Feuing, the most significant of these issues, can be considered first. It was into the hands of feuars that the estates of church and crown fell. The feuars became the heritable proprietors of the lands in return for paying a feu duty—

[104] Whyte, *Agriculture and Society*, 192–4.
[105] A. Gibson and T. C. Smout, 'Scottish Food and Scottish History, 1500–1800', in Houston and Whyte (eds.), *Scottish Society*; Goodare, 'Parliament and Society', ch. 8; T. C. Smout, 'Famine and Famine-Relief in Scotland', in L. M. Cullen and T. C. Smout (eds.), *Comparative Aspects of Scottish and Irish Economic and Social History, 1600–1900* (Edinburgh, n.d. [1977]), 22–3; T. C. Smout et al., 'Scottish Emigration in the Seventeenth and Eighteenth Centuries', in N. Canny (ed.), *Europeans on the Move: Studies on European Migration, 1500–1800* (Oxford, 1994), 78–86.

usually equivalent to the original rent or slightly more, but fixed in perpetuity and thus liable to diminish through inflation. The former landlords remained the nominal superiors of the feuars, but had little control over them so long as the feu duties were paid; feuars could bequeath or sell their lands freely. It was the signal achievement of Margaret Sanderson to show in detail that there were two kinds of feuars on the church lands: about a third of estates were feued to the peasant tenants themselves, while the rest went to outsiders in large blocks.[106] Peasants who obtained feus of their holdings thus gained additional legal security, status, and independence; a larger number saw their lands feued over their heads, and thus acquired a new landlord seeking a return on his outlay.

The government thus had to decide how it was going to regulate feuing. Or at least, it did after the Reformation. Before 1560, feus of church land were supposed to be confirmed by the pope, though this was not common, and most feus were not confirmed at all; the crown also confirmed some. The first policy enactment on feuing came in 1559, when the general council of the church banned feuing over tenants' heads for the next five years.[107] This became a dead letter with the Reformation next year, whereupon parliament and privy council began to interest themselves in the subject. They began with a series of temporary orders trying to restrict feuing and to prevent evictions of tenants from feued church lands. But in 1564 there was a shift from restricting feuing to profiting from it through the sale of licences; as large cash sums flowed in to the treasurer, concern about evictions evaporated.[108]

Having invested in their feus, the new landlords might well seek to raise rents or otherwise alter their relationship with their tenants. If so, they soon came up against the issue of 'kindly tenants'.[109] Kindly tenancy (meaning to do with kinship) was a type of tenure that was seen as conferring rights of occupancy on the tenant—rights that might not be complete, but were heritable. Although the details were complex, Scottish kindly tenants occupied a similar tenurial position to English copyholders, though they were less numerous and had fewer rights. In particular, the rights could be regulated by the landlord, and could be held to exist only with his concurrence. Still, kindly tenants' rights did exist. The privy council recognized a tenant's 'richt and lang continewit kyndnes' to his lands in 1581.[110] The law, however, turned against kindly tenants in the early seventeenth century, with a series of decisions construing their rights restrictively.[111] Moreover, many Scottish peasants were

---

[106] Sanderson, *Scottish Rural Society*, chs. 6–7 and *passim*. Peasants received larger numbers of feus, but only for small acreages.

[107] *Statutes of the Scottish Church, 1225–1559*, ed. D. Patrick (SHS, 1907), 179–81.

[108] R. K. Hannay, 'On the Church Lands at the Reformation', *SHR* 16 (1919), 52–72 at 54–60; Goodare, 'Scottish Parliamentary Records', 250.

[109] For this complex subject, see Sanderson, *Scottish Rural Society*, ch. 5; Whyte, *Agriculture and Society*, 30–1. [110] *RSS* viii. 630.

[111] Stair, *Institutions*, II.9.15–21 (where the term used for a kindly tenant is 'rentaller').

tenants at will, with no right to their holding beyond the end of the agricultural year.

A landlord's ultimate sanction against a recalcitrant tenant was eviction. This would not need to be exercised often, but it had to be available. Evictions had rarely been heard of before our period, because demand for land had been low and few landlords had wanted to revise their relationship with their peasant tenants. Instead, evictions had been linked with disputes among the elite, as lords changed their relationship with elite tacksmen (leaseholders) whose armed resistance to removal sometimes caused 'grete trubill' and 'slauchter'. As late as 1546, the most significant statute on evictions had sought to regulate this.[112] Few peasants held tacks, however. Only in 1555 was a statute passed that laid down clear rules for evicting peasants: it had to be done at Whitsun, and forty days' notice was required. This was soon being elaborated by a series of legal decisions.[113] The government had provided landlords seeking rent increases with a clear legal means of dealing with uncooperative tenants.[114]

Finally we come to the issue of farming practice and organization. Ian Whyte's analysis of policies on this concludes that apart from regulating teinds, parliament gave no statutory support to the restructuring of agrarian practices and relationships before 1647, and that the period 1661–95 was most significant. It was then, for instance, that pioneering acts on enclosure, crop rotation, and division of commonties were passed. On the other hand, he sees the main agrarian developments as being 'organisational changes' rather than what people did in fields—restructuring of tenancies, for instance, to create enlarged farms with single tenants.[115] This broad picture is certainly convincing, but in connection with government policy on 'organisational changes' there is a case for considering also a statute of 1621. It announced itself as a measure to aid the 'pure laboreris of the ground', husbandmen, who, it said, were suffering from the 'fraude and malice of servandis', men and women, who demanded high wages and agreed to be hired only from Martinmas to Whitsun, at which time they

cast thame lowse of purpois and intentioun to mak thair gayne and advantage by the extraordinarie warkis whiche befall in that seasone betuix Witsonday and Mertimes . . . for doing quairoff they knaw the saidis husband men . . . wilbe forced to hyre them at daylie and oulklie wages, and [at] such heigh raite as they pleis.

[112] *APS* ii. 476, c. 13; R. K. Hannay, 'A Fifteenth-Century Eviction', *SHR* 22 (1925), 193–8.

[113] *APS* ii. 494, c. 12; Balfour, *Practicks*, ii. 456–65.

[114] How they used this legal machinery is beyond the scope of this chapter, and further research is needed, but see I. Whyte, 'Poverty or Prosperity? Rural Society in Lowland Scotland in the Late Sixteenth and Early Seventeenth Centuries', *Scottish Economic and Social History*, 18 (1998), 19–32, and K. M. Brown, *Noble Society*, 42–6.

[115] Whyte, *Agriculture and Society*, ch. 4; I. Whyte, 'The Emergence of the New Estate Structure', in M. L. Parry and T. R. Slater (eds.), *The Making of the Scottish Countryside* (London, 1980).

To prevent this, it was made illegal for wage labourers hired from Martinmas to Whitsun to leave at Whitsun, unless they had a contract with another employer from Whitsun to Martinmas. Justices of the peace were given power to compel them to continue in service with the previous master at the same wages.[116] As we have seen, this was exactly the kind of law that led, rigorously interpreted by the judges, to the enserfment of the colliers and salt workers.

The statute casts a new light on the tradition of legislating in favour of the 'pure laboreris of the ground'; the farmers on whose behalf the 1621 act was passed were obviously prosperous employers. In the Beauvaisis, the term 'laboureur' meant a rich peasant, a member of the village aristocracy; this sense of the word seems detectable in Scotland too.[117] What we have, in fact, is the beginning of a system of agriculture organized by large tenant farmers employing labour. Eventually they would obtain labour without coercion: the 1621 statute was transitional. But when in Shetland in 1613 a local statute ordered that none were to set up households until they were worth £72, so as to ensure a labour supply, it was a sign of the times.[118] Subsistence farming would fade out, with encouragement from the authorities.

This chapter has surveyed the people's experience of government. One final issue remains to be investigated: their response to it. Although they did not participate in the governing process, which was something done *to* them without their consent, they might occasionally say what they thought about it—even going to the highest levels to do so.

To ask whether peasants petitioned the crown or parliament is not as unreasonable as it might seem. English and Continental evidence suggests that peasants oppressed by their own lords would perceive these high and remote authorities as likely to be sympathetic to their cause.[119] Any approaches they made to them, in moments of stress, were likely to have disappointing results; nevertheless, belief in the ultimate justice of the king was an efficacious stabilizer of feudal society. As we have seen, the Scottish government occasionally made symbolic gestures indicating its willingness to listen to poor folks' complaints. These gestures did not have to be followed by actual complaints, and their main effect was to project an image of the monarch's ultimate justice, but there was always the possibility that they would be interpreted literally. And while some grievances were individual ones, others were collective.

Two examples are known of collective petitioning by the lower orders. In 1578, the 'native tenants and kyndlie possessouris' of the bishopric of

---

[116] *APS* iv. 623–4, c. 21. For the implementation of this, see Gibson and Smout, *Prices, Food and Wages*, 267.

[117] H. Kamen, *The Iron Century: Social Change in Europe, 1550–1650* (2nd edn., London, 1976), 228. [118] *Court Book of Orkney and Shetland*, 20.

[119] R. Hilton, *Bond Men Made Free: Medieval Peasant Movements and the English Rising of 1381* (London, 1973), 225.

Dunblane managed to petition parliament against the prospect of eviction. The earl of Montrose, having engineered the appointment of Andrew Graham as bishop, had received from him a feu charter of much of the bishopric, and was planning to restructure his newly acquired estates. Parliament ordained that Montrose's charter should not be confirmed until the tenants were 'satisfeit for thair kyndnes'—that is, given guarantees that their traditional tenures would be respected. But in the subsequent parliament of October 1579, a furious Montrose claimed that such guarantees should be imposed only as 'ane universall law', and that he would accept the ruling only 'gif the remanent nobilmen within this realme havand sic infeftmentis will consent to sic conditionis'. The tenants counter-petitioned but were dismissed, and the issue had in fact been decided beforehand. Montrose had already made an 'act of cautioun' in January 1579, when he had received a precept for confirming his feu charter, and the tenants 'neidis na confirmatioun' of the 1578 act.[120] Parliament was bound to favour landlords in any fundamental conflict of interest with their tenants. In 1582, evictions of the Dunblane tenants had already begun.[121]

There was also a radical petition from urban artisans in the late 1550s; its intended recipient is unclear, and the nature of the document itself is what mainly matters. It was drawn up in a period when the early Protestant movement gave people the confidence to believe that things might be about to change drastically. Protestant artisans involved in a campaign to defend their right to hold burgh offices produced a manifesto, the 'Grounds of the Debate Between Merchants and Craftsmen in Burghs'. It attacked hierarchy among men, since all men were brothers: two examples of illegitimate hierarchy were the placement of the churchman above others, and the merchant above the craftsman. Equality was justified by the 128th Psalm. It also attacked idleness in society, dividing society into five groups of which four were idle: those who could not or would not work; churchmen; emperors, kings, and nobles; soldiers; and 'labourers of the world', including particularly craftsmen, but also merchants. Rural workers were not mentioned explicitly, although by implication they were among those who worked to support the rest—in a system which was regarded as unjust. Mary Verschuur, who has uncovered the document, suggests that it was drawn up for presentation to the convention of royal burghs—the only likely set of authorities who might be sympathetic (crown or parliament clearly would not be).[122] This interpretation need not be incorrect, but it does treat the 'Grounds of the Debate' as hard-headed and

---

[120] *APS* iii. 111–12, c. 32; 165–6, c. 48; *RSS* vii. 1795.

[121] *Stirling Presbytery Records*, 71. Jenny Wormald, who did not have access to this document, treated the Dunblane case as favouring the tenants, but this is untenable: Wormald, *Court, Kirk and Community*, 54.

[122] M. B. Verschuur, 'Perth Craftsmen's Book: Some Examples of the Interpretation and Utilization of Protestant Thought by Sixteenth-Century Scottish Townsmen', *Records of the Scottish Church History Society*, 23 (1987–9), 157–74 at 163–7.

practical when it was in many ways idealistic and almost millenarian—a kind of manifesto for a revolution that never occurred.

The common folk were less likely to communicate their wishes to government through revolution than through riot. Evidence for this is scanty, but one cannot conclude with confidence that riots were rare. In Edinburgh in 1570 there was a grain riot very much in the style familiar in eighteenth-century England: a crowd blocked the export of a consignment of grain and forced its sale locally.[123] Whether this was a unique event, or whether it was recorded because of unusual circumstances, is unknown. There were frequent protests against debasement of the coinage in the 1570s. Debasement led to higher prices, and coins of low silver content were more easily counterfeited, leaving poor people with coins which they could not pass for full value. The Regent Morton's 'sophisticat coyne' of 1572 was soon largely held by the poor, who 'outcryit sa odiously aganis the Regent and his counsillors, with execrations and maledictions, as is odious to reherse'. A debasement of 1575 'procured great invy and hatred of the commouns against the erle of Morton, for the people's hands were full of that money', wrote David Calderwood, while the anonymous Edinburgh chronicler noted that 'the pure veriit and band the regent and haill lords oppenlie in thair presentis, quhen ever thai past or repast . . . quhilk wes havie and lamentable to heir'. In 1578, over-stamping of older coins at a higher rate was said to be 'altogither mislykit be the commone pepill'.[124]

As far as is yet known, this unrest was an urban phenomenon, and perhaps even an Edinburgh one.[125] Riots did happen in other towns, on a variety of issues. A riot in Burntisland against a programme of evictions was led by 'ane multitude of weemen, above ane hundir, off the bangstar Amasone kinde'. The ringleader was a bailie's wife, instigated by the parish minister.[126] As usual, there is less evidence for what happened in the countryside. In the famine year of 1596, it was reported that 'the discontent of the poor commons, with their present poverty thro' the dearth of corn', made them 'wish for some alteration, and desire rather a good war than a cruel peace'.[127]

Prosecutions of gypsies could have unexpected results, and there is little evidence of popular hostility to them. When a group of gypsies were about to be executed in Edinburgh in 1624, the officers were attacked by a crowd of local people who tried to prevent the execution. They succeeded in liberating

---

[123] Richard Bannatyne, *Memorials of Transactions in Scotland, 1569–1573*, ed. R. Pitcairn (Bannatyne Club, 1836), 26–7.

[124] *Historie and Life of King James the Sext, 1566–1596*, ed. T. Thomson (Bannatyne Club, 1825), 106, 152; Calderwood, *History*, iii. 302; *Diurnal of Remarkable Occurrents*, 345; Moysie, *Memoirs of the Affairs of Scotland*, 18. 'Veriit and band' = cursed and swore at.

[125] Cf. Lynch, *Edinburgh and the Reformation*, 155.

[126] Chancellor Dunfermline to Viscount Fenton, 30 Apr. 1615, *Eccles. Letters*, ii. 433–6.

[127] Mr James Colville to Francis Bacon, 11 Mar. 1596, T. Birch, *Memoirs of the Reign of Queen Elizabeth from the year 1581 until her Death*, 2 vols. (London, 1754), i. 446–7.

one of the gypsies, Gavin Trotter.[128] Governments have often tried to boost their popularity by playing on racial prejudices; this may sometimes have worked in early modern Scotland, but on this occasion it failed badly.

Although this chapter has had a consistent overall theme, the materials from which it has been fashioned have sometimes seemed like a motley patchwork. Between women and gypsies, or between gypsies and peasants, there may not seem to be any essential unity, apart from the basic fact of their exclusion from political life. But the fact that their experience of government had varied textures is an effective illustration of the threefold nature of state power. Women felt state power as an ideological force, demanding godliness and moral conformity; peasants felt the impact of economic policies, as tenures were restructured; gypsies were on the receiving end of the state's physically coercive power, as were the highlanders, examined in Chapter 10 above. But while this diversity was real enough, so was the unity of the power of the state. These three forms of power—ideological, economic, and military—were in fact the basis of the authority of the state.[129] Ideology represented the persuasive power of ideas, which so far as women were concerned was a way of legitimizing the regulation of their behaviour. Economic power represented the ability to extract and control resources; the state did not extract resources directly from the peasants, but it provided machinery whereby landlords were enabled to do so. And physically coercive sanctions, while not taking priority over ideological or economic ones, could be effective against some of those with no voice in government, notably the gypsies.

Although conceptually distinct, these three forms of power could also overlap or be converted into one another. The ideological subjection of women underpinned their vital contribution to the economy and their relative inability to control economic resources. The prosecution of witches, also primarily ideological, culminated in dramatic displays of physical coercion as witches were publicly burned at the stake. The 'new violence of the state' in the late sixteenth and early seventeenth centuries was not just about violence: it was about government as a whole.

Since so much of the coercive power that the state began to wield in this period was new, it may be asked whether it was also modern. Michael Braddick has discussed this question in connection with England. He sees the growth of fiscal and military power as the central line of development for English state power, but notes that 'those who felt the impact of state authority most sharply' were sexual offenders, witches, vagrants, and other groups similar to those discussed in the present chapter. Fiscal and military development, which have been continuous and closely linked ever since the early modern period, are certainly 'modern' trends; overtly repressive regulation of

---

[128] *RPC* xiii. 392–3, 406, 408, 410–11.
[129] Cf. Goodare, *State and Society*, ch. 9.

the common people's lives has not grown in the same linear fashion.[130] Modernity here is associated with ideological and cultural pluralism, not with the persecution of ever-widening categories of deviance and dissent. Perhaps this was achieved only once persecution had been tried and found wanting in the course of the seventeenth century. However, there are enough examples of persecution in more recent times for the link between modernity and toleration to be complex and sometimes fraught. In Scotland it was at any rate the post-Reformation state that first launched a programme of ideological and cultural conformity, raising issues that have been with us, in some form, ever since.

[130] Braddick, *State Formation*, 435–6.

CHAPTER TWELVE

A Stewart Revolution
in Government?

Iff Ovid wer to lyfe restord
  to see which I behould
he might inlairge his pleasant taels
  of formis manifould
be this which now into the court
  most plesantlie appeirs
to see in penners and in pens
  transformed all our speirs
and into paper all our jaks
  our daggs in horns of ink
for knapstafes, seals and signateurs
  to change ilk man dois think.

William Fowler[1]

A restored Ovid might not have agreed with William Fowler that what he
beheld at the emerging court of the young James VI was a metamorphosis in
the full sense. Fowler probably wrote between two baronial revolts, the
Ruthven Raid of 1582 and the Stirling Raid of 1584; political power could
still manifest highly traditional forms. But his little verse does somehow encapsulate some of the ways in which the government of Scotland was beginning to change. Fowler felt that government was becoming a matter of settled
bureaucracy, focused on the royal court and council, animated by royal
largesse ('signateurs'), and sustained by national taxation.

Fowler tells us less about changes that had already happened than about
the direction in which he thought things were moving. Of course, future
trends may be extrapolated from past ones (which is one of the reasons why
history is useful), but his verse is essentially about the future *ideal* of a stable,
peaceful, wealthy, centralized, and well-administered monarchy. That ideal
was being confidently discussed and sought after at James's recently established court, now settled at Holyrood. Fowler apparently had mixed feelings

---

[1] Quoted and discussed in H. M. Shire, *Song, Dance and Poetry of the Court of Scotland
under King James VI* (Cambridge, 1969), 100. 'Jaks' = armoured tunics; 'daggs' = pistols; 'knapstafes' = batons; 'signateurs' = warrants for royal grants.

about the trend, for his poem went on to comment wryly on the greedy jostling for royal patronage to which it was giving rise. But James, who also recognized the trend, welcomed it. It was at this time, in 1583, that he announced his intention to rule as a 'universal king', above noble faction.[2] The intention became a reality. The Stirling Raid of 1584 failed. After 1594, baronial revolts ceased altogether.[3] James's adult reign would bring sweeping changes to the government of Scotland.

When assessing these and related changes, it is useful to adapt a familiar historiographical phrase and ask, cautiously: was there a 'Stewart revolution in government'? The historiography of this question leads back initially to Maurice Lee's stimulating book of 1959 in which he argued that the late 1580s and early 1590s, the period in power of James VI's great minister, John Maitland of Thirlestane, saw the foundation of a 'Stewart despotism'. Professor Lee's book leads back in turn to Geoffrey Elton's 1953 argument that a 'Tudor revolution in government' occurred in England in the 1530s—an argument with which Tudor historians have been grappling ever since.[4]

This chapter can hardly review the English debate in full, but some salient points should be touched on. For one thing, Scottish debate has followed similar lines. English medievalists argued against Professor Elton that the alleged novelties of the 1530s had existed long before: Jenny Wormald contended against Professor Lee that James VI's regime was an entirely traditional one. And the debate, similarly, was inconclusive.[5] Christopher Coleman observed in 1986 that 'while there has been a confusing range of responses to the concept of "Tudor Revolution", it has only extended from the dismissive to the guardedly and selectively supportive'.[6] Although this observation was made in a book designed to put an end to the concept, it attracted the same range of responses in 1997 and even more recently.[7] What follows will be 'guardedly

---

[2] J. Goodare and M. Lynch, 'James VI: Universal King?', in eid. (eds.), *The Reign of James VI*, 5.

[3] Whatever the so-called 'Gowrie conspiracy' of 1600 was, it was not a baronial revolt, as no troops were raised. Revolts in the Highlands continued, because they were not fully integrated into the structure of the state.

[4] Lee, *John Maitland*; Elton, *Tudor Revolution*. Professor Lee has confirmed to me in conversation that he had Elton's book in mind when writing his own. While retaining the substance of his 1959 views, he has discarded the term 'despotism' and it will not be used here. The term 'revolution in government' brings problems too, as we shall see.

[5] J. Brown (now Wormald), 'Scottish Politics, 1567–1625', in A. G. R. Smith (ed.), *The Reign of James VI and I* (London, 1973); M. Lee, 'James VI and the Aristocracy', *Scotia*, 1 (1977), 18–23; J. Wormald, 'James VI: New Men for Old?', *Scotia*, 2 (1978), 70–6.

[6] C. Coleman, 'Professor Elton's "Revolution"', in id. and Starkey (eds.), *Revolution Reassessed*, 5.

[7] See the papers on the 'Eltonian legacy', *Transactions of the Royal Historical Society*, 6th ser. 7 (1997). 'Dismissive': R. W. Hoyle (p. 200); 'guardedly and selectively supportive': C. S. L. Davies (p. 178). (The 'Eltonian legacy', as these papers show, ranges much more widely than the 'revolution in government' hypothesis.) Perhaps cautiously dismissive is Gunn, *Early Tudor Government*, 209. For detailed supportive responses see A. G. R. Smith, *The Emergence of a Nation State: The Commonwealth of England, 1529–1660* (2nd edn., London, 1997), ch. 11, and P. Edwards, *The Making of the Modern English State, 1460–1660* (Basingstoke, 2001),

and selectively supportive'—not concerning the original English concept directly, but concerning its applicability to Scotland.

Which aspects of the postulated 'revolution in government' can be identified as potentially relevant to Scotland, and thus requiring full assessment? Above all there is the establishment of parliamentary sovereignty. Parliament's right to control the church is the single most important aspect of this. Parliament also grows in scope as a body actively shaping the law. Sovereignty means that all must ultimately obey parliament, and parliament alone. Although the crown is a component of parliament and thus participates in these processes (perhaps even playing a leading role), the crown alone is not sovereign. Linked to parliamentary sovereignty comes the creation of a territorially unified state. Local privileges and immunities are reduced, and a single law operates throughout the realm. The role of parliament also appears in finance, with a new importance for parliamentary taxation. Taxation comes to be more regular, and is recognized to be appropriate for the ordinary needs of government rather than for occasional exigencies like warfare.

As well as these parliamentary aspects, the theory postulates change in daily government. Bureaucracy grows in size. More importantly, bureaucratic departments grow in scope. No longer do they merely carry out routine tasks; they plan the making of policy. Coordinating the policy-making process is a new body consisting primarily of the heads of these departments: the privy council. Meanwhile the royal household, previously the mainspring of policy-making, is sidelined, and concentrates on providing for the monarch's personal needs. Headed by the privy council, the governmental system can now function efficiently even without the guiding hand of an active and conscientious monarch.

In its full form, the 'revolution in government' can seem like a carefully designed programme, and it becomes natural to seek the designer. The king himself is an unlikely candidate in view of the programme's effects on his position. Instead this role is posited in England for Thomas Cromwell, Henry VIII's principal secretary. In Scotland, as we have seen, the statesmanlike planner is seen as Maitland, who was secretary and later chancellor. The parallel was drawn closer by Professor Lee, who regarded Maitland as having been more effective as secretary than as chancellor. He compared Maitland to Cromwell and to Cardinal Richelieu 'as one of the significantly creative state-builders of early modern Europe'.[8]

Yet in England this has proved the weakest part of the 'revolution in government' case. Cromwell left no document proving that he had an overall plan for such a revolution. His creative role has to be inferred from scattered

---

115–22; for a briefer but sympathetic one, Braddick, *State Formation*, 20–2. No study of Tudor government can ignore the 'revolution in government' question, which helps to show why it is worth asking the question for Scotland.

[8] Lee, *John Maitland*, 117–18, 298.

remarks and reconstructed from the record of his actions.[9] Indeed, even the attribution of governmental initiatives to him can be problematic. Thus the case for Cromwell's determining role in the 'Tudor revolution' is an *ex post facto* reconstruction that depends not only on prior acceptance of other elements of the 'revolution', but also on a willingness to believe in the decisive influence of great men on history. A consensus has developed that the evidence for Cromwell's determining role is insufficient. The only recent scholars willing to attach him firmly to the 'Tudor revolution' have been those who have hoped thereby to sink the entire concept. Those more sympathetic to the 'Tudor revolution' have stressed contingency, pressure of events, and evolutionary development in explaining its individual components. The same ideas can be applied, *mutatis mutandis*, to Maitland.

Maitland was indeed a statesman of ability, as Professor Lee's detailed narrative of his career shows. The parliament of 1587 did pass much reforming legislation in which his hand can be detected.[10] The policy of cooperation with the presbyterian movement, pursued by him and the king, probably did help to foster political stability.[11] But while numerous measures of administrative reform and centralization occurred during Maitland's tenure of office, they cannot all be attributed to him. The upgrading of the powers of the admiral's court in July 1587 was probably not his work.[12] It was argued in Chapter 3 that the whole programme of legislation ran counter to the desire of the legal thinkers of his period for codification of the old laws, rather than their piecemeal replacement by new statutes. In his wide-ranging and assiduous activities, Maitland's energies were directed largely to immediate ends— the search for political stability, and the maintenance of his own position in power. Scottish politics in his time was a faction-ridden switchback ride in which keeping one's seat could be an achievement in itself. It is surely preferable to explain early modern European state formation primarily in terms of broad circumstances rather than through the fortuitous advent of individuals, however creative.[13]

Professor Elton's ideas on parliamentary sovereignty, by contrast, have won wide acceptance. Statute law, as the ultimate authority shaping the common law, triumphed over its rivals—local custom and supranational canon law. The direct subjection of the church to statute law was a revolutionary event.[14] This happened in Scotland too. The Reformation Parliament

---

[9] G. R. Elton, 'The Political Creed of Thomas Cromwell', in his *Studies in Tudor and Stuart Politics and Government*, 4 vols. (Cambridge, 1974–92), ii. 215–35.

[10] For his sponsorship of the important act for shire commissioners see Goodare, 'Admission of Lairds', 1115–18.

[11] Lee, *Great Britain's Solomon*, 66–8. Again, though, Maitland's share of responsibility for the policy cannot be gauged with precision.

[12] Macpherson, 'Francis Stewart', 161–3; cf. Ch. 7 above.

[13] This is why it is better to speak of 'state formation' than 'state building': Braddick, *State Formation*, 7.

[14] Elton's case here was silently conceded by his most fundamental critics: Coleman and Starkey (eds.), *Revolution Reassessed*. Cf. G. R. Elton, '*Lex terrae victrix*: The Triumph of

of 1560 established its power to define religious doctrine, and although the queen refused to ratify its legislation, she accepted its *de facto* authority. The pope vanished abruptly from the scene.

There was one temporary difference from England. Scotland's new Protestant church tended to claim its own sources of authority, and many of its leaders distanced themselves from the 'civil magistrate', especially in the first two decades. But even in these decades, the church always sought statutory backing for its programme, from the Confession of Faith itself to issues of revenue and moral discipline. It took a high view of the primacy of divine law, but it was not seeking ecclesiastical independence or separation from the 'state'.[15] After 1584, parliament successfully enacted something very like a royal supremacy over the church. Those who objected to this usually did so by selective citation from the statute book itself, claiming that certain religious statutes were authoritative while omitting to mention others.[16] Even while the government was legislating to control the church and to determine ecclesiastical policy, therefore, its critics were not saying that parliament should keep its hands off; instead they argued about what kind of church its legislation should control. Whether parliament legislated for episcopacy or presbytery, parliamentary supremacy over the church was unquestionable.[17]

Meanwhile, more of the law was parliamentary legislation. In Hector MacQueen's study of the medieval common law, the king could legislate in parliament, but legal change was not primarily driven forward by legislation or indeed by governmental activity at all; rather it was autonomous and custom-based.[18] National customary law or common law remained important to the early modern state, but it was shaped through legislation. During the Jacobean debate on Anglo-Scottish union, it was accepted that national parliaments presided over the two countries' laws, even though most union proposals stopped short of calling for parliamentary union, contenting themselves with bringing the two countries' laws into line with each other.[19] Even so, the idea of 'union of laws' was stronger in 1604–7 than after 1689, when union would mean simply union of parliaments. This may be because Jacobean lawyers still tended to perceive the law as autonomous, rather than as the creation of parliament. In 1681, Viscount Stair wrote of 'our ancient and immemorial customs, which may be called our common law' (here he instanced some standard rules on transmission of landed property) as 'anterior

[15] J. Kirk, 'Minister and Magistrate', in his *Patterns of Reform: Continuity and Change in the Reformation Kirk* (Edinburgh, 1989).

[16] They also maintained that this legislation was only ratifying a position mandated by God, but the legislation itself had not said this, and even if it had, historians can concern themselves only with terrestrial manifestations of divine authority.

[17] Goodare and Lynch, 'James VI: Universal King?', 28; Goodare, *State and Society*, 192–203.

[18] MacQueen, *Common Law and Feudal Society*, 247, 265–6, and *passim*.

[19] Levack, *Formation of the British State*, 69–72.

to any statute, and not comprehended in any, as being more solemn and sure than those are'.[20] What Stair carefully did not say was that these customs were *superior* to statute; he surely knew that they were not.

Another aspect of Professor Elton's 'revolution in government' concerned the reduction of provincial autonomies, such as those of Wales and Cheshire. This process was also evident in Scotland, especially in the Highlands and Borders. In fact there were several processes, which although overlapping should be distinguished. One, most visible in the Borders, was common to the whole of Scotland—the weaning of the nobility away from the autonomous dispute settlement of the bloodfeud. Because the Borders were so heavily militarized, this process was particularly painful. There was also the reduction of purely administrative autonomy, achieved by the dismantling of the Border wardenships and the conversion of the region into the 'Middle Shires'.

Versions of these processes operated in the Highlands, but in distinctive ways. The Highlands were neither separated completely from Scotland—as might have happened if the lordship of the Isles had been allowed to develop its full fifteenth-century potential—nor integrated fully within it—as might have happened if the region had followed the same political trajectory as Wales within the sixteenth-century English state. The example of Wales reminds us that language alone need not form a barrier to administrative and political absorption; continuing Highland distinctiveness needs to be accounted for at least partly on other grounds. One of those grounds, as argued in Chapter 10, was the experience of colonization. Here the parallel is not so much with Henrician Wales as with Elizabethan Ireland. The Scottish state did not *want* to absorb Highland elites peacefully; it wanted ultimately to extirpate them. Some were indeed extirpated, although most survived. This survival was perhaps a failure of state formation, but there was no need for the process to be total. Cheshire was integrated into England during the 'Tudor revolution', but the palatinate of Durham was only partly absorbed, and further integrative measures remained to be taken in 1672 and 1836. The Isle of Man has still not been absorbed. What matters in state formation is not just the completeness of the process but also the direction and strength of the dominant trend.

The trend was visible elsewhere in Scotland, where further provincial autonomies were being reduced. The 'principality' of Scotland, a collection of royal estates centred on Ayrshire and Renfrewshire, had shown signs in the fifteenth century of developing into a devolved apanage for a royal prince. Its inhabitants were granted exemption from parliamentary attendance in 1490, a crucial act showing vividly that the late medieval parliament was not conceived as an integrative body for a sovereign state. This planned exercise in provincial devolution was postponed through the dynasty's failure to

---

[20] Stair, *Institutions*, I.1.16.

produce an adult prince until 1619—by which time things were very different. When Prince Charles was created prince of Scotland, the act of 1490 was ignored and his jurisdictional rights were minimized.[21] Another quasi-dynastic apanage was carved out in Orkney and Shetland in the 1560s and 1570s by Robert Stewart, an illegitimate son of James V who had himself created earl of Orkney. But his successor's casual assumption that he was above the law in his own domains led to his imprisonment in 1609 and execution in 1615.[22] Orkney and Shetland had enjoyed a large measure of autonomy even before the Stewart earls' advent; they retained their own Norse laws and customs. After the second earl's downfall, the islands were subjected to Scots law and integrated into the state.

In Chapter 6 we saw the development of an executive privy council, with its most important members being the heads of administrative departments. This sometimes technical subject was at the heart of Professor Elton's original 'revolution', as he contended that such a council had emerged in England to replace the monarch and royal household as the mainspring of executive decision-making. In Scotland one would have to agree with those of his critics who responded that the privy council supplemented traditional forms of influence. The separation of government institutions from the royal household has been described as 'perhaps the clearest long-term change between the twelfth and the seventeenth centuries' in European governments.[23] This may be too sweeping for any early modern government, since while the major states were absolute monarchies they had to retain a major role for kings and their friends. Professor Elton himself came to see a continuing role for the royal court.[24]

So the issue is not one of the privy council replacing the royal court—but there certainly were two significant and related changes. First, a privy council was created: this was new and very important. Second, as the state became more centralized, the role of kings and their friends might actually increase, since government in the localities was less autonomous, and nobles had to exercise influence via the centre—which often meant the royal court. There may have been a demarcation of functions between governmental bureaucracy and royal household; and more government was carried out *through* the institutions, even if some decisions were still taken in the household. Amy Juhala's study of James VI's household is not primarily a study of government, and deals mainly with the creation of splendid physical and cultural surroundings for the king and his family.[25] More work is required on James's

---

[21] *APS* ii. 221, c. 17; Goodare, *State and Society*, 239–40.

[22] P. D. Anderson, *Robert Stewart, Earl of Orkney, Lord of Shetland, 1533–1593* (Edinburgh, 1982), chs. 5–7; id., *Black Patie*, chs. 6, 9.

[23] W. Reinhard, 'Power Elites, State Servants, Ruling Classes, and the Growth of State Power', in id. (ed.), *Power Elites and State Building*, 14.

[24] G. R. Elton, 'Tudor Government: The Points of Contact: iii: The Court', *Transactions of the Royal Historical Society*, 5th ser. 26 (1976), 211–28.

[25] Juhala, 'Household and Court of James VI'.

gentlemen of the chamber, but it does not seem that they were themselves governors. Rather than making policy directly, they facilitated connections between the king and the nobility. Of course this still contributed to government. There could be no sharp separation between government and household so long as absolute monarchy lasted. James said that his 'government by pen' meant that he governed Scotland 'by a clearke of the councell', but he also had his son and heir wet-nursed by the clerk of the council's wife.[26]

How far was this style of government bureaucratic? It was not a fully modern bureaucracy, with a separation between official and post; officials tended to treat their posts as possessions, and they often operated as clients of patrons. Those patrons, who were often courtiers or aristocrats, formed a link between the administration and the royal court. Still, there are other aspects of the question. In particular we may focus on outcomes rather than on processes—thus observing one of the features of bureaucracy itself, in that a bureaucracy is concerned to achieve specific outcomes. Two other related attributes are that it functions by gathering and processing of information, and that it possesses clear chains of command. It is therefore worth asking how far the Scottish administration was bureaucratic in these three senses.[27]

The first characteristic of bureaucracy, then, is rational organization directed towards the achievement of specific goals. In this it differs from law courts, which have more concern for 'due process' than for outcomes. Courts are not expected to want one side to win the case, or to be influenced by non-judicial considerations like the possible costs of the verdict to the state. A government that uses law courts to implement its policies will tend to create statutory duties (or rights) for *individuals*, whereupon they can be sued (or sue others) if the requirements of the statute are not met. A government that uses bureaucracy will create an *institution* with statutory duties, leaving it to carry these out in the ways it finds best. Often the duties will be broadly expressed, using criteria of reasonableness and efficiency (a service is to be provided as long as its cost is reasonable). This distinction between legal process and bureaucracy is not absolute; administrative structures generally involve both, but have tendencies towards one or the other. Yet although the distinction was developed with modern public-service bureaucracies in mind, aspects of it are highly pertinent to the processes of early modern government. Bureaucratic administration creates its own decision-making structures and criteria in order to reach its goals. These are internal to the organization rather than specified by the law; the law merely lays down the goals. So long as it pursues these goals, the bureaucracy has space to operate, unconstrained

---

[26] James VI & I, speech to parliament, 1607, in *Political Writings*, 173; *RPC* v. 200. They were James Primrose and his wife Margaret Masterton.

[27] What follows on this owes much to J. L. Mashaw, *Bureaucratic Justice* (New Haven, 1983), ch. 2 and *passim*.

by outsiders with the right to force it to act in a particular way. It has *discretion*.

The use of this kind of discretion will readily be recognized in the work of the central Scottish executive, especially the privy council. Statutes might lay down precise requirements and duties, but for many of them it was understood that their enforcement was discretionary. The rule might be clear, but it was applied flexibly. It was argued in Chapter 5 that all those sweeping statutes, making (to modern eyes) impossibly unreasonable demands, were really creating space for executive authorities to decide which aspects of the demands were reasonable under the circumstances.

The application of such discretion is found even in the fiscal administration. In some branches of revenue, the government aimed to get as much as it could, as quickly as it could; but not in all. The system of fiscal feudalism, in which the crown collected a rake-off from the lottery of inheritance, is an example. The crown's legal rights on the entry of an heir to landed property were definite, and specified by charter—but the practice was to take a negotiated 'composition' rather than to exact the full amount theoretically due. A memorandum of advice to a new treasurer showed a repeated concern for what was 'raisonable' in fixing this. In entering a feuar to lands of the crown, it recommended a composition that was three or four times the feu duty; but some feu duties were exceptionally high, and 'in sutche landis nather the dowble nor the single of the few dewatie awcht to be exacted but sum discreit consideratioun, quhilk must be altogither rewled be the thesaurer['s] discretion'.[28]

Bureaucracy operates by collecting and processing information. It does not wait for others to bring petitions or complaints, but decides itself what information it needs, and obtains it. The exchequer had always kept records, but mainly as a check against fraud; the ancient exchequer rolls were preserved as talismans rather than being used regularly as current office files. When Sir John Skene became clerk register in 1594, he took a different attitude. He burrowed energetically into the records, arranging and cataloguing them in order to improve internal procedures and to identify ancient royal rights that might be revived. In 1608–10 he compiled a list of 'proposalls' for exchequer reform, most of which related either to the gathering of information (collecting registers of hornings) or to processing it (comparing present and past accounts).[29] In later ages, governments would demand statistics; in this period, they wanted reports from subordinate officials and institutions.

This information-gathering campaign was particularly noticeable in the fields of revenue and criminal justice. In 1592 the treasurer was required by parliament to keep registers of licences for export of forbidden goods, of

---

[28] Goodare (ed.), 'Fiscal Feudalism'.

[29] A. L. Murray, 'Sir John Skene and the Exchequer'. For an elaborate but apparently highly exceptional search of the exchequer rolls in 1501, see Madden, 'The Finances of the Scottish Crown', 8.

monks' portions, of first fruits of benefices, and of licences of exemptions from military service. The justice clerk was ordered to compile a list of all re-missions granted since the king's majority in 1578. In 1597, more statutes demanded yet more red tape. Rentals of church temporalities were to be given in by ministers provided to any benefice, and feuars of church lands were to give in copies of their titles. All feuars were ordered to hand in copies of their titles to the clerk of the temporality in 1599.[30] It was first suggested that Border wardens should make regular reports in 1579; their English counter-parts had been doing so since 1536. It was also in 1579 that a programme of getting sheriffs to send in their registers of hornings was launched. Better recording of people at the horn was a constant demand on the local authori-ties thereafter—an aspect of the pressure on traditional local government discussed in Chapter 8.[31]

Regional magnates were no longer the only ones who knew about their regions—the government regularly learned a lot more about local political geography. This made government more effective, not just in remote regions but also in the core of the state. In 1591 the government compiled a list of about five hundred Lowland lairds who could be summoned to join a planned military expedition to the Western Isles. Strikingly, although the list was compiled by sheriffdom, it could distinguish those who lived in the Lowland part of the sheriffdom of Perth.[32] Even today, it would be much easier for someone in Edinburgh to compile such information on a county basis than to ransack maps and gazetteers to replicate this administrative achievement of 1591.

In its early years, the privy council did not write everything down. This can be seen from the treasurer's accounts, which did write down the money spent on implementing decisions that look like the council's. No council decisions were minuted between 29 February and 19 May 1562. Yet on 18 April a pursuivant and three messengers received £10 for 'passand of Edinburght . . . to summond ane assis upoun certane personis that abaid fra the raid of Jedburght', clearly a political initiative taken in Edinburgh. Several other such initiatives were taken during this period; they must have been decided by the council, or by some councillors.[33] The silence of the council register was probably connected with the absence of the queen. Although she attended neither the 29 February nor the 19 May meeting, she was at Holyrood on those dates, while passing almost all the intervening period in Fife (mainly at St Andrews and Falkland).[34] Perhaps some councillors were away with her, or

---

[30] *APS* iii. 556, c. 30; 575, c. 67; iv. 133, cc. 15–16; NAS, treasurer's accounts, 1599–1600, E21/73, fo. 42ʳ.

[31] Rae, *Administration of the Scottish Frontier*, 82.

[32] NAS, Cunninghame of Caprington letter book, GD149/265, part 3, fos. 58ʳ–59ᵛ.

[33] *RPC* i. 204–6; *TA* xi. 155–8, 161–2, 168–9.

[34] E. M. Furgol, 'The Scottish Itinerary of Mary Queen of Scots, 1542–8 and 1561–8', *Proceedings of the Society of Antiquaries of Scotland*, 117 (1987), 219–31 and attached microfiche.

those in Edinburgh were neglecting their paperwork in her absence, or both. But if so that would represent a reversal of the pre-1545 trend, in which it was the monarch's *presence* that led to a relaxation of corporate conciliar government. At any rate, the identifiable silences of the council register seem to become fewer over time, indicating an increase in the corporate character of conciliar government.[35]

The third attribute of the ideal bureaucracy is the possession of clear chains of command, usually in a hierarchical organization. Administrators have precise powers and duties, and know to whom they are answerable. Here, early modern Scotland did not make such significant advances, partly because aristocratic government was sometimes carried out by deputy. Some offices required personal attendance, but offices that were likely to be held by nobles did not, because nobles did not necessarily have the time or ability to carry out difficult tasks. Prestigious offices like admiral, chamberlain, constable, or justice general; financial offices like treasurer or collector general; and key local offices like sheriff: all could be exercised by deputy. Once appointed, the sheriff depute was basically invested with the authority of the sheriff, subject only to the sheriff principal's intervention. Such intervention might be frequent, or it might be non-existent; it might be constructive, or it might be capricious.[36]

Chains of command were also blurred at the highest level. The privy council itself was a permeable body, open to periodic influence both from the royal household and from the leading nobility. Even the chancellor, Sir George Hay, was unsure whether his scheme to feu the earldom of Orkney in 1624 had failed because Lord Kinclevin had pulled strings at court to block it, as he claimed.[37] Kinclevin's alleged contact was the earl of Annandale, one of James's grooms of the bedchamber. In 1615, Annandale (then John Murray of Lochmaben) had processed the scheme to prosecute Catholics with which Chapter 5 began. These two examples concern royal patronage and religious affairs, probably the two areas of government in which the privy council was least involved; on the other hand, the council was not wholly disconnected even from these areas, and could exert influence if it chose. But so long as government was a partnership with the landed nobility, the nobility had to have channels of influence. Such influence did not preclude chains of bureaucratic command, but it inevitably diminished their clarity.

---

[35] The relationship between the council register and the treasurer's accounts (the latter at present unpublished after 1580) would repay further study on this and other issues.

[36] Cf. the cooperation in witch-hunting between the sheriff of Aberdeen and his depute, the earl of Huntly, and Thomas Leslie. Leslie usually acted, but Huntly was sometimes involved personally: J. Goodare, 'The Aberdeenshire Witchcraft Panic of 1597', *Northern Scotland*, 21 (2001), 17–37 at 24, 30. For sheriff deputes generally see *Fife Court Book*, pp. liv–lix.

[37] NLS, Hay to James, 8 Nov. 1624, Denmylne MSS, Adv. MS 33.1.1, vol. xi, no. 36. Kinclevin was heir-apparent to the forfeited earldom, and was manoeuvring to stop it passing into anyone else's hands. Hay thought he was bluffing, but could not be sure.

Once it is accepted that there was bureaucracy, the question of whether there were bureaucrats may seem redundant. But it is still worthwhile to glance at James VI's senior administrative staff. Were they 'new men', or a '*noblesse de robe*'? This was an important aspect of the debate between Dr Wormald and Professor Lee referred to above. The concept of a *noblesse de robe* can be discarded, since this French term refers to a hereditary caste of royal judges; no such heritability of office arose in Scotland, where administrators were recruited individually from among the landed elite.[38] The more important question of 'new men' has been addressed in detail by Ried Zulager. Were James VI's senior administrative staff more educated or professional than their predecessors? Did they come from a different, perhaps lower, social background? Dr Zulager finds many continuities between James VI's administrators and those of the previous three monarchs. What was new was the general growth in importance of the law and legal education to the propertied elite; royal administrators fully reflected this. About half of the administrators he studied had been trained in law. Others performed other tasks: they were primarily financial specialists, or military officers, or simply political or ecclesiastical fixers. Their functions were increasingly differentiated. They were not wholly 'professional', since they were willing to bend the law to suit their royal master's interests; in that, Dr Zulager concludes, they were undoubtedly 'bureaucrats'.[39]

In the field of taxation, Scotland was more 'revolutionary' than England in some ways, though less in other ways. Professor Elton's original concept included the idea that parliament accepted that taxation should be granted for ordinary governmental purposes. While this has been controversial, it has been supplemented by the recognition that an important revision of the tax system occurred between 1512 and 1523. A new tax, the subsidy, was introduced on the basis of a direct assessment of the wealth of each propertied individual. At the time this was a notable fiscal advance, tapping people's wealth more effectively than fifteenth-century taxes. By the end of the century, taxation was being levied more frequently—almost every year.[40]

Parliamentary taxation was similarly boosted in Scotland, with the gradual introduction of taxes that were first (from the early 1580s) small but frequent, and then (from 1588 onwards) sizeable.[41] Taxes came to be demanded

---

[38] Goodare, *State and Society*, 88–9. Heritable jurisdictions still existed in Scotland but were declining, and the state never harnessed them as it did in France.

[39] Zulager, 'A Study of the Middle-Rank Administrators', 85–108, esp. 97.

[40] R. Schofield, 'Taxation and the Political Limits of the Tudor State', in C. Cross et al. (eds.), *Law and Government under the Tudors* (Cambridge, 1988). The early Tudor period has been reasserted as fiscally revolutionary by P. Cunich, 'Revolution and Crisis in English State Finance, 1534–1547', in W. M. Ormrod et al. (eds.), *Crises, Revolutions and Self-Sustained Growth: Essays in European Fiscal History, 1130–1830* (Stamford, 1999).

[41] Goodare, 'Parliamentary Taxation'; for the main early 17th-c. taxes, see *APS* iv. 289–92, cc. 18–19 (1606); 475–80, cc. 12–13 (1612); 581–5 (1617); 597–605, cc. 2–3 (1621); v. 167–74 (1625); 209–17 (1630); 13–20, cc. 1–2 (1633).

over several years in annual instalments, with the gross revenue settling at about £100,000 per year when levied. There were few non-tax years after 1606, and none after 1621. As in England, these taxes (except in royal burghs) were directly assessed on individuals, rather than imposing quotas on counties or districts and leaving the communities to apportion the burden. A belated but arguably comparable advance in government power had been achieved.

But the Scottish tax assessments, although established much later than the English ones, were much less durable; they were erected on flimsy and uneven foundations. The Tudor subsidy assessments gradually crumbled between about 1590 and 1629, but in their time they had been solid and effective.[42] The Scottish assessments were outdated from the moment they were established, being based not on valued rent but on 'old extent', an antiquated valuation that sometimes bore little relation to current land values. The government tried to introduce a new assessment system in 1600, but a convention of estates rejected it amid acrimonious scenes.

Scotland did conform, more clearly than England, to one of the original models of the 'revolution in government': the acceptance that taxation should be levied to meet the peacetime needs of government. The stated purposes of taxes varied widely—royal ceremonial, embassies, even repayment of royal debts, as well as warfare. It was conventional to offer some reason for each individual tax, and this reason never quite became 'to pay for the government'.[43] But some of the reasons were manifestly spurious. The tax of 1612 was officially for the marriage of Princess Elizabeth—but it was established policy that Scottish money was not remitted south.[44] As taxation became a regular annual event, the reality of taxes funding the government was ever more obvious. As yet it was far from being the whole of the government's funding, but it was an integral and essential component of it. By contrast, English governments could usually say that they were involved in warfare, or at least warlike preparations. It is not surprising that they put this justification for taxes in the shop window, especially when English wars were capable of swallowing all the taxes that parliaments could offer and more.[45] But perhaps there was an underlying recognition, even in England, that taxes were levied to pay for the government.

The period covered by this book witnessed a dramatic expansion in the daily business of central government. Centralization was described in Chapter 5 as people adopting a single, national standard to regulate their affairs.

[42] M. J. Braddick, *Parliamentary Taxation in Seventeenth-Century England* (Woodbridge, 1994), 78–117.   [43] Goodare, 'Parliamentary Taxation', 48–52.
[44] *APS* iv. 475, c. 12; Goodare, *State and Society*, 129–30. For the multifarious purposes on which the money was actually spent, including the royal visit of 1617, see NAS, taxation accounts, 1612, E65/6.
[45] R. W. Hoyle, 'Crown, Parliament and Taxation in Sixteenth-Century England', *English Historical Review*, 109 (1994), 1174–96.

Something of this may be charted through the rise of the courts in Edinburgh. If they came to a single place to ascertain that standard, or to seek its application, then that place was Edinburgh. The town's life pulsated to the rhythm of the law courts, especially the court of session. 'The pacquet rynnis not now in vacance so oft as in sessioun,' wrote Sir Thomas Hope to a London correspondent; 'the nixt will not go befoir the 28 of this instant.'[46] The wealth of Edinburgh's judges, writers, and advocates, already considerable in 1565, had increased markedly by 1635. By the latter date, the total wealth of the capital's lawyers had reached about half that of the merchants themselves.[47] Whether this wealth came from official salaries or fees from clients, it displayed a power to extract resources from society. People felt it increasingly necessary to seek decisions from the central courts, and to pay handsomely for the privilege.[48]

The privy council generated less work for lawyers, since it did not admit advocates to plead before it.[49] But the expansion of the council's business was equally remarkable—like the court of session, its business more than quadrupled—and perhaps even more significant. Along with the exchequer and court of session, the privy council established its role at the heart of the executive in our period. They eclipsed the old, informal royal council, and pushed many local jurisdictions (notably sheriffs) into a clearly subordinate position. At the outset of our period, it was not preordained that this would happen. Mary's advent as an adult personal monarch in 1561 might have been like the personal rule of James V in 1528, which had led to the dissolution of the regular conciliar body back into the amorphous 'lords of council'. Instead, the privy council continued. Probably this was assisted by a feeling that a female ruler ought to take as much male counsel as possible.[50] But the steady growth of conciliar business surely shows that there was an underlying logic to the system of conciliar government.

In the process, the executive role of the crown shifted, and it lost much autonomy. The privy council got into its stride gradually as the central executive agency during the 1570s and 1580s; by the end of that period it could act effortlessly as *the* government. No regent was needed during James VI's absence in Denmark in 1589–90. James retained an important role in the council, and could usually get his way if he really wanted. But that did not

---

[46] NLS, Hope to Viscount Annan, 1 Aug. 1622, Denmylne MSS, Adv. MS 33.1.1, vol. x, no. 60.

[47] Donaldson, 'Legal Profession', 13–16; W. Makey, 'Edinburgh in Mid-Seventeenth Century', in Lynch (ed.), *The Early Modern Town*, 208. The Edinburgh merchants' wealth had itself grown substantially.

[48] Finlay, *Men of Law*, 38–47; K. M. Brown, 'Aristocratic Finances and the Origins of the Scottish Revolution', *English Historical Review*, 104 (1989), 46–87 at 64–5.

[49] A procurator or other representative (who might be an advocate) could be admitted in the absence of the principal; but the council normally expected people to plead their cases in person.

[50] For such a feeling in the early years of Queen Elizabeth, see Smith, *De Republica Anglorum*, 65.

make his government 'personal' in the sense that his grandfather's had been. In decision-making by a consensus-seeking committee like the privy council, any member could assert himself and try to bring his colleagues round to his view. Although the king was in an exceptionally good position to do this, it was exceptional for him to do so. Government by consensus had become the norm. And while the council could govern in this way without active input from the king (it required only his name), the king could not govern without the council. He could browbeat it or purge it, but not bypass it.

The king's departure to England did not shift the council from its entrenched position; it reinforced it. A constant stream of councillors' letters besought James to vouchsafe his princely wisdom to them while humbly recommending a course of action which they knew he would usually accept. They knew better than he what was going on; and they, not he, would have to implement the policy once decided. On the occasions when James overruled the council's advice, he still had to make it do what he wanted. Things might have been different if the Regent Moray had reconstructed the council into four separate bodies in 1569, as discussed in Chapter 6; that, by creating alternative channels for executive action, would have given the monarch room for manoeuvre. This was what Charles I was seeking when he separated the membership of the privy council and court of session in 1625; but by then the council was too deeply rooted. The radical options for assertion of the monarch's personal authority had been closed off.

Individual monarchs did still matter, of course, but the history of Scottish government is not primarily the history of what James VI himself did. As pointed out in Chapter 4 above, the expression 'James VI' can symbolize the government that operated in his name, but it is the purpose of this book to get beyond the symbol and to expose the variety of personnel and processes at work. This does not reduce King James to insignificance, but any case for his personal initiative has to be argued specifically rather than merely by reference to the fact that it was done in his name. This case has been argued effectively in the crucial matter of the eradication of feuding.[51] James also exercised personal influence to encourage witch-hunting, incurring much criticism.[52] However, some of his other personal pursuits, such as the 'reunion of Christendom', involved little or no Scottish governmental activity.[53]

The privy council's scope for action grew partly because parliament passed more and more statutes; it was the council that steered the process of enforcing them. The strategy of discretionary enforcement, described in Chapter 5 above, was essentially its strategy. Discretionary enforcement succeeded because it worked within the existing structure of local particularism. Executive

[51] K. M. Brown, *Bloodfeud*, 240–3.

[52] J. Goodare, 'The Scottish Witchcraft Panic of 1597', in id. (ed.), *The Scottish Witch-Hunt in Context* (Manchester, 2002), 60–70.

[53] W. B. Patterson, *James VI and I and the Reunion of Christendom* (Cambridge, 1998).

authorities, local and even central, could decide whether or not to enforce the law in a particular locality. This might even create new forms of regional distinctiveness. Witch-hunting was discretionary, and there evolved a marked regional pattern to it, with the most intense activity in the south-east.[54] There eventually emerged a more generous poor-relief policy in southern Scotland, where most parishes opted for compulsory local assessments.[55] Still, all these new laws were central ones, pointing towards a future of full and literal enforcement. The more statutes there were, the more they tended to circumscribe and even to undermine traditional particularism.

Statute law was not just handed down from on high; it emerged through a process of negotiation among the political classes represented in parliament. This is not to say that everyone wanted all the laws (any more than they do today), but people put up with them, as we saw in Chapter 1, because they accepted the process of parliamentary legislation as legitimate. Even in the ideal absolutist state, where orders were formally issued by the king, there was a royal court where negotiations were constantly in progress on what the king would be best advised to order; that, too, was legitimate. When the implementation of the law was also subject to negotiation, the legitimizing process was continued.

The successful expansion of the law of the state created an ideological climate in its favour. Enforcing the law and implementing government policy became familiar and normal. Not everybody hunted witches or organized poor relief in seventeenth-century Scotland, but it was harder for members of the elite to doubt the value of these activities when the government was publicly promoting them through its executive agencies. Government actions may not always have been effective, but they pointed in a clear direction and probably usually had at least some effect. How much the statute of 1579 requiring possession of Bibles and psalm books did for sales of these items is unknown, but it can only have been positive, not negative.[56] Any negative impact would have been felt instead on sales of missals and saints' lives. This particular law probably had only a small impact, but it was one of many—and these proliferating laws did not generate a hostile reaction to the concept of statute law as such. Through sensitive implementation, statutes became part of people's lives.

One line of criticism of the 'Tudor revolution' is that of Steven Gunn, who argues a need to adapt Professor Elton's model to that provided by Bruce McFarlane. McFarlane offered a persuasive interpretation of late medieval government as essentially a matter of lordship over people, while Professor Elton saw sixteenth-century government as a matter of evolving institutions.

---

[54] Goodare et al., 'Survey of Scottish Witchcraft'.

[55] R. Mitchison, 'North and South: The Development of the Gulf in Poor Law Practice', in Houston and Whyte (eds.), *Scottish Society*. This development post-dated our period, but was based on discretionary enforcement of legislation of 1575 and 1579.

[56] *APS* iii. 139, c. 10; cf. Ch. 5 above.

The suggestion can be made that there was a transition (perhaps in 1485) from one to the other, but evidence for such a transition has proved elusive. Alas, neither Elton nor McFarlane provided an account of the *end* of the world in which the king was essentially the lord of other lords (and preferably the good lord of other good lords).[57] When this subject is tackled by Michael Hicks, the results seem limited in their applicability to Scotland. Indentured retainers and other means of paid military recruitment, so important in late medieval England, had no direct parallel in Scotland, where military service was largely unpaid until the early seventeenth century.[58]

It is fortunate that we in Scotland need not share these problems of English historiography, since we have an excellent account of how the nobility were weaned away from autonomous dispute-settlement and persuaded—or sometimes forced—to accept the authority of the courts. Some of it has explicitly followed the model of Mr McFarlane in tracing the lineaments of traditional lordship.[59] Keith Brown, whose detailed study of the subject has become a classic, emphasizes not only the innovatory character of the attack on feuding, but also the way in which James VI emphasized traditional lordship even as he undermined essential aspects of it. In his intervention to settle local feuds he was even 'acting as a feudal overlord'. Professor Brown also points to James as capable of conscious innovation, as when he condemned 'the olde Scots fashion' as a worthless argument in defence of the indefensible.[60] The king as the apex of feudal society was indeed a traditional ideal; when to this was added an unprecedented royal monopoly on legitimate violence, it became the ideal of the absolutist state.

The reconstruction of the nobility meant, above all, their abandonment of private warfare and acceptance that their military future lay in armies organized by the state. This was already beginning in the sixteenth century, when there was a bifurcation between the tower-houses of lords and the fortifications built by the crown. The latter were no longer designed like baronial residences, and were sometimes described as 'blok houssis'. They concentrated on providing defensive housings for artillery. Lordly residences, meanwhile, had gunports for handguns; but they no longer maintained a common architectural tradition with royal fortifications. Indeed these architecturally sophisticated Renaissance 'châteaux' had symbolic, rather than practical, defences. Their gunports did not have to command real sight-lines, or even to have room for a gunner behind them. Fighting of various kinds occurred in our period, but little of it was siege warfare.[61]

---

[57] Gunn, *Early Tudor Government*, 2–6; cf. K. B. McFarlane, *The Nobility of Later Medieval England* (Oxford, 1973), 119.

[58] M. Hicks, *Bastard Feudalism* (London, 1995).

[59] Wormald, *Lords and Men*, 7–8 and *passim*; K. M. Brown, *Bloodfeud*; Wasser, 'Violence and the Central Criminal Courts'.   [60] Brown, *Bloodfeud*, 218, 205.

[61] J. Zeune, *The Last Scottish Castles* (Buch am Erlbach, 1992), 275–84; C. McKean, 'The Scottish Château', *Review of Scottish Culture*, 12 (1999–2000), 3–21; R. Samson, 'Tower-

Reconstruction of the nobility also involved a change in the way that they organized their estates. In late medieval times, the lord was all in all to his tenants and dependants. An estate was a power base: from it, fighting men were raised to protect the estate itself and to advance the lord's career. It also provided money rents, but these were secondary. This pattern continued longer in the Highlands, and is well brought out in an account of the sixth Lord Lovat, whose lands lay on the Highland Line and who died at a great age in 1633:

> This nobleman . . . was never known to raise [the rent of] a tennant for any mans pleasure for brib or grassom, which he never sought nor tooke; and, if a gentlemans sone would seeke to raise a tennant in the incountry, he would flattly deny him, telling that he would give him land in the Highland, for gentlemen are appointed to watch and guard the country, and therefor ought to live uppon the marches, skirts, and extremitics thereof to keep of[f] theeves and sorroners.[62]

But Lovat was recognized as old-fashioned; and he was heavily in debt.

With the decline of private warfare, money slowly became central to landlordism. As a result, the possession of an estate became a way of making money: and the point is that it was now one way among several. Fewer landlords exercised such traditional lordship; instead, some of them began to manage their estates for profit.[63] As for power, they now exercised more of this indirectly, using their money. The fact that they had acquired their money through rent did not distinguish them so firmly from those whose fortunes rested on other foundations. Money did not confer directly the right to command others, but it purchased prestige and access to the machinery of the state. It was that machinery which possessed direct coercive power.

Fynes Morison, who visited Scotland in 1598, knew that much had changed by 1617 when he published his account of his travels. He wrote of aristocratic warfare in the past tense, and noted an economic implication of it: 'The Scots, living then in factions, used to keepe many followers, and so consumed their revenew of victuals, living in some want of money.'[64] Money was increasingly requisite for litigation; there is no full scholarly study of this, but some work has been done on the employment of lawyers by Highland chiefs. In 1620, Sir John Grant younger of Freuchie spent £1,358. 6s. 5d. on legal fees, apparently for just one case. Having had to visit Edinburgh twice, he must have had other costs too.[65]

Nobles who failed to adapt to all this could sometimes fail spectacularly— and the leading failures were seen as examples at the time. The overthrow

Houses in the Sixteenth Century', in S. Foster et al. (eds.), *Scottish Power Centres from the Early Middle Ages to the Twentieth Century* (Glasgow, 1998).

[62] Fraser, *Chronicles of the Frasers*, 250. 'Grassom' = entry fine; 'sorroners' = fighting clansmen seeking free quarters.

[63] Whyte, 'Poverty or Prosperity?', 23–9; K. M. Brown, *Noble Society*, ch. 2.

[64] P. H. Brown (ed.), *Early Travellers in Scotland* (Edinburgh, 1891), 88–9.

[65] D. A. Watt, 'Chiefs, Lawyers and Debt', 200–1.

of the earl of Orkney in 1609–15 has already been noted as a phase in the reduction of provincial distinctiveness, but it was also part of the process of reducing noble autonomy. The earl of Caithness was exiled in 1623 for various minor crimes but mainly for bankruptcy. Sir Robert Gordon, who contributed to his downfall, noted sententiously: 'Neither could the earle of Orknaye's exemple (which wes recent befor his eyes) divert him from the course which broght him to this extremitie. A notable warning to posteritie.'[66]

Most nobles heeded the warning and welcomed the opportunity to adapt, for instance embracing the higher standards of education called for by a life in state service.[67] The reconstructed Scottish state machine *used* the nobility rather than replacing them. Once they ceased feuding and submitted their disputes to the law courts, they did not necessarily need to discover the virtues of impartial justice. To be sure, there was no longer anything like the co-option of the judicial system witnessed in 1501, when the justice clerk, Richard Lawson, acted as an advocate for the earl of Errol and gave him a bond of manrent, making him as much a member of the earl's affinity as his armed servants.[68] By the end of James VI's reign, nobles' client networks had lost their military function, but they had not ceased to exist; they had been transferred from the field of battle to the institutions of government. The court of session, for instance, was open to the influence exerted by powerful men. Lord President Spottiswoode upbraided the advocates in 1633:

There is never interlocutor or decreet given in matters of any importance, but the party that is prejudged by it doth proclaim loud enough that his cause was good, but he was borne down by the credit and friendship of his adversaries. We owe this to you, I will not stick to tell it, that the people is possessed with this opinion of us, that there is little regard had before us to the justice and equity of causes, but that we are more led with by-respects.[69]

Although public opinion was ominously sceptical about Spottiswoode's commitment to 'justice and equity' when faced with aristocratic interference, the precise nature and extent of that interference would be hard to assess. But 'credit and friendship' were undoubtedly real forces.

Nor were they necessarily malign forces. Sir Robert Gordon's advice of *c*.1620 to his nephew, the earl of Sutherland, may not reveal an intention to pervert the course of justice, but it does bring out the importance of a noble's active involvement in law and administration:

Be suir also to hawe some of the ringleaders both in counsell and session to be your assured freinds. Retein still the best men of lawe and advocats in Edinbrugh for

---

[66] Gordon, *Sutherland*, 382.   [67] Brown, *Noble Society*, ch. 8.

[68] Finlay, *Men of Law*, 45.

[69] 'Address of Sir Robert Spottiswoode to the members of the faculty of advocates, summer session 1633', *Spottiswoode Miscellany*, i, ed. J. Maidment (1844), 195.

your counsell. Hawe a good, diligent, skillfull and faithfull agent still resident in Edinbrugh, who shall be your pensioner, and shall advertise yow from tyme to tyme of all occurrences there. Besyds this, yow shall still hawe in your owne companie a man expert in the laws and statutes of the kingdome, whom yow shall retaine alwayes with your selfe as your domestick serwant. Let him be a publick noterie, and a messenger at armes. It is best to hawe him a borne Southerland man, if it be possible, for so shall he be trustiest to yow.[70]

A nobleman thus expected to cultivate both privy council and court of session.[71] Gordon's 'best men of lawe' were writers to the signet, equivalent to modern solicitors, who dealt with non-litigious conveyancing and contractual matters as well as arranging litigation with advocates. Such high-powered legal expertise was unnecessary in the locality, but a notary and messenger at arms were always needed. Local influence was detectable in Gordon's wish for a 'borne Southerland man', though this to him was not an essential requirement.

So landlords never became politically insignificant: on the contrary, the state was largely run by landlords for at least two centuries after our period had ended. There were two main reasons for this. Firstly, landlords were often successful at the business of making money, so when power was conferred by money they were bound to get a lot of it. Secondly, there were still some special features of landed wealth. It carried greater prestige than wealth from trade or even law. It was longer-lasting, as no special skill was required to be a landlord, enabling landed wealth to be transmitted through many generations. It also retained some direct connection with political power. Peers, who sat personally in parliament, had to be landlords. The parliamentary franchise in the counties, too, was attached to land. The position would have been different if the nobility itself had been more urban, as it was in Italy. The distinction between nobles and burghs might have been blurred if government had been a matter of urban elites dominating the countryside in their own interests.[72] As it was, the Scottish nobility was very much a *landed* class.

Was there, then, a 'revolution in government' in the Scotland of Mary and James VI? This is partly a matter of how one defines one's terms. 'Revolution in government' is not a phrase I would have chosen; I would rather have kept the term 'revolution' for sudden and coercive changes of regime, such as occurred in Scotland in 1560, 1638, and 1689.[73] Nevertheless, 'revolution in

---

[70] Fraser, *Sutherland Book*, ii. 355.

[71] The court of session was formally known as the 'lords of council and session', but Gordon here referred to two bodies and so must have meant the privy council. At this date, there was much overlap in the two bodies' membership.

[72] Cf. P. Burke, 'City-States', in J. A. Hall (ed.), *States in History* (Oxford, 1986). Scottish burgesses were beginning to take on wadsets (mortgages) of land, but that is another issue.

[73] For some studies of real revolutions see C. Tilly, *European Revolutions, 1492–1992* (Oxford, 1993), and R. Porter and M. Teich (eds.), *Revolution in History* (Cambridge, 1986). Historians have sometimes been over eager to attach the term 'revolution' to their findings—

government' is a recognized phrase to describe a cluster of constitutional, legal, and administrative developments that can be argued to have occurred in early Tudor England. Subsequent research on Professor Elton's original concept has modified and refined it, often reducing his original claims but still demonstrating the fruitfulness of the concept as a way of understanding governmental developments. Something similar occurred in Scotland, about half a century later than the equivalent developments in England. If the term 'revolution in government' is used with these reservations, as a phrase to describe a cluster of governmental developments, then there was indeed a 'Stewart revolution in government'.

The key development, linked to numerous others, was the establishment of an executive privy council as a corporate decision-making body, rather than having a king advised by 'lords of council', usually individually. Below the privy council came more active administrative departments, notably the late sixteenth-century exchequer and then the early seventeenth-century treasury. Bureaucracy grew. Centralization grew, with more of the governing that local elites did being subject to national standards (statute law, and the practice of the court of session) rather than local custom. The territory of the state became more integrated, with the subjugation of the elites of the Borders. Highland elites were not fully integrated, but they were no longer left to their own devices for long periods, and were subject to frequent central interference. This interference, discussed in Chapter 10, was also more consistently and openly hostile than it had been before or indeed than it would be later.

Fiscal developments form a second group of changes. Taxation, both direct and indirect, grew. The state now drew its revenues from the propertied classes rather than having its own separate property. These revenues were modest by English or indeed by overall European standards. The emerging Scottish state was fiscally weak; nobody needed it to be otherwise, sheltered as it was by England from the worst effects of participation in Continental warfare. The increases in taxation still transformed patterns of political participation, as larger numbers of the propertied classes came to parliament in order to supervise grants of taxation.

Finally, therefore, there was a transformed role for parliament. Parliamentary sovereignty was established—not just over the church, but over the magnates too. This led to an explosion of statute law, and a recognition that such law, rather than traditional custom, was *the* law. The magnates had a leading share in making the new and multiplying statutes by which they were governed, but they did have to recognize that they were subject to those statutes and could no longer be autonomous in their own regions. This gives a distinctively sharp edge to Scotland's 'revolution in government'. Private

'educational revolution' and 'price revolution' are two examples. For scepticism about a 'military revolution', see Goodare, *State and Society*, 169.

warfare had already largely ceased in the England of Henry VIII, but it was an unavoidable reality in the Scotland of James VI. Yet by the end of James's reign it had, finally, been superseded by a newly established monopoly of public warfare.[74] The significance of this was not immediately apparent, since James did not require his government to undertake much warfare, but by the covenanting period it would be crucial. The chronology of governmental developments will be discussed further in the Conclusions below.

[74] Except in the Highlands, where state structures were not fully operative.

Conclusions

The successful centralizing state which followed feudal fragmentation [in Europe] was law-abiding rather than confiscatory. It may have been due to a cultural survival related to the Roman legal heritage. It may, more plausibly, be connected with the fact that the new commercial and eventually industrial wealth is confiscation-elusive or fragile. Unlike a sack of potatoes, it cannot easily be seized, and, if interfered with, it withers. The rulers may have found that the tax-potential of their subjects diminishes if they are brazenly or arbitrarily oppressed.

Gellner, *Plough, Sword and Book*, 159

Government is vital to human society, and raises large questions. Let us begin by revisiting a small question of definition: the question of who or what the 'government of Scotland' actually was. Not one definition but three may be offered.

The first definition is a narrow one; it focuses on the everyday business of central government and on the people and institutions most responsible for it. These people were the monarch, plus his or her officers of state and other privy councillors, and leading courtiers and nobles resident at court. These groups usually overlapped, although there was an occasional tendency for the royal court to form an alternative centre of power to the bureaucracy. Still, they were all the monarch's advisers and they all helped to exercise royal authority. An additional interest exercising often decisive advice consisted of English diplomatic representatives, or (after 1603) the king himself on the occasions when he acted as a channel for English interests.[1] The concept of 'the crown' signifies the public manifestation of the collective and (usually) consensual activities of these groups. They were all recognized as being in charge of the government. Indeed, they made headlines, being named and discussed personally in administrative records, ambassadors' despatches, chronicles, memoirs, and correspondence. In the full sense of the phrase, these people were in power.

The second definition is broader, and focuses on the large-scale, setpiece occasions when the political community assembled to deal with the big issues. These were parliaments. Parliaments passed the legislation that so many of these issues called for; they also exercised a check on the crown's advisers, partly for that reason (it could never be taken wholly for granted

---

[1] Cf. Nicholls, *Jacobean Union*, and the 'dynastic state' adumbrated by Braddick, *State Formation*, 337.

that a controversial legislative proposal by the crown would be passed by parliament), but also because the crown's day-to-day exercise of authority required money—taxes—that parliaments could choose to grant or withhold. The lesser members of parliament, burgh and shire commissioners, sometimes functioned as lobbyists of government, in a similar way to the lawyers and church ministers who hovered round parliament without actually being members of it. Whether members of parliament or not, as lobbyists they aimed to persuade government to sympathize with their interests. But when a decision on legislation was called for, membership of parliament mattered because the members had a vote. When they agreed to legislation (or, much more rarely, when they rejected controversial legislation proposed by the crown), the members of parliament were governing directly. Legislative sovereignty was parliamentary sovereignty. Parliament, and thus the political community represented in it, possessed power.

The third definition is not so broad, but goes deeper. It focuses on power as it was experienced directly by most people—local power. To ordinary people it was their immediate superiors who mattered. Crown and parliament were less prominent than baron court and kirk session. The bailie and officers of the former, and the elders of the latter, were the crucial figures. Of course the lord of the baron court might be a member of parliament, or even a courtier, but that would not necessarily be relevant to his tenants, even if it was an important aspect of the articulation of government. Closer still to the common people, and to some extent drawn from them, were the birlawmen, or the bailies of the burgh of barony. Ordinary folk were probably more familiar with the power of their own bosses than with that of the bosses' bosses— though Chapter 11 has pointed to a number of ways in which central power penetrated deeply into society.

So power was exercised at every level. Threads of authority extended upwards and outwards from the locality—linking baron court to sheriff, kirk session to presbytery and synod, local landlord to the client network of some great magnate, and then linking these to the people in the first of these three definitions of government: the monarch, and his or her privy councillors, officers of state, and leading courtiers. Meanwhile, monarchs and advisers were linked back to people in the localities—not the common people, but the leaders of local society who attended parliament. Prominent among these were the nobility. They exercised a dual local and national role, making the early modern state a fundamentally aristocratic one. Power was exercised in an interconnected web. The three definitions of 'government' turn out to be three components of a single matrix of power.

This matrix of power has been analysed in the preceding chapters from several angles. If we take its first component, the everyday government, we have seen in Chapter 1 that it had to be legitimized. Everyday government, because it was headed by a monarch, was particularly easy to justify in religious terms;

the ideology of divine right favoured monarchs. Monarchs also had to be seen to take good advice, and this was legitimized in aristocratic terms—the best advice was that obtained from the nobility. Chapter 2 takes this further by showing that the most important groups in Scottish society, especially the nobles, were also best connected when it came to influencing government, either from the inside or from the outside. It might sometimes be hard to say whether a given noble was inside or outside the government. The connection of such people with the monarch has been discussed in Chapter 4, where the 'crown' is seen as an institution that was operated, usually at the royal court, by the monarch in conjunction with a varying combination of advisers—high-born companions, nobles, and councillors—who usually cooperated with one another, but not always.

Everyday government was often a matter of implementing laws—applying general rules to specific situations. The various ways in which this could be done have been set out in Chapter 5, using the concepts of 'discretionary enforcement'—in which executive agencies set high and low priorities in the enforcement of different laws—and 'negotiated implementation'—in which they sought consensus with those they were governing on the extent to which laws would be applied to the latter. Discretionary enforcement and negotiated implementation occurred at all levels of government, from the crown to the local court. It was, however, particularly characteristic of the privy council, the subject of Chapter 6. The privy council, as a corporate body created in 1545, marked the later sixteenth century firmly off from what had gone before (a point to which Chapter 12 returns). The council, more than any other body, steered the everyday government, meeting regularly throughout the year and taking hundreds of policy decisions. Moreover, Chapter 7 has shown that the council was not just a matter of the councillors as individuals. The leading councillors were departmental heads, responsible for particular branches of the administration. Because the executive departments were controlled by the council, Scottish government was often remarkably well integrated.

The impact of government beyond the political elite has been the subject of Chapters 10 and 11. Chapter 10, on the Highlands, has shown the council as constantly involved both in the making and in the implementation of Highland policy from the late 1580s onwards. This is especially noteworthy because before then, Scottish governments had not regularly felt the need to have a Highland policy at all. Chapter 11, on the common people, has found considerably less involvement of everyday central government with them. There were perhaps two main exceptions. The feuing of church land in the late sixteenth century required a royal licence after 1564, involving the crown indirectly in the restructuring of tenurial relationships which feuing often brought. And witch-hunting was carried out by commission from the privy council, involving it regularly in detailed reviews of relationships between witchcraft suspects and local elites.

Conclusions 301

Turning from everyday government to parliament, this too has been discussed in most of the book's chapters. Parliament had to be legitimized, as we have seen in Chapter 1; this was achieved in the most basic sense when people actually turned up when it was summoned. In this period they came with enthusiasm and in unprecedented numbers. An entire new estate, that of shire commissioners, was admitted to membership in 1587, and the noble estate also grew to a record size. The increasingly confrontational nature of political processes within parliament placed strains on many members' goodwill, but in our period the government was still usually winning the votes and even perhaps the debates.

The nobles were the most important estate in parliament, as has been shown in Chapter 2. The clerical estate was almost eclipsed in the later sixteenth century, as bishops were downgraded and monastic commendators became secular nobles. Lesser members of parliament, the burgh and shire commissioners, sometimes lobbied in the same way that non-members might do, and the most influential non-members—lawyers and the English ambassador—were often more successful. The parallel today would be the backbench Member of Parliament who exercises less influence than the well-connected corporate lobbyist. The Protestant church sometimes sought official representation in parliament but was more interested in lobbying, although its success in this was as mixed as its political fortunes were varied.

Parliament was not seen primarily as a supreme legislative body at the outset of our period, when the law was not conceived as something that had been legislated into existence. Instead the 'old laws' were regarded as the theoretical basis of law, deriving their authority from virtually immemorial antiquity. Chapter 3 has discussed the efforts at codification of the old laws, in order to make them usable, and the explosion of statute into supremacy when the codification efforts failed and parliament instead began to pass a large volume of legislation. The flow of new statutes slackened after the 1590s, and Chapter 4 has shown that the crown (the king and his advisers in court and council) thereafter sought to restrict parliament's competence and to exalt the royal prerogative as a means of government. But such efforts had limited success. Much though James VI would have liked to tax or legislate by royal edict, he never could.

Laws, once passed, had to be implemented. The central institutions which carried this out, discussed in Chapters 5–7, have all been discussed above as part of everyday government, but much of Chapter 5 has been about statutes and the intentions of the legislators who framed them. A traditional line of criticism of the Scottish parliament has been that its laws were ineffective; this, it has been argued in Chapter 5, often rests on a misunderstanding of what people thought laws could achieve. Laws were passed demanding total obedience—what other formula could have been used?—but in practice they were usually expected to be implemented with discretion.

Parliament passed some landmark statutes relating to the Highlands. Although these have come into Chapter 10 they have not been its main focus; they have been discussed at greater length elsewhere.[2] What Chapter 10 has sought to do is to establish a framework for interpreting both legislative and executive actions of government. The clan elites of the Highlands began to be treated as actual or potential targets for colonization, sometimes directly, but increasingly by means of client clans who were expected to implant 'civility' and to pay higher royal rents. This policy had only modest success on its own terms, but it resulted in a lasting polarization among the clan elites.

The relationship between parliament and the common folk, discussed in Chapter 11, was less direct. Statutes periodically claimed to favour the 'pure laboreris of the ground', but these were mostly about teinds and their primary beneficiaries were landlords. Statutes on moral discipline—adultery, fornication, incest, pilgrimages, witchcraft—were inspired by the Reformation, but moral discipline was generally in the hands of kirk sessions, which did not necessarily take their guidance from the statute book. Other executive agencies too could deal with poor folks on their own account. Prosecution of gypsies (for the crime of being gypsies) had been carried on for some years on privy council authority before parliament passed a statute on the subject, in 1609.[3] The enserfment of the colliers derived from a statute of 1606 but depended on creative interpretation by the courts, especially to make the serfdom hereditary.

The legitimation of local government has not been discussed directly in Chapter 1, and there is scope for further research on this. One possible line of enquiry would be to ascertain the extent of the contrast between rural local government, all traditionally in the hands of nobles and legitimized by chains of individual dependence,[4] and urban local government, thoroughly corporate and legitimized by the collective status of a wealthy oligarchy. Rural local government was at any rate the norm, both in quantitative terms and in being aristocratic.

Local government was run by members of the political community, but (as mentioned in Chapter 3) the leaders of the community were no longer using parliament to keep the government off their local patch. In the fifteenth century there had been a distinct trend for the magnates assembled in parliament to regard proposals for royal provision of justice with suspicion as undermining their local jurisdictions. By the late sixteenth century, the political community that has been discussed in Chapter 2 had acquiesced in the transfer of extensive jurisdiction from sheriff courts to the court of session, and

---

[2] Goodare, *State and Society*, ch. 8; Lynch, 'James VI and the "Highland Problem" '.

[3] *APS* iv. 440, c. 20.

[4] At the outset of our period there were still non-noble corporate landlords, the church and the crown, but the estates of both were pervaded by nobles' influence, typically as hereditary bailies or other officials. Cf. P. J. Murray, 'The Lay Administrators of Church Lands in the Fifteenth and Sixteenth Centuries', *SHR* 74 (1995), 26–44.

was happy to use parliament to *govern* rather than to provide a check on the government. Local elites lobbied for more statutes, not for fewer statutes. The loose framework of the 'old laws', discussed in Chapter 3, had allowed local autonomy, but statutes did not.

In practice, however, when statutes were implemented, this required the acquiescence of local elites. Chapter 5 has shown that the implementation of statutes was often intended to be discretionary, and that the privy council or other central body responsible for implementing the law would often be flexible in doing so. Moreover, the related concept of negotiated implementation has recognized that local authorities had a real input into the question of how statutes would be applied to them and the people of their locality. They could often choose to make particular statutes high priorities, and other ones low priorities. The increase in the density of executive government at the centre, discussed in Chapters 6 and 7, surely reduced local autonomy here but did not abolish it.

The crucial chapters on local government have been Chapters 8 and 9. The former of these has discussed the local authorities that existed in 1560, and the way in which they adapted to a more intense regime of central authority. Hardly any authorities were abolished (apart from the diocesan officials of the Catholic church) and few were even significantly downgraded, but they lost much practical autonomy. Chapter 9 has shown that the traditional local authorities were supplemented by a range of new ones—especially the ministers and courts of the Protestant church, but also justices of the peace, registers of sasines, and various monopolistic projects. The density of administration was greatly increased, and most of the new local authorities were more closely connected to the centre than the old ones had traditionally been.

Local government in this sense did not exist in the Highlands. Instead, governmental functions were retained in the hands of Highland chiefs. One reason that this did not change much during our period has been explained indirectly by Chapter 10: central government did not trust the chiefs and was unwilling to endow them with institutional authority. Instead, central government sponsored external attacks on the chiefs. By the last decade of our period, there were more systematic efforts to get chiefs to answer for their followers, but this scarcely amounted to the creation of structures of governmental authority that would include the chiefs.

Turning to the relations between government and ordinary folk, Chapter 11 has discussed this but has had rather more about central than about local government; again further research is required on the latter. There have, however, been valuable studies of the moral discipline enforced by the local courts of the Protestant church, on which Chapter 11 has been able to draw. The chapter has also outlined a framework for understanding the increased involvement of government with women, a large and far from exhausted topic. Both Chapter 10 and Chapter 11 are indeed outline treatments of topics on which far more deserves to be said. Rather than dealing solely with the impact of everyday central government, or of parliament, or of local government, these chapters have combined aspects of all three. This integrated discussion may at least help to support the argument that everyday central government, parliament, and local government all formed an integrated matrix of power.

Thus defined, the matrix of power is a functioning thing but not per se an evolving one. We can see how it operated, but we also want to know how it developed. This is where Chapter 12 comes in. Both governmental operation and governmental development have been discussed in the core chapters of this book; Chapter 12 has focused on development, and on the question of how the increasing elaboration of governmental machinery affected the nature of the state. Its entry point has been the question of whether there was a 'revolution in government' along the lines of the much-discussed Tudor 'revolution' in England; the answer (rather as in England) is yes and no. Government did become more centralized, more bureaucratic, more territorially integrated, and more focused on a single sovereign body—the crown in parliament. The territorial nobility were integrated into it. But they were not superseded, and indeed their client networks animated the state. The church, too, was integrated into the state, but the way in which this had happened was a source of conflict rather than stability. By 1625, the state that had emerged was dynamic but fragile.

At this point it is worth looking at these governmental developments in another way, by providing a straightforwardly chronological account of the main changes that occurred in Scottish government between 1560 and 1625. This has the advantage that it need not confine itself to the 'revolution in government' model but can take in any and all relevant changes. Some of the changes would not be predicted by that model but were contingent on specific episodes of Scottish political history; they nevertheless had a part to play. What follows will continue beyond 1625, in order to compare the developments of the period 1560–1625 with those of the next few decades.[5]

The fundamental context of the development of government was provided by the Reformation, established dramatically in 1560 and working itself out thereafter for the whole of the rest of our period and beyond. The authority of the pope was abrogated, removing the single most significant supra-national authority from government and thus promoting the sovereignty of the state.[6] The Reformation also divided the political community, with disputes over religion cutting across allegiances based on more traditional patterns of locality, kinship, and clientage.[7] Finally, the Reformation

---

[5] The reference notes to this chronological account indicate some of the main works in which these developments have been discussed. See also the historiographical section of the Introduction above.

[6] Goodare, *State and Society*, ch. 1.   [7] Donaldson, *All the Queen's Men*.

gradually created a new network of powerful church courts, especially kirk sessions and presbyteries.[8]

The Reformation did not achieve its full aims of producing a godly society. But at least at state and institutional level, it was remarkably successful. If it had failed, Scotland would probably have remained within the French rather than English orbit, and perhaps even the Franco-Scottish union of crowns would have continued. Instead, Protestantism became and remained the official religion, helping to give England and Scotland a common diplomatic orientation. A radical Protestant movement grew up to trouble the regime, which meanwhile sought what its critics perceived as a *rapprochement* with Catholicism. The success with which it distanced itself from its radical critics meant that the state could continue in an absolutist direction, basing itself on the nobility.[9]

The growth of an integrated sovereign state was further promoted at the time of the 'Black Acts' of 1584, asserting royal and parliamentary power over the church. This proved enormously controversial because the assertion of supremacy was linked to episcopacy, and there were periods in the 1590s when a resurgent presbyterian movement seemed likely to lead the church away from secular control. However, the government was able to reimpose episcopacy in the decade or so after 1596, and it lasted until 1638.[10] Episcopacy itself was never stable or likely to be long-lasting—but the period before 1638 did show that a church fully independent from the secular state (as the presbyterian 'two kingdoms' theory demanded) was impractical. When the covenanting revolution overthrew episcopacy, it paid lip-service to the 'two kingdoms' theory but rapidly developed new mechanisms for governmental control of the church—notably the new office of 'ruling elder', allowing the politicians to appoint themselves as ecclesiastical governors.[11] The 1584 act establishing parliamentary power over the church was actually reasserted.[12]

The incorporation of the church into the state was not something that the early Protestant movement intended; if anything, they envisaged the state being incorporated into the church. In 1560 the Scottish church found itself largely autonomous, having ceased to be governed by a supra-national authority; by 1625 it was a department of state. This had happened, not simply by weakening the church—for in many ways it had been strengthened—but by the creation of a more dense network of interlinked sources of authority. Links were not just forged between kirk sessions and the high commission, and between justices of the peace and the privy council; if these had been the only links, one might have been able to treat 'church' and 'state' as separate

---

[8] Graham, *Uses of Reform*; Todd, *Culture of Protestantism*.
[9] A. R. MacDonald, *Jacobean Kirk*.   [10] Mullan, *Episcopacy in Scotland*.
[11] W. Makey, *The Church of the Covenant, 1637–1651* (Edinburgh, 1979), chs. 9–10.
[12] *Records of the Kirk of Scotland, 1638 downwards*, i, ed. A. Peterkin (Edinburgh, 1838), 149–50. The immediate aim was to invalidate the prerogative court of high commission.

entities. In practice there were also links between kirk sessions and JPs, and between the council and high commission. All were interested in the creation of a Christian polity in which the authority of the state as a whole was under-pinned by divine sanction, and in which all agencies of government would cooperate to punish sin.

There were still problems over this, but they were over the kind of state there was going to be. In the view of the early seventeenth-century presbyte-rian movement, which had inherited the radical cutting edge of the early Protestants, it would have to be a dynamic, committed, godly state, hard at work purging the nation of its sins in preparation for the coming millennium. Such a state would have been hard to imagine a century earlier—or, indeed, a century later. The episcopalians tried to adopt as much as possible of this programme, but were constrained by their commitment to the absolutist state, an aristocratic polity.

A further aspect of sovereignty related to the autonomous local power of the nobility, based on their ability to wage private war. The symbolic date at which this was curbed was 1598, when the 'Act anent Feuding' ordered the submission of feuds to royal justice. The determination of the government to enforce this appeared over the next two decades, during which bloodfeud was slowly but surely terminated.[13] This was not simply an assertion of governmental power *over* the nobility, however, since it was made clear that the new governmental structures were being created *for* the nobility. They would be involved in governmental decision-making, and supported financially.[14]

This then leads on to the question of finance. In the development of the fiscal resources of the state there is no single symbolic date; rather there may be several. The first is a primarily constitutional development: the admis-sion of lairds to parliament in 1587. This was the result of pressure from lairds ever since 1560, but it was successful because the government needed lairds to legitimize parliamentary taxation.[15] The first really large tax was raised in 1588, and parliamentary taxes became gradually larger and more regular until by the 1610s they were usually raised every year. This was a substantial achievement, though the structure of direct taxation was erected on the weak foundation of outdated assessments that could not tap landed wealth efficiently. There were also indirect taxes. In 1597 customs were imposed on imports and some duties rose, and in 1612 the customs rates were raised drastically. A further significant fiscal date was 1603, when the union of crowns removed the cost of the court from the Scottish treasury. Thereafter the government was able to escape from the chronic indebtedness and near-bankruptcy of the 1590s and developed

---

[13] K. M. Brown, *Bloodfeud*.
[14] Goodare, *State and Society*, ch. 3; id., 'The Nobility and the Absolutist State'.
[15] Id., 'Admission of Lairds'.

sizeable revenue surpluses, which largely went towards subsidizing the nobility.[16]

The regal union was also important in its own right, though it was not wholly new in 1603. Its outlines were discernible as early as 1561, with the establishment of a working diplomatic relationship between Elizabeth and Mary. Once Scottish monarchs adopted the diplomatic stance of seeking recognition as heirs-apparent to the English crown, they had to maintain Scotland's satellite status. From some points of view the regal union simply consummated and confirmed Scotland's position as an English satellite. James in 1603 placed closer union on the agenda; so long as the regal union endured, the possibility of amalgamation could never be entirely removed. On the other hand, he soon accepted the failure of his own schemes for closer union, and discovered that a looser form of regal union could work.[17] He continued to govern both England and Scotland directly, a point often obscured by the careless use of phrases like 'absentee monarchy'.[18]

The late sixteenth and early seventeenth centuries fostered Anglo-Scottish union through closer religious and cultural contacts. However, neighbours sharing a common culture may still detest one another cordially. The union of 1707, like the convergence of state structures in the seventeenth century, is best seen as a union of states rather than one of nations. This required some kind of consensus over religion, but linguistic and cultural union was unnecessary.[19]

The reign of James VI also saw significant steps taken towards the integration of the Highlands into the state. A series of military expeditions from the 1590s to the 1620s cowed several clans, and large territories were forfeited by the most intractable opponents of state power. Efforts at direct colonization were defeated, so the government had to settle for the aggrandizement of the more cooperative clans rather than the destruction of the clan system.

One area in which nobles were recruited into state service was in warfare. In the first two decades of the seventeenth century, the traditional, unpaid 'common army' was silently abandoned, and warfare became a matter of paid regiments. This development was limited partly through fiscal weakness (the pre-covenanting Scottish state was solvent only so long as it was not asked to pay for serious warfare), but mainly because Scotland saw very little warfare and large armies were unnecessary.

From the point of view of state structure, James's reign launched Scotland down the absolutist road already being taken by England. This model of state formation was dominant until 1638, and influential down to 1689 at least. The weaknesses of the absolutist state in Scotland were also those possessed by the contemporary state in England. The lack of a standing army; the

---

[16] Id., 'Parliamentary Taxation'; id., *State and Society*, ch. 4.

[17] Wormald, 'Creation of Britain'; B. Galloway, *The Union of Scotland and England, 1603–1608* (Edinburgh, 1986).   [18] See Ch. 6 above, and Lee, *Government by Pen*.

[19] Levack, *Formation of the British State*.

inability to tax peasants directly; the reliance on local property-holders, rather than salaried agents of the crown, to govern the localities: these are commonplaces of English history of the Tudor and early Stuart period. There were possibilities for governmental failure in Scotland in the 1590s and early 1600s simply through the crown's increasing inability to make ends meet. There was a worrying royal bankruptcy in 1598; such bankruptcies were never total, but a really serious one might have led to a temporary collapse in central authority.[20] It is not impossible to imagine a restoration of stability in which the magnates retained their autonomy and the monarchy was reduced in power. Scotland could have gone the way of Poland—but it did not.

So central state power survived. It also reached into the localities more intimately than before, through the creation of new forms of local authority that were answerable to central institutions and not to local magnates. As was shown in Chapter 9, the number of local public administrators was multiplied almost fourfold in our period in proportion to the population, a remarkable achievement at a time when that population was itself growing.

On the other hand, centralization of the state was not wholly successful. If all authority—including fiscal authority—had been concentrated in the hands of the crown, then Scotland could have gone the way of France. As it was, the absolutist state constructed in the late sixteenth and early seventeenth centuries was more like the circumscribed version of absolutism seen in England. In both states, the early stages of absolutism enhanced the role of parliament, and the crown thereafter was never quite able to dispense with this inconveniently consultative institution.

The accession of Charles I in 1625 is often regarded as a new development in Scottish politics, but its significance for the development of government is more indirect. Its strident promotion of episcopacy may be seen as ephemeral, since bishops were abolished by the covenanters and never regained the influence that they had had under Charles. Other than that, the main governmental development was the royal revocation of 1625. It was part of a process of restructuring of land tenures, teinds, and office-holding. Although it soon became bogged down in bureaucratic complexity, some of it continued into the 1640s and later. The personal reign of Charles I can largely be seen as continuing the tendencies of his father towards an absolutist state, in which power was focused on the crown and managed by the nobility through patronage and clientage. The regime did not dispense with parliament, although it would presumably have made efforts to do so eventually, as it did in England. The Scottish parliament of 1633 was induced to grant six years of parliamentary taxation rather than the conventional four, and Charles might well have asked a future parliament to grant him this revenue for life or

---

[20] Goodare, 'Thomas Foulis and the Scottish Fiscal Crisis'.

in perpetuity, as was done after the Restoration. But before this could happen, his regime was overthrown by the covenanting revolution.[21]

The regime of the covenanters made a series of crucial contributions to the development of Scottish government. Some of them built on previous achievements while others reversed them. The covenanters established a much more effective fiscal regime, enforcing a new assessment system for the land tax and establishing an excise—a new tax on domestic sales. This built on and extended, rather than reversing, the fiscal growth of the period since 1587. The covenanters succeeded with their new taxes because they were faced with a series of wars which (initially at least) were popular; people were willing to pay to support the cause. Large, modern armies were raised for the first time.[22]

It is hard to assess the long-term effectiveness of the covenanting regime because it never functioned for long in peacetime. It is all very well to mobilize for a popular war, but in the short term, wars tend to be paid for by borrowing, with new taxes being used to repay the debts gradually during the succeeding period of peace. The regime was overthrown before it had a chance to show whether it had developed sufficient economic resources to repay its debts.[23] But the later seventeenth and early eighteenth centuries, when a similar parliamentary regime was revived and then (after 1707) upgraded to ruthless English standards of resource-extraction and military mobilization, may provide some indication that the covenanters were building an effective state.

In doing so, the covenanters reversed some of the governmental innovations made under James and Charles. In particular they established a fully parliamentary regime, nullifying the tendency towards autonomous royal power and promoting instead the power of an institution containing all the main propertied classes, not just the nobility. They also abolished episcopacy. The first of these moves undermined the privileged position of the nobles, while the second arguably benefited them by removing a powerful group that nobles had found hard to control. Both moves replaced the ideological legitimation of the absolutist state, with its insistence that power flowed downwards from God to the king and then to the political classes, with an ascending ideology in which the political classes formed and controlled government in their own legitimate interests. This was not turning the clock back to the late medieval period of parliamentary prominence. Ascending ideology

---

[21] Lee, *Road to Revolution*; Macinnes, *Charles I and the Making of the Covenanting Movement*.

[22] D. Stevenson, 'The Financing of the Cause of the Covenants, 1638–1651', *SHR* 51 (1972), 89–123; id. (ed.), *The Government of Scotland under the Covenanters, 1637–1651* (SHS, 1982); E. M. Furgol, 'Scotland turned Sweden: The Covenanters and the Military Revolution, 1637–1651', in J. Morrill (ed.), *The Scottish National Covenant in its British Context* (Edinburgh, 1990).

[23] Part of the covenanting war effort was also paid for by English subsidies: Stevenson, 'Financing of the Cause of the Covenants'.

as the covenanters used it had been developed only in the later sixteenth century, as a combination of the secular humanism of George Buchanan and the ideas of radical presbyterianism.[24] The late medieval parliament was a gathering of magnates whose primary power was local, while the covenanting parliament was an instrument of central state power.[25] As such it looked forward to modern times.

Simplistic either-or comparisons, whereby the creation of the modern Scottish state is ascribed either to James VI or to the covenanters exclusively, are therefore unhelpful. The process was a cumulative one in which both regimes had a contribution to make. A covenanting-style regime could not have been created in the mid-sixteenth century, when power was still far more fragmented; an attempt in 1556 to do what the covenanters did by revising the tax assessment system was a complete failure.[26] The covenanters took over, modified, and extended a successful government, rather than abolishing an unsuccessful one and replacing it with something different.

The conclusion, therefore, is that the government of Scotland travelled a long way during the reigns of Queen Mary and her son. This abstract statement can be illustrated in a concrete way by an episode during Charles I's early effort to embroil his northern kingdom in his Continental wars. Warfare was, after all, one of the basic activities of the early modern state, and mobilization for war involved a variety of governmental interventions in society. The earl of Nithsdale was one of those who promoted Scotland as a recruiting-ground for regiments to be sent to Germany, and Lord Ogilvy wrote to him in 1627 about some of the administrative arrangements. He wanted clothing for the soldiers he had already recruited, 'for they will not imbark with good will except they get thair clothes', but was even more concerned about continuing rights to recruit. Ogilvy warned Nithsdale that the chancellor was manoeuvring to channel recruits towards Nithsdale's rival, Lord Spynie, and that it 'consernes both your lordship's awin credeit, and the credeit of your freindis' that this should be thwarted. He wanted Nithsdale to persuade the council to order 'ane divisione of the shyres be lottes'. Ogilvy, whose lands and connections were based in the shire of Angus, hoped that Nithsdale would thereby gain that shire and allocate it to him, but failing Angus, he offered to take on recruitment in any nearby shire—he mentioned 'Fyff, Stretherne, Mar, Buchan, or Abberdeine'.[27]

This episode reveals a good deal about the way in which government had come to operate. The first point concerns the troops' need for clothing. This

---

[24] Mason (ed.), *Scots and Britons*.

[25] Tanner, *Late Medieval Scottish Parliament*; J. R. Young, *The Scottish Parliament, 1639–1661: A Political and Constitutional Analysis* (Edinburgh, 1996).

[26] Goodare, 'Parliamentary Taxation', 23.

[27] Lord Ogilvy to earl of Nithsdale, 22 June 1627, W. Fraser, *The Book of Caerlaverock: Memoirs of the Maxwells, Earls of Nithsdale, Lords Maxwell and Herries*, 2 vols. (Edinburgh, 1873), ii. 82–3.

illustrates state power, since a late medieval government could not recruit troops unless they were already fully armed, let alone clothed. By the early seventeenth century, the government expected to be able to equip them itself, and indeed to pay them. Paid military service, bypassing nobles' retinues, was something new.

But military recruitment did not bypass the nobility altogether. Ogilvy and Nithsdale were nobles. They had special influence—'credeit'—in government. They used networks of kinship and clientage in government service. Ogilvy was not a bureaucrat who could be posted anywhere; he wanted to recruit in the shire of Angus because his connections were there. But he was not entirely restricted to those connections, and was certainly not raising a traditional armed retinue from his own followers. The council had stopped him recruiting in the lordship of Coupar, of which he was bailie, in 1625—a dispute continuing in 1627.[28] Moreover, he was willing to move to a nearby shire if necessary.

So bureaucracy was involved. The arrangements for dividing up the recruiting territories illustrate the power of the privy council, for it alone could decide the issue. No doubt Nithsdale deployed his 'credeit' to influence the decision, but it was for all that a decision made at the centre, not in a locality which he could control. The basic point to grasp about the role of the nobility in the emerging absolutist state is that they exchanged one form of power for another. Instead of exercising untrammelled power in their own local domains, they gained a share of influence over the whole country through participation in government at the centre. An indication of bureaucratic initiative is detectable in Ogilvy's list of 'shyres'; three of the six he mentioned (Strathearn, Mar, and Buchan) were not actually shires but districts of other kinds. They seem to have been chosen as recruiting areas for administrative convenience, ignoring tradition. At this point the story can be rounded off by mentioning that Ogilvy's and Nithsdale's lobbying efforts seem to have succeeded. The council divided up all the shires of Scotland between Nithsdale, his rival Spynie, and a third recruiter, Sir James Sinclair of Murkill. This may well have been done by casting lots; all at any rate received widely scattered territories.[29]

None of this reflected traditional patterns of magnate power. In the allocation of shires, Nithsdale did get Angus (and so could presumably devolve it to Ogilvy), but it is questionable whether Nithsdale was really a regional magnate in the traditional sense, and even if he was, his region was Dumfriesshire, far removed from Angus. His much-mistrusted fellow-recruiters, Spynie and Sinclair, were not major figures in any region. They were even clearer examples of the tendency noted in Chapter 2 for royal administrators to have central connections but not local ones. Traditional magnate power had been

---

[28] *RPC*, 2nd ser., i. 214–15; ii. 30–1.
[29] *RPC*, 2nd ser., ii. 32–4. Ross-shire seems inadvertently to have been omitted.

supreme at the outset of our period, when all armies raised in Scotland (royal or non-royal) were composed of unpaid noble retinues. Even in the 1590s this had been so. Nithsdale's own father, the eighth Lord Maxwell, had been killed in 1593 at the head of a private army of Maxwells in pursuit of a private feud. Lord Maxwell had been warden of the west march, a royal office, but his connections had still been predominantly local. His son, Nithsdale, had no private army and few local connections; instead he exercised power at a national level, helping to integrate the localities of Scotland into the national state.

By 1625, the state that had emerged was dynamic but fragile. Charles I's Scottish war effort did not display his government at its most effective; rather it revealed fiscal weakness and political unpopularity. Once his first convention of estates had rejected a special military tax, merely continuing the taxes already in force, the government was left to organize a war with no extra resources. But its need for those resources shows that it was trying to operate an up-to-date system of administration and military organization. Having abolished nobles' retinues, it had lost touch with traditional means of unpaid warfare relying on those retinues. It would be left to the covenanters, with God more conspicuously on their side, to find more effective ways of mobilizing the political, fiscal, and military resources of Scottish society. In doing so, the covenanters built on governmental foundations that had been laid between 1560 and 1625.

Select Bibliography

I. MANUSCRIPTS

Aberdeen City Archives

William Kennedy, 'Alphabetical index to the first 67 volumes of the council register of the city of Aberdeen, 1398–1800'.
Kirk session accounts, 1617–18.

British Library, London

'Forme of the coronation of the kings of Scotland', 1625 × 1685, in Add. MS 19797.
Copies of documents relating to the revenues of Scotland, Add. MS 24275.
David Chalmers, 'Dictionary of Scots law' (1566), Add. MS 27472.
Earl of Dunfermline to Earl of Salisbury, 13 July 1608, in Add. MS 32476.
State papers and correspondence relating to the affairs of Scotland, 1449–1594, Add. MS 33531.
State papers relating to Scotland, 1572–5, Cotton MSS, Caligula, C.iv.
'Proposalls for reformation of certain abuses in the state', in Harl. MS 4612.
'Notes furth of the registers of exchequer, 1583–1674', in Harl. MS 4628.
Earl of Salisbury to Sir Thomas Edmondes, 11 May 1605, in Stowe MS 168.

Dundee City Archive and Record Centre

Dundee council minutes, vols. i–ii.
Miscellaneous burgh papers.

National Archives of Scotland, Edinburgh

Exchequer auditors' act book, 1584–6, E4/1.
Treasurer's accounts, E21.
Comptroller's accounts, E24.
Decreets on the taxations, E62.
Taxation accounts, E65.
Leven & Melville muniments, GD26/7/393.
Cunninghame of Caprington letter book, GD149/265.
Justiciary court books, JC1.
Books of adjournal, JC2.
Account of fines, in circuit court minutes, JC10/29.
Protocol books, NP1.
Miscellaneous parliamentary papers, PA7/1.
Register of commissions, 1607–16, PC7/1.

National Library of Scotland, Edinburgh

'Ane abbreviat of the registers of the high court of admirality', 1613–73, in Adv. MS 6.2.1

Adv. MS 22.3.14.

'Ordour to be observit in the stewart court of Annandaill', in MS copy of Balfour's 'Practicks', Adv. MS 24.6.3 (3).

Denmylne MSS, Adv. MSS 33.1.1, 33.1.15.

'The wayes quhairby the rentis of the quenis grace croun may be augmentit', in Adv. MS 34.2.17.

2. PRINTED PRIMARY SOURCES

(a) Public and Administrative Records

Aberdeen Council Letters, 6 vols., ed. L. B. Taylor (London, 1942–61).

Accounts of the Collectors of Thirds of Benefices, 1561–1572, ed. G. Donaldson (SHS, 1949).

Accounts of the (Lord High) Treasurer of Scotland, 13 vols., ed. T. Dickson et al. (Edinburgh, 1877–).

Actis and Constitutionis of the Realme of Scotland . . . (Edinburgh, 1566), copy in NLS, H.33.c.24.

Acts of the Lords of Council in Public Affairs, 1501–1554, ed. R. K. Hannay (Edinburgh, 1932).

Acts of the Parliaments of Scotland, 12 vols., eds. T. Thomson and C. Innes (Edinburgh, 1814–75).

Acts of Sederunt of the Lords of Council and Session (Edinburgh, 1790).

Admiral. *Acts of the Admiral's Court of Scotland (Acta Curiae Admirallatus Scotiae), 1557–1562*, ed. T. C. Wade (Stair Society, 1937).

Balgair. *Court Minutes of Balgair, 1706–1736*, ed. J. Dunlop (Scottish Record Society, 1957).

Booke of the Universall Kirk: Acts and Proceedings of the General Assemblies of the Kirk of Scotland, 3 vols., ed. T. Thomson (Bannatyne and Maitland Clubs, 1839–45).

Calendar of State Papers . . . *in the Archives and Collections of Venice*, 38 vols., ed. R. Brown et al. (London, 1864–1940).

Calendar of State Papers, Domestic Series, 94 vols., ed. R. Lemon et al. (London, 1856–).

Calendar of the State Papers Relating to Scotland and Mary Queen of Scots, 1547–1603, 13 vols., ed. J. Bain et al. (Edinburgh, 1898–1969).

Carnwath. *Court Book of the Barony of Carnwath, 1523–1542*, ed. W. C. Dickinson (SHS, 1937).

Criminal Trials in Scotland, 1488–1624, ed. R. Pitcairn, 3 vols. (Bannatyne and Maitland Clubs, 1833).

Dumbarton Common Good Accounts, 1614–1660, ed. F. Roberts and I. M. Macphail (Dumbarton, 1972).

Edinburgh. *Extracts From the Records of the Burgh of Edinburgh*, 13 vols., ed. J. D. Marwick et al. (SBRS and Edinburgh, 1869–1967).

Exchequer Rolls of Scotland, 23 vols., ed. J. Stuart et al. (Edinburgh, 1878–).

Falkirk. *Court Book of the Barony and Regality of Falkirk and Callendar*, i: *1638–1656*, ed. D. M. Hunter (Stair Society, 1991).

Fife. *Sheriff Court Book of Fife, 1515–1522*, ed. W. C. Dickinson (SHS, 1928).

'The Incorporated Trade of Skinners of Edinburgh, with Extracts from their Minutes, 1549–1603', ed. W. Angus, *Book of the Old Edinburgh Club*, 6 (1913), 11–106.

Kirkintilloch. *Court Book of the Burgh of Kirkintilloch, 1658–1694*, ed. G. S. Pryde (SHS, 1963).

Lothian and Tweeddale. *Records of the Synod of Lothian and Tweeddale, 1589–1596, 1640–1649*, ed. J. Kirk (Stair Society, 1977).

Orkney and Shetland. *Court Book of Orkney and Shetland, 1614–1615*, ed. R. S. Barclay (SHS, 1967).

Quoniam Attachiamenta, ed. T. D. Fergus (Stair Society, 1996).

Records of the Convention of Royal Burghs of Scotland, 7 vols., ed. J. D. Marwick and T. Hunter (Edinburgh, 1866–1918).

Regiam Majestatem, ed. Lord Cooper (Stair Society, 1947).

Register of the Great Seal of Scotland (Registrum Magni Sigilli Regum Scotorum), 11 vols., ed. J. M. Thomson et al. (Edinburgh, 1912–).

Register of the Privy Council of Scotland, 37 vols., ed. J. H. Burton et al. (Edinburgh, 1877–).

Register of the Privy Seal of Scotland (Registrum Secreti Sigilli Regum Scotorum), 8 vols., ed. M. Livingstone et al. (Edinburgh, 1908–).

Sadler. *State Papers and Letters of Sir Ralph Sadler*, 3 vols., ed. A. Clifford (Edinburgh, 1809).

St Andrews Kirk Session Register, 2 vols., ed. D. H. Fleming (SHS, 1889–90).

The Second Book of Discipline, ed. J. Kirk (Edinburgh, 1980).

Shetland. *Court Book of Shetland, 1615–1629*, ed. G. Donaldson (Lerwick, 1991).

Skene, John (ed.), *Regiam Majestatem* (Edinburgh, 1609).

Spynie. 'Extracts from the Register of the Regality Court of Spynie, 1592–1601', ed. J. Stuart, in *Miscellany of the Spalding Club*, ii (1842).

Stirling Presbytery Records, 1581–1587, ed. J. Kirk (SHS, 1981).

Stirling. *Earl of Stirling's Register of Royal Letters, 1615–1635*, 2 vols., ed. C. Rogers (Grampian Club, 1885).

Stuart Royal Proclamations, i: *1603–1625*, ed. J. F. Larkin and P. L. Hughes (Oxford, 1973).

(b) Narratives, Tracts, etc.

[ANDERSON, PATRICK], *The Copie of a Baron's Court, Newly Translated by What's-you-call-him, Clerk to the Same*, ed. D. Webster (Edinburgh, 1821).

BALFOUR OF DENMILNE, Sir JAMES, *Historical Works*, 4 vols., ed. J. Haig (Edinburgh, 1824–5).

BALFOUR OF PITTENDREICH, Sir JAMES, *Practicks*, 2 vols., ed. P. G. B. McNeill (Stair Society, 1962–3).

BANNATYNE, RICHARD, *Memorials of Transactions in Scotland, 1569–1573*, ed. R. Pitcairn (Bannatyne Club, 1836).

BRUCE, ROBERT, *Sermons: With Collections for his Life by Robert Wodrow*, ed. W. Cunningham (Wodrow Society, 1843).

BUCHANAN, GEORGE, *The History of Scotland*, 6 vols., ed. J. Aikman (Edinburgh, 1830).

CALDERWOOD, DAVID, *History of the Kirk of Scotland*, 8 vols., ed. T. Thomson and D. Laing (Wodrow Society, 1843–9).

COWPER, WILLIAM, *Workes* (2nd edn., London, 1629).

CRAIG, THOMAS, *De Unione Regnorum Britanniae*, ed. C. S. Terry (SHS, 1909).

——*Jus Feudale*, 2 vols., ed. J. A. Clyde (Edinburgh, 1934).

'Diary of the Convention of Estates, 1630', ed. J. Goodare, in *SHS Miscellany*, xiv (forthcoming).

Diurnal of Remarkable Occurrents . . . Since the Death of King James the Fourth till the year 1575, ed. T. Thomson (Bannatyne Club, 1833).

FRASER, JAMES, *Chronicles of the Frasers, 916–1674*, ed. W. Mackay (SHS, 1905).

GORDON, Sir ROBERT, *Genealogical History of the Earldom of Sutherland* (Edinburgh, 1813).

HAMILTON, Sir THOMAS, 'Memoriall anent the progres and conclusion of the parliament haldin at Edinburgh in October 1612', in *Maitland Club Miscellany*, iii (1843).

HERRIES, LORD, *Historical Memoirs of the Reign of Mary Queen of Scots*, ed. R. Pitcairn (Abbotsford Club, 1836).

Historie and Life of King James the Sext, 1566–1596, ed. T. Thomson (Bannatyne Club, 1825).

HOPE, Sir THOMAS, *Major Practicks*, 2 vols., ed. J. A. Clyde (Stair Society, 1937–8).

——*Minor Practicks*, ed. J. Spotiswood (Edinburgh, 1734).

KING JAMES VI & I, *Political Writings*, ed. J. P. Sommerville (Cambridge, 1994).

KNOX, JOHN, *History of the Reformation in Scotland*, 2 vols., ed. W. C. Dickinson (London, 1949).

——*Works*, 6 vols., ed. D. Laing (Bannatyne Club, 1846–64).

LESLIE, JOHN, *Historie of Scotland*, 2 vols., ed. E. G. Cody and W. Murison (STS, 1888–95).

LINDESAY OF PITSCOTTIE, ROBERT, *Historie and Cronicles of Scotland*, 3 vols., ed. Æ. J. G. Mackay (STS, 1899–1911).

LINDSAY OF THE MOUNT, Sir DAVID, *Works*, 4 vols., ed. D. Hamer (Scottish Text Society, 1931–6).

MACGILL, JAMES, and BELLENDEN, JOHN, 'Discours particulier d'Escosse', ed. P. G. B. McNeill, in *Stair Society Miscellany*, ii (1984).

MACKENZIE, Sir GEORGE, *Laws and Customes of Scotland in Matters Criminal* (Edinburgh, 1678).

——*Observations on the Acts of Parliament* (Edinburgh, 1686).

MAJOR (MAIR), JOHN, *A History of Greater Britain*, ed. A. Constable (SHS, 1892).

MELVILLE, JAMES, *Autobiography and Diary, 1556–1610*, ed. R. Pitcairn (Wodrow Society, 1842).

MELVILLE OF HALHILL, Sir JAMES, *Memoirs of His Own Life*, ed. T. Thomson (Bannatyne Club, 1827).

MOYSIE, DAVID, *Memoirs of the Affairs of Scotland, 1577–1603*, ed. J. Dennistoun (Bannatyne Club, 1830).

The Muses Welcome to the High and Mighty Prince James (Edinburgh, 1618).

ROW, JOHN, *History of the Kirk of Scotland, 1558–1637*, ed. D. Laing (Wodrow Society, 1842).

SCOT, WILLIAM, *An Apologetical Narration of the State and Government of the Kirk of Scotland since the Reformation*, ed. D. Laing (Wodrow Society, 1846).

SKENE, Sir JOHN, *De Verborum Significatione: The Exposition of the Termes and Difficill Wordes Conteined in the Foure Buikes of Regiam Majestatem and Uthers . . .* (Edinburgh, 1599).

SMITH, Sir THOMAS, *De Republica Anglorum*, ed. M. Dewar (Cambridge, 1982).

SPOTTISWOODE, JOHN, *History of the Church of Scotland*, 3 vols., ed. M. Napier and M. Russell (Spottiswoode Society, 1847–51).

STAIR, JAMES, VISCOUNT, *Institutions of the Law of Scotland*, ed. D. M. Walker (Edinburgh, 1981).

WELWOOD, WILLIAM, 'The Sea Law of Scotland', ed. T. C. Wade, in *Scottish Text Society Miscellany* (1933).

(c) Source Collections

Ancram. *Correspondence of Sir Robert Kerr, First Earl of Ancram, and his Son William, Third Earl of Lothian*, 2 vols., ed. D. Laing (Bannatyne Club, 1875).

Clan Campbell Letters, 1559–1583, ed. J. E. A. Dawson (SHS, 1997).

Dunvegan. *The Book of Dunvegan*, 2 vols., ed. R. C. Macleod (Third Spalding Club, 1938–9).

FRASER, W., *The Douglas Book*, 4 vols. (Edinburgh, 1875).

—— *Memoirs of the Maxwells of Pollok*, 2 vols. (Edinburgh, 1863).

—— *The Sutherland Book*, 3 vols. (Edinburgh, 1892).

GOODARE, J. (ed.), 'Fiscal Feudalism in Early Seventeenth-Century Scotland', in *SHS Miscellany*, xiii (2004, forthcoming).

GOULDESBROUGH, P. (ed.), *Formulary of Old Scots Legal Documents* (Stair Society, 1985).

Highland Papers, 4 vols., ed. J. R. N. Macphail (SHS, 1914–34).

HMC, *Calendar of the Manuscripts of the Marquis of Salisbury*, 24 vols., ed. S. R. Bird et al. (London, 1883–1976).

HMC, *Report on the Manuscripts of the Earl of Mar and Kellie*, 2 vols., ed. H. Paton (London, 1904–30).

The Jacobean Union: Six Tracts of 1604, ed. B. R. Galloway and B. P. Levack (SHS, 1985).

Letters and State Papers during the Reign of King James VI, ed. J. Maidment (Abbotsford Club, 1838).

MACQUEEN, H. L. (ed.), 'Two Visitors in the Session, 1629 and 1636', in *Stair Society Miscellany*, iv (2002).

NAPIER, M. (ed.), *Memorials of Montrose and his Times*, ed. M. Napier, 2 vols. (Maitland Club, 1848).

Orain Iain Luim: Songs of John MacDonald, Bard of Keppoch, ed. A. M. Mackenzie
  (Scottish Gaelic Texts Society, 1964).
Original Letters Relating to the Ecclesiastical Affairs of Scotland, 2 vols., ed. D. Laing
  (Bannatyne Club, 1851).
State Papers and Miscellaneous Correspondence of Thomas, Earl of Melros, 2 vols.,
  ed. J. Maidment (Abbotsford Club, 1837).
'The Straloch Papers', in *Spalding Miscellany*, i (1841).
The Warrender Papers, 2 vols., ed. A. I. Cameron (SHS, 1931–2).

3. SECONDARY WORKS

ADAMS, S., 'James VI and the Politics of South-West Scotland, 1603–1625', in
  Goodare and Lynch (eds.), *Reign of James VI*.
—— 'A Regional Road to Revolution: Religion, Politics and Society in South-West
  Scotland, 1600–1650' (Ph.D. thesis, Edinburgh, 2002).
ANDERSON, P., *Lineages of the Absolutist State* (London, 1974).
ANDERSON, P. D., *Black Patie: The Life and Times of Patrick Stewart, Earl of Orkney,
  Lord of Shetland* (Edinburgh, 1992).
—— *Robert Stewart, Earl of Orkney, Lord of Shetland, 1533–1593* (Edinburgh,
  1982).
AUSTIN, JOHN, *The Province of Jurisprudence Determined*, ed. W. E. Rumble
  (Cambridge, 1995).
AYLMER, G. E., *The King's Servants: The Civil Service of Charles I, 1625–1642*
  (London, 1961).
BARDGETT, F. D., 'The Monifieth Kirk Register', *Records of the Scottish Church
  History Society*, 23 (1987–9), 175–95.
BARKER, R., *Political Legitimacy and the State* (Oxford, 1990).
BEETHAM, D., *The Legitimation of Power* (London, 1991).
BOARDMAN, S. I., 'Politics and the Feud in Late Medieval Scotland' (Ph.D. thesis,
  St Andrews, 1990).
BRADDICK, M. J., *Parliamentary Taxation in Seventeenth-Century England*
  (Woodbridge, 1994).
—— 'State Formation and Social Change in Early Modern England: A Problem Stated
  and Approaches Suggested', *Social History*, 16 (1991), 1–17.
—— *State Formation in Early Modern England, c.1550–1700* (Cambridge,
  2000).
BROOKS, C. W., *Pettyfoggers and Vipers of the Commonwealth: The 'Lower Branch'
  of the Legal Profession in Early Modern England* (Cambridge, 1986).
BROWN, K. M., 'Aristocracy, Anglicisation and the Court, 1603–1637', *Historical
  Journal*, 36 (1993), 543–76.
—— *Bloodfeud in Scotland, 1573–1625* (Edinburgh, 1986).
—— 'Courtiers and Cavaliers: Service, Anglicisation and Loyalty among the Royalist
  Nobility', in J. Morrill (ed.), *The Scottish National Covenant in its British Context*
  (Edinburgh, 1990).
—— 'From Scottish Lords to British Officers: State Building, Elite Integration and the
  Army in the Seventeenth Century', in N. Macdougall (ed.), *Scotland and War,
  AD 79–1918* (Edinburgh, 1991).

—— 'A House Divided: Family and Feud in Carrick under John Kennedy, Fifth Earl of Cassillis', *SHR* 75 (1996), 168–96.

—— 'Noble Indebtedness in Scotland between the Reformation and the Revolution', *Historical Research*, 62 (1989), 260–75.

—— *Noble Society in Scotland: Wealth, Family and Culture, from Reformation to Revolution* (Edinburgh, 2000).

BROWN, M., 'The Taming of Scotland? Kings and Magnates in Late Medieval Scotland: A Review of Recent Work', *Innes Review*, 45 (1994), 120–46.

BRUNTON, G., and HAIG, D., *An Historical Account of the Senators of the College of Justice* (Edinburgh, 1836).

BURGESS, G. (ed.), *The New British History: Founding a Modern State, 1603–1715* (London, 1999).

BURKE, P., *Popular Culture in Early Modern Europe* (London, 1978).

BURNETT, C. J., 'Early Officers of Arms in Scotland', *Review of Scottish Culture*, 9 (1995–6), 3–13.

BURNS, J. H., *The True Law of Kingship: Concepts of Monarchy in Early-Modern Scotland* (Oxford, 1996).

CAIRNS, J. W., et al., 'Legal Humanism and the History of Scots Law: John Skene and Thomas Craig', in J. MacQueen (ed.), *Humanism in Renaissance Scotland* (Edinburgh, 1990).

CAMERON, J., *James V: The Personal Rule, 1528–1542* (East Linton, 1998).

CANNY, N., *Making Ireland British, 1580–1650* (Oxford, 2001).

CHALMERS, T. M., 'The King's Council, Patronage, and the Government of Scotland, 1460–1513' (Ph.D. thesis, Aberdeen, 1982).

CLANCHY, M. T., *From Memory to Written Record: England, 1066–1307* (2nd edn., Oxford, 1993).

COLEMAN, C., and STARKEY, D. (ed.), *Revolution Reassessed: Revisions in the History of Tudor Government and Administration* (Oxford, 1986).

COLLINSON, P., 'The Monarchical Republic of Queen Elizabeth I', in his *Elizabethan Essays* (London, 1994), 43–56.

COOPER, T. M., 'The King versus the Court of Session', *JR* 58 (1946), 83–92.

CORMACK, A. A., *Teinds and Agriculture* (Oxford, 1930).

COWAN, E. J., 'Clanship, Kinship and the Campbell Acquisition of Islay', *SHR* 58 (1979), 132–57.

—— 'Fishers in Drumlie Waters: Clanship and Campbell Expansion in the Time of Gilleasbuig Gruamach', *TGSI* 54 (1984–6), 269–312.

COWAN, I. B., *The Scottish Reformation* (London, 1982).

—— and SHAW, D. (ed.), *The Renaissance and Reformation in Scotland* (Edinburgh, 1983).

CRICK, B., *In Defence of Politics* (5th edn., London, 2000).

CUDDY, N., 'Anglo-Scottish Union and the Court of James I, 1603–1625', *Transactions of the Royal Historical Society*, 5th ser. 39 (1989), 107–24.

—— 'The Revival of the Entourage: The Bedchamber of James I, 1603–1625', in D. Starkey et al. (eds.), *The English Court from the Wars of the Roses to the Civil War* (London, 1987), 174–95.

DAWSON, J. E. A., *The Politics of Religion in the Age of Mary Queen of Scots: The Earl of Argyll and the Struggle for Britain and Ireland* (Cambridge, 2002).

DELLA FAVE, L. R., 'Towards an Explication of the Legitimation Process', *Social Forces*, 65 (1986), 476–500.

DENNISON, E. P., et al. (eds.), *Aberdeen before 1800: A New History* (East Linton, 2002).

DESBRISAY, G., 'Twisted by Definition: Women under Godly Discipline in Seventeenth-Century Scottish Towns', in Y. G. Brown and R. Ferguson (eds.), *Twisted Sisters: Women, Crime and Deviance in Scotland since 1400* (East Linton, 2002).

DIETZ, F. C., *English Public Finance, 1558–1641* (2nd edn., London, 1964).

DILWORTH, M., 'The Commendator System in Scotland', *Innes Review*, 37 (1986), 51–72.

DODGSHON, R. A., *From Chiefs to Landlords: Social and Economic Change in the Western Highlands and Islands, c.1493–1820* (Edinburgh, 1998).

DONALDSON, G., *All the Queen's Men: Power and Politics in Mary Stewart's Scotland* (London, 1983).

——'The Legal Profession in Scottish Society in the Sixteenth and Seventeenth Centuries', *JR*, NS 21 (1976), 1–19.

——*Scotland: James V–James VII* (Edinburgh, 1965).

——*Scottish Church History* (Edinburgh, 1985).

DOUCET, R., *Les Institutions de la France au XVIᵉ siècle*, 2 vols. (Paris, 1948).

DURKAN, J., 'The French Connection in the Sixteenth and Early Seventeenth Centuries', in T. C. Smout (ed.), *Scotland and Europe, 1200–1850* (Edinburgh, 1986).

——'The Royal Lectureships under Mary of Lorraine', *SHR* 62 (1983), 73–8.

ELLIOTT, J. H., *The Count-Duke of Olivares: The Statesman in an Age of Decline* (New Haven, 1986).

——*The Revolt of the Catalans: A Study in the Decline of Spain, 1598–1640* (Cambridge, 1963).

ELLIS, S. G., 'The Collapse of the Gaelic World, 1450–1650', *Irish Historical Studies*, 31 (1999), 449–69.

ELTON, G. R., '*Lex terrae victrix*: The Triumph of Parliamentary Law in the Sixteenth Century', in D. M. Dean and N. L. Jones (eds.), *The Parliaments of Elizabethan England* (Oxford, 1990).

——*Studies in Tudor and Stuart Politics and Government*, 4 vols. (Cambridge, 1974–92).

——*The Tudor Revolution in Government* (Cambridge, 1953).

——(ed.), *The Tudor Constitution* (2nd edn., Cambridge, 1982).

ERTMAN, T., *Birth of the Leviathan: Building States and Regimes in Medieval and Early Modern Europe* (Cambridge, 1997).

EVANS-JONES, R. (ed.), *The Civil Law Tradition in Scotland* (Stair Society, 1995).

EWAN, E., and MEIKLE, M. M. (eds.), *Women in Scotland, c.1100–c.1750* (East Linton, 1999).

FINLAY, J., 'James Henryson and the Origins of the Office of King's Advocate', *SHR* 79 (2000), 17–38.

——*Men of Law in Pre-Reformation Scotland* (East Linton, 2000).

FLETCHER, A., *Reform in the Provinces: The Government of Stuart England* (New Haven, 1986).

FOSTER, W. R., *The Church before the Covenants, 1596–1638* (Edinburgh, 1975).

FRASER, A., *The Gypsies* (Oxford, 1992).

GATRELL, V. A. C. et al. (eds.), *Crime and the Law: The Social History of Crime in Western Europe since 1500* (London, 1980).

GELLNER, E., *Plough, Sword and Book: The Structure of Human History* (London, 1988).

GIBSON, A. J. S., and SMOUT, T. C., *Prices, Food and Wages in Scotland, 1550–1780* (Cambridge, 1995).

GILLIES, W., 'Gaelic: The Classical Tradition', in R. D. S. Jack (ed.), *The History of Scottish Literature*, i: *Origins to 1660* (Aberdeen, 1988).

—— 'Some Aspects of Campbell History', *TGSI* 50 (1976–8), 256–95.

GODFREY, (A.) M., 'Arbitration and Dispute Resolution in Sixteenth-Century Scotland', *Tijdschrift voor Rechtsgeschiedenis*, 70 (2002), 109–35.

—— 'The Assumption of Jurisdiction: Parliament, the King's Council and the College of Justice in Sixteenth-Century Scotland', *Journal of Legal History*, 22 (2001), 21–36.

—— 'Jurisdiction in Heritage and the Foundation of the College of Justice in 1532', in *Stair Society Miscellany*, iv (2002).

GOLDSWORTHY, J., *The Sovereignty of Parliament: History and Philosophy* (Oxford, 1999).

GOODARE, J., 'The Aberdeenshire Witchcraft Panic of 1597', *Northern Scotland*, 21 (2001), 17–37.

—— 'The Admission of Lairds to the Scottish Parliament', *English Historical Review*, 116 (2001), 1101–33.

—— 'The Estates in the Scottish Parliament, 1286–1707', *Parliamentary History*, 15 (1996), 11–32.

—— 'The First Parliament of Mary Queen of Scots', *Sixteenth Century Journal*, 36 (2005, forthcoming).

—— 'The Framework for Scottish Witch-Hunting in the 1590s', *SHR* 81 (2002), 240–50.

—— 'The Nobility and the Absolutist State in Scotland, 1584–1638', *History*, 78 (1993), 161–82.

—— 'Parliament and Society in Scotland, 1560–1603' (Ph.D. thesis, Edinburgh, 1989).

—— 'Parliamentary Taxation in Scotland, 1560–1603', *SHR* 68 (1989), 23–52.

—— 'Scotland's Parliament in its British Context, 1603–1707', in H. T. Dickinson and M. Lynch (eds.), *The Challenge to Westminster: Sovereignty, Devolution and Independence* (East Linton, 2000).

—— 'The Scottish Parliament and its Early Modern "Rivals"', *Parliaments, Estates and Representation*, 24 (2004, forthcoming).

—— 'The Scottish Parliament of 1621', *Historical Journal*, 38 (1995), 29–51.

—— 'The Scottish Parliamentary Records, 1560–1603', *Historical Research*, 72 (1999), 244–67.

—— 'The Scottish Political Community and the Parliament of 1563', *Albion*, 35 (2003), 373–97.

GOODARE, J., 'Scottish Politics in the Reign of James VI', in id. and Lynch (eds.), *The Reign of James VI.*

—— *State and Society in Early Modern Scotland* (Oxford, 1999).

—— 'The Statutes of Iona in Context', *SHR* 77 (1998), 31–57.

—— 'Thomas Foulis and the Scottish Fiscal Crisis of the 1590s', in W. M. Ormrod et al. (eds.), *Crises, Revolutions and Self-Sustained Growth: Essays in Fiscal History, 1130–1830* (Stamford, 1999).

—— 'Witch-Hunting and the Scottish State', in id. (ed.), *The Scottish Witch-Hunt in Context.*

—— 'Women and the Witch-Hunt in Scotland', *Social History*, 23 (1998), 288–308.

—— (ed.), *The Scottish Witch-Hunt in Context* (Manchester, 2002).

—— and LYNCH, M., 'James VI: Universal King?', in eid. (eds.), *The Reign of James VI.*

—— (eds.), *The Reign of James VI* (East Linton, 2000).

—— et al., 'The Survey of Scottish Witchcraft, 1563–1736' (Jan. 2003), www.arts.ed.ac.uk/witches/.

GRAHAM, M. F., 'Equality before the Kirk? Church Discipline and the Elite in Reformation-Era Scotland', *Archiv für Reformationsgeschichte*, 84 (1993), 289–310.

—— *The Uses of Reform: 'Godly Discipline' and Popular Behavior in Scotland and Beyond, 1560–1610* (Leiden, 1996).

GRAVES, M. A. R., *The Parliaments of Early Modern Europe* (London, 2001).

GUNN, S. J., *Early Tudor Government, 1485–1558* (London, 1995).

HAMILTON-GRIERSON, P. J., 'The Judicial Committees of the Scottish Parliament, 1369–70 to 1544', *SHR* 22 (1925), 1–13.

HANNAY, R. K., *The College of Justice: Essays by R. K. Hannay* (Stair Society, 1990).

—— 'The Early History of the Scottish Signet', in his *College of Justice.*

—— 'The Office of the Justice Clerk', *JR* 47 (1935), 311–29.

—— 'On the Church Lands at the Reformation', *SHR* 16 (1919), 52–72.

HARDING, A. (ed.), *Law-Making and Law-Makers in British History* (London, 1980).

HARRIS, T. (ed.), *The Politics of the Excluded, c.1500–1850* (London, 2001).

HARRISON, J. G., '"Policing" the Stirling Area, 1660–1706', *Scottish Archives*, 7 (2001), 16–24.

HARRISON, P., and BRAYSHAY, M., 'Post-horse Routes, Royal Progresses and Government Communications in the Reign of James I', *Journal of Transport History*, 18 (1997), 116–33.

HECHTER, M., *Internal Colonialism: The Celtic Fringe in British National Development, 1536–1966* (London, 1975).

HEWITT, G. R., *Scotland under Morton, 1572–1580* (Edinburgh, 1982).

HINDLE, S., *The State and Social Change in Early Modern England, c.1550–1640* (London, 2000).

HINTON, R. W. K., 'The Decline of Parliamentary Government under Elizabeth I and the Early Stuarts', *Cambridge Historical Journal*, 13 (1957), 116–32.

HOUSTON, R. A., and WHYTE, I. D. (eds.), *Scottish Society, 1500–1800* (Cambridge, 1989).

JUHALA, A. L., 'The Household and Court of King James VI of Scotland, 1567–1603' (Ph.D. thesis, Edinburgh, 2000).

KIERNAN, V. G., *State and Society in Europe, 1550–1650* (Oxford, 1980).

KOENIGSBERGER, H. G., 'Monarchies and Parliaments in Early Modern Europe: *Dominium regale* or *dominium politicum et regale*', *Theory and Society*, 5 (1978), 191–217.

LARNER, C., *Enemies of God: The Witch-Hunt in Scotland* (London, 1981).

LEE, M., *Government by Pen: Scotland under James VI and I* (Urbana, Ill., 1980).

—— *Great Britain's Solomon: James VI and I in his Three Kingdoms* (Urbana, Ill., 1990).

—— *John Maitland of Thirlestane and the Foundation of the Stewart Despotism in Scotland* (Princeton, 1959).

—— *The Road to Revolution: Scotland under Charles I, 1625–1637* (Urbana, Ill., 1985).

LENEMAN, L., and MITCHISON, R., *Sin in the City: Sexuality and Social Control in Urban Scotland, 1660–1780* (Edinburgh, 1998).

LEVACK, B. P., *The Formation of the British State: England, Scotland and the Union, 1603–1707* (Oxford, 1987).

LOACH, J., *Parliament under the Tudors* (Oxford, 1991).

LOUGHLIN, M., 'The Career of Maitland of Lethington, *c.*1526–1573' (Ph.D. thesis, Edinburgh, 1991).

LYNCH, M., *Edinburgh and the Reformation* (Edinburgh, 1981).

—— 'James VI and the "Highland Problem" ', in J. Goodare and M. Lynch (eds.), *The Reign of James VI* (East Linton, 2000).

—— (ed.), *The Early Modern Town in Scotland* (London, 1987).

—— and DINGWALL, H. M., 'Elite Society in Town and Country', in E. P. Dennison et al. (eds.), *Aberdeen before 1800: A New History* (East Linton, 2002).

—— et al. (eds.), *The Scottish Medieval Town* (Edinburgh, 1988).

LYTHE, S. G. E., *The Economy of Scotland in its European Setting, 1550–1625* (Edinburgh, 1960).

MACDONALD, A., and MACDONALD, A., *Clan Donald*, 3 vols. (Inverness, 1896–1904).

MACDONALD, A. A., et al. (eds.), *The Renaissance in Scotland* (Leiden, 1994).

MACDONALD, A. R., 'Deliberative Processes in Parliament, *c.*1567–1639: Multi-cameralism and the Lords of the Articles', *SHR* 81 (2002), 23–51.

—— 'Ecclesiastical Representation in Parliament in Post-Reformation Scotland: The Two Kingdoms Theory in Practice', *Journal of Ecclesiastical History*, 50 (1999), 38–61.

—— *The Jacobean Kirk, 1567–1625: Sovereignty, Polity and Liturgy* (Aldershot, 1998).

—— 'James VI and the General Assembly, 1586–1618', in Goodare and Lynch (eds.), *Reign of James VI*.

—— ' "Tedious to rehers"? Parliament and Locality in Scotland, *c.*1500–1651: The Burghs of North-East Fife', *Parliaments, Estates and Representation*, 20 (2000), 31–58.

MACDONALD, F. A., 'Ireland and Scotland: Historical Perspectives on the Gaelic Dimension, 1560–1760' (Ph.D. thesis, Glasgow, 1994).

MACDONALD, S., *The Witches of Fife: Witch-Hunting in a Scottish Shire, 1560–1710* (East Linton, 2002).

MACDOUGALL, N., *James IV* (Edinburgh, 1989).

——(ed.), *Church, Politics and Society: Scotland, 1408–1929* (Edinburgh, 1983).

MACFARLANE, L. J., *William Elphinstone and the Kingdom of Scotland, 1434–1514* (Aberdeen, 1985).

MACGREGOR, M. D. W., 'A Political History of the MacGregors before 1571' (Ph.D. thesis, Edinburgh, 1989).

MACINNES, A. I., *Charles I and the Making of the Covenanting Movement, 1625–1641* (Edinburgh, 1991).

——*Clanship, Commerce and the House of Stuart, 1603–1788* (East Linton, 1996).

McKECHNIE, H. (ed.), *Introductory Survey of the Sources and Literature of Scots Law* (Stair Society, 1936).

MACKIE, J. D., and PRYDE, G. S., *The Estate of the Burgesses in the Scots Parliament and its Relation to the Convention of Royal Burghs* (St Andrews, 1923).

McLACHLAN, H. V., and SWALES, J. K., 'Sexual Bias and the Law: The Case of Preindustrial Scotland', *International Journal of Sociology and Social Policy*, 14 (1994), 20–43.

MACLEAN, L. (ed.), *The Seventeenth Century in the Highlands* (Inverness Field Club, 1986).

McMAHON, G. I. R., 'The Scottish Courts of High Commission, 1610–1638', *Records of the Scottish Church History Society*, 15 (1963–5), 193–209.

McNEILL, P. G. B., 'The Jurisdiction of the Scottish Privy Council, 1532–1708' (Ph.D. thesis, Glasgow, 1960).

——'The Scottish Regency', *JR*, NS 12 (1967), 127–48.

——and MACQUEEN, H. L. (eds.), *Atlas of Scottish History, to 1707* (Edinburgh, 1996).

MACPHERSON, R. G., 'Francis Stewart, 5th Earl Bothwell, c.1562–1612: Lordship and Politics in Jacobean Scotland' (Ph.D. thesis, Edinburgh, 1998).

MACQUEEN, H. L., *Common Law and Feudal Society in Medieval Scotland* (Edinburgh, 1993).

MADDEN, C., 'The Finances of the Scottish Crown in the Later Middle Ages' (Ph.D. thesis, Glasgow, 1975).

MALCOLM, C. A., 'The Office of Sheriff in Scotland: Its Origin and Early Development', *SHR* 20 (1923), 129–41, 222–37, 290–311.

MANN, M., *The Sources of Social Power*, i: *A History of Power to AD 1760* (Cambridge, 1986).

MASHAW, J. L., *Bureaucratic Justice* (New Haven, 1983).

MASON, R. A., *Kingship and the Commonweal: Political Thought in Renaissance and Reformation Scotland* (East Linton, 1998).

——(ed.), *Scotland and England, 1286–1815* (Edinburgh, 1987).

——(ed.), *Scots and Britons: Scottish Political Thought and the Union of 1603* (Cambridge, 1994).

——and MACDOUGALL, N. (ed.), *People and Power in Scotland* (Edinburgh, 1992).

MATTINGLY, G., *Renaissance Diplomacy* (Pelican edn., Harmondsworth, 1965).

MEMMI, A., *The Colonizer and the Colonized*, trans. H. Greenfeld, introductions by J.-P. Sartre and L. O'Dowd (2nd edn., London, 1990).

MERRIMAN, M., *The Rough Wooings: Mary Queen of Scots, 1542–1551* (East Linton, 2000).

METCALF, D. M. (ed.), *Coinage in Medieval Scotland, 1100–1600* (British Archaeological Reports, no. 45, 1977).

MITCHISON, R., *Lordship to Patronage: Scotland, 1603–1745* (London, 1983).

——*The Old Poor Law in Scotland: The Experience of Poverty, 1574–1845* (Edinburgh, 2000).

——and LENEMAN, L., *Girls in Trouble: Sexuality and Social Control in Rural Scotland, 1660–1780* (2nd edn., Edinburgh, 1998).

MORRILL, J., 'A British Patriarchy? Ecclesiastical Imperialism under the Early Stuarts', in A. Fletcher and P. Roberts (ed.), *Religion, Culture and Society in Early Modern Britain* (Cambridge, 1994).

——'The Formation of Britain', in S. G. Ellis and S. Barber (eds.), *Conquest and Union: Fashioning a British State, 1485–1725* (London, 1995).

MULLAN, D. G., *Episcopacy in Scotland: The History of an Idea, 1560–1638* (Edinburgh, 1986).

MURRAY, A. L., 'The Comptroller, 1425–1488', *SHR* 52 (1973), 1–29.

——'The Customs Accounts of Dumfries and Kirkcudbright, 1560–1660', *Transactions of the Dumfriesshire and Galloway Natural History and Antiquarian Society*, 3rd ser. 42 (1965), 114–32.

——'The Customs Accounts of Kirkcudbright, Wigtown, and Dumfries, 1434–1560', *Transactions of the Dumfriesshire and Galloway Natural History and Antiquarian Society*, 3rd ser. 40 (1963), 136–62.

——'Exchequer, Council and Session, 1513–1542', in J. H. Williams (ed.), *Stewart Style, 1513–1542* (East Linton, 1996).

——'Huntly's Rebellion and the Administration of Justice in North-East Scotland, 1570–1573', *Northern Scotland*, 4 (1981), 1–6.

——'The Lord Clerk Register', *SHR* 53 (1974), 124–56.

——'Notes on the Treasury Administration', *TA* xii (1980).

——'The Procedure of the Scottish Exchequer in the Early Sixteenth Century', *SHR* 40 (1961), 89–117.

——'The Scottish Chancery in the Fourteenth and Fifteenth Centuries', in K. Fianu and D. J. Guth (eds.), *Écrit et pouvoir dans les chancelleries médiévales: Espace français, espace anglais* (Louvain-la-Neuve, 1997).

——'The Scottish Treasury, 1667–1708', *SHR* 45 (1966), 89–104.

——'Sir John Skene and the Exchequer, 1596–1612', in *Stair Society Miscellany*, i (1971).

MURRAY, D., *Early Burgh Organization in Scotland*, 2 vols. (Glasgow, 1924–32).

NICHOLLS, A. D., *The Jacobean Union: A Reconsideration of British Civil Policies under the Early Stuarts* (Westport, Conn., 1999).

NORMAND, LORD (ed.), *An Introduction to Scottish Legal History* (Stair Society, 1958).

O'BRIEN, I. E., 'The Scottish Parliament in the 15th and 16th Centuries' (Ph.D. thesis, Glasgow, 1980).

OCKRENT, L., *Land Rights: An Enquiry into the History of Registration for Publication in Scotland* (London, 1942).

OHLMEYER, J. H., ' "Civilizinge of those rude partes": Colonization within Britain and Ireland, 1580s–1640s', in N. Canny (ed.), *The Oxford History of the British Empire*, i: *The Origins of Empire* (Oxford, 1998).

OLLIVANT, S. D., *The Court of the Official in Pre-Reformation Scotland* (Stair Society, 1982).

O'MAINNÍN, M., ' "The same in origin and in blood": Bardic Windows on the Relationship between Irish and Scottish Gaels, c.1200–1650', *Cambrian Medieval Celtic Studies*, 38 (Winter 1999), 1–51.

PAGAN, T., *The Convention of the Royal Burghs of Scotland* (Glasgow, 1926).

PARKER, D., *The Making of French Absolutism* (London, 1983).

PARKER, G., 'Success and Failure during the First Century of the Reformation', *Past and Present*, 136 (Aug. 1992), 43–82.

PATON, G. C. H. (ed.), *Introduction to Scottish Legal History* (Stair Society, 1958).

PEARCE, A. S. W., 'John Spottiswoode, Jacobean Archbishop and Statesman' (Ph.D. thesis, Stirling, 1998).

PERCEVAL-MAXWELL, M., *The Scottish Migration to Ulster in the Reign of James I* (London, 1973).

POCOCK, J. G. A., *The Ancient Constitution and the Feudal Law* (2nd edn., Cambridge, 1987).

PRYDE, G. S., 'Scottish Burgh Finances before 1707' (Ph.D. thesis, St Andrews, 1928).

RAE, T. I., *The Administration of the Scottish Frontier, 1513–1603* (Edinburgh, 1966).

RAIT, R. S., *The Parliaments of Scotland* (Glasgow, 1924).

REINHARD, W. (ed.), *Power Elites and State Building* (Oxford, 1996).

RIBALTA, P. M., 'The Impact of Central Institutions', in Reinhard (ed.), *Power Elites and State Building*.

RITCHIE, P. E., *Mary of Guise in Scotland, 1548–1560* (East Linton, 2002).

ROBERTSON, D., 'The Burlaw Court of Leith', *Book of the Old Edinburgh Club*, 15 (1927), 165–205.

RODRÍGUEZ-SALGADO, M. J., 'The Court of Philip II of Spain', in R. G. Asch and A. M. Birke (eds.), *Princes, Patronage and the Nobility: The Court at the Beginning of the Modern Age, c.1450–1650* (Oxford, 1991).

ROPER, L., *Oedipus and the Devil: Witchcraft, Sexuality and Religion in Early Modern Europe* (London, 1994).

SANDERSON, M. H. B., *Cardinal of Scotland: David Beaton, c.1494–1546* (Edinburgh, 1986).

——*A Kindly Place? Living in Sixteenth-Century Scotland* (East Linton, 2002).

——*Mary Stewart's People* (Edinburgh, 1987).

——*Scottish Rural Society in the Sixteenth Century* (Edinburgh, 1982).

SCHOFIELD, R., 'Taxation and the Political Limits of the Tudor State', in C. Cross et al. (eds.), *Law and Government under the Tudors* (Cambridge, 1988).

SCHULZE, W., 'Estates and the Problem of Resistance in Theory and Practice in the Sixteenth and Seventeenth Centuries', in R. J. W. Evans and T. V. Thomas (eds.), *Crown, Church and Estates: Central European Politics in the Sixteenth and Seventeenth Centuries* (London, 1991), 165–71.

The Scots Peerage, ed. J. B. Paul, 9 vols. (Edinburgh, 1904–14).

SCOTT, W. R., *The Constitution and Finance of English, Scottish and Irish Joint-Stock Companies, to 1720*, 3 vols. (Cambridge, 1912).

SCOTTISH RECORD OFFICE, *Guide to the National Archives of Scotland* (Edinburgh, 1996).

SELLAR, W. D. H., 'The Common Law of Scotland and the Common Law of England', in R. R. Davies (ed.), *The British Isles, 1100–1500* (Edinburgh, 1988).

SHARPE, J. A., *Crime in Early Modern England, 1550–1750* (London, 1983).

SHAW, D., *The General Assemblies of the Church of Scotland, 1560–1600* (Edinburgh, 1964).

SHIRE, H. M., *Song, Dance and Poetry of the Court of Scotland under King James VI* (Cambridge, 1969).

SKINNER, Q., *The Foundations of Modern Political Thought*, 2 vols. (Cambridge, 1978).

SMITH, A. G. R., *The Emergence of a Nation State: The Commonwealth of England, 1529–1660* (2nd edn., London, 1997).

SMITH, D. B., 'The Spiritual Jurisdiction, 1560–1564', *Records of the Scottish Church History Society*, 25 (1993–5), 1–18.

SMITH, T. B. (ed.), *The Laws of Scotland: Stair Memorial Encyclopedia*, 25 vols. (Edinburgh, 1987–95).

SMOUT, T. C., 'Famine and Famine-Relief in Scotland', in L. M. Cullen and T. C. Smout (eds.), *Comparative Aspects of Scottish and Irish Economic and Social History, 1600–1900* (Edinburgh, n.d. [1977]).

—— 'Peasant and Lord in Scotland: Institutions Controlling Scottish Rural Society, 1500–1800', *Recueils de la Société Jean Bodin pour l'Histoire Comparative des Institutions*, 44 (1987), 499–524.

—— (ed.), *Scotland and Europe, 1200–1850* (Edinburgh, 1986).

—— et al., 'Scottish Emigration in the Seventeenth and Eighteenth Centuries', in N. Canny (ed.), *Europeans on the Move: Studies on European Migration, 1500–1800* (Oxford, 1994).

SOMMERVILLE, J. P., *Royalists and Patriots: Political Ideology in England, 1603–1640* (2nd edn., London, 1999).

STEVENSON, D., *The Scottish Revolution, 1637–1644* (Newton Abbot, 1973).

STEWART, J. A., 'The Clan Ranald: History of a Highland Kindred' (Ph.D. thesis, Edinburgh, 1982).

TANNER, R., *The Late Medieval Scottish Parliament: Politics and the Three Estates, 1424–1488* (East Linton, 2001).

—— 'The Lords of the Articles before 1540: A Reassessment', *SHR* 79 (2000), 189–212.

TAYLOR, W., 'The King's Mails, 1603–1625', *SHR* 42 (1963), 143–7.

—— 'The Scottish Privy Council, 1603–1625: Its Composition and its Work' (Ph.D. thesis, Edinburgh, 1950).

THOMSON, T., *Memorial on Old Extent*, ed. J. D. Mackie (Stair Society, 1946).

TODD, M., *The Culture of Protestantism in Early Modern Scotland* (New Haven, 2002).

VERSCHUUR, M. B., 'Perth Craftsmen's Book: Some Examples of the Interpretation and Utilization of Protestant Thought by Sixteenth-Century Scottish Townsmen', *Records of the Scottish Church History Society*, 23 (1987–9), 157–74.

WALKER, D. M., *A Legal History of Scotland*, iii: *The Sixteenth Century* (Edinburgh, 1995), and iv: *The Seventeenth Century* (Edinburgh, 1996).

WASSER, M. B, 'The Pacification of the Scottish Borders, 1598–1612' (M.A. diss., McGill University, 1986).

—— 'Violence and the Central Criminal Courts in Scotland, 1603–1638' (Ph.D. diss., Columbia University, 1995).

WATT, D. A., 'Chiefs, Lawyers and Debt: A Study of the Relationship between Highland Elite and Legal Profession in Scotland, c.1550 to 1700' (Ph.D. thesis, Edinburgh, 1998).

WATT, D. E. R., *Medieval Church Councils in Scotland* (Edinburgh, 2000).

WELLS, V. T., 'The Origins of Covenanting Thought and Resistance, c.1580–1638' (Ph.D. thesis, Stirling, 1997).

WHATLEY, C. A., 'The Dark Side of the Enlightenment? Sorting out Serfdom', in T. M. Devine and J. R. Young (eds.), *Eighteenth Century Scotland: New Perspectives* (East Linton, 1999).

WHYTE, I. D., *Agriculture and Society in Seventeenth-Century Scotland* (Edinburgh, 1979).

—— 'The Function and Social Structure of Scottish Burghs of Barony in the Seventeenth and Eighteenth Centuries', in A. Maczak and C. Smout (eds.), *Gründung und Bedeutung kleinerer Städte in nördlichen Europa der frühen Neuzeit* (Wiesbaden, 1991).

—— 'Poverty or Prosperity? Rural Society in Lowland Scotland in the late Sixteenth and Early Seventeenth Centuries', *Scottish Economic and Social History*, 18 (1998), 19–32.

WILLIAMS, P., *The Council in the Marches of Wales under Elizabeth I* (Cardiff, 1958).

—— *The Tudor Regime* (Oxford, 1979).

WILLIAMSON, A. H., 'Scots, Indians and Empire: The Scottish Politics of Civilization, 1519–1609', *Past and Present*, 150 (Feb. 1996), 46–83.

—— *Scottish National Consciousness in the Age of James VI* (Edinburgh, 1979).

WILLOCK, I. D., *The Origins and Development of the Jury in Scotland* (Stair Society, 1966).

WINCHESTER, A. J. L., *The Harvest of the Hills: Rural Life in Northern England and the Scottish Borders, 1400–1700* (Edinburgh, 2000).

WORMALD, J., 'Bloodfeud, Kindred and Government in Early Modern Scotland', *Past and Present*, 87 (May 1980), 54–97.

—— *Court, Kirk and Community: Scotland, 1470–1625* (London, 1981).

—— 'The Creation of Britain: Multiple Kingdoms or Core and Colonies?', *Transactions of the Royal Historical Society*, 6th ser. 2 (1992), 175–94.

—— *Lords and Men in Scotland: Bonds of Manrent, 1442–1603* (Edinburgh, 1985).

WRIGHTSON, K., 'Two Concepts of Order: Justices, Constables and Jurymen in Seventeenth-Century England', in J. Brewer and J. Styles (eds.), *An Ungovernable People: The English and their Law in the Seventeenth and Eighteenth Centuries* (London, 1980).

YOUNG, M. D. (ed.), *The Parliaments of Scotland: Burgh and Shire Commissioners*, 2 vols. (Edinburgh, 1992–3).

ZULAGER, R. R., 'A Study of the Middle-Rank Administrators in the Government of King James VI of Scotland, 1580–1603' (Ph.D. thesis, Aberdeen, 1991).

Index